Duncan Campbell has been writing about crime for nearly half a century. He was the crime correspondent of the *Guardian* and chairman of the Crime Reporters' Association. He has written extensively on the subject of crime for various publications, including the *Observer, Esquire, New Statesman, London Review of Books, Radio Times* and *Oldie*.

Campbell was the first presenter of BBC Radio Five Live's Crime Desk and the winner of the Bar Council newspaper journalist of the year award. He has appeared in numerous documentaries about crime and was the consultant on the 2018 film, *King of Thieves*, about the Hatton Garden burglary, which was partly based on an article he wrote about the case for the *Guardian*.

Other books written by the author include *That Was Business, This Is Personal, A Stranger and Afraid, If It Bleeds* and *We'll All Be Murdered in Our Beds!*

UNDERWORLD

DUNCAN CAMPBELL

EBURY
PRESS

1 3 5 7 9 10 8 6 4 2

Ebury Press, an imprint of Ebury Publishing
20 Vauxhall Bridge Road
London SW1V 2SA

Ebury Press is part of the Penguin Random House group of
companies whose addresses can be found at
global.penguinrandomhouse.com

Penguin
Random House
UK

First published by BBC Books in 1994
This revised and updated edition published in 2019

www.penguin.co.uk

A CIP catalogue record for this book is available from the British Library

ISBN 9781529103656

Typeset in 11.75/16.5 pt New Caledonia LT Std
by Integra Software Services Pvt. Ltd, Pondicherry

Printed and bound in Great Britain by Clays Ltd, Elcograf S.p.A.

Penguin Random House is committed to a sustainable future
for our business, our readers and our planet. This book is
made from Forest Stewardship Council® certified paper.

CONTENTS

ACKNOWLEDGEMENTS

Many people helped with this book. I would like to thank particularly Hélène Mulholland for her diligent research, my agent Andrew Lownie and the publishers, Sara Cywinski and Emma Smith of Ebury Press, and Helena Caldon. I am indebted to the members of *The Underworld* team at the BBC responsible for the many original interviews with the main players in the history of gangland: Lorraine Heggessey, Andrew Weir, Louise Norman, Frank Simmonds, Jonathan Dent and Sarah Horsfall.

Others assisted with advice, information, interviews, research and in other ways. They include the late Bobby King, Jonathan Green, Eric Allison, Ralph Edney, Torquil Crichton, Clive Christie, Ray Baron, the late Alex Marnoch, Neil Darbyshire, the late Brian Hilliard, Wally Probyn, Kathy Bailey, Veronica Forcella, John Masterson, Andy Malone, Rosa Bosch, John Hodgman, Brendan Gibb-Gray, Rosanna Lusardi, Jim Dickinson, the late Pat Kavanagh, John Grieve, Stewart Tendler, Ed Upright, David Bailey, Henry Vaughan, Ian Cobain, Peter Huck, Nur Laiq, Rob Evans, Helen Pidd, Lorna Macfarlane, Sheila Ableman, Deborah

Taylor, David Cottingham, Ron McKay, Linda Blakemore and Ruby Crystal.

I would also like to thank the staff of the National Archives, the British Library, Colindale Newspaper Library, the *Guardian* Library, the Mitchell Library and the *Herald-Evening Times* Library in Glasgow, the Bramshill Police Staff College Library, the late Camille Wolff of Grey House books and the staff of Broadway Books. I have referred to many books in the course of the research and their titles, for readers seeking greater detail, appear at the back of the book.

There will inevitably be omissions and errors. This is, in part, due to the fact that the hardest three words for villains, police officers and crime reporters to say are: 'I don't know'. Also, many memories have become clouded by time and nostalgia. A plea of mitigation rather than a defence.

CHRONOLOGY

23 December 1911 East End Vendetta trial.

27 November 1918 Billie Carleton dies of supposed drug overdose.

19 November 1922 Frattelanza Club fight.

18 January 1923 Cortesi brothers sentenced for Frattelanza fight with Sabinis.

18 April 1925 'Brilliant' Chang deported.

8 February 1931 Eddie Manning dies in prison.

24 October 1933 Kray twins born.

18 January 1934 Charlie Richardson born.

24 January 1936 Body of 'Red Max' Kassel found.

8 June 1936 'The Battle of Lewes' between racetrack gangs.

4 October 1936 Jack Spot leads attack on Blackshirts' march in the East End.

10 January 1940 Ruby Sparks escapes from Dartmoor Prison.

1 May 1941 Murder of 'Little Hubby' Distleman in Soho.

31 October 1941 'Babe' Mancini hanged for murder of 'Little Hubby' Distleman.

5 December 1945 Kidnapping of Irene Coleman.

31 December 1945 Ghost Squad formed.

29 April 1947 Alex d'Antiquis shot dead by armed robbers.

9 July 1947 Billy Hill claims London gangland take-over in the 'battle that never was' against the Whites.

19 September 1947 Charles Jenkins and Chris Geraghty hanged for d'Antiquis killing.

3 September 1950 Sunday People exposes Messinas.

19 March 1951 Alfredo Messina arrested.

21 May 1952 Eastcastle Street mail van robbery: £287,000 stolen from ambushed mail van, biggest robbery of its time.

2 November 1952 PC Sidney Miles shot. Christopher Craig and Derek Bentley arrested for his murder.

24 September 1953 Maples store burgled.

21 September 1954 KLM bullion raid.

21 October 1954 People reporter Duncan Webb attacked.

11 August 1955 The 'fight that never was': Jack Spot and Albert Dimes's battle in Soho.

31 August 1955 Carmelo and Eugenio Messina arrested.

2 May 1956 Jack Spot attacked by Frankie Fraser and others.

25 June 1956 Tommy Smithson murdered.

21 July 1957 Jack Spot's Highball club burned down.

14 December 1958 Ronald Marwood stabs PC Raymond Summers to death.

8 May 1959 Ronald Marwood hanged.

16 August 1959 Street Offences Act changes face of prostitution.

7 February 1960 Pen Club shootings.

28 May 1960 Peter Scott/Gulston steals Sophia Loren's jewels.

11 October 1962 John Gaul fined £25,000 for living off immoral earnings.

11 July 1963 Harry Challenor plants half-brick on Donald Rooum.

8 August 1963 The Great Train Robbery.

15 April 1964 The Great Train Robbers convicted and gaoled for up to thirty years.

12 June 1964 Jack 'The Rat' Duval beaten.

18 June 1964 Lucien Harris beaten.

12 July 1964 'Peer and Gangster' story published in *Daily Mirror.*

2 January 1965 Ginger Marks murdered.

20 April 1965 Reg Kray marries Frances Shea.

29 June 1965 Thomas Waldeck murdered.

8 July 1965 Ronnie Biggs escapes from Wandsworth Prison.

24 July 1965 Freddie Mills found dead in car.

7 March 1966 Mr Smith's: Dickie Hart killed in gangland fight.

9 March 1966 George Cornell killed in the Blind Beggar.

2 May 1966 John Bradbury sentenced to death for Waldeck murder.

12 August 1966 Three policemen shot dead in Shepherd's Bush.

11 November 1966 Harry Roberts caught for murder of three policemen.

12 December 1966 Harry Roberts, John Duddy, Jack Witney gaoled for life for the murder of three policemen; Frank 'The Mad Axeman' Mitchell escapes from Dartmoor.

24 December 1966 Frank Mitchell killed.

4 April 1967 Richardson gang 'torture' trial starts at the Old Bailey.

28 October 1967 Jack 'The Hat' McVitie murdered.

25 January 1968 Charlie Wilson recaptured.

8 May 1968 Ron and Reg Kray arrested.

7 January 1969 Krays' trial starts at the Old Bailey.

8 March 1969 Ron and Reg Kray gaoled for life.

26 March 1969 Ralli Brothers' robbery.

29 November 1969 *The Times* allegations on police corruption.

9 February 1970 Ilford bank robbery: £237,000 stolen from Barclays Bank, Ilford, at that time the largest daylight bank robbery since the World War II.

7 May 1970 David Knight killed in fight.

5 March 1971 Vic Kelaher arrested by Customs.

22 April 1971 Car bomb placed under Jimmy Tibbs's car.

23 August 1971 Fred Sewell murders Supt Gerald Richardson in Blackpool.

25 August 1971 Dixons arrested.

18 February 1972 Trial of Bernie Silver.

27 February 1972 Commander Ken Drury exposed by *Sunday People*.

17 April 1972 Robert Mark becomes Commissioner of the Metropolitan Police.

10 August 1972 Wembley Barclays Bank robbery.

5 November 1972 *Sunday Times* exposé of Drugs Squad.

23 December 1972 Bertie Smalls arrested.

March 1973 Bertie Smalls becomes a supergrass.

5 June 1973 'Chris' Krishnarma arrested. Later given what was then the longest ever cannabis sentence of ten years.

31 December 1973 Bernie Silver arrested.

1 February 1974 Ronnie Biggs arrested in Rio de Janeiro.

25 April 1974 Jimmy Humphreys, pornographer, gaoled for eight years for attacking wife's lover.

11 June 1974 Maurice 'King Squealer' O'Mahoney arrested.

4 September 1974 Alfredo 'Italian Tony' Zomparelli murdered at the Golden Goose, Soho.

1/2 November 1974 Terence Eve murdered.

19 December 1974 Bernie Silver gaoled for six years on vice charges.

4 January 1975 George Brett and son Terry murdered.

24 April 1975 Bank of America robbery in Mayfair.

8 July 1975 Bernie Silver convicted of Smithson murder.

12 January 1976 Barbara Gaul murdered by hitmen.

28 February 1976 Members of Scotland Yard's Obscene Publications Squad arrested.

24 June 1976 Edgeler brothers gaoled for Barbara Gaul murder.

18 October 1976 Bernie Silver's murder conviction quashed on appeal.

8 November 1976 'Dirty Squad' trial opens.

26 March 1977 Operation Julie LSD raids: 120 arrested.

7 July 1977 Kenneth Drury gaoled for eight years.

23 September 1977 George Davis arrested on Bank of Cyprus robbery.

8 March 1978 Operation Julie team gaoled.

19 October 1979 Customs officer Peter Bennett shot dead.

17 January 1980 George Piggott gaoled for murder of Alfredo Zomparelli.

24 March 1980 £3.5 millions' worth of silver bullion hijacked on way to Tilbury Docks.

4 April 1980 Charlie Radcliffe arrested on Operation Yashmak.

23 May 1980 Charlie Richardson escapes.

19 November 1980 Ronnie Knight cleared of murder of Zomparelli; Leonard 'Teddy Bear' Watkins gaoled for life for murder of Peter Bennett.

28 November 1980 Henry MacKenny and Terence Pinfold convicted of contract killings and gaoled for life.

3 December 1980 Colin 'Duke' Osbourne found dead in Hackney.

18 January 1981 Charlie Richardson recaptured.

24 March 1981 Ronnie Biggs kidnapped and taken to Barbados.

27 June 1982 Nicky Gerrard murdered.

28 January 1983 David Martin captured.

11 October 1983 David Martin gaoled for twenty-five years for attempted murder and robbery.

26 November 1983 £26-million Brink's-Mat robbery at Heathrow.

10 October 1984 Glasgow's Ice-Cream War trial.

2 December 1984 Brian Robinson and Micky McAvoy convicted of Brink's-Mat robbery.

26 January 1985 DC John Fordham murdered in West Kingsdown, Kent.

10 June 1985 Johnny Knight and Terry Perkins gaoled for twenty-two years for Security Express robbery.

13 October 1986 Supergrass Dave Smith cuts his own throat.

12 July 1987 Knightsbridge Safe Deposit Centre robbed.

25 July 1988 Howard Marks arrested in Palma.

18 February 1989 Police informer Alan 'Chalky' White murdered in Gloucestershire.

13 April 1989 Jimmy Farrell and Terry Dewsnap shot dead on North Harrow post office robbery.

28 July 1989 Freddie Foreman returned to England from Spain.

4 August 1989 Train robbers Tommy Wisbey and Jimmy Hussey gaoled for cocaine dealing.

19 January 1990 Ron Cook murdered by Linda 'Black Widow' Calvey.

23 April 1990 Charlie Wilson shot dead in Spain.

2 May 1990 £292-million bearer bonds stolen in City of London.

13 July 1990 Howard Marks pleads guilty to cannabis charge, gaoled for twenty-five years.

28 September 1990 Roy Adkins murdered in Amsterdam.

27 November 1990 Armed robber Kenny Baker shot dead during Securicor raid in Woodhatch, Surrey.

11 March 1991 'Abbi' Abdullah murdered in Walworth betting shop.

28 April 1991 Police informer Dave Norris shot dead in Belvedere, south London.

3 August 1991 David Brindle and Stanley Silk shot dead in The Bell, Walworth.

17 August 1991 Arthur 'Fat Boy' Thompson Jnr. killed.

12 June 1992 Paul Ferris cleared of murder of Arthur Thompson Jnr.

30 October 1992 Joey Pyle and Pete Gillett convicted of drug dealing.

26 November 1992 Frank Sims gaoled for amphetamine operation.

13 March 1993 Arthur J. Thompson dies.

1 June 1993 James Moody shot dead in Royal Hotel, Hackney.

24 January 1994 Largest-ever drugs haul (1,300 kilos of cocaine) seized at Birkenhead. No arrests.

17 March 1994 Mehmet Kaygisiz shot dead in Islington café.

13 June 1994 Jimmy and Rusty Humphreys convicted of prostitution offences.

29 November 1994 Buster Edwards hangs himself.

4 January 1995 Ronnie Knight gaoled for seven years on Security Express charge.

17 March 1995 Ronnie Kray dies.

1 May 1995 Liverpool gang leader David Ungi killed in armed ambush in Liverpool.

7 December 1995 Tony Tucker, Patrick Tate and Craig Rolfe shot dead in Range Rover near Rettendon, Essex.

7 November 2000 Millennium Dome diamond robbery thwarted.

22 December 2003 Luan Plakici jailed for ten years for smuggling and exploiting women.

18 March 2005 Burger Bar Boys members convicted of the Shakespeare/Ellis Shootings.

21/22 February 2006 £53-million Securitas depot robbery.

9 March 2007 Terry Adams jailed for money laundering.

22 August 2007 Rhys Jones, aged eleven, killed in Liverpool.

16 December 2008 Sean Mercer jailed for twenty-two years for murder of Rhys Jones.

7 October 2009 Curtis 'Cocky' Warren convicted of cannabis offences, jailed for thirteen years.

12 January 2010 Heathrow armed robbery: first criminal trial in 400 years heard without a jury.

28 March 2014 Francis Brennan found murdered in Spain.

11 November 2014 Harry Roberts released after forty-eight years served for the murder of three police officers.

2 April 2015 Hatton Garden safe deposit centre burglary.

24 June 2015 John Palmer shot dead at his Essex home.

26 July 2015 Paul 'Mr Big' Massey murdered.

9 March 2016 Hatton Garden burglars jailed at Woolwich Crown Court.

30 March 2016 Bekir 'Dukie' Arif jailed for conspiracy to supply drugs.

4 August 2016 Tristen Aslanni jailed for twenty-five years for drug dealing and firearm offences.

21 December 2017 Antique firearms dealer Paul Edmunds jailed for thirty years.

4 February 2018 Terry Perkins dies in prison.

5 May 2018 'Scouse John' Kinsella shot dead.

22 January 2018 First known Bitcoin armed robbery.

15 March 2019 Michael 'Basil' Seed convicted of Hatton Garden £14 million burglary and jailed for ten years.

INTRODUCTION

Over the Easter weekend in 2015 a gang of elderly burglars broke into a safe deposit centre in London's Hatton Garden jewellery district, drilled their way through a wall and stole £14 million worth of gold, diamonds and cash, thus winning for themselves the nickname of the 'Diamond Wheezers'. Within three years their exploits had been translated into three films, five books, a television series and a song. At their trial the judge noted that they had been described as 'analogue criminals in a digital age'.

The men found guilty were paid-up life members of the underworld. One of them, Terry Perkins, had taken part in a robbery of the £6-million Security Express depot in east London in 1983, and another, Brian Reader, had been gaoled for his part in the £26-million Brink's-Mat robbery at Heathrow in the same year. Both men had spent time on the run in mainland Europe, both came from a criminal tradition where people did not 'grass' or inform, and they used to meet, chat and plot together in a north London pub.

Nearly three hundred years earlier, the Essex Gang, as they were known, a group of robbers and poachers, also used to meet and plot in a hostelry to the north of London, also used to pop across the Channel on smuggling trips to France, and knew that George II was offering pardons for whoever informed on them. Their leader, who was executed in 1739 on what is now York racecourse, was Dick Turpin.

Now, in a new millennium, gangs still meet and plot, informers still seek milder sentences for helping the Crown and, although the footpads and smugglers are not hanged any more, the names of the best-known villains still exercise the sort of fascination that has enabled Dick Turpin to live on in legend and song. Just as Turpin was not averse to holding old ladies over a fire to persuade them to tell him where their savings were hidden, so Perkins's gang had been happy to pour petrol over the staff in the Security Express robbery and threaten to strike a match if the combination number for the vaults was not forthcoming. Criminals had moved from robbing stage coaches into internet fraud. They dealt in crack cocaine and Bitcoin rather than game and guineas, and they escaped in stolen cars rather than on Black Bess. But the underworld that kings and sheriffs sought to crush, which detectives and Home Secretaries have harried and hounded, which fascinated writers from John Gay and Charles Dickens to Graham Greene and Martina Cole, has survived. Its structures have changed and its nets spread wider, but it remains as sturdy as ever.

Revenue from crime now runs into billions of pounds every year, and attempts to put an exact figure on it seem fruitless. Crime spawns hundreds of thousands of jobs, whether for drug dealers and bank robbers, police and prison officers, or lawyers and the ever-growing army of security guards. It shows no signs of abating as punishments from the seventeenth-century's hanging of pickpockets to the indeterminate sentences and electronic tagging of the twenty-first century are tried and seen to fail.

There are many obvious ways in which the underworld has changed: through the motor car and the aeroplane criminals became more mobile and elusive; the introduction of drug laws from the 1920s onwards has unwittingly created the most lucrative of all black markets; and, of course, the internet has opened up countless new opportunities to smuggle, defraud and recruit. This book is about the British underworld, the people who chose and choose to live outside the law. There are other types of criminals, of course: the corporate swindlers and City fraudsters who often make far larger illegal sums, robbing with the pen rather than the sword and taking far fewer personal risks. And there are other murderers more calculating, sadistic and brutal than those within the underworld. But this book is not about them. We deal here with those who have chosen skulduggery as a profession – the career criminals, those who have decided to live outside the law – and the world that they inhabit.

Some are the iconic names of crime and detection: the Brilliant Chang and Darby Sabini, 'Mad Frankie' Fraser and Albert Dimes, the Great Train Robbers and the Brummagem Boys, Eddie 'the King of the Safecrackers' Chapman and 'Taters' Chatham, cannabis smuggler Howard Marks and cocaine trafficker Curtis Warren. On 'the other team' are the likes of 'Slipper of the Yard' and 'Nipper' Read. Some have never troubled the public consciousness. Some have ended their days watching satellite television on their patio in Puerto Banus; others will continue to give pleasure to Her or His Majesty, uncomforted by the old maxim they learned on their first job: 'If you can't do the time, don't do the crime'.

But there are strands that run almost unchanging through the underworld's history. There have, for instance, always been groups of 'aliens' at whose doors the blame for much of our organised crime has been placed. Russians, Jews, Chinese, Italians, Maltese, Turks, Pakistanis, Jamaicans, Colombians, Russians again, Travellers and Albanians have all at various times been seen as the leading players in protection rackets, drugs, vice, robbery and violence.

Certainly, pockets of immigrant groups, excluded sometimes from the more traditional ways of making money, have profited from their initial anonymity and the protection offered by a close-knit community; but at the heart of the underworld has always been the British criminal who has co-opted or imitated the new arrivals and, in the twenty-first century, joined forces with them. And nothing has transformed the underworld so massively as the drugs business, where international contact of some kind is essential.

Although Great Train Robber Tommy Wisbey said that there was no such thing as 'the underworld – just known criminals', that elusive universe and the country of Gangland does still exist. It may not be as definable as in the days before the Second World War when the Sabinis and the Hoxton Mob could be traced to a few streets of east London, or when the Glasgow gangs were as well organised as Rotary Club branches. Most modern criminals have no great desire to court the sort of publicity that Billy Hill and Jack Spot, the Krays and Richardsons attracted. But there are still extended families where the main income is not entered on a tax-return form; and there are still plenty of clubs and pubs that provide the ambience for drug dealing and money laundering in the same way that the old spielers housed gaming parties and illegal drink-ups.

The underworld remains a man's world. There have been some remarkable women inhabitants, from the 'Queen of the Forty Elephants' and the 'Bobbed-Haired Bandit' in the thirties to the 'Queen of the Shoplifters' and the 'Queen of the Underworld' in the fifties, the 'Black Widow' in the nineties and the drugs 'queen-pins' of the new millennium. But only two women appeared on the Serious and Organised Crime Agency list of 145 leading criminals in 2013, and women make up less than 5 per cent of the prison population. Essentially, crime remains a boys' game, with the most prominent roles for women being that of loyal mum, long-suffering 'widow', youthful transporter of drugs or exploited prostitute.

As one armed robber remarked, if you take into account the unprofitable years most criminals have spent behind bars, they could have made as much money working part-time on a building site as they did with all their heists. For the vast majority of prisoners, the romance of crime is illusory and the reality of gaol is one of boredom. But it is partly through gaol that the underworld hierarchy is established and its pecking order, as strict as anything Debrett's could devise, is maintained.

The notion of the 'underworld' first surfaced, according to lexicographer Jonathan Green, in 1874, in the *Manchester Evening News*, in a story headlined 'Criminal Manchester', which refers to 'this hidden underworld', although the reference may cover both criminals and a poverty-stricken underclass. By 1900, the American monthly magazine, *McClure's*, was offering its readers 'True stories from the underworld', and the fascination has continued to this day. When Charles Dickens wrote *Oliver Twist* he was criticised by his contemporaries for glamorising crime. Television programmes, films and music videos in the twenty-first century face the same criticism. Certainly, many criminals are ruthless, lazy bullies, some on the edge of psychopathy, but equally some are charming rogues who prefer the risks and rewards of what the poet Robert Browning called 'the dangerous edge of things' to what they see as the hypocrisies and tedium of the overworld. They are citizens of the underworld. This book is about them.

1

THE BEGINNINGS

THE RACETRACK GANGS, THE MOBS AND THE SMASH-AND-GRABBERS

Mr Justice Hilbery was in stern mood as he surveyed the sixteen prisoners in the dock of Lewes Assizes. 'You had armed yourselves with weapons which have been aptly described as villainous instruments to use upon any fellow human being,' he told them. 'You showed no mercy to your victim and you intended to show no mercy. Crimes of gang violence in this country will be met with no mercy.' He sentenced the wielders of hatchets and knuckle-dusters, truncheons and chisels to a total of fifty-three years in gaol for the part they had played in the Battle of Lewes. Its date, June 1936, might not be in the same history books as another, more famous, Sussex battle but it marked a high-water mark of violence that was to have resonances for more than the next half-century. Britain now had her own very public gangsters.

But the story of the modern underworld starts in the previous century, in fiction rather than in fact. For so powerful was the effect on the public consciousness of the criminal life portrayed in Charles Dickens's *Oliver Twist* that many of the imaginary haunts of the book's characters were razed to the ground. When the London street clearances of the 1840s and 1850s took place Saffron Hill, where Fagin instructed his apprentice pickpockets, and Jacob's Island, where Bill Sikes met his death, were symbolically cleansed. But the Victorians were to learn, as would their descendants up to the present day, that it takes more than a slum demolished or a short, sharp shock to trouble one of the most enduring features of the capital.

The Seven Curses of London, which James Greenwood published in 1869, suggested that as many as 20,000 criminals, emboldened by the end of transportation to Australia and the inadequacies of the police, were at large in London at the time. Indeed, the police had scant notion of how to counteract the growth of the smarter villain. There was little in the way of detective work and the Criminal Investigation Department was not formed until 1878. The first commissioner at Scotland Yard, Sir Richard Mayne, had been opposed to the notion of such an outfit because of public fears that the new police would be a body of spies.

One of the best-known criminal figures in east London in the early part of the twentieth century was Arthur Harding, who was born in 1886 and who, unlike many of his contemporaries, lived to tell his tale. He received his criminal baptism in 1902, at the age of sixteen, when he was sentenced to twelve months' penal servitude for helping a man called 'One-eyed Charlie' steal a bale of rags worth 18s. from a cart. After three months in Wormwood Scrubs, Harding was transferred to the first of the new Borstals. These establishments had been set up to cater to young offenders and initially strove to provide training for a trade, along with physical exercise and the reading of improving literature. But if prisons were later to be seen as universities of crime, the new Borstals were to become elite boarding schools, turning out the hardened little villains who became the underworld figures of the twentieth century. 'Borstal made me fitter, stronger, taller and when I went back to my associates I found I was something of a hero,' Harding told his biographer, Raphael Samuel. His progression was typical of the career criminal of the time. He became the 'captain' of a group of thieves and an active participant in protection rackets and armed robbery.

There were violent, if infrequent, skirmishes between rival gangs. Around 1907, Harding and his friends became involved in a running battle against a team led by Isaac 'Ikey' Bogard, better known as 'Darky the Coon'. Bogard was a 'shundicknick', a pimp, by trade but renowned as a hardman who affected an American accent and dressed like a cowboy in an open-necked shirt, leather chaps and Stetson, with a gun – still legal in those days – stuck nonchalantly in his belt. He had a number of ex-boxers in his ranks and had been gaoled for punching a policeman in the face, escaping to a rooftop and then pelting the pursuing officers with tiles.

Harding claimed that the feud had been sparked when a former associate of his, George King, joined up with Bogard and another gangster, Philip Shonck, who planned to kill him. Before he could do the deed, Shonck was shot by one of Harding's henchmen, Tommy Taylor. This led to a series of shoot-outs in the East End.

Acquiring firearms seemed not to be a problem: some were stolen from a lax Irish constabulary and imported and others were seized in raids on local gunsmiths. Although he was proud of his Irish police revolver and happy to 'glass' an adversary in the face, Harding apparently had his standards: 'As an Englishman, I would never use a knife.'

The culmination of the feud was the 'Vendetta Affair' of 23 December 1911, which began with an argument over a woman and ended in a showdown between Harding and Bogard in the Bluecoat Boy pub in Bishopsgate, east London. Each side was about a dozen strong. Bogard offered Harding a drink which

Harding, true to form, threw in his face, following up with the glass. 'The Coon had a face like the map of England,' he recalled of the aftermath. When Bogard and King asked for police protection at Old Street police court a few days later, Harding's team tried to ambush them as they came out and Harding was arrested. Eight of the miscreants stood trial at the Old Bailey. The evidence was shaky and the Bluecoat Boy manager was too frightened even to stay in London; he moved out to run a club in Southend, which gradually became a popular resting place for villains who found the nearby capital too warm. Harding was gaoled for three years for causing an affray and possession of a firearm in a court of law.

The *Illustrated Police News* reported the trial under the heading: 'East End Vendetta. Gang of Ruffians Broken Up At Last'. Mr Justice Avory issued a suitably bench-like condemnation in his summing-up: 'I wish to say that the condition of things disclosed by the evidence – that a portion of London should be infested by a number of criminal ruffians armed with revolvers – ought not to be tolerated further and if the existing law is not strong enough to put a stop to it some remedial legislation is necessary.'

Harding went to gaol but returned to the area to become a well-known East End figure. Bogard fought in the First World War, won the Military Medal and ended up working for the former head of the Flying Squad, Fred 'Nutty' Sharpe, who had become a bookmaker in Wandsworth and always had a soft spot for villains – 'a colourful rascally lot, these "wide 'uns"', as he described them.

The police were less tolerant of some of the other more desperate robbers at work at that time. They had already arrested, in 1902, members of rival Russian gangs, the Bessarabians and Odessians, who were early proponents of protection rackets in London but they became more engaged after what was later known as the Tottenham Outrage.

On 23 January 1909 two men arriving with the wages for Schnurmann's rubber factory in Tottenham, north London, were ambushed by two Latvian immigrants, Paul Hefeld, who was armed, and Jacob Lepidus. In the struggle and ensuing chase a policeman, PC William Tyler, and a ten-year-old schoolboy, Ralph Jocelyn, who had joined in the hue and cry, were shot dead and two people were injured. The robbers fled, commandeering a tram, whose conductor was forced at gunpoint to drive it, and a milk-cart and a van before being cornered at a high fence by the banks of the River Ching. Unable to scale the fence, Hefeld encouraged Lepidus to flee and then shot himself in the head; he died in hospital nineteen days later. Lepidus took refuge in a cottage, where he was surrounded by both police and the outraged – and armed – locals who fired haphazardly into the house. As the police entered the back of the cottage, Lepidus either shot himself or was killed by a fusillade from two police officers who fired blind into the room where he was hiding.

Two years later, in January 1911, a wanted poster offering a £500 reward appeared in London, seeking information about another gang involved in a botched robbery of a jeweller's in Houndsditch, east London, during which three police officers had been killed. 'Peter Piatkow, a native of Russia,' it read, 'Joe Levi, foreign appearance, speaking fairly good English, thickish lips, erect carriage ... A woman 26–27, fairly full breasts, sallow complexion, face somewhat drawn ... Foreign appearance'. Suspects were eventually tracked down to 100 Sidney Street, in Stepney, which was soon surrounded by police and soldiers from the Scots Guards, where the Home Secretary, Winston Churchill, directed operations in a top hat. When the house caught fire amidst the fusillade, Churchill prevented the fire brigade from extinguishing it: 'I thought it better to let the house burn down rather than spend good British lives in rescuing those ferocious rascals.'

The groups involved in such enterprises, many of them immigrants from eastern Europe, were anarchists and radicals, regarded as suspicious in both criminal and political terms and seen as threatening the stability of the capital because of their easy access to guns.

'Flocks of aliens, mostly Russians, were arriving at Irongate Wharf at the foot of Tower Bridge and were being housed in the Docks area,' wrote 'Nutty' Sharpe in his memoirs. 'Russians in top-boots and leather leggings and little round fur hats, wild-looking people from the most outlandish parts of that great uncivilized land, a lot were desperadoes and went in for crime straight away.' They were blamed for robberies and shootings, and the line between the professional crook and the committed anar-chist became blurred, not least because of a tendency to lump them all together in the press and Parliament.

Gambling of one kind or another played a major part in the life of the underworld: street bookmaking was illegal (until 1960) and the police were obliged to arrest a certain number of bookies every week. Consequently, the senior bookies would pay hard-up men to be arrested on their behalf rather than face gaol themselves. Bribery of the low-paid police officers was routine, with fixed rates of a shilling a day for constables and so on, depending on rank. The charismatic Edward Emmanuel led the Jewish bookies of the day and also organised boxing bouts, often rigged ones. Boxing started to establish itself as a backdrop against which both criminals and policemen socialised, a role it still plays.

Few of the underworld in the early years of the century en-joyed a reputation outside their own circle but one who did was Eddie Guerin. Born in London in 1860, he emigrated to Chicago with his parents as a child and his international approach to crime was about a century ahead of its time. He was a bad boy. He fell foul of the American police and Pinkerton's private detectives in Pittsburgh and St Louis, Toronto and Ohio. But he clearly rev-elled in the role of the young tearaway: 'What a red-hot game it was,' he later enthused of his time in New York. On the run, he returned to England in 1887 and made for the Criterion bar in Piccadilly, which was then the haunt of 'the boys' or 'the heads', as villains were known. (They did not become the 'faces' until after the Second World War.) He was gaoled for attempting to break into a post office and sent to Holloway Prison, where he was one of its last male prisoners.

Guerin's celebrity in the London underworld came from the widely held belief that he had escaped from Devil's Island, off the coast of French Guiana, in a rowing boat and had had to eat his companions in order to survive. The true story was more prosaic: he never actually went to Devil's Island, which was no longer used as a penal colony. Instead he was sent, as punishment for carrying out a robbery of American Express in Paris in 1901, to two of its neighbouring Îles du Salut. Money was smuggled to him by friends who sent him copies of the *Illustrated London News* and *Scientific American* stuffed with banknotes and he was able to make good his escape through a combination of bribery and cunning.

Back in Britain in 1906 after his escape, he briefly tried to earn an honest living as a tailor in Leeds, in Yorkshire, before returning to London. By now the French authorities wanted him back and on 29 April 1906 he was arrested at one of his regular haunts, a French newsagent in Charlotte Street, where he was buying *Le Matin* in an effort to discover whether he was indeed a wanted man. His former sweetheart, a prostitute called 'Chicago May', had betrayed him. He was successful in an action to avoid extradition on the grounds that he had been born in England, and was freed, but was later shot outside Russell Square underground station by the angry May and her new beau, a drunken hoodlum called Charlie Smith or Cubine Jackson. Guerin managed to square his dislike of 'snitching' enough to give evidence against the pair at the Old Bailey, and Smith – 'I'm Mr Smith of Nowhere,' he said, when asked to identify himself at the London Sessions – was gaoled for life and 'Chicago May' for fifteen years.

Good escape yarns have always won the admiration of the criminal fraternity and Guerin's notoriety gave him an entrée to the British underworld, many of whose members became his friends: the bank robber Walter Sheridan, the Bidwell brothers, who were regarded as the best forgers of Bank of England notes, and 'Moocher' Wigram, who had a reputation for planning some of the major jobs of the era. But Guerin drifted into petty crime and was gaoled in 1917 for trying to break into the Metropole hotel in Brighton. What hurt more was that when he went to the American Bar in London's Savoy hotel after his release, he was asked to leave as an undesirable.

By 1928, Guerin was able to write nostalgically of the 'good crooks' and say how he and the Scotland Yard men with whom he would occasionally drink had little respect for the new breed of criminal who had 'no skills'. Touchingly, he believed he was one of a dying breed: 'No doubt education is playing its part. "Honesty is the best policy" is one of the fundamental principles of the compulsory learning with which the younger generation of today are brought up.'

The Great War had its impact on the underworld just as the Second World War would in its time. Charles Leitch, an inter-war Scotland Yard detective, noted in his memoirs that the 'battalions of crime have been further swollen by the "new criminal" who in most cases is a criminal *"malgré lui"* – one who is driven into crime against his will by the fatal urge of an economic situation which he does not pretend to understand'.

Leitch and his colleagues believed that these men were unafraid of battle and killing and bitter at the failure to find them a role in society after the hell of the trenches. The detective saw a new generation of villain, brought up in the time of post-war uncertainty and disillusionment: the 'Legion of the Lost', he called them, men who wanted not just *'panem* (bread) but a large measure of *circenses* (circuses)'. These were to become the motor bandits and the confidence tricksters, the smash-and-grab artists and the cat burglars.

In the overheated post-war atmosphere of the early twenties, the alien criminal took on a special aura: a gang of 'international coiners and anarchists', as the police described them, established themselves in Hampstead. They were led by a Frenchman called Bonnot, the Red Bandit, who was, according to Leitch, the first 'motor bandit'. White Russians fleeing the Revolution could not be deported, a loophole exploited by criminals. And there was more than a whiff of anti-Semitism around the attitude to the Jewish criminals of the time. In *Crooks of the Underworld*, published in 1929, 'Charles Gordon' talks about the managers of night-clubs who, 'being of Jewish persuasion', advised people on how to carry out insurance frauds with their stolen jewels.

But it was on the racetracks in the 1920s and 1930s that the idea of organised crime and gang warfare was to have its modern birth. Street gambling was illegal and the large sums that bookies at racecourses could make drew a criminal element who offered what amounted to protection. Bookies would be charged for the chalk for their boards showing the odds, the stools on which they stood and the sponging down of their boards between races. They were also expected to dawdle about their work with clients so that the pickpockets could get to work. These 'dips' were described by Detective Superintendent Charles Vanstone as 'feral, shifty little men, they darted about all over the place'. The gangs also asked bookies to buy tickets in aid of the 'distressed wife' of any of the gang members unfortunate enough to be gaoled. It was simple enough to disrupt the pitches of bookmakers who would not co-operate.

Young lads worked for the gangs 'on the bucket', which meant they assisted in sponging down the boards. 'They [the bookies] could have done it themselves quite easily,' says Frankie Fraser, who did the job as an eight-year-old, 'but it was part of the ritual that they had to pay for this wonderful benefit.' He would take home 7s. 6d at the end of the day and the sponge man would do much better. To a young Fraser, whose father worked honestly for £2 10s. a week, it was clear that virtue was not its own reward: 'I thought to myself – this is the game to be in.'

Billy Kimber, a Birmingham-based bookie who had been born in south London, ran the Brummagem Boys and from around 1910 controlled the racecourses at Newbury, Epsom, Alexandra Park, Earls Park and Kempton Park. He had rivals, including a team from Leeds, one from the East End and the 'Italians'. Razor slashings were a regular occurrence and a bookie was killed at Sandown Park. One favourite weapon was a razor blade stitched into the peak of a cap.

In 1921 the Birmingham and Leeds mobs decided to take on the 'Italians' – Kimber hated all foreigners – on the last day of the Derby meeting at Epsom, but the Birmingham Boys ambushed their Leeds allies by mistake, only realising their error when a Leeds man shouted out, 'You have made a bloomer. We are Leeds men.' The pitched battle lasted ten minutes and twenty-three men were convicted of offences relating to it. The Home Secretary, Sir William Joynson-Hicks, responding to public expressions of out- rage at the mayhem, announced that he intended to smash gang- dom: 'It may be difficult to get rid of these gangs all at once but give me time.' He needed it.

The 'Italians' who enjoyed such a fearsome reputation were better known as the Sabinis. Darby (Charles), Joe, Fred, George and Harry Boy Sabini were an Italian immigrant family who launched their Bookmakers and Backers Racecourse Protection Society to challenge Kimber's hegemony on the tracks. They worked closely with the Jewish bookies and there was a series of pitched battles between the two gangs in the early twenties. The Sabinis operated from their base in Clerkenwell, in east London, the Little Italy of the era. Darby, a former boxer who had worked as a bouncer at the boxing halls in nearby Hoxton, held the posi- tion of paterfamilias in the local community. He sorted out internal conflicts and defended the honour of the young Italian women, most notably, so the story went, that of a barmaid whose dress had been stripped from her by a local bully. While most of his men were of Italian origin, Darby also worked with the Jewish bookmaker Alf Solomons, a local streetfighter called Georgie Sewell and the man who was later to take over some of his territory: Alf White. In the end, the Sabinis were more than a match for the Birmingham mob who, as Arthur Harding saw it, were 'all "rough house", they weren't as clever as the Darby Sabini lot'.

The Sabinis had a menacing reputation: 'Darby Sabini and his thugs used to stand sideways-on to let the bookmakers see the hammers in their pockets,' recalled ex-Detective Chief Superintendent Edward Greeno of the Flying Squad, who described another Italian member of the gang as having a 'name like a mineral water'. He claimed to have driven Darby Sabini away from Ascot on one occasion after the gang leader had been knocked unconscious by the Hoxton Mob. He had followed him to the gents, where Sabini's lieutenants were 'twisting his ears, a painful but effective way of bringing a man out of a fist-induced coma'.

The Sabinis were not above co-operating with the police when it suited them, specifically in helping them to arrest members of the Birmingham Mob so effectively that Kimber eventually decamped back to the Midlands. Sometimes the Sabinis would assist the constabulary by chalking the palms of their hands and slapping a known thief on the shoulder, thus identifying him to the racecourse police. One of the more colourful villains on the racetracks was known as 'The Policeman' because he posed as an undercover officer; when a victim had grabbed hold of a pickpocket, he would 'arrest' the culprit and take him off to 'the station' (railway rather than police).

The financial rewards were great, and at their peak in the thirties gangs reckoned to take upwards of £5,000 a day from the courses. But some criminals looked down on them. They were

suspicious of the close relationship they often had with the police
and accused them of being bullies because they tended to hunt in
packs of twenty or so. The Jockey Club asked the police for help,
without great effect initially. It remained a violent world, one
touched on by Graham Greene in *Brighton Rock*, and there were
many aspiring 'Pinkies' about as legitimate work dried up during
that decade.

The Sabinis brooked no argument and defended their reputation fiercely. But there was dissension within the Italian criminal
community, specifically between the Sabinis and the Cortesis
(another Italian gang), after Harry Boy Sabini had been shot
and wounded in the Frattellanza Club in Clerkenwell in
November 1922.

Louisa Doralli, the daughter of the club's manager, told in the
subsequent trial how she had noticed the arrival of the five members of the Cortesi gang: Gus, Paul and George Cortesi, Harry
'Frenchie' (which was another name by which the Cortesis were
known) and Alexander Tomaso, known as Sandy Rice. She had
grabbed 'Frenchie' as he pulled a revolver out of his pocket but he
wrenched it free. 'I didn't think they would shoot at a woman,' she
said. Gus Cortesi had then hit Darby Sabini with a lemonade bottle and fired at him, but the bullet went through the window.
Harry 'Frenchie', who had shot and wounded Harry Sabini, went
on the run and the *Daily Express* advised its readers how to spot
him: 'He walks with a Charlie Chaplin step, the result of a combination of flat feet and knock knees, but he is able to disguise not
only his walk but his features.' Not for long.

At the trial, George and Paul Cortesi and Tomaso were cleared
but two of the Cortesis, Gus and Harry 'Frenchie', were gaoled for
three years. Inspector Grosse told the court that there had been a
number of fights between the two gangs and that there was 'a
feud the bottom of which was difficult to fathom'. In sentencing
Gus and Harry, Mr Justice Darling remarked: 'I look upon this as

part of a faction fight which has raged between you and other Italians in consequence of some difference which the police do not entirely understand. You appear to be two lawless bands – the Sabinis and the Cortesis. Sometimes you are employed together against the Birmingham people and sometimes you are employed against each other … I do not think there is much to choose between you but the Sabinis are within the King's peace while in England and people must not be allowed to shoot them or at them.' He warned the 'Italian colony' that if such conduct continued, those responsible would be turned out of the country with their wives and children.

In its reports on the case the *Empire News* discreetly referred to Darby as 'one of the most talked-of men in London'. The Sabinis certainly made frequent appearances in court following similar feuds, often over the honour of women. On one memorable occasion the judge, Mr Justice Darling, who was proud of his linguistic abilities, addressed one of the Sabinis in Italian, which most of the gang did not understand, informed the jurors helpfully that the name derived from the Sabines and retold the story of the rape of the Sabine women.

The Sabinis were also victims of an anti-Italian feeling abroad in the thirties. In one Soho incident, thugs had entered a club asking, 'Are there any raddies here?' ('Raddies' was short for radicals, the name given to the Italian followers of Garibaldi.) The severe beating of an unfortunate Italian with 'life-preservers' (coshes) and chair legs followed. Pitched battles continued. One of the Sabinis' juvenile recruits was Umberto 'Battles' Rossi, who got his nickname because his mother would shout his name 'Berto!' from the window when he was playing football in the street and, with her Italian accent, it sounded to the English boys like 'Battles'. Since he was constantly at war – on one occasion splitting open another boy's head because he had mimicked his mother – the name stuck. 'That boy was in hospital for ten days,' he said.

'Through an incident like that people say "be careful" of him so I gained a reputation. I wanted to kill him but Albert Dimes (or Alberto Dimeo, one of the main London gangsters of the era) was there and he grabbed my hand and stopped it.'

Rossi's own family were law-abiding. 'I was the only villain. Our parents couldn't buy us a bike and I thought – this won't do me, I'll go out and nick a few quid. Then you get recognised by the Sabinis and they say "this kid's a tough kid". Clerkenwell was like a large family – there were straight-goers working in asphalt and marble but one or two families took up another way of life and were gangsters.' As a young man, he duly acted as a driver for 'Harry Boy' Sabini and was close to the gangster, Bert Marsh, a Soho bookie who had changed his name from Pasqualino Papa and who James Morton in *Gangland* suggests might be a more genuine contender for the title of 'godfather' at that time.

The most celebrated of the many conflicts was the Battle of Lewes in June 1936, mentioned at the start of this chapter. A gang of around thirty Londoners, mainly from Hackney and Hoxton, attacked a Sabini-protected bookie, Alf Solomons, and his clerk, Mark Frater. The aggressors had realised that undercover police were present – 'It's no good here, there are too many top-hats [detectives],' said one – but chanced their luck anyway. Police reported later how they had followed the gang and had heard one of its members, James Spinks, shouting, 'There they are, boys, get your tools ready.' Frater was lucky to be wearing his bowler hat, which partly deflected a hatchet blow from Spinks, whom police regarded as a ringleader. Someone in the crowd shouted a warning of 'Here they are, boys. Blow!' But a total of sixteen of the fighters were later gaoled by the solemn Mr Justice Hilbery. Not all the press saw it as a moment of great significance at the time: the *Daily Telegraph* gave it only a couple of paragraphs on its back page beside the stop-press news of the Lindbergh kidnap in

America. But the after-effects were great, both for the Sabinis and in terms of the public's attitude to organised gangs.

The Sabinis' power was already waning. Darby unwisely sued for libel after an unflattering profile appeared in the DC Thomson publication, *Topical Times*, in 1924, but he lost and was declared bankrupt. In court he denied being the 'king of the Sabini gang', saying, 'I am just a humble, peace-loving man.'

The Second World War was the final leveller. Some of the brothers were interned as enemy aliens. Harry Boy took over from Darby, who had moved to the South Coast of England, and recruited desperadoes from Sicily. Darby went briefly to gaol for receiving and while he was inside his beloved son was killed in action with the Royal Air Force. Darby died in Hove in 1950, a broken man. His funeral was not a gangland extravaganza, but crime correspondent Edward T. Hart reported that his old adversary, the detective Jack 'Charlie Artful' Capstick, who had founded the Ghost Squad at Scotland Yard in 1946, threw a red rose from his buttonhole onto the grave.

The White family from King's Cross gradually took over the racetracks and some of the streets with a casual brutality. As safe-cracker Eddie Chapman, later to emerge as one of the underworld's best-known characters, recalled, 'They had a team of little villains who would go and cut off anybody's head for about a tenner.'

The key development for the criminal between the two world wars had undoubtedly been the motor car, which made speedy escapes possible. The police response was the formation in 1919 of the Flying Squad, a mobile squad that initially used a covered wagon from the Great Western Railway for surveillance and two RAF vans, one to patrol north of the Thames and one south. The name came from a *Daily Mail* journalist, W. G. T. Crook, who referred to a 'flying squad' of picked detectives. There were eighteen in the initial squad – later to acquire the nickname

'Sweeney' from the rhyming slang of Sweeney Todd, the Demon Barber, and distinguished by its swooping eagle emblem. It would never be short of potential prey and one of its earliest targets was the twenties' best-known smash-and-grabber, one John 'Ruby' Sparks.

Born in Bermondsey, in south-east London, with a bare-knuckle fighter for a father and a receiver of stolen goods as a mother, Sparks began his apprenticeship as a junior mail-train robber, hiding in a hamper with the mailbags and sprinting out later with the loot. He was supposedly nicknamed 'Ruby' after he had stolen real rubies from a maharajah but been assured by an incompetent receiver that they were artificial; Sparks casually handed them out to friends, losing himself thousands of pounds in the process. He was also known as 'Rubberface' because of his habit of contorting his features whenever police tried to take a mug shot.

He first became a cat burglar, learning the tricks of the trade from an Australian wide boy called Georgie McCaig, but in about 1923, he teamed up, famously, with the 'Bobbed-Haired Bandit', a young woman called Lilian Goldstein, née Kendall, who drove a Mercedes and wowed the popular prints, one of which described her thus: 'She is often dressed in a red beret and motoring coat of the same colour, or in an all-green motoring outfit, and she is believed to be the brains behind recent country-house raids which have resulted in losses running into several thousands of pounds.' Goldstein came from a respectable family – her father was a house painter – and was a dressmaker before she fell for Harry Goldstein, as a teenager, and, according to the police, earned money for him by travelling round Hyde Park with clients in the backs of taxis. She had had a brief gaol sentence and a period of working as a saleswoman in London before meeting the dashing Sparks and acting as his driver. According to Sparks, it was Goldstein who persuaded him to give up 'that climbing lark' and get into a form of villainy as novel as cyber-crime would become nearly a century later – carrying out a robbery and fleeing in a motor car. As Sparks described it in his ghosted autobiography, 'nobody had thought of using motor-cars to commit thieving. It was practically sacrilege, as motor-cars were highly respectable things in 1920.' They worked together on smash-and-grabs and robberies for half a dozen years until they were arrested.

It could be a messy business. Sparks reckoned he had a 'handful of diamonds for each scar' and would carry bulldog clips in a clean handkerchief to keep the cuts he received on smash-and-grabs together until Goldstein could stitch them up. He also took advantage of the louche young men who liked to slum it in the West End: 'Upper-crust teddy boys prepared to betray the whereabouts of their own mother's tiara for the price of a night at Quo Vadis.'

Even the police were in awe of Goldstein's driving skills. 'Nutty' Sharpe recalled: 'She could whiz that great long tourer about with the skill of an artist ... her trouble was that she ought to have been a boy.' The Bobbed-Haired one, for her part, objected when Sparks's friends greeted her with 'Hi, doll'; her nickname was borrowed by the press from a notorious American, Celia Cooney, who robbed New York drugstores with her husband in the 1920s. They could not escape the law for ever and, although Goldstein was cleared of her part in the robberies, Sparks received a three-year term in 1927. His escape from Strangeways in 1927 was accompanied by a rhyming farewell note:

'The cage is empty
The bird is flown
I'm gone to a place
Where I'm better known.'

More sentences were to follow. He did not sit placidly in gaol and was a leading figure in the 1932 Dartmoor Prison mutiny.

On 10 February 1939, he was gaoled for five years. Sparks escaped from Dartmoor on 10 January 1940 with two fellow convicts, no mean feat then or now, and remained at large for five months. There was a poignant reunion with the Bobbed-Haired Bandit in whose Wembley Park home he hid. He had become involved with more ruthless, young gangsters and was slowing down. Goldstein was sentenced to six months for harbouring him but served only three weeks, as she was deemed to have acted only because of her long-term and 'womanly' attachment to Sparks: 'I can understand the human element in this case,' said the judge. 'He was an escaped convict to the rest of the world but that is not how she viewed him.' They parted, however, and Sparks eventually married a respectable woman called Anne, with whom he ran first an ice-cream business and then, at the end of the Second World War, the Penguin Club in Regent Street, complete with waitresses dressed as musical comedy sailorettes.

As for Lilian Goldstein, she bowed out with typical panache, telling Sparks as she explained her unwillingness to take part in a robbery with two young criminals which would involve throwing ammonia in someone's face: 'I've had this Bandit Queen lark, crime is for kids – like those two greasy-haired spiv wonders – not for grown-ups.'

Elsewhere in the underworld, there were very different larks afoot.

2

THE MASTER CRAFTSMEN – AND WOMEN

SAFE-BREAKERS AND CAT BURGLARS

'There was a hell of a lot of depression hitting the country but we lived like multimillionaires,' said Eddie Chapman. 'We used to motor down to Brighton in a drophead Ford Sedan which cost £120 brand new. They did ninety miles an hour and we used to smash them up and just buy another one.' He had met two chorus girls from a show called *Panama Hattie*. 'The one thing we had was money. Whenever we ran out, we used to go out and blow another safe. Life was a bit fast and furious then.'

Alongside the racetrack gangs of the twenties and thirties had developed a new breed – the artisan criminals, the master craftsmen, the specialists with their own skills and techniques. Foremost amongst them was the safe-breaker, traditionally the brain surgeon of criminal society. He was by now so prolific that security firms were having to invent ever more elaborate ways of trying to combat him: spinning safes, sinking safes that dropped underground, sliding safes with spring-loaded money boxes, even the Trusty Alarm Box 'which growls like an angry mastiff if any unauthorised person picks it up'. The cracksmen were undeterred.

In the 1930s Chapman came into this arena. A young man from a small mining village outside Newcastle, Chapman had been an apprentice in the shipbuilding trade before lying about his age and joining the Guards. He found protecting the Tower of London a tedious job and on his first leave headed for the West End. A Marble Arch prostitute introduced him to a new world: 'I met a lot of small-time villains and did one or two things with them. I bought a civilian suit and I never went back.' But the military came back for him and he was sentenced to 112 days in the glasshouse. After his release he drifted back to his new friends, and soon to prison in Lewes, where he met his partner-to-be, Jimmy Hunt. Hunt took him on his first serious job, a break-in of Fyffe's banana factory, where he learned how to rip the backs off safes with screwdrivers.

Chapman and Hunt became more daring. On one occasion they knocked a hole through the wall of a furriers in broad daylight, pretending they were watermen who had come to repair the mains. They stole to order – lipsticks, fur stoles, yeast tablets, whatever the customer had asked for.

The thirties were innocent times and when an American crook arrived on the scene in an underworld club the locals were amazed at his ideas on crime: 'He was sounding off about "Don't you guys ever do any heists?" We said, "What's that?" He said, "Just knock on the door and hold a fucking gun there and they'll fall apart." We said no, we never carry guns. There was an unwritten rule.' But the American did ask, more pertinently, if they blew up safes and, having learned of the rather primitive methods then used, suggested that they explore the possibilities offered by gelignite.

Chapman and Hunt set off to Wales to find the explosives in the quarries and mines there and stole 400 detonators and two packets of gelignite. They practised in the countryside and, having brought down a mighty tree, decided they were ready to blow up safes. Their journey began at Edgware Road underground station, which was relieved of its takings, and they travelled onwards and upwards from there: 'Every week we were knocking something out. The papers got hold of it and every time there was a job it was on the BBC – "There's been another attack by the gelignite gang."' A specially formed police squad initially thought an American gang was at work because of the traces of chewing gum used to fix the explosive. The press speculated that the IRA could be involved.

Odeon cinemas were a popular target. Chapman would hide in the gents, perched above a cubicle, until the cinema was closed and then break into the manager's office and set to work on the safes. On one occasion, robbing the Odeon at Swiss Cottage, he miscalculated the timing on one of the two safes and was bowled over and injured. After he had recovered himself, he stuffed the money into a bag and made his escape. On the underground he realised that the office cleaners who were staring at his dishevelment were noting the suspicious words 'Odeon Cinema' on the bag on his knee.

The safe-breaking method was basic: 'It was simply a matter of filling the keyhole up with gelignite.' One trick was to hang a typewriter on the handle of the safe so that when the blast weakened the lock the extra weight would open the door before too much damage was caused. After overdoing the amount of explosive on a few occasions, he decided to keep a methodical list of how much had been used each time and its subsequent effect. 'Each safe used to boast it was "in-built explosive-free",' said Chapman. 'This wasn't true. We had a few failures but not many. Most of the errors were to do with using too much explosive.' The French letter now came into its own as something for the safe-breaker's weekend: it would be filled with gelignite and water, knotted and then poked through a lock. The condom kept the explosive together, preventing it from dropping into the safe.

The attractions of the life were obvious. For a while in the thirties Chapman lived in a hotel by the Burlington Arcade: 'We were kids. We had a suitcase full of silver, half-crowns, sixpences, shillings, and every time I went out I'd say take a handful. We over-tipped everyone.' It was a time when Fats Waller and the Four Flash Devils were playing at The Nest, when Lady Mountbatten would arrive with a black escort and a bottle of whisky was 12s. 6d. The police knew what he was up to, but could never catch him in the act: 'They started to come round the clubs and pubs we were using. Fabian [Superintendent Robert Fabian, the Scotland Yard detective] used to walk in and say, "I know you've had it off, you bastard, buy me a drink."'

When other criminals complained about the additional police activity generated by all the safe-breaking, Chapman moved up to Scotland, having read about a record dividend being paid at a Co-operative store in Edinburgh. With a couple of accomplices, he drove north with gelignite and tools stashed in golf bags; their cover story was that they were off to a tournament. In the store, they found a half-ton Chubb safe in the office, and a difficult job was made more so when the look-out failed to spot a lurking policeman. One accomplice was caught in the Co-op itself, crashing into the pyramids of fresh fruit and tins as the policeman summoned help by 'playing his flute' (blowing his whistle). Chapman leapt aboard a slow train in his getaway and the team eventually drove south. They made it to Newcastle Corner, where they were spotted by police and arrested. Two of the Yard's big names, Edward Greeno and Fabian, arrived on the scene, but the local magistrate ruled that the robbers should stand trial in Scotland first and Chapman was granted bail. He raised bail for his confederates by breaking into another Odeon cinema.

Back in London, at Smokey Joe's club, he was warned that the Yard were looking for him and retreated to the Regent Palace Hotel: 'Written on the menu was "Come to sunny Jersey". I thought – that's a good idea.' And off he went with some accomplices.

The robbers' cover story in Jersey was that they were in the film business. The eventual plan was to head for South America. But their attempts to lie low were blown when one of the team sent some perfume to a new girlfriend he had met tea-dancing in Bournemouth. The faithless doxy told her brother, who was in the CID, and the hunt moved to Jersey. When his waiter's hand started shaking badly as he poured the wine, Chapman realised that the hotel must be under surveillance and fled along the beach. He told a local landlady he was just 'off the boats' and needed a bed for the night. He then broke into a handy cinema and stole £1,200, planning to ship out to Dieppe at dawn. But he was hardly in bed when the police burst in, shouting: 'Come on, you bastard, put the bracelets on.' He confessed that he had just broken into a safe so the local police insisted that he stay and stand trial. He was gaoled for two years.

But the war intervened. The Germans invaded the Channel Islands in 1940 and Chapman, not wanting to return to the British mainland and gaol, offered himself as a spy and was recruited as a German agent in 1941 with the code-name 'Fritz'. When they sent him back to England to carry out sabotage, he informed the intelligence services and became 'Zigzag', a double agent. As Ben Macintyre noted in his biography, *Agent Zigzag*, 'the instincts of the spy and the thief are not so different: both trade in stolen goods.' The unsuspecting Germans awarded him the Iron Cross while the British authorities, in recognition of his service, withdrew the outstanding charges against him, sparing him a possible sentence of twenty years for more than forty cracked safes. His story was later filmed as *Triple Cross*, starring Christopher Plummer, Romy Schneider and Trevor Howard.

'The deal was that any money I made with the Germans I kept,' says Chapman. 'I was working under British Intelligence and they behaved like a lot of Boy Scouts.' Chapman followed the motto of Do-Your-Best and kept safe-breaking, with jabs of cocaine before a big job to ease the pain of a bad back and give him the two hours he needed to operate: 'It was murder. If there had been a man-hunt, I would never have got away.'

Finally, after serving a total of only around four years for all his time safe-cracking, Chapman packed in crime and started a health farm – he had always kept in trim with boxers, believing a good criminal is a fit criminal. Amongst those who were to patronise his legitimate venture were boxers John Conteh and Frank Bruno. The *Sunday Telegraph* made him their 'honorary crime correspondent' and he and his businesswoman wife, Betty, invested wisely, buying a castle in Ireland and a yacht and sending their daughter to a good school.

If Chapman was the champion in the safe-blowing division, the most famous house-breaker of the post-Second-World-War period, and burglar to the gentry – 'His crime sheet read like *Debrett's*,' according to Chapman – was George 'Taters' Chatham. But Chatham lacked Chapman's ability to remain at large and was arrested so often he was rumoured to have his own room, 'Chatham's cell', in Chelmsford gaol. His first conviction was in 1931 and he spent a total of thirty-five years inside.

Chatham specialised in robbing the rich and famous and titled. He would break into a house and, if it did not live up to his expectations, he would try the one next door. Mr 'Teasy Weasy' the hairdresser and Madame Prunier, the restaurateur, were two of his victims. With the proceeds he ran a 12-cylinder Lagonda and a sports Mercedes. He had a certain sense of honour: on one occasion he had stolen an eternity ring and a fur coat from Lady Rothermere, wife of the chairman of Associated Newspapers. He was approached by one of the family's editors and asked if he could recover the items, which he duly did, complaining only at the cheap quality of the coat, which he said he would never have dreamed of giving to any of his girlfriends.

On one of his profitable expeditions his only accomplice was the London smog, a pea-souper so dense that people could not see more than a few feet in front of them. Using the cover provided by nature he broke into houses around Hyde Park, leaping from balcony to balcony and gaining meteorological recognition in the newspapers as the cat burglar who had 'made hay while the sun wasn't shining'. In December 1938 he was gaoled for six years.

One of Chatham's most famous heists, in April 1948, was that of the Duke of Wellington's swords from the Victoria and Albert Museum, into which he broke via a window 12 metres up by tying two ladders together. It was a simple job: 'I smashed the glass, took the swords and was away.' He removed the stones, sold some and gave others to his girlfriend. He had no regrets: 'I was sort of besotted by them and thought I had to have them. I was a rebel against authority and I had no respect for the police. If I could outwit them in any way, I would.' He rationalised the burglaries thus: 'They were usually very, very rich people, millionaires. Some of them regarded it as a nice thing to talk about at dinner parties.' He once attempted to break into the home of Raine Spencer, Princess Diana's stepmother, but inadvertently walked off the roof and fell four floors. He was in hospital for six weeks but was determined, like a rider thrown by a horse, to get back on the roofs. In plaster, bandages and great pain he broke into another house and was in the process of putting jewellery in his pocket when the maid walked in and alarmed her employers with her scream.

Chatham's tools were a screwdriver, gloves and a tiny torch, and he preferred to break in while everyone was at home at a dinner party so that there would be no alarms and the jewellery would be on the premises. Belgravia, Mayfair and Regent's Park formed his golden triangle. He picked his targets carefully, spending time in the public library examining reference books like *Who's Who* and *Burke's Peerage*, and glossy magazines like the *Tatler* and *Country Life*, which acted as a sort of *Exchange & Mart* for thieves.

He also had his inside men. An ex-captain in the Blues, who claimed to have escorted the young Princess Elizabeth and her sister, would tip him off as to where money and jewellery might be found and a Lloyd's clerk 'borrowed' confidential reports on insured premises, smuggling them out for Chatham to examine in a lunch hour.

But while Chapman had accumulated his money and spent little time inside, he gambled his loot as fast as he acquired it, reckoning to have stolen and spent several million pounds. In his sixties he was still stealing furs and jumping red lights to escape pursuing police cars. At seventy-six he was arrested for shoplifting: 'What have I got? A lot of sad memories. And thirty years inside.'

The inheritor of Chatham's mantle was Peter Gulston, who changed his name to Scott, an Irishman whose teenage apprenticeship involved burgling houses in the wealthy Belfast suburbs, with his Belfast Royal Academy college scarf, rugby bag and debonair manner as disguise. He reckoned to have carried out more than 150 such thefts by the time he was finally arrested in 1952 and sent to Crumlin Road gaol for six months. At his trial a policeman described him as a 'natural thief', which he took as a compliment. Scott's mainland career started when he was working in London as a doorman at a club and a 'suave, trench-coated guy' approached him with an offer of openings. He moved speedily into the first division of burglars. Although he was informed by a London criminal that he could never be 'one of the chaps' because he was Irish, his combination of charm and aggression secured him a permanent niche in the underworld.

It was not only the money that motivated him: 'Fear is a very private form of excitement and it's sexual in its context.' He soon moved into the homes of the rich, buying a new suit so that he

felt properly dressed. He recalls an early job: 'The butler was lay-
ing a majestic table laden with food and silverware and I felt a bit
like a missionary seeing my flock for the first time. I realized this
was my life's work, persecuting the rich and the opulent.' He
knew he had a talent for his chosen career: 'As soon as Lester Piggott throws a leg over a horse, you can see the magic. As soon as
I climbed up a drainpipe, my confederates could see the magic.'

His informants included chauffeurs from Knightsbridge, who
let him know the addresses of the wealthy and when functions
were being held. Scott was modest about his skills: 'The term "cat
burglar" has been romanticized. You're really only a dishonest
window cleaner. I actually watch window cleaners doing much
more dangerous things than I've ever done.' Although he had
given the fur trade 'the benefit of my degeneracy' for a number of
years, he was principally a jewel thief, moving on to antiques,
silverware and paintings. Mayfair was his private oyster and
the pearls were real. He learned where the rich hid their jewels;
one in soiled sanitary towels, others in the airing cupboard.

He lived on his wits. During one break-in 'a titled lady had
come to the top of the stairs and I shouted up, "Everything's all
right, madam" and she went off to bed, assuming I was the butler.'
(An earlier, notorious burglar had the almost endearing trade-
mark of reassuringly remarking, when he heard the burgled resident stirring upstairs, 'It's only me'!) Scott took a number of bad
falls, nearly impaling himself in Bond Street and falling through a
canopy in Viceroy Court. His career was the subject of a film
called *He Who Rides the Tiger*, starring Tom Bell and Judi Dench,
but Scott was in Dartmoor when they were filming and made no
money from it.

His other connection with the film world came when he
robbed Sophia Loren at the Norwegian Barn, in the Edgeware-
bury County Club, when she was making a film in England. He
had read that she would be paid in jewels and thought he would

have some for himself. On 28 May 1960, he drove into a garage in the area with a press card in the window of his stolen 2.4 Jaguar, pretending to be a journalist, and was tipped off as to her where-abouts by the petrol pump attendant. He spotted Ms Loren put-ting empty Chianti bottles in a bin and remembers her as 'an attractive peasant girl'. He broke in and removed a briefcase with cash and jewels and he recalls that the robbery was listed as the largest jewel theft in the world, worth about £200,000. On televi-sion subsequently, Ms Loren told the thief that she had put a curse on him as she came from old Gypsy stock, a curse that Scott ruefully admitted was successful, since he proceeded to lose all the money in the casinos. But he defended his calling.

'The police don't get terribly excited about people who burgle prefabs in Catford, whose owners don't have the ear of the Home Secretary. All my victims were very prestigious people – the only people who end up with vast amounts of money or jewellery are very greedy predatory people and it's been one of the great privi-leges of my life to persecute them. I almost feel as though I was an agent of God bringing retribution to the self-satisfied. I used to go to Ascot quite frequently and you'd meet them all in their top hats and their finery, prats chattering in monosyllables. I had an endemic hatred for them. I don't think I was very greedy. I spent my life giving money to head waiters, tarts and the needy book-makers. Of the two thieves on the cross with the Nazarene, I rather see myself as the one who didn't get into heaven.'

The solo professionals and the heavy gangsters did not mix too much. Gangsters, Scott believed, were parasites and predators to be avoided by the jobbing thief. On one occasion when a couple of gangsters wanted to join him on a raid because of his high suc-cess rate, he took them to a remote country mansion, placed them at the front of the building, went round the back and smashed a window to set off the alarm. Lights went on and the group sped away, relieved to have escaped. He asked the young gangsters to come again the next week but they had decided it was not the game for them.

In his memoirs, *Gentleman Thief,* published in 1994, he admitted to 'an obscene passion for larceny' but claimed to have given up thieving: 'There was no road to Damascus, no burning bush, I simply didn't fancy getting locked up again.' This was wishful thinking. In 1998 he was involved in the theft of Picasso's *Tête de Femme* from a Mayfair gallery. When arrested, he quoted W. E. Henley's poem, 'Invictus', to the officers: 'under the bludgeonings of chance, my head is bloody but unbowed.' They were unimpressed. Gaoled for three and a half years for handling stolen goods, he explained that he had been 'poaching excitement'. He spent his later years coaching tennis in Regent's Park and tending to the gardens of a local church. 'I used to think I was one of the most attractive men in London,' he said. 'I was never short of beautiful women on my arm. It wasn't until I ended up hitting tennis balls for a tenner an hour that I realized how totally unattractive I was. You almost become invisible in poverty. The number of people I've seen in recent years – the Rolls-Royce slows when it sees me, and I can almost feel them thinking – "there's no mileage in talking to Peter now" – and it glides away. But I was only a very modest performer in the sin business. I have a suspicion that if the Nazarene is in residence he might remand me in custody for a while but he'll talk to me again.' He died in 2013. At his small funeral, the songs 'Steal Away', 'They Can't Take That Away from Me' and Woody Guthrie's 'The Unwelcome Guest' were played. His ashes were scattered in the Secret Garden in Regent's Park, within sight of some of London's most expensive houses, which would once have been his happy hunting-ground.

A contemporary of Chatham and Scott was the Sheffield-born safe-cracker, Albert Hattersley, who learned his trade, as it were, in the mines as a young man when he worked as a shot-firer – using explosives to dislodge rock – in Thorpe colliery. He came from a hard-working, religious family and said in his memoir that his only explanation for choosing a life of crime was 'the craving for excitement'. Starting with cracking safes in post offices and branches of the Co-op in the north of England, he gained such a reputation as a 'peterman' that London gangsters recruited him in the 1950s and he was much in demand. Sometimes he was hired to blow up an empty safe to cover up for an inside job.

An early example of the British criminal happy to travel abroad for work, Hattersley graduated to small banks in Belgium and France, with help from a crooked Belgian jeweller to whom he had previously sold some of his loot. Late in his career, during the 1984 miners' strike, he was stopped by the police after he had cracked a safe in Woolworth's in Barnsley and offered a deal: if he would break into a mineworkers' union safe – to find evidence that the strikers were receiving financial support from Libya – he could be on his way. He turned the offer down. Hattersley, who died in 2017, aged ninety-five, also claimed to have broken into a safe on one occasion for honourable reasons: a woman friend was being blackmailed into continuing a relationship by a man who had some mildly pornographic photos of her; apart from destroying the photos, he felt he was justified in taking £1,000 he also found there. Scott, Chapman, Chatham and Hattersley were part of a long line of individual underworld entrepreneurs. There were others whose portraits would hang alongside them in a rogues' gallery of the first half of the twentieth century.

'Gentleman George' Smithson was one of the best-known of the country-house burglars. He lived respectably in Kensington, where he consulted *Burke's Landed Gentry* and *Debrett's* to see who had property where. He arrived at his chosen targets by bicycle and mixed little with the traditional underworld. But despite his discretion, he was gaoled three times between 1911 and 1929.

'Flannelfoot', the nickname of Edward Vicars, carried out hundreds of burglaries in the London suburbs in the thirties.

He covered his feet with cloth so that he could move silently about a house, burgling it and then making his getaway on a stolen bicycle. He was so successful that a special squad was set up at Scotland Yard to trace his muffled footsteps. He was caught in 1937, credited with 135 burglaries that year, gaoled for five years and died in prison.

One of the most celebrated teams, who operated after the Second World War, consisted of Johnny 'No Legs' and Harry 'The Doctor' Bass. Their technique was more Ealing than stealing: the legless Johnny, an Italian by birth, would approach a jeweller's at closing time in his electric wheelchair. He would ask for assistance because he had lost the key to his tool-box. The jeweller would oblige by lending him his bunch of keys to try. At this stage 'the doctor', wearing 'an Anthony Eden' hat, as one colleague described it, and with a stethoscope round his neck, would arrive and ask for directions to Acacia Avenue. During the course of this conversation Johnny 'No Legs' would make an impression of the keys. They would then wait six weeks or so, checking that there was sufficient jewellery to be worth stealing. Bravingtons in Blackpool was their Waterloo. Jewellers had exchanged information and the police were waiting. Both were gaoled.

Another high-profile criminal of the forties was Bert Holliday, also known as 'the Gentleman Cracksman'. Four police forces hunted him but he was only caught when he was spotted in 1949, stealing a cheese from the Dumb Bell Inn in Taplow, in Buckinghamshire. Although he came from a poor Elephant and Castle background, Holliday was a jewel thief in the Raffles mode. He posed as a retired jeweller, lived in a house called Jour de Fête on Friary Island on the Thames, rode to hounds and mixed with a southern county set. He also stole guns, antiques and petrol coupons. In his house the police found stolen goods that stretched back to 1932. Working sometimes with 'Poofy Len' Oades, Holliday was an expert climber and always carried a gun on his jobs.

For a while he baffled the police. Four forces hunted him and men were drafted into hunt balls to try to spot 'Johnny the Gent', as their suspect came to be called. When finally arrested, he was granted £2,000 bail and disappeared for three days before shooting himself in a hotel in Virginia Water with a gun he concealed in a walking stick. A suicide note expressed elegant regret that he would be unable to go fishing that day.

The thirties and forties were also the era of the conman. Many ruses were of touching simplicity, involving plausible rogues showing bogus newspaper cuttings that indicated they had inherited a fortune but needed a few quid to tide them over. The standard one required the conman to be possessed of a 'good' accent, an accomplice who would add authenticity to his story and a just-plausible hard-luck tale with the promise of easy riches for the victim. Many seemed to involve 'colonials' and one of the most successful in Britain was an Irishman, Fermoy-born Michael Corrigan or Cassidy, who worked under the name of Major Corrigan. He persuaded gullible souls to put money into Mexican oil concessions. In 1930, after promoting himself to Chief Inspector in Canada's North West Mounted Police and then General in the Mexican army, he was gaoled for five years. He bounced back as a supplier of aircraft to the Australian government, selling non-existent arms to the French government in the thirties.

Sir Richard Jackson, whose career spanned both the office of the Director of Public Prosecutions and the CID at Scotland Yard, bumped into Corrigan in the Carlton Bar after his release from gaol. He recalled: 'He greeted me most affably, recalling that we last met "at the Old Bailey" as though it had been the Athenaeum.' Corrigan thrived in the forties, claiming a concession for exporting balsawood on behalf of the Guatemala government, selling 145 Piccadilly and bulk-purchasing army surplus stores. Arrested for fraud in 1946, and facing a long sentence, he hanged himself with his tie in Brixton Prison, leaving a library book called *Hangman's Tie* by his bed and a contrite note to his solicitors, which said, 'I deserve everything for being such a greedy fool.'

The thirties and forties were an innocent time. Some people even fell for the cherishable 'Burn Up', in which the victim was shown a machine, not unlike the one that brought Frankenstein to life, which could reproduce money. All he had to do was provide the ready cash and it would then be doubled. Alas, in the midst of the transaction the machine would 'blow up' and the money would be 'lost'.

In the late thirties Eustace Hamilton Stewart Hargreaves, whom the press called 'The Biggest Spiv of All', profited from pre-war gullibility to con investors out of hundreds of thousands of pounds by selling a bogus liqueur which tasted revolting, and which he advised should be taken 'only in moderation because of its aphrodisiac qualities'. He was finally gaoled after the Second World War, in 1953, for eight years.

Most of the famous solo criminals were men but there have been some notable women thieves. When a beautiful artist's model called Mary Carr appeared in court in London in 1896, dressed in a velvet cloak and a hat with ostrich feathers, she was described as 'the Queen of the Forty Thieves', a title that was to be given to a number of women over the next three decades. Perhaps the woman with the greatest claim to the title was Alice Diamond, though, who was born in the same year that Mary Carr was sentenced to three years of penal servitude. Gaoled as a sixteen-year-old for stealing blouses from Gamages department store, she was soon described as 'the Queen of the Forty Thieves' by police and was seen as the head of a shoplifting crew which included the hard-drinking, no-nonsense Maggie Hill, sister of gangster Billy Hill. Neither of the two women was afraid of violence if caught and Alice used her vast rings as knuckledusters, according to her biographer, Brian McDonald, while Maggie armed herself with a razor. They were also known as the 'Forty Elephants'. (The *Daily Telegraph* crime correspondent of the time, Stanley Firmin, suggested that the 'Forty Elephants' came partly because of an association with the Elephant and Castle and partly because the shoplifters were mainly large women: 'some being nearly six foot tall'. Firmin claimed that these women would beat up young crooks who trespassed on their patch.) Maggie Hill had also made a name for herself by teasing a judge who gaoled her; she responded to his instruction of 'Take her down' by shouting out: 'You didn't say that last night when you were making love to me!'

Another prolific thief who called herself 'the Queen of the Underworld' was Zoe Progl, née Tyldesley, who embarked cheerfully on a criminal career, having been disowned by her parents after losing her virginity as a teenager to a GI on VE-Day in 1945. She worked first as a 'come-on' girl in post-war nightclubs and helped a junkie boyfriend steal furs, which gave her a taste for the high life and the company of gangsters; she had a child by Tommy Smithson, who would later meet a notoriously violent end. She would also lead on drunk American servicemen and relieve them of their wallets and trousers. As a woman she invited less suspicion than a male burglar when she broke into wealthy apartments in London to steal jewellery. In her memoir, *Woman of the Underworld*, she recalled her various essential disguises: 'the schoolmarmish look... for this I donned a sporty tweed suit, semi-rimless spectacles, a false hairbun.' Perhaps her greatest claim to fame was to escape, via a rope ladder and some trusty accomplices, from Holloway Prison in 1964, the first woman to do so.

A contemporary was Margaret Dowse. Known for her great charm, she worked with her boyfriend, Stanley Trinder. They would move to a town, find Dowse a job in a post office or shop, win the trust of the proprietors and eventually manoeuvre the situation for her to be allowed to take the cash to the bank. Then she would disappear and the couple would move on. By the time she was caught, in 1960, Dowse was wanted in forty-one different towns, and selection boards for CID officers were asked: 'What would you do about Margaret Dowse?' Gaoled at Lewes Crown Court for five years for larceny, forgery and falsification of accounts, she asked for another thirty-seven offences to be taken into account. The police were shocked that a woman should be such a prolific criminal: 'She was scarcely an ornament to her sex,' remarked Sir Richard Jackson.

One of Alice Diamond's young recruits in the 1940s was Shirley Pitts, who would go on to win the title of 'Queen of the Shoplifters'. She came from a criminal family – her brother, 'Adgie', was a well-known safe-cracker, a member of what was known as 'the Wine Gang' because they would take wine with them on their jobs – and was gaoled early in her career for pushing a store detective through a shop window. By the time she was in her twenties she had a reputation for being one of the most skilled shoplifters in the country.

Pitts had a special pair of custom-made bloomers into which she would stuff the stolen merchandise and which she never washed because she was superstitious. She would organise the teams which attacked Harrods, her favourite, and other major stores, using two or three accomplices to act suspiciously while the other went for the perfume counters. When electronic security tags were introduced, she would use foil-lined bags to get the goods past security or would snip off the tags and slip them into the shopping bags of the most respectable-looking customers. When the European Common Market was still only being discussed by politicians, she was organising shoplifting expeditions to Paris, Geneva and Berlin. Gaoled three times, she escaped once while pregnant with one of her seven children, who all went on to respectable careers. When she died in 1992, she was buried in a blue Zandra Rhodes creation, which friends said was stolen. A cortège of fifteen Daimlers cruised nearly twenty miles through

London to her resting place in a Tooting cemetery, where a trumpeter and guitarist played the 'Heaven, I'm in heaven ...' lines from Irving Berlin's 'Cheek to Cheek'. There was a floral tribute in the shape of a Harrods' shopping bag. Her epitaph was spelled out in flowers on her grave: 'Gone shopping', which became the title of Lorraine Gamman's biography of her.

3

KINGS OF THE UNDERWORLD

FROM BILLY AND SPOT TO THE PEN CLUB

Frankie Fraser was typical of many of his colleagues in pretending to be mad to avoid the call-up for the Second World War. His most convincing move was to assault a doctor and leap out of a window in the Bradford hospital where he had been taken for assessment. Taken to the Royal Infirmary in Edinburgh for further tests, he was told that he would have the waves in his brain electronically examined: 'So I thought to myself, "Let's kill the General! Let's kill the General!" It must have worked. They said that, owing to my condition, I was discharged from the army.' Thus was born 'Mad' Frankie.

But if Fraser and many like him opted out of the war by pretending to be two mailbags short of a heist, the war was still to have an enormous effect on the underworld.

'War at any time is not calculated to foster a respect for life and property and a war to the death like the last one, in which the

State perforce made great inroads on the liberty of the subject and the rights of property, was hardly the school in which one could expect respect for the law and the rights of others to flourish,' concluded Sir Harold Scott, Commissioner of the Metropolitan Police from 1945 to 1953, as he surveyed the steady climb of criminality. He believed that the introduction of widespread restrictions during the war, for reasons which were not always apparent to the average citizen, had bred a new lack of respect for law in general; evasions of petty rules were not regarded as 'crimes' in the old sense.

War had also uprooted hundreds of thousands of people, stability had been disrupted and children had grown up at a time of confusion and fear. There was the inevitable lack of respect for property, with the notion of 'to the victor the spoils' justifying what was essentially stealing and with looting in bombed cities seen as a minor peccadillo amidst the mighty evils of war. A large number of deserters who had neither identity cards nor ration books turned inevitably to villainy.

Rationing itself spawned crime, with ration books becoming a lucrative form of currency: in 1944, 100,000 food ration books were stolen from the Romford food office in Essex, a haul reckoned to be worth £500,000. The forging of clothing and petrol coupons was widespread. There were also extensive frauds in surplus vehicle deals and on the black market, currency fiddles, and illicit sales of gun carriers, rifles, lorries, food and raw materials from army dumps; even Ivor Novello, the composer of 'Keep the Home Fires Burning', was gaoled for four weeks for misuse of petrol coupons – and was looked after in prison by 'Mad Frank'. More significant were the wilder reaches of crime encouraged by the war. Some servicemen had acquired a knowledge of explosives and commando techniques which was not always discarded with the khaki. They joined the criminal who had either been in gaol for most of the war or who had dodged the call-up. Many career criminals, like Fraser, had feigned illness or mental instability.

The end of the conflict brought inter-gang rivalries into sharper focus. The White family from Islington, in north London, had emerged as the leading racetrack gang just prior to and during the war. The paterfamilias was 'Big Alf' White, the old confrère of the Sabinis and now a bookie whose star had waned somewhat after a bad beating at Harringay Greyhound Stadium in 1933. It was against the Whites that a young man, who was to emerge as one of the major figures in the post-war underworld, was to win his spurs.

Billy Hill, one of twenty-one children, was born in 1911 in London and grew up in Camden. His father was a painter and decorator who had served time for assaulting the police and his mother was a receiver (of stolen goods). One brother, Jimmy, was already a major pickpocket and many other members of the extended family were criminals. His brother-in-law, 'Brummy' Sparkes, was a well-known villain and sister Maggie was already an expert shoplifter. Eddie 'Devil's Island' Guerin was a family friend.

Compared in looks to Humphrey Bogart, Hill took a pride in his appearance and was a graduate of the birch. This brutal form of punishment involved a Home Office-approved implement soaked in brine. It was administered by a prison officer whom the prisoner was not allowed to see, and attended by a doctor who would afterwards dress the wounds with medicated pads. The cat, which was the other main form of official corporal punishment, was sometimes used so violently that a man's nipples would be torn off. A little leather singlet was provided to prevent this. As with the birch, there would be a large turn-out of officials to spectate.

Hill received his first sentence at fourteen and was to spend a total of seventeen years inside during his career. In the thirties he formed his own gang, the 'heavy mob' as they liked to be called, and he liked to give his team Runyonesque nicknames like 'Bear's Breath', 'Franny the Spaniel' (Franny Daniels), 'Horrible Harry' and 'Teddy Odd Legs' (Teddy Machin).

Seeking to establish himself as a major force in the underworld, Hill suggested in his autobiography, *Boss of Britain's Underworld*, that in 1947 he became the 'bandit king' of London by winning a historic showdown with the Whites. He claimed that he assembled 150 thieves and tearaways who were unhappy about the power wielded by the Whites, who were taking protection money in the West End and charging a percentage to people using the illegal clubs. They included gangs from the Elephant and Castle, Kilburn, Paddington and Essex. Hill recounted that the Whites, confronted by this show of strength, tacitly relinquished claims to the leadership of gangland. There was, indeed, a meeting of sorts but it seems to have been neither as large nor as epic as he recalled. Frankie Fraser, one of Hill's lieutenants, remembers only some of White's people being cut and Harry White hiding under a table in a club called the Nuthouse.

If the Whites had showed, Hill said, 'St Valentine's Day in Chicago would have looked like a Girl Guides' picnic.' However, it is more likely that the result of such a contest would have been a lot of striping and slashing, the favoured weapon of the time being the 'chiv' or knife. Hill claimed to have always slashed downwards, so that if his hand slipped he could not cut an artery, and he liked to leave his signature – a V for victory sign – on an enemy's cheek. He seems to have revelled in it: on one occasion he had been attacked by a man who shoved a broken glass in his face in a north London pub appropriately called the Butcher's Arms: 'I pulled the glass out of my face with one hand and the chiv out of my pocket with the other. Then I got to work doing a bit of hacking and carving. I don't know how many blokes I cut that night. I didn't care. When you get a jagged glass shoved into your face you don't bother about counting the blokes you chiv. You just hack away until your knife gets blunt or the others swallow it.'

Hill's smash-and-grab raids were a feature of London criminal life and he used to claim he had so many villains anxious to work with him that he had to put them on a rota. He claimed, too, to have invented the 'run-out'. This method of stealing from jewellery shops used the most respectable-looking of the thieves – one young 'screwsman' even had his hair waved to make him look like a toff who might be interested in an expensive engagement ring. Hill claimed that he used young blades from Eton and Dulwich College. The smart young man would go into a shop carrying *The Times* and a briefcase and ask to see some rings. Having won the confidence of the jeweller, he would then grab the rings and sprint out of the shop to the waiting getaway car.

Guns, mainly .45s, Lugers, Smith & Wessons and Colt revolvers, were easy to come by. Ex-servicemen had brought them back from the theatres of war and a post-war amnesty revealed no fewer than 30,000 in circulation. A revolver cost £5, an automatic £10.

Hill's lieutenants were a mixed crew. One, Bobby Ramsey, found God while in Dartmoor in the mid-fifties and would be seen calling on his Maker as he marched round the prison's football pitch. He beat up one cynic who thought it was a pose to fool the chaplain. (Finding God was a popular method of trying to obtain an early release, which some chaplains did little to discourage. One at Pentonville Prison, in the days before radios and Sunday papers were allowed, ensured a full house in the chapel by reading out the football results in the Sunday morning service, between the hymns and the lessons.)

Not a man plagued by self-doubt, Hill claimed to have set up a business called Murder Inc. in 1952/53 which involved not murder, but merely 'warning' lovers away from unfaithful wives and collecting money from the husbands. His claim that around 300 such jobs were carried out seems fanciful to say the least.

The other major gangland figure of the fifties was Jack Comer, better known as Jack Spot, the nickname coming either from a prominent black mole on his cheek or – the version he preferred – that whenever there was a fight, he was 'on the spot'. He was born into a Polish Jewish immigrant family in 1912 and had won his awesome reputation by leading the attack on Oswald Mosley's fascist Blackshirts when they tried to march through the East End on 4 October 1936, threatening the Jewish traders in the area; he armed himself for the fray with a sofa leg topped with lead, constructed for him by a sympathetic cabinet-maker.

It was the Hill–Spot axis that was finally to supersede the Whites in terms of influence and power. Initially, the two men were friends and close colleagues. Spot even met Hill at the prison gates when he came out in 1949 and they and their partners holidayed together in the south of France.

'Spotty' had fought briefly in the war, although he seems to have been at odds with the authorities for much of the time over discipline and was eventually discharged, like so many of his associates, on grounds of mental instability. Most of his family were killed in the Blitz and, after a violent argument with an anti-Semitic thug in a London spieler, he decamped to Leeds, where he worked with émigré Poles who had established themselves in the underworld there and who protected the Regal Gaming Club. At the end of the war, Spot returned to London and set about re-establishing himself in the criminal fraternity. He ran a successful illegal gambling club using the Aldgate Fruit Exchange as a front, complete with bogus staff whom he gleefully described: 'All these geezers with respectable ties and tea-shop manners who acted as clerks [and] were on my payroll.' He reckoned to make £2,000 a week from the *chemin de fer*, faro and rummy tables and boasted that 'Monte [Carlo] would look like a funfair compared with my spieler'.

He was also taking part in racetrack rackets and enforcing his position with selected attacks on associates of the Whites. His version of the fight for ascendancy with the Whites was that there was a pitched battle between the two gangs in a club off Piccadilly in January 1947. Each side had a different version of who started the slashing but Spot came out on top and claimed later: 'Coshes and knives were flashing about ... the King's Cross boys couldn't take it.' He claimed, without much evidence, that he could assemble 1,000 fighting men armed with grenades, Sten guns and service revolvers to finish the job. However, there was to be no final confrontation. He told *Daily Sketch* readers, who were treated to his memoirs in 1955, that he was 'the king who kept his crown by being tougher than the other toughs'. (The *Sketch* cheerfully ran Spot's memoirs alongside stern editorials entitled 'Smoke Out The Rats', in which it said that gangland should be purged: 'We expect the police to clean up these vermin and to crush them for ever ... the jealous rats fighting it out on the streets and the alleys could in a short time make Soho a desert where no respectable citizen would risk his reputation or personal safety.')

Married to the beautiful Rita, a young Irish woman who had fallen for his undoubted charm and style, Spot played the part of the gang leader to perfection. Leonard 'Nipper' Read, the detective who made a name for himself tackling London's later gangs of the sixties, recalled Spot at the height of his power in the forties and early fifties: 'He dressed in beautifully-cut suits and always wore a brown fedora and he had a religious way of progressing through the day. He would go to the barber's in Edgware Road station and they would shave him and when he felt immaculate, he would walk down the Edgware Road, waving and saying good morning to people. He would go into the Bear Garden at the Cumberland Hotel and would sit there for the rest of the morning.

People would come up and ask his advice about various matters and he would give it much in the way that Don Corleone did in *The Godfather*.'

Occasionally, Spot had to make his presence felt personally. In 1947, he beat up Johnny Warren, a member of the Whites' extended family, in a pub toilet in Soho. As he explained to writer Robert Murphy years later: 'I used to knock 'em out in the lavatory. That was my surgery. I used to go into the toilet and Bomp! Leave 'em in the piss.'

Spot hired young heavies for protection work and as bodyguards, amongst them Joe Cannon, a west London hardman, who was later to spend many years in gaol for armed robbery. He made a niche for himself in British penal history by relieving himself over the desk of the governor of Brixton Prison.

A familiar, cigar-smoking figure in Soho, Spot used the Modernaires Club in Old Compton Street as one of his offices. When the telephone rang for him, he silenced the musicians' rehearsals of what he called their 'heeby-jeeby music' with an imperious wave of the hand. Spot liked people to do as he said. When pianist and trumpeter Denis Rose arrived two hours late for a gig, he told him he would never work in the West End again. The rest of the band played 'Please Don't Talk About Me When I'm Gone'.

One of the other main figures of the forties and fifties was Alberto Dimeo, or Albert Dimes, an Italian-Scottish ex-Borstal boy, RAF deserter, racing man and impetuous gambler. He was a respected figure in Soho and renowned for a sense of humour: he gave jazz club owner Ronnie Scott, with whose father he went racing, a magnum of champagne to open whenever the club started making money. It gathered dust for many years.

Dimes had been charged with the murder on 1 May 1941 of Harry 'Little Hubby' Distleman, the doorman of the West End Bridge and Billiards Club – known to its regulars as the Old Cue Club – who had been stabbed to death on its Wardour Street premises. There had been a fight, probably over the barring of a man from another club a few nights earlier, and Antonio 'Baby' or 'Baby-face' Mancini, who managed the club downstairs, said he had slipped off his dinner jacket and gone to investigate. He claimed that he had heard a voice shouting 'There's Babe! Let's get him!' and had stabbed Distleman in the chest in self-defence.

Distleman collapsed, crying, 'He has stabbed me in the heart. I am dying.' The *Daily Express* reported laconically: 'This is a crime Hitler did not commit... It was just a good old-fashioned Soho crime.' The paper commented that 'Soho, well hit by the raids, chatted more over Hubby Distleman's death than of the night they hit the hospital on the corner. For they knew Hubby was just the victim of an internal war between gangs that have run through Soho even in the Blitz.' Mancini, Joseph Collette and Dimes were charged with the killing and Mancini, whom detective Edward Greeno described as 'a highly-strung individual with a habit of assault-and-wounding', was convicted and hanged. Dimes and Collette were convicted of unlawful wounding. Greeno concluded: 'The hanging of Mancini put the fear of God into the racecourse riff-raff. Soho could now look forward to a nice quiet war.'

The rifts in the underworld were becoming apparent by the fifties and Hill, Spot and Dimes all had parts to play in the ensuing bloodshed. Hill had already written his 'Boss of the Underworld' story in the *People*, along with *People* reporter Duncan Webb, and Spot had penned his less fluent 'King of Soho' tale for the *Daily Sketch*. Frankie Fraser and the Hill team were becoming less impressed with Spot's tactics: 'He would terrorize a thief into giving him something, but he wouldn't go and thieve it himself,' said Fraser.

Hill and Spot drifted further apart, and the latter had also fallen out with Dimes. According to Frankie Fraser, Dimes's deceptively easygoing manner – he would allow people to tease him about money they owed him – fooled Spot into thinking he was weak and had 'lost his bottle'. In 1955, the wily Hill was able to discredit Spot. He had found out that Spot had given evidence against three men in an assault case back in 1937. Although this was nearly twenty years earlier, Hill got hold of the depositions of the committal proceedings which showed Spot up as an informer and had copies made and pasted up in underworld pubs. Spot was livid at this blow to his image and thought that a fight with Dimes would improve his sinking status. He had already suffered the indignity of being arrested in 1953 for possession of a knuckleduster.

On 11 August 1955, Spot approached Dimes in Frith Street, in Soho, and stabbed him in the thigh and stomach. Dimes fled to a fruit shop on the corner of Old Compton Street, where he knew he would find an industrial can-opener to use as a weapon. Spot pursued him with a potato knife but was waylaid by the shop-keeper, a woman friend of Dimes, who cracked him over the head with a set of scales. Dimes grabbed the knife and slashed Spot, who collapsed in a nearby barber shop. Spot was taken to the Middlesex Hospital. *Daily Express* reporter Frank MacGarry, who tried to enter the ward, asked one of Spot's associates what was being discussed: 'Peace, chum. Just peace,' came the reply, which MacGarry recorded in an article headlined 'The Drape-Suit Men Take Presents to Spot'. Dimes was treated in Charing Cross Hospital.

The fight itself was heralded as an outbreak of gang war. The *Daily Express* report set the scene: 'The hands of the clock above the Italian Espresso coffee bar pointed to 11.40. Mambo music was blaring from the juke-box ...' The spilt blood in the heart of the city seemed to authenticate the notion of a London gangland for a public that had resigned itself to celluloid gangsters with American accents. There was even a hint of pride in the reports. Britain had its own gangsters at last. The BBC News and Infor- mation Unit opened a 'gang warfare' file for the first time. 'The fight completely put the underworld, as they call it, right into focus and it hasn't stopped,' said Fraser.

Spot was tried for attacking Dimes and cleared – it became known as 'the Fight that Never Was' – thanks to the intervention of Parson Basil Andrews, an eighty-eight-year-old cleric who was down on his luck, having welshed on a number of betting debts, and who seemed to have wandered into the Old Bailey off the set of an Ealing comedy. Adjusting his dog collar, Andrews told the court that Dimes had been the aggressor and had attacked Spot first.

It later emerged that Andrews had been given £63 by one of Spot's associates, Morris 'Moishe Blue Boy/Blue Ball' Goldstein, to ignore the commandment about bearing false witness. Andrews admitted the deception and was then used as a major prosecution witness against Goldstein, Rita Comer (Mrs Spot) and two others: Peter MacDonough and Bernard 'The Yank' Schach. Andrews gave moving evidence: 'I was tempted and I fell.' Goldstein was gaoled for two years, Schach and MacDonough for a year and Mrs Comer, so striking a woman that even the detectives fancied her, was not gaoled. (Goldstein was a successful criminal and once bought himself a flash Mercedes; when he drove it home his mother, seeing the German-made vehicle, shouted at him: 'There's blood on the hands that made that car!')

The Hill–Spot feud rumbled on. In May 1956, Hill found that Spot was planning an attack on him and persuaded some of the latter's disloyal men to tip him off about their boss's movements so that he could get his revenge in first. Spot was well aware of what was now afoot and asked the police for help, which they felt unable to give. Fraser, on the run on a charge of grievous bodily harm at the time, was one of the hit squad, armed with a shillelagh. When he saw Spot and Rita and two of the Spot team, he shouted, 'Right, it's on you, Jack!' and promptly set about him. 'He must have been practising his scream because it was louder than his wife's,' said Fraser of Spot's reaction. 'Hers was quite loud but his was even better. I just whacked him with the shillelagh a couple of times and someone else cut him and that was that.' Fraser said he would cheerfully have killed Spot because of his attack on Dimes. He had planned to humiliate him by cutting a noughts and crosses pattern on his face 'but unfortunately there wasn't that amount of time'.

Fraser and Bobby Warren were each gaoled for seven years for their part in the attack, despite Fraser's counsel's plea that he was 'a weaker vessel of mankind who has been used for a foul purpose'. 'Billy Boy' Blythe was sentenced to five years and two others, William 'Ginger' Dennis and Bert 'Battles' Rossi, to four. One of the accused, Tommy Falco, giving evidence, complained to the prosecution: 'Would you like to speak less big words? I can't understand them.' During the trial Spot was described as 'a corner boy of the lowest ilk' and 'the man who prides himself as being the King of the Underworld – the scum of the earth'. Mr Justice Donovan told the jury: 'The civic value of the man Comer [Spot] is neither here nor there. If this sort of thing is allowed to spread it will not be safe for any of us to walk the streets.'

Hill waited outside the court, dressed in a grey slouch hat and brown linen suit, sitting on a bench marked 'Remembrance' in a nearby churchyard, his left-hand-drive Buick parked ready for departure after the verdict. Spot, who had not given evidence against his assailants, said as he left the court, 'I ain't afraid of anyone but I want a quiet life now.' The reaction from the press was unsympathetic. Cassandra of the *Daily Mirror* referred to 'the scum of the earth flaunting their mob rule in London town'. Hill had made his point and the underworld joke of the time – 'Billy Hill's the boss – Jack Spot was very cut up about it' – marked the end of the Spot era.

Talking just before his death in 2017, at the age of ninety-four, 'Battles' Rossi was still angry that Spot had identified his attackers:

'you don't expect someone to do that if they're a gangster and they put it about that they're king of London. He was a rat.' He added: 'I was the Mafia's man over here,' but was cagey about what his work for them actually involved. He said that he would receive a call to come to the US and be put up in a hotel. 'Next morning, someone would pick me up and drive me wherever and then point out the subject. It might be the day after that I'd get a call: "nice bit of work." I'd be picked up, given an envelope and driven to the airport.' Interviewed by the police over many murder cases, he was charged along with another man, John Heibner, with the murder of Biddy Gold in 1975 in the basement of the clothing business she ran in Clerkenwell. The prosecution suggested that Rossi gave the murder weapon to Heibner, who was convicted. Rossi, defended by Jeremy Hutchinson, QC, was acquitted after he claimed that the package he had been seen handing to Heibner contained jewellery, not a gun.

But the battle in Soho was not over yet. When Tommy Falco was slashed outside the Astor Club the following year and required forty-seven stitches, he named Spot as his attacker. In fact, Falco was involved in a devious plot to have Spot gaoled in retaliation for what had happened to Fraser, Warren and Co. Falco had been slashed by Hill's side with instructions to inform the police that Spot had done it. 'It's a diabolical liberty,' were Spot's immortal words when he was arrested. This elaborate plan emerged during Spot's trial, when the appropriately nicknamed Victor 'Scarface' Russo gave evidence that Dimes and Hill had asked him if he would agree to have his face slashed for £1,000 and say that Spot had done it. Russo, a flyman down to his knuckle-bones, had taken half the money but he changed his mind about taking any further facial surgery. His evidence cleared Spot. The judge, Mr Justice Streatfield, said in his summing-up: 'There has been something like gang warfare going on – and heartily sick of it all respectable people are becoming.'

Spot moved into clubs, but his first venture, the Highball in Bayswater, went up in flames shortly after it opened. He ran into heavy financial problems over misguided legal actions and was evicted from his West End flat. In 1958 he did a deal with pulp-fiction writer Hank Janson and published *Jack Spot – the Man of a Thousand Cuts*. He slipped from view, living quietly in Ireland and London, where he was cared for by his loyal daughters and seen occasionally at boxing matches. He had the satisfaction of outliving Dimes, who died of cancer in 1972 and whose Kent funeral was attended by the actor Stanley Baker.

Others liked to claim a place in the criminal aristocracy. For instance, the *Daily Sketch* in 1959 carried a boast from a young man called Joseph Francis Oliva: 'I am the leader of a gang 400 strong. They call me King Oliva ... I am going to be the boss of the nightclubs round the West End. I have got to shift one or two big gang leaders to do it. But I have got a man behind me financing me.' He claimed he could raise his 400 foot-soldiers with just fifteen or twenty telephone calls. But when he was later arrested for other, less spectacular, matters the 'King' abdicated and said he only made the claims for money. The most notorious battles for ascendancy may have been fought on the streets but the underworld was attempting to acquire its big money elsewhere, not always successfully.

In the summer of 1948 the police were tipped off that a raid on a bonded warehouse at London Airport was being plotted. The plan was to drug the tea of the BOAC staff in charge of the warehouse and steal a million dollars' worth of bullion and around £500,000 worth of other goods. On 24 July, seven masked men, armed with iron bars and bludgeons, broke in and found undercover police officers who had taken the place of the BOAC staff and were pretending to be drugged. The officers allowed themselves to be tied up and gagged with adhesive tape. One who did not seem drowsy enough was coshed into unconsciousness. But when the robbers were about to start opening the safe other policemen entered with the words: 'We are police of the Flying Squad. Stay where you are.'

There was then a wild fight between the two sides, immortalised as the Battle of Heathrow, and complicated by the fact that both sides had dressed up in BOAC uniforms. Eight gang members were arrested and charged, along with the airport loader who had tipped them off about the warehouse. There was a cherishable tale that one man did escape and thereafter became known as 'Handy Henry' because he had hidden under a police van, clinging to its axle all the way from the airport to Harlesden police station, where he made his getaway. Spot claimed later that Teddy Machin also escaped and fell in a ditch, where pursuing police failed to see him. Those arrested received sentences of from five to twelve years' penal servitude. The loader, who co-operated with the police by identifying the gang, received only a bind-over.

But the symbolic robbery of the period was the Eastcastle Street mail-bag heist in 1952, in which an estimated £287,000 was stolen. It was, as one crime reporter recorded, carried out with 'Montgomery-like thoroughness ... it went off as smoothly as any of our commando raids during the war'. Indeed, the actual raid on the van had been practised with precision on roads outside London, with the cover that the robbers were a film unit making a crime movie.

It was 4.17 a.m. on 21 May 1952 when a post office mail-van on its way from Paddington Station to St Martins-le-Grand general post office yard was held up in Eastcastle Street in the West End. When the van stopped at the lights, which had been tampered with, one car, a black Riley, blocked it in front and another, a green Vauxhall, at the rear. Each car had four men in it. The men in the front car leapt out and attacked the post office men while those behind went to work on the back door of the van. One of the van crew, Henry Syms, was heavily coshed and two others hurt. Three of the robbers then drove the van, which had already had its alarm disconnected, to a yard in Augustus Street in Camden Town. There, two other men helped transfer eighteen mailbags – another thirteen had been abandoned – to a fruit and vegetable van already prepared with hidden panels. This van was driven to Spitalfields Market in east London and watched until it was felt that it would be safe to move it. The rest of the team sped off in their stolen cars to Covent Garden, where they dumped the vehicles and were picked up by other members of the gang.

From the start, it was clear that there had been inside information. It was also obvious that serious professionals were at work. The *Daily Mirror* speculated that those involved must be 'aged about twenty, probably ex-Borstal boys, expert motor drivers'.

Ronald Howe, the head of the CID, took personal charge of the investigation with Detective Chief Superintendent Bill 'Cherub' Chapman of the Flying Squad and Superintendent Bob Lee running the operational side. The insurance assessors offered £25,000 for information leading to the recovery of the money. So seriously was the crime seen nationally that the Prime Minister, Sir Winston Churchill, asked for daily reports on the inquiry and the Postmaster-General, Earl De La Warr, had to give explanations to Parliament.

More than a thousand police officers were involved in the hunt, scores of villains were rounded up and 400 police cars carried out a sweep of arrests. None of the main robbers was ever caught but it was widely accepted that Billy Hill had organised the heist. *People* reporter Duncan Webb suggested that the job had been masterminded by a man to whom he gave the not very subtle pseudonym of 'Bill'. Hill himself could not resist bragging about the job in his memoirs, and told how a man had disconnected the van's alarm by walking into St Martins-le-Grand yard and tampering with the relevant wires in the targeted vehicle.

The man was 'Taters' Chatham. Another of the participants was Terry Hogan, who fell to his death from a flat in Brentford in 1995 after suffering from depression. After being a highly successful criminal in the fifties and early sixties he went straight and was never linked to the Eastcastle Street job.

Frankie Fraser said that Hill was so anxious to avoid the sort of tip-off to the police that had scuppered the Heathrow robbery that he summoned his team on the eve of the heist, told them their roles and then allowed no one to leave, even to get their masks or their gloves. Hill had fixed up alibis for the gang, adamant that no one should stray outside the premises: 'Even if someone went to the toilet, someone stood outside. That's how thorough it was,' said Fraser.

The robbery was regarded by the police as the start of a new era, the beginning of 'project' crime. The message to the criminal fraternity was that crime was now big business, that planning and patience paid off.

Two years later, in 1954, a lorry belonging to KLM Dutch airlines stopped outside the KLM office in Jockey's Fields, Holborn, in central London. As its tailboard dropped, a smaller van backed on to it, a man jumped from van to lorry, shouted, 'Hold on, hold on a minute' and threw two boxes containing £45,000 of gold bullion into the van, which then sped off. Hill was an obvious suspect. His warehouse – he was then in a legitimate business selling toys – was searched and every doll and teddy bear inspected, providing some comic relief: these were 'talking' dolls and bears which said 'Oooh' and 'Aaah' when picked up. Again, he was never charged but the word amongst his associates was that he had masterminded all three of these first large post-war operations.

Hill had a faithful wife, much admired by his criminal friends, who only left him after twenty long-suffering years. He let her keep one of his Soho clubs and gave her a poodle called Chico as a going-away present. He embarked on a new relationship with Gypsy, a striking beauty who attracted Hill's attention by belting three women with a high heel after she had seen them mocking a deaf mute in the street. In 1955, the couple tried to move to Australia but, by the time they reached New Zealand via the Pacific, it was clear the country would not admit them. 'It makes you sick when you think we have come this far,' Gypsy told the *Daily Express*. 'If only we had known sooner, we could have got off earlier – in Tahiti.' Gypsy spent time in prison awaiting trial for smashing a table lamp into the face of a man who made a mocking reference to her fur coat – 'look at her, in her rabbit' – in a nightclub in Paddington in 1957. She was later cleared after witnesses suffered mysterious memory losses. The couple moved to Marbella in the sixties then returned to England to run a club in Sunningdale until the mid-seventies. Hill died in 1984.

Armed robberies were rare in the post-war years: there were nineteen in 1950, ten in 1951 and nineteen in 1952. Money was moved from bank to bank in brown vans or hired cars, some of whose drivers used to tip off criminals as to when and where they were going, even indicating by the use of the brake light whether or not the bank manager had handcuffed himself to the bag. As Frankie Fraser explained, it was necessary to beat up the inside man to make it realistic: 'You not only took his ignition key so that they couldn't follow, you took some of his blood.' (A sawn-off starting handle encased in rubber was a favourite weapon.) This was to persuade the police, who were invariably looking for an inside man, that the recipient of such a beating could not have been involved. Robbers were still reluctant to use firearms.

Robert Fabian, one of the Yard's most famous detectives and no shrinking violet, had a helpful theory that all gunmen had grey eyes: 'Unless he is insane, the brown-eyed criminal does not carry a gun with intent to use it. He may think he does but the showdown proves him wrong. The man who shoots to kill has grey eyes.' Fatal shootings were rare, one of the reasons why those that happened received so much publicity.

On 13 February 1948, in Southgate, PC Nathaniel Edgar, patrolling with a colleague, was shot three times in the groin and thigh and died of his wounds. The man who killed him was a deserter named Donald Thomas. The hunt for Thomas is significant for students of police semiotics: in the press release the phrase 'a man believed to be able to help with their inquiries' was used for the first time. Thomas was found at a boarding-house in Clapham. A Luger with eight rounds in its magazine and one in its breech was hidden under his pillow, and by his bed was a book called *Shooting to Live with the One-Hand Gun.* He was arrested after a short struggle. His death sentence was commuted to life imprisonment and he served only fourteen years.

A notorious killing a year earlier had involved Harry Jenkins, a member of a Bermondsey criminal family, who killed a motorcyclist called Alec d'Antiquis, who had tried to stop him escaping from a hold-up at a pawnbroker's shop in Charlotte Street in London's West End. Jenkins was a self-confident young criminal, known as the 'King of Borstal'. At twenty-three, he knew all the tricks of the trade. He sent out for a lunchtime edition of an evening paper before the identification parade and shoved it in his jacket pocket; his idea was that a witness might spot it and reckon that he could hardly be the suspect if he had been out on the street so recently. He was nonetheless charged with his associates, Christopher Geraghty and Terence Rolt, and executed with Geraghty in Pentonville Prison in September 1947 after a six-day trial; Rolt was too young to hang. The shooting shocked even some members of the criminal fraternity. 'Most of the people in the underworld abhorred it as much as ordinary people,' said Eric Mason, a gangland figure. 'It wasn't the done thing.'

One shooting which was to be remembered decades later was that of PC Sidney Miles on 2 November 1952. Two young men, Christopher Craig and Derek Bentley, had been caught red-handed on the roof of a Croydon warehouse. Bentley was arrested and uttered the immortal words, 'Let him have it, Chris.' His family argued that he meant Craig should surrender the gun, but the police claimed it amounted to an instruction to fire. Craig shot Miles fatally but was too young to hang, a penalty given instead to the luckless Bentley. His execution at Wandsworth Prison in January 1953 provoked angry demonstrations and was a major factor in the abolition of the death penalty. Craig served his sentence and re-emerged to live a quiet life as a plumber in the Home Counties. Bentley received a conditional posthumous pardon in 1993, after forty years of campaigning by his sister, Iris.

While racetrack crimes had receded, the booming greyhound racing business offered openings. In December 1945, bookies paid out £100,000 in one night when a dog called Bald Truth won the last race at White City after starting at odds of eight to one. An intruder had hidden in an empty kennel beside the dogs that were due to run in the race and had fed all but the winner morsels of doped fish. The only clues were malted-milk tablets that the doper had eaten because there was no room to unwrap a sandwich. He was identified, but never charged, and dog-track security was sharply tightened.

The underworld was growing. Scots who had drifted to London during the war, and had access to gelignite in Highland quarries, were regarded as expert safe-blowers and the trade continued to be highly revered. An article in the weekly magazine *Weekend* in 1963 was even able to observe: 'Why is the British safe-breaker so good? One reason is that cracking a crib requires characteristics in which the British excel – skill, tenacity, stamina and patience.'

'Jump-ups' were another popular crime in the late forties. The style was to drive behind a lorry until its driver stopped for a cup of tea and then steal his load – hence the 'fell off the back of a lorry' tradition. More imaginative techniques developed: in the fifties, thieves would print a bogus numberplate identical to that of a targeted lorry and drive in front of the vehicle, waving it. The driver would think his numberplate had fallen off and would stop – and be robbed. Cigarettes were a popular haul. Eric Mason recalled that a team would know where a lorry was delivering and would wait until the driver was entering a shop. They would then grab cartons from the tailboard, sling them in a car and speed off.

'At Christmas time, you'd always look for a vanload of turkeys because you sold plenty, made a few quid and all your friends would get a turkey for Christmas so you'd make yourself a good fella.' The procedure was to take the stolen van to a 'slaughter', a warehouse either leased from or owned by a crooked farmer, where there would be a secure barn for unloading and the loot divided.

This period also saw the expansion of the Flying Squad. Within it was the Ghost Squad, formed on 1 January 1946 to infiltrate the gangs by using around thirty undercover officers who never revealed themselves or appeared in court. Its chief, Detective Inspector Jack Capstick, was told by the Deputy Commander of the CID, Percy Worth, that 'as far as the underworld is concerned, you will have no more material existence than ghosts'. But the Ghost Squad was disbanded four years later, amidst hints that some of the officers had taken their undercover role a little too literally. They claimed to have seized 780 villains in their brief history and recovered £300,000 in stolen goods. But their informers' bill of £20,000 was a high one.

Sporadic violent incidents involving known criminals continued. On 14 December 1958 there was a fight between two gangs, whom the police described as 'the Finsbury' and 'the Angel Mob', outside Grey's Dance Academy in Holloway, north London, a favourite haunt of the winkle-pickered wide boys of the time. A young police constable, Ray Summers, broke up the fight and was marching off one of the leaders when he was stabbed by a young man called Ronnie Marwood, who was hanged the following year at Pentonville despite a campaign for a reprieve. It was a forerunner of more violent times, encapsulated by a killing at the start of the new decade.

On 7 February 1960, Jimmy Nash, a member of the Nash family who were gradually moving into London clubland, walked into the Pen Club in Spitalfields, east London, with his girlfriend, Doreen Masters, and a couple of friends, Joey Pyle and John Read. The club, which was so named because it had been financed with the proceeds of a robbery on the Parker Pen Company, was owned by Billy Ambrose, an ex-boxer, and was a haunt of villains. A fracas started almost immediately and Ambrose, who was on home leave from a gaol sentence, was shot and wounded as he tried to intervene. But the target of the attack was a cheery York-shireman, Selwyn Cooney, who ran the Cabinet Club in the West End for Billy Hill. Cooney was shot twice in the head and fell over a television set with a bullet lodged fatally in his brain. There was a violent fight and the attackers fled, leaving the dead and wounded in their wake. The manager of the club, Fay Sadler, cleaned the place up and Cooney was carried out and laid on the pavement while an ambulance was called.

Views differ as to why he was shot. One suggestion is that he had been involved in an altercation with Nash's brother Ronnie about a car accident involving a woman friend called 'Blonde Vicky' James. Cooney was said to have sent her a bill for the dam-age to his Vauxhall Victor and to have taken the matter up in a club with Ronnie, even coming to blows. The claim was that boxer Jimmy Nash was seeking retribution on behalf of his brother.

Jimmy Nash, who worked as a steeplejack and was known as the most peaceful of six Nash brothers, went briefly into hiding then turned himself in, accompanied by Manny Fryde, his astute and legendary legal representative, who announced that his client would say nothing and would not go on an identification parade. The police were given little help. Out of thirty-six people in the club, only four could remember seeing anything. Nash, wearing his lucky gold tiepin, said that he had struck Cooney on the nose but denied having a gun. One witness retracted his evidence and there was a brilliant speech from defence counsel Victor Durand, QC. Nash was cleared of murder but convicted of grievous bodily harm and gaoled for eighteen months for his part in the fight. There was a furious reaction to the verdict from Cooney's father. The *Sunday Pictorial* commented laconically: 'As far as the law is concerned, all that happened to Cooney is that he leaned on a bullet that happened to be passing.'

The Scotland Yard detective Bert Wickstead, who enjoyed the nicknames of 'The Old Grey Fox' and 'Gangbuster', believed that the murder of Cooney was an attempt to remove a man who had remained loyal to Billy Hill and who, after the latter's humiliating return from Australia, was still faithful. 'Hill had left a vacuum when he went into which tried to step all sorts of parties including the Nash family,' said Wickstead. But few members of the underworld gave any credence to this neat theory.

The case was a watershed in that it led to the formation of the Criminal Intelligence Branch (first C11, now SO11) at Scotland Yard to co-ordinate information on known criminals involved in organised crime; the Cooney murder investigation had demonstrated that the police lacked basic key intelligence on gangland. Young CID officers were encouraged to attend courts where known gangland figures were appearing so that they would learn their faces. It was also the start of jury protection, whereby jurors in major trials are taken off to dine at lunchtime, protected from the public and potential nobblers.

The public gallery at Nash's trial was the criminal equivalent of the members' enclosure at Ascot. Wickstead recalled that, 'It was full of unsavoury characters. It's a great pity the devil couldn't have cast his net then because it would have saved London a hell of a lot of trouble.'

Indeed, double trouble with a capital K was on its way.

4

GANGLAND

THE KRAYS AND UNTIMELY ENDS

While the Pen Club was writing itself into the history of the underworld, two young men were already making a name for themselves in another part of clubland. In 1954, the twenty-one-year-old Kray twins, Ronnie and Reggie, had taken over the running of the Regal billiard hall on the Mile End Road in the East End. They established their reputation when Ronnie cutlassed a Maltese gang that tried to extract protection money, and when both brothers beat up some docker heavies, one of whom had unwisely said to Ronnie, 'Here you are, sonny, you're just about old enough for a shandy.'

Most people in the neighbourhood already knew the twins well enough to know they were an altogether headier brew than lemonade shandy. Born in October 1933 into a close-knit family with Gypsy, Irish and Jewish roots, the sons of the feckless Charles and the fiercely protective Violet, they had established themselves as up-and-coming boxers. They often shared the billing at bouts, turning professional at the age of sixteen, and had been gaoled for assaulting a policeman before they were out of their teens. The fact that they were twins gave them an added aura, which their older brother Charlie believed made them a target for contemporaries who wanted to test themselves: 'It was like the Wild West – let's kill Billy the Kid and then we'll be Billy the Kid.'

The twins had already crossed more than cutlasses with the authorities and their National Service was divided between going AWOL, assaulting NCOs and kicking their heels in the glasshouse. They ended up in Shepton Mallet military prison, which unintentionally acted as a sort of Sandhurst for the training of the officer class of the underworld. Not for nothing did Ronnie eventually become known as 'The Colonel'. By the time they emerged they were ready for the action to which Ronnie's fascination with gangster movies was leading them.

They were noted early on by the older criminals and over the next few years were to receive assistance and advice from Jack Spot, who offered them a pitch at Epsom, from Billy Hill, now in semi-retirement, and from Tommy 'Scarface' Smithson, a loner involved in the vice trade, whose fearlessness the twins admired.

Clubs, both their own and others whose safety they guaranteed for a regular payment, were to be the stepping stones in their rise to fame. They acquired the one with which they were most widely associated in 1957. The Double R – 'a cowboy, lone plains drifter tribute' was how Charlie described the name he said he invented – was a modest enough drinking spot in Bow Road, east London, for those on the edges of crime. The Glaswegian heavy, 'Big Pat' Connolly, and Tommy 'the Bear' Brown were employed as bouncers.

Ronnie was actually in gaol as the club was expanding, serving a three-year sentence for slashing and stabbing a young man called Terry Martin, who was a victim of a complex grudge-settling operation. Arrested by police with Martin's blood still fresh on his shirt, Ronnie explained: 'I've had a nose-bleed.' Even in the early days, he was starting to show signs of the unbalanced personality that was eventually to derail the twins. He used disproportionate violence to settle disputes, even shooting a man in the motor trade in the leg over a minor argument about payment. After starting his sentence in Wandsworth Prison, Ronnie was moved to the gentler environs of Camp Hill gaol on the Isle of Wight. But the delusions from which he had started to suffer were worsening and he became violent. Once removed from the calming influence of his twin and unsettled by the death of his beloved Aunt Rose – who had told him so presciently when he was a small boy, 'Ronnie, love, you were born to hang' – he finally became dangerously irrational. He was eventually certified insane at Winchester Prison and in February 1958 he was moved to Epsom's Long Grove hospital prison, the 'nuthouse' as he called it.

But he did not stay long. During a visit from Reggie and some friends, the twins swapped places and Ronnie escaped before the authorities realised the switch had taken place. The escape took him to a safe house in Walthamstow and then to a caravan in Suffolk, where he entertained himself by riding in an appropriately ramrod-straight fashion. Bored with country life, he would emerge periodically at the Double R after a decoy car had tested whether the police were watching for him. However, his mental health was deteriorating. He suffered frightening paranoid delusions, became suicidal and believed that relatives had become police informants or Russian spies. Harley Street psychiatrists were consulted and 'minders' tried to pacify him by indulging his whims but his worried family finally agreed that he was 'barmy' and in 1958 decided he should give himself up.

His period back inside seemed to have stabilised him slightly and he was eventually released in 1959 to find that Reggie, freed from his brother's erratic moods, had been able to consolidate the business. Ronnie bought himself a Dobermann Pinscher and entered the profession 'dog breeder' in his passport.

By now, however, the Krays were breeding something more powerful than big German dogs: what they saw as 'respect' and what others saw as fear. 'The Firm', as it was called, was being born. Amongst those recruited were the Scottish muscle of Ian Barrie and 'Scotch Jack' Dickson, an ex-marine from Leith, who had served with 45 Commando in Malaya; an admiring cousin, Ronnie Hart; financial advisers Leslie Payne and Freddy Gore; ex-boxer Billy Exley; Freddie 'the Mean Machine' Foreman and hardmen Connie Whitehead and Albert Donoghue. An impressive network of informers included young men who took Ronnie's fancy and were known as his 'spies'.

Albert Donoghue was one of the Krays' inner circle who had been recruited because of his reputation as a fearsome East End fighter, one who would battle for unofficial titles like 'King of the Teddy Boys'. 'To be told the twins were taking note of you was something to be proud of,' he recalled. But he committed a minor indiscretion which offended Ronnie and was punished with a shot in his leg. He told curious police that he thought he had been hit by a firework – it was November – and his refusal to grass impressed the brothers, who duly put him on a pension of £15 a week, with specific responsibility for looking after Reggie and collecting the various dues paid to the gang. 'I could eat and drink for nothing and I could get my clothes made to measure for next to nothing,' said Donoghue. 'If you needed a car, you just went to a car site and frightened the guv'nor and pulled one off the front for a couple of weeks and run it into the ground.'

The twins' method of dealing with miscreants was straightforward: 'The guy would be kidded, made to feel easy. "All right? What you drinking?" That sort of thing. Then one would walk away from him this way and one that way. When everyone was out of the way, they would just spring the guy. He would be done first with a weapon and then what you call "obliged". He would be seen to. Ronnie liked to be involved personally.' The twins delivered the punishments dispassionately: 'Imagine you were fitting a new lock to your door, you'd be concentrating. They had the same sort of look. No horror or anything, just plain business. You're doing a little job.' Bizarrely, some of those who felt as though they might have offended became upset if they were not singled out for punishment: 'It made them feel small, insignificant.' But those receiving major beatings could act strangely, too: 'One guy tried to get away from his kicking by crawling up the return slot on a jukebox, which is only so wide. He must have imagined in his head it was some sort of a door. He must have been terrified.' Sometimes violence was not necessary. 'Ronnie could just sit there and stare at a person for half an hour and that person would go away thoroughly cowed. That was how much fear they generated.' The members of the Firm knew enough not to get involved: to them, the relationship between the twins was like a marriage; outsiders did not interfere in its violent rows. But it was Leslie 'The Brain' Payne who was to prove crucial in the transition of the Krays from East End tough guys to gang leaders. From Paddington in west London, Payne was ten years older than the twins and had drifted into crime at the end of his war service as a sergeant in Greece. He had bumped into the Krays when he was in the motor trade and their name had been taken in vain by someone seeking to avoid paying a debt. 'They seemed to grow fond of me,' he wrote in his memoirs. However, when they viciously beat someone up for him he realised that their affection had its disadvantages – and that it was better to have them as friends than enemies.

Payne introduced the twins to the 'long firm fraud', which was to provide much of their early cash. Long Firms, or LFs, were essentially corporate con tricks: a bogus company would be set up, which would start buying the relevant goods; the first bill would be paid promptly and the confidence of the suppliers won. After a few months, much larger orders would be placed and the firm would disappear with the goods, leaving nothing but an empty warehouse and unpaid bills behind it.

The Krays needed the readies. They gradually acquired about thirty people on their payroll, each of whom was paid about £20 a week in cash. The money was generated by three long firm frauds, four clubs and a percentage of stolen property. Payne claimed that a subsidiary robbery team, with Freddie Foreman to the fore, also contributed. The Firm even had its formal 'board' meetings. The business side met at 11 a.m. on Monday mornings when the club managers handed over their profits – or what they thought the twins would accept as their profits. On Monday evenings the 'muscle' met in a pub to find out if anyone had been arrested or had run away. Reggie apparently thought that keeping formal ledgers with all transactions was a good idea; Payne told him that entering 'long firm' and its weekly income might not be the soundest business practice.

One regular earner was the Kentucky Club in Stepney, east London, smarter and more ambitious than the Krays' earlier efforts: black leather, red walls, *trompe-l'oeil* windows, danceband stage and a clientele that included actress Barbara Windsor, theatre director Joan Littlewood, trumpeter Eddie Calvert and actor Roger Moore. It was the beginning of a love affair, often reciprocated, with show business. Judy Garland might even have married Reg, claimed Charlie, although that may now seem as fantastical as finding the end of the rainbow. At the Old Bailey trial that was to end their career, Ron told the judge offhandedly that if he had not been in court he would probably have been taking tea with Miss Garland.

Ronnie loved the club ambience and encouraged smokers to smoke harder so that the establishments would achieve a suitably fuggy atmosphere. In the meantime, Reg had developed his famous 'cigarette punch' whereby he would offer an intended victim a cigarette and, when the man accepted, would sock him hard, breaking his jaw; the secret of the trick was that the jaw was loosened when the cigarette was in the man's mouth and was therefore easier to break.

Payne recorded that Reggie often told his twin to relax and enjoy himself and that on one occasion Ronnie responded by treating the company to a manic version of 'Knees Up Mother Brown'. His favourite song of the time, which he would frequently request of singers in the various clubs, was 'Mack the Knife'.

Tales like these did the Krays' reputation no harm, nor did the pitched battles which Ronnie occasionally favoured, most notably against a bunch known as the Watney Street Mob, who came off second best in a bloody clash with the Krays at the Hospital Tavern in 1959. But it was minor 'mistakes', not these public displays of violence, that took the Krays to court. Reggie was gaoled for eighteen months in 1960 along with a small-time crook called Danny Shay after a botched attempt at extracting protection money.

Esmeralda's Barn, a gambling club in Wilton Place, Knightsbridge, with a restaurant and, originally, a lesbian cellar bar, was their attempt in 1960 to move further upwards and westwards. According to one story, they acquired it in a roundabout way from the slum landlord Peter Rachman, who had passed it on in exchange for peace and quiet in his neck of the Notting Hill woods. (Payne suggested later that Rachman backed out of a possible joint venture when he realised what the Krays were like.) The twins loved the glamour of a West End club, particularly with a toff, Lord Effingham, whom they patronised – 'Effy, get the effing tea' – on the board. But Ronnie had no business sense and, while Reggie was serving his eighteen months, was granting credit and opening bottles of bubbly with abandon.

'They thought they were immune from prosecution and could actually walk on water,' said 'Nipper' Read, the detective who was to pursue them. He recalled the effect they had on people: 'If they drove down Commercial Road, everybody waved to them. If somebody had a drink with them, it was like having tea with Princess Margaret.'

He remembered his first sighting, in 1964, when working undercover, of Ron Kray at the Grave Maurice, a Whitechapel pub which the twins frequented: 'There was a big American car and a guy stepped out with his hand in his pocket as though he had a gun there and sort of swept the street, making sure there was no one in sight and then gave a signal and the back door opened and out stepped Ronnie Kray. He was dressed like a 1930s Chicago gangster, with a long, long cashmere coat that reached to his ankles, tied in a loose belt at the waist. His hair was greased and parted and he wore his glasses. He looked like Al Capone without his fedora.' The style was important: 'Italian elegance with British bite, a Whitechapel translation of second-generation Mafia mufti,' as writer Iain Sinclair has since described it. Leslie Payne was not entirely convinced: 'They were fairly hygienic although they weren't very clever with their fingernails.'

Certainly, the twins had a presence which was particularly attractive in the austere fifties. 'Crooks are like everyone else,' said Read. 'They like to belong. The Krays called themselves the Firm and generated this feeling of fatherly protection or comfort to other crooks who felt that if they belonged to an organization of that kind, then they were subscribing to something worthwhile.'

At the time, it must have seemed that they were. More clubs were being tapped for protection money. The twins took over the Cambridge Rooms in Kingston, on the western outskirts of London, a venture mainly remembered now because a racehorse, Solway Cross, was raffled there for charity – the twins were great fund-raisers and did not mind people knowing this – and was won by the actor Ronald Fraser after a night of booze and bidding. Another club, Le Monde, in Chelsea, had become part of the portfolio. Payne suggested that in the mid-sixties the Firm was taking protection money from between a third and a half of all the illegal gaming clubs in London. Elsewhere they came briefly unstuck when the owner of the Hideaway Club, Hew McCowan, the son of a baronet, gave evidence against them in January 1965 on charges that they had demanded money with menaces. But one of the witnesses, Sidney Vaughan, had a change of heart after what was described as a 'visitation from God' that required him to recant his original story; and McCowan was undermined in court, partly because of the irrelevant introduction of his homosexuality. The case fell apart and the twins threw a rowdy celebration party. Later, they took over the Hideaway Club, turning it into the El Morocco.

They also had dreams of larger empires. In 1964, they attempted to expand into Africa, attracted by tall tales from Ernest Shinwell, son of the Labour peer 'Manny' Shinwell. The idea was to invest in a massive construction plan for 3,000 houses and a shopping precinct in Enugu, in Nigeria, where Ronnie enjoyed himself snacking on monkey meat and palm wine and briefly pondered the idea of bringing a Nigerian manservant home with him. But this scheme turned into fiasco. They had to rescue Leslie Payne from the local gaol, where he had been held under the charge of 'impersonating a company director', and withdraw. Further north, Tangier had become a popular watering-hole for the 'chaps'. Gypsy Hill ran a club called Churchills, a favourite haunt with both European and North African villains. Morocco became Ron's favourite country because of the young men there; he was already, remarkably for a criminal of that era, known as homosexual.

Back in England, the twins' associations with the powerful were not without embarrassments. In 1964, Ron met Lord Boothby at the latter's Belgravia home to discuss a business deal which never went through and the meeting was recorded for posterity in photographs. Rumours spread and the *Sunday Mirror* of 12 July splashed with a tale of the 'Peer and a Gangster'. The *Daily Mirror* followed suit with a story about 'the picture we dare not print' and hints of Mayfair high jinks. Lord Boothby responded with a long letter in *The Times* in which he explained that Ron Kray had asked him to take part in a business venture, that he had been unaware that Ron was the 'king of the underworld', that he was not homosexual and 'I have not been to a Mayfair party of any kind for more than twenty years'. The *Mirror* contritely paid £40,000 damages.

Nearly thirty years later, the Krays' biographer, John Pearson, suggested that Boothby had 'enjoyed the devil's own luck' in getting his apology and damages. Just after the twins were gaoled in 1969, Pearson was given a suitcase by Violet Kray, which Ronnie wanted him to have. It contained friendly letters from Boothby, thanking Ronnie for a box of Corona cigars, for instance, and showing that he had known Ronnie for much longer than he claimed. There was also a photograph, taken at the Society Club in Jermyn Street, in the West End, of Boothby with Ronnie, Billy Exley and other members of the Firm. In the centre of the photograph, as Pearson put it, 'was a teenage boy. On either side of him sat Ronnie Kray and Boothby, looking as if unable to decide which of them would eat him first.' Pearson suggests that the dishonest libel action not only cost the *Mirror* editor, Reg Payne, his job, but put the Krays 'off limits' to other journalists for a time: 'To confront the Krays might have raised awkward questions of their involvement with Boothby and to re-open that affair might have sparked off an uninviting scandal.'

The twins had also contacted Tom Driberg, the Labour MP, who had been introduced to them by Joan Littlewood at the Kentucky Club in Stepney, east London, and who shared Ronnie's interest in young men. He became a regular attender at Ronnie's parties where, as Driberg's biographer, Francis Wheen, recorded,

'rough but compliant East End lads were served like so many can-
apés'. Driberg was persuaded to make representations to the
Home Office on behalf of gaoled friends of the Krays and did not
desert the twins, even after their incarceration, although he
slightly played down his connection with them, saying he had a
'very slight acquaintance with them'.

In the mid-sixties the Krays were taking their role extremely
seriously, even travelling in different cars, as members of the royal
family use different planes, so that if one was killed the other
would be able to carry on running the Firm. They also aspired to
be mobsters on the scale of their celluloid heroes. Charlie Kray
claimed that a number of deals were done with the Mafia whereby
the Krays helped dispose of stolen bearer bonds in the English
banking system. But he also says that one of their largest transactions, the handling of $250,000 worth of 'hot' bonds that he had
been sent to Paris to fetch, ended with them becoming literally
too hot to handle. He burned the bonds in his mother's dustbin.

Payne was dispatched to conduct business with a criminal family in Montreal but the team was eventually deported back to
England. Ron was briefly wined and dined in New York and came
home entertaining grand notions of running a Mafia franchise in
England. However, the indication is that the Krays, who provided
entertainment and some forms of protection and escort services
for visiting hoodlums and their show-business allies, were seen as
small bananas by the American Mafia, who regarded England as
not worth the effort.

The Krays did, however, enjoy the company of the Mafia-
connected George Raft, who tried to set up his Colony Club as a
going concern in Britain but was banned from re-entry by the
Home Secretary, Roy Jenkins, in 1967 on the grounds that his
continued presence in the United Kingdom would not be condu-
cive to the public good. The Colony Club closed two years later.
Reg idolised Raft and would quote him admiringly in later life:

'He told me that his philosophy of life is that it is better to social-
ize every night rather than watch television and that's the way he
keeps young.'

Had the Krays been content to take the considerable earnings
that their protection racket brought them, both in London and
increasingly in excursions into places like Birmingham and Leicester, and not sought an empire which they were ill-equipped to
sustain, they might have ended their days buffing up their tans on
the south coast of Spain. But it was not to be. Cat burglar Peter
Scott reckoned that the police initially did not bother prosecuting
them and other gangsters because the gangs were mainly fighting
amongst themselves: 'It wasn't until they moved into the elegant
areas and saw themselves as [being] as good as the righteous that
wrath descended on them. What happened in the sixties was that
the gangsters failed to recognise the guidelines and started to push
the perimeters out. Society blew the whistle and said enough is
enough. They had one brandy too many and it went to their head.'

It was more than brandy the Krays were downing. Ronnie had
a ferocious capacity for drink – everything from brown ale to bottles of gin would be dispatched in the long erratic nights of clubbing. In contrast, Reggie seemed to have settled down slightly
and in 1965 married Frances Shea, whom he had been courting
in chivalrous fashion. The wedding was photographed by David
Bailey, who took the most iconic of the shots of the twins. Frances
left the marital home within eight weeks, dismayed by the other-
worldly atmosphere of lurking menace and the constant presence
of the Firm's foot-soldiers. She committed suicide in 1967, an
event that Charlie Kray believed was pivotal in the final collapse
of the twins: 'When that happened, Reg had a death wish, he really didn't care what happened to him.'

The twins still hankered after a larger empire and uncondi-
tional respect. When George Cornell, or Myers, one of the outspoken henchmen of the rival south London Richardson family,

made it clear that he had little of the latter for Ron, even calling him a 'fat poof' behind his back, action became inevitable. An additional factor may have been that Cornell was putting the squeeze on an East End warehouseman who was already paying the twins for protection, and indicated that he had no intention of backing off. Albert Donoghue is adamant that the 'poof' insult was not the reason for the death: 'Cornell was a loner and he had come over to our territory. It was an insult and Ronnie took it as an insult.' Two days after a shoot-out involving the Richardson gang in Mr Smith's nightclub in south London, in which Dickie Hart, an ally of the Krays, had died, Ron decided to cross a fresh boundary.

On 9 March 1966, Albie Woods, a bookmaker friend of Cornell, was only killing time when he agreed to spend an hour or so with him in the Blind Beggar on the Mile End Road. They had just been to visit a mutual friend, Jimmy Andrews, who was in hospital suffering from gunshot wounds. Cornell suggested a drink in what might have been seen as the heart of enemy territory. Woods noticed three men walk in, have a drink then leave. Shortly after, two men entered. 'All of a sudden, George said, "Look who's here." Then I realized that someone had stopped behind me. I saw a fellow taking aim at George. George was sneering at him. At that instant it was – BANG – the shot was fired and all I could see was a massive flame and smoke.'

Woods slid off his bar-stool and ducked behind the bar. There was a second shot: 'George was lying down beside me and I saw two pairs of legs walk across the middle of the bar, the next thing there's BANG BANG BANG BANG. I could hear the barmaid screaming. I put my arm underneath George's head and shouted, "Get an ambulance quick."' Woods had no desire to be there when the police arrived so he left Cornell with two men and went to phone Olive, Cornell's wife. 'I said, "I have some bad news. George has been shot." She said, "Who done it?" I said, "I don't really know, but you'll find him if you go to the hospital opposite the Blind Beggar."' Woods then drove to south London and eventually to Charlie Richardson's house, his blue mohair suit stained red with Cornell's blood. 'I told Charlie what had happened and he said, "You'd better have a wash and brush up." He wasn't very pleased that George had been shot. A couple of news flashes came on. One said that a man had been shot in the Blind Beggar, another, an hour later, said he had been transferred to a hospital in Maida Vale. Then we got another flash which said he died.'

But Woods says he was unable to identify the two men and that even when the police finally persuaded him to attend an identification parade and asked him if he could tap the gunman on the shoulder, he was unable to assist: 'The police looked at me and I know they didn't believe me. If looks could kill, I would have been dead there and then. I don't think George would have wanted me to pick them out anyway. They say that those that live by the sword, die by the sword.'

One of the Krays' firm, Eric Mason, a Portland Borstal old boy and reputedly the last man to have received the cat in a British prison, recalled the night of the murder. He had been driving home with his girlfriend, a dancer at the Pigalle in Piccadilly, when news of the killing came on the car radio. 'She said to me, "You've gone very quiet. Was that something to do with what was said on the radio? That's where you and your friends drink, isn't it?"' After Mason returned to his flat there was a call from Reg Kray, telling him to go to a safe house the twins had in Walthamstow.

'I looked up at the flat and I saw Ronnie Kray's silhouette in the window. He came to the door and it was as if he had just returned from holiday,' said Mason. 'He said: "I've got some right good news for you." And I said: "Oh, yeah, what's that?" So he said: "Here you are, have a gin and tonic." He had an ironing board and there was a bottle of gin on it. He had his jacket off, he was in his shirtsleeves and braces. He said, "I've just put a couple of bullets in that Cornell's head, I took his fucking head off." I went – "Phew ..."

'He said, "You'd have been well pleased, if you'd have been there." So I said, "Yeah, I heard something on the radio." And he said, "Anyway, that mob know now that we don't mess about with mugs like them." I sat there and I was thinking to myself – any minute now the law could arrive and we are nicked. And Ronnie, it was as if he had said, "I've just run over a cat." There was absolutely no emotion whatsoever.'

Ronnie had good reason to be calm. None of the witnesses could remember seeing anything and the police inquiry ground to a halt. The Krays seemed genuinely untouchable. In any case, a few months later they had other cod to fry.

Frank Mitchell, known as the 'mad axeman' and famed for his brute strength and awesome lack of fear, was sprung from Dartmoor by the twins on 12 December 1966. It was suggested that the Krays wanted him as a counterweight to the Richardson gang's own unguided missile, 'Mad' Frankie Fraser. Charlie Kray denied this: 'The twins had all the respect or fear; they didn't need Frankie Mitchell.' Anyway, by the time of his escape, the Richardsons had been weakened by the bloody battle at Mr Smith's club and Mitchell was now regarded as something of an inconvenience. But the twins had promised Mitchell that they would help and he gradually put pressure on them to honour their word as he became increasingly impatient at not being given an official release date.

The escape was not particularly complex. Mitchell was the beneficiary of a liberal regime at Dartmoor that allowed him enough laxity to spend lunchtime in the pub on the edge of the moor. He would emerge with a crate of beer, which he was allowed to take back to prison – 'an incredible state of affairs', as the judge, Sir Frederick Lawton, later described it. The Krays had to do little more than provide a getaway car and a hide-out.

Tucked into his safe house, Mitchell, a simple soul who had been classified subnormal as a child, was supplied with a striking woman from the West End club scene, Lisa Prescott, with whom he promptly fell in love. Letters written on his behalf by 'Mad' Teddy Smith, one of the Firm's brighter recruits, or Lennie Dunn, a book-stall owner who had arranged the hide-out, were signed with the Mitchell thumbprint and sent to *The Times* and the *Daily Mirror*, suggesting he would return to gaol if he was told when his final release date would be: 'Sir, the reason for my absence from Dartmoor was to bring to the Notice of my unhappy plight to be truthful, I am asking for a possible Date of release. From the age of nine, I have not been completely free, always under some act or other. Sir, I ask you, where is the fairness in this? I am not a murderer or a sex maniac, nor do I think I am a danger to the public. I think that I have been more than punished for the wrongs I have done.'

Little did Mitchell know that a more final form of punishment awaited him. When the twins decided that he should return to gaol, Mitchell refused and took a gun from one of his minders. He had become a nuisance and, after being told that he was going to be taken to a fresh hiding place, he was escorted to a van and shot dead. Albert Donoghue who, with Teddy Smith, had helped Mitchell escape in the first place told later that the 'mad axeman' had been shot in the chest and head while the van moved down through Barking.

As Albert Donoghue said: 'He wanted to circulate and he said that if the twins won't organize it, I'll go to them. This was relayed back and that was it. He signed his death warrant.' Mitchell was dissuaded from taking a jungle knife with him and told that Lisa could not come with them in case they ran into the police and because of Ronnie's attitude to women. He was accompanied to a waiting van by Donoghue, Alfie Gerrard and three others and he sat on the right wheel casing. As the passenger door was shut and the engine turned on, the first shots rang out.

'Two guns just opened up,' said Donoghue, who witnessed two Kray henchmen carry it out and who died in 2016. 'BAH – BAH – BAH – BAH. Mitchell's on his knees and I can see them hitting him. He just fell back. As he started groaning, one of them went BANG BANG BANG around the heart. You could see his shirt jumping. Quiet. He starts groaning again. We're coming back on to the main road. As we do a left into the tunnel, he starts groaning again. The gun went under his ear and BANG, that was the last one. Now we're on the main road so I said right, stop here. Common sense told me I should be next and I was waiting for a bullet.' He lived to tell the tale: 'I had a big old Crombie overcoat on and I had to walk along with it wide open to get rid of this smell of cordite and gunpowder... They must have taken the body to pieces.' He returned to carry out a 'wet and dry' clean-up of the flat where Mitchell had been hidden, taking care to wipe the fingerprints off the headboard of the bed which, Lisa had helpfully informed them, Mitchell used to grip.

The 'mission accomplished' code phoned through to the Krays was supposedly along the lines of 'the geezer's gone' or 'the dog is dead'. His body has never been found. Less attention was paid to what happened to Teddy Smith, who also disappeared shortly afterwards.

Frank Mitchell's death was to become the Turin Shroud of the underworld, surrounded by myth and speculation. Ron claimed in his version of events that 'Mitchell wasn't mad, he wasn't an axeman and one day he will reappear and the world will know the truth.' Two years later, Reg dismissed the idea of the resurrection of Mitchell as 'sad to say, ridiculous' but provided a new scenario which suggested that he had been shot by 'an ex-boxer and three Greeks ... [he was] so strong that he was still alive after being shot three times'. 'Scotch Jack' Dickson said that Mitchell was probably cremated, although it had been put about that he was in the cement holding up the Box flyover in east London. But in his 1997 memoir, *Respect*, Freddie Foreman, who was acquitted of involvement in the murder, acknowledged his role in it: 'I took part in his killing as a favour to the twins. There was no financial incentive whatsoever.' Foreman, who spent a total of sixteen years behind bars and was an adviser on *Legend*, the 2015 film about the Krays, starring Tom Hardy as both twins, would later say that he regretted ever meeting them and described them as 'bad news'. Of Mitchell's last days, he wrote: 'he threatened to kill a dozen policemen rather than go back to prison. He wanted to go out at night with a mask on his face, saying he wouldn't be recognised. He would demonstrate his strength by heaving up his minders by their belts and do 100 press-ups after having it off with his bird all day and all night.'

There was no investigation into Mitchell's death since, as far as the police knew, he was still alive and on the run. The twins, fuelled perhaps by their apparent invulnerability, carried out another murder in October the following year. The victim was a big, stroppy, hard-drinking, pill-popping villain called Jack 'the Hat' (which covered his premature baldness) McVitie, who had crossed the twins. (He had also blotted his social copy-book by turning up at one of their clubs on a hot day dressed in his hat, Bermuda shorts and with a machete.) The theory behind the murder has traditionally been that Ron, having 'got his button' by killing Cornell, egged his brother on to prove himself in the same way. McVitie was the chosen victim because he not only owed the twins money, which he had been too casual about repaying, but he had also been heard making threats against them when in his cups. He had supposedly been given the money to kill Leslie Payne, about whom the twins were already suspicious, and had clearly not carried out the job.

One of the Krays' men, Tony Lambrianou, was present at the McVitie killing and had a different explanation: 'The idea that there was a pressure on Reggie to kill somebody was a total fallacy.' McVitie, whom Lambrianou described as a Jekyll and Hyde character, had offended the Krays by misbehaving violently and upsetting women guests in the Regency club, run by an underworld family called the Barrys, when out of his head on amphetamines. 'How far could they let him go? There might just be a time when they couldn't turn a blind eye any more. It meant people losing respect for them. There was no intention to murder anyone that night.'

Earlier in the evening, Lambrianou and his brother, Chris, had gone to meet some other associates, the Mills brothers, at a pub called the Carpenter's Arms in Bethnal Green, east London. They had instructions to bring McVitie for a meeting with the twins. As Lambrianou told it, it was just another Saturday in the pub when they set off in their two-tone Zodiac Mark II to the Stoke Newington flat in north London where Ronnie and Reggie were waiting. 'Reggie started to shoot him in the head but the gun failed to go off. There was a bit of talk from McVitie – "What have I done?" – and Reg told him, "You know what you've done, Jack." Jack sat down on the sofa and said, "I'm sorry, it won't happen again," but they had heard it all before. All of a sudden, Jack stood up and walked to the window and he punched the pane out. It was said that he tried to dive for it but, in fact, he punched it out of sheer frustration that he had been set up. There was a carving knife, a normal carving knife, and the next thing, it was over. I didn't actually see it because I turned away. It was said that Reggie pinned him to the floor with the knife through the throat but that never happened. McVitie had been stabbed three times and I think the first stab killed him.'

Tony Lambrianou said that Kray did not intend to kill McVitie at first. 'He said to him, "I've had enough of you, you fucking cunt, now fuck off and never let me see you again." McVitie could have avoided the aggravation but we're talking about a man who couldn't let go. I would have done exactly the same as Reggie that

night, he couldn't let it get any further.' There were strangers in
the room, he says, which Reg would have been smart enough to
see as a potential problem if the murder had been premeditated.
Lambrianou and his brother were detailed to clean up and get rid
of the body, which was wrapped in an eiderdown. The body would
not fit in the boot of the car so it was put in the back seat and the
car was driven through the Blackwall Tunnel and left beside a
church. There it was picked up, wrapped in chicken-wire attached
to weights and dumped at sea. The car was crushed into a
90-centimetre cube, which was referred to afterwards as 'the Oxo'.

Donoghue shared the popular view on why McVitie died:
'When Ronnie got drunk, when he was heavy on pills, he would
be screaming at Reg, "You cowardly bastard, I've done mine now
it's time you, you skinny slag, about time you done yours." Simple
as that.' According to Donoghue, there had been previous plans
for Reggie to kill Joey Cannon, another heavy and former Jack
Spot man. McVitie and Donoghue were given the job of taking
the intended victim to a flat in Hackney.

'Before Cannon arrived, Reggie got this gun wrapped up in a
bath towel to silence it and said, "D'you reckon this will be all
right?"' Reggie was to hide in one room while McVitie and Donoghue kept Cannon talking. In the event, when Cannon arrived,
there was a staged scuffle and McVitie and Donoghue tipped him
the wink to escape. 'When Reggie came out of the room, we said
we'd had a scuffle and he'd gone. I think he was a little
bit relieved.'

John Pearson in *Profession of Violence* wrote that Ron Kray
enjoyed spreading rumours about what had happened to McVitie:
that he had been fed to the pigs in Suffolk or to the furnaces of
Bankside Power Station or buried in the foundations of a City
block or in Epping Forest. When Pearson, invited to be the official biographer of the twins and still unaware of their activities,
met Reggie shortly after the killing he noted he had a bandaged

hand and asked politely how he had injured himself. 'Gardenin',' came the reply.

'Murder is a very gory scene, a terrible, terrible thing that you never forget,' said Tony Lambrianou. As far as he was concerned, McVitie was a violent man who had once thrown a woman out of a car, had insulted the twins and who deserved a spot of discipline. 'It was too dangerous to leave him on the loose, he'd come back at you. It was just an unfortunate error.'

Eric Mason thought that the killing was slightly more than an inconvenient mistake. 'He was taken to his death as drunk as a sack. He should never have died that way. Reg Kray's got a lot of nice things about him but he did a lot of things in his life that, if he'd thought about them, he wouldn't have done. He was very much under the influence of his brother who was, without a doubt, a psychopath.' As the blood flowed, even the twins themselves were seen by some of the Firm as expendable and there was talk of Reggicide and Ronnicide in the ranks, as Albert Donoghue recounted: 'We knew it couldn't last. The Colonel was going crazy.' After the Cornell murder and the rumour that Cornell's brother was seeking revenge, Ronnie decided a change of tactics was in order: 'He said, "There's too much shooting going on." So he bought four axes, gave us each an axe to go and track him down. It would make a "change of pattern" is how they put it. That's crazy, isn't it?' It proved to Donoghue that the twins were not really equipped to run the show: 'Ronnie should have just been brought out like a pit bull dog. They couldn't organize a piss-up in a brewery. They should have been lieutenants or sergeants with someone else organizing.'

Another strange death some two years earlier was also linked, without evidence, to Ronnie Kray. Freddie Mills, a former world light heavyweight boxing champion and one of the most popular of British post-war sportsmen, had been found dead in his car on 24 July 1965, near the Freddie Mills Nite Spot in Soho. There was a Belgian .22 rifle by his side. Originally the death was treated as murder and it was suggested that Ronnie Kray had had him killed because he owed the twins money and because the killing would establish Ronnie as untouchable. But this was speculation and after the owner of the rifle was traced and said he had loaned the boxer the gun so that he could go to a fancy-dress party as a cowboy, it was concluded that Mills had died by his own hand.

Theories as to why Mills should kill himself were legion: that he was gay and was about to face a charge for propositioning a man in a toilet; that he had enormous debts which he could not repay; that he had been depressed after the suicide of his friend, the crooner Michael Holliday; that he had a call-girl racket that was about to be exposed; and, most persistently, that he had been the man behind the Nude Prostitute or Jack the Stripper murders, which were never solved and which appeared to cease after his death. (The murders of Irene Lockwood, Helene Barthelemy and Mary Turner had been seen as different from other sex crimes. One or two of the women killed were known to criminals and some of the underworld were under suspicion.)

The author Tony Van Den Berg came out with a fresh theory in 1993 that Mills might have been murdered by a Chinese gang seeking an entrée into clubland. In 2018, a fresh claim was made in a BBC4 documentary: that Mills had been murdered by a Mafia hitman because he was threatening to expose a promoter called Benny Huntman as the Mafia's man in Britain, and as someone who was working with them to bring their casinos into London. The claim was made by Huntman's son, Roger, who said that his father was 'heartbroken' at having arranged Mills's murder and died of a heart attack three months later.

Another odd underworld death of the time, with a loose Kray link, was that of Ginger Marks in January 1965. Marks, a minor crook, was killed because of his connection with another criminal, Jimmy Evans, who had shot Freddie Foreman's brother,

George, in the groin for having an affair with his wife. Freddie Foreman was later acquitted of the murder but wrote about it graphically – 'I let fly a hail of bullets' – in his memoir, in 1997. Under the old 'double jeopardy' laws, no one could be charged with the same offence twice, but the 2003 Criminal Justice Act allowed a retrial if 'compelling' new evidence came to light; Foreman declined to discuss it in the 2018 documentary, *Fred – Godfather of British Crime*.

Leonard 'Nipper' Read had been given the responsibility by Scotland Yard of nailing the twins after McVitie's death: 'The Krays were both idolized and feared. People either loved them or were terrified of them. Either way, no one was going to talk about them. And so I decided to go back to basics.' He set off after those who had drifted out of the Krays' circle.

He eventually struck gold with Leslie Payne, who had detached himself from the Firm and believed that the Krays had advanced plans to see him dead. McVitie had already been asked to do the job and Payne now believed that an American hitman called 'Junior', with a panther tattoo on his arm, had been hired. He made a 146-page statement to Read in the quiet of the library of a police section house in Marylebone. Payne would arrive from his Tulse Hill home every day and for three weeks told the tale. He was joined in his work by Freddy Gore, the other half of the Krays' financial team. The two were known as 'Laurel and Hardy'. Payne was granted immunity and Read used him to reassure other potential witnesses that it was safe to inform. Read believed his inquiry was hampered by the early leaking of his work by the 'mandarins' at Scotland Yard, who liked to boast of corporate successes. He heard that there was a contract on his life and started looking under his car before setting off for work.

Read also tracked down Lisa Prescott, Mitchell's companion. Unfortunately, she mistook the detectives for gangsters and tried to escape them by jumping out of the police car and into the

Thames when they were taking her to Tintagel House, where the inquiry was based for security reasons; she had realised they were going in the opposite direction from Scotland Yard and therefore believed they must be impostors.

Albert Donoghue assisted the police after he had been told by the twins that he would have to take responsibility for the murder of Frank Mitchell. Donoghue had initially refused to co-operate with the authorities but, after his family had been threatened, he changed his mind and named Freddie Foreman as Mitchell's killer.

A shadowy American criminal called Alan Cooper, who had arrived on the scene at the time of the Krays' tentative relationship with the Mafia and had taken over Payne's role as adviser, was to act as a further plank in the ramp now being erected against the twins. His part would appear to have been that of *agent provocateur*, although it is hard to separate the fantasy from the reality in a man who once offered the Krays such handy hardware as a pigskin attaché case with a built-in hypodermic syringe, suitable for carrying out underworld hits.

The Krays themselves seem to have taken the news of the pursuit phlegmatically down at Fort Vallance. They bought two boa constrictors and named them Read and Gerrard after the two men tracking them: 'Nipper' and Chief Superintendent Fred Gerrard. But, early in the morning of 9 May 1968, as they lay in bed after a heavy night at the Astor Club, the police struck. Many of those arrested with them were offered deals if they co-operated.

It was clear that, with the Krays arrested and behind bars, tongues were being loosened. By the time the twins' trial started at the Old Bailey many of their old comrades had seen the writing on the wall and realised that it said 'co-operate or rot'. Billy Exley, who had helped run the long firm frauds, 'Scotch Jack' Dickson and cousin Ronnie Hart, who had enjoyed the high life with the twins, all agreed to help the police, earning the undying hatred of the brothers, who described them as 'rats'. Hart later attempted suicide.

Lambrianou was one of those who did not cross over. 'I can look in the mirror and say I never pointed the finger or put them away.' He was puzzled that Donoghue should be one of the ones who did: 'He was the one that surprised me ... "Scotch Jack" Dickson has had to live with himself for what he did.'

Dickson retired from view after the trial and went into the ladies fashion business in the south of England. He kept a low profile after his days with the Krays, emerging only to publicise his memoirs – but refusing to be photographed – and died in 2014. (He is not to be confused with 'Scotch Jack' Buggy, a hot-tempered Glasgow heavy who operated in London at that time. Buggy was killed in 1967 and his bound body dumped in the sea, where it was found by two off-duty policemen on a fishing trip. Two men were charged with the murder years later but acquitted. Why he was shot has never been satisfactorily explained, although the most persistent rumour was that his death was connected in some way with Great Train Robbery money. The Krays inevitably came into the frame because Buggy was involved in protection racketeering.)

Neither Cornell nor McVitie, the men for whose murders the twins were gaoled for life, may have been, as Charlie Kray put it, 'nice people' and both had suggested that they would get the Krays. But the second murder was last orders for the twins: 'When the McVitie thing happened,' Charlie said, 'I really knew it was the beginning of the end. You're waiting. At any moment they're going to come for you. It's a terrible feeling.' He denied that the twins operated through fear: 'The twins never asked anyone to do anything, if there were fights or whatever, they did it themselves.' The people who eventually gave evidence against them were 'the ones wanting to be gangsters, walking around being heavy with people. If people were nervous or frightened of the twins they

must have had a guilt complex because if you haven't done anything wrong there's no need to be afraid of anybody.'

The Krays' trial opened at the Old Bailey on 7 January 1969
with eleven men in the dock. Court officials tried to hang num-
bered placards round the defendants' necks to identify them to
the jury but the Firm objected strongly, with Ronnie shouting,
'This is not a cattle market' as he ripped his up. After Ronnie's
barrister, John Platts-Mills, QC, had remarked to the judge, Mr
Justice Melford Stevenson, that the placards smacked of ancient
colonial practices, the court relented and the jurors were given a
plan of the dock with the names marked on it. The twins tried to
tough it out, but the testimony of more than twenty of their former associates was too detailed for them to escape. Ron and Reg
were duly convicted of the murders of Cornell and McVitie respectively and cleared, along with Foreman, of the killing of
Mitchell. They were gaoled for life with a recommendation from
the judge, whose country home was called 'Truncheons', that they
serve at least thirty years. They were joined inside by brother
Charlie, the Lambrianous, Freddie Foreman and Ian Barrie, who
were gaoled for their various roles in the mayhem. Donoghue was
sentenced to two years for his part in Mitchell's death.

The Krays' melody has lingered on. They became the royal
family of the underworld, their slightest moves and moods catalogued, and by 1990 there was the first of many films of their
lives. The première of *The Krays* was remarkable for the dozens
of gangsterly dressed young men arriving by limousine, an effect
only partially marred by the fact that close inspection showed that
they had all hired the same vehicle, which was doing a discreet
circuit between the front of the Leicester Square cinema and a
nearby pub.

The books poured out year after year. In 1990, in *Born Fighter*,
Reg Kray announced that he had become a born-again Christian
and wanted to be used as a 'vehicle for God ... I cannot become a

saint overnight but I leave it all in God's hands'. His favourite reading had become Kahlil Gibran's *The Prophet* and he stunned prisoners in Parkhurst by saying grace before their Christmas dinner. He also castigated his fellow inmates for reading pornography to satisfy their 'filthy, lustful desires' and attacked men who bullied gay prisoners. Contrition for the murder of McVitie was not part of his new religious baggage. He likened it to the killing of Argentinian troops in the Falklands War: 'I would sooner see the loss of the McVities of this world than the deaths of innocent young soldiers plucked from the joys of life by the bullets of war.'

Reg 'adopted' various young men inside. One of these new 'sons' was Pete Gillett, whom Reg met in Parkhurst and whose career as a singer he tried to promote. Gillett did make a couple of singles but they did not sell and despite proclamations of going straight – 'my life is now show business and watching out for Reg's best interests out here' – he was to find himself back in gaol in October 1992 on a major drug-dealing charge.

In 1991 a slim volume of the philosophy and poetry of Reg Kray, entitled *Thoughts,* was published in London. In the introduction the publishers, River First, informed readers: 'This book contains the thoughts, ideas and writings of Mr Reginald Kray. The main text was created over a nine-hour period which gives an insight into this man's unique mind, hence textual and grammatical anomalies remain.' What followed was sixty pages of poems like:

> Puppy dog be my friend
> I know you are loyal
> And will stay with me till the end
> I know I cannot ask for a better friend.

Even Tony Lambrianou, who died in 2004, was puzzled that the Krays' mystique still hung over parts of east London like old aftershave: 'I have met people who have got shrines to them in their homes.'

Tony's brother, Chris Lambrianou, found shrines of a different kind in gaol. One Sunday in 1977, while serving his sentence in Wormwood Scrubs, he heard the Bob Dylan song 'Knockin' on Heaven's Door' being played on the landing below him. The words in the song 'Ma, take these guns off of me, I can't use them any more... ' had a profound effect on him and he heard a voice telling him to kill himself. His hand fell on a Gideon Bible, which he had not realised was in the cell, and he started reading the Book of Genesis. Shortly afterwards, in Maidstone Prison, he had what he said was a vision in which three Middle Eastern-looking men appeared, one of whom told him: 'Follow us.' Although the prison chaplain was unimpressed by what Lambrianou told him he had seen, the former 'arrogant, selfish thug', as he put it, became a 'caring Christian' and he regarded his time with the Krays as a wasted period of mindless stupidity. After his eventual release he worked as a special needs officer at a rehabilitation centre in Oxford, helping people deal with addiction problems.

Ron Kray died in March 1995 without ever being released from Broadmoor, where, still immaculately turned out in pinstripe suit and silver sixpence cufflinks, and as ramrod-straight as one would expect of a retired colonel, he had played host to visitors. The former model, Maureen Flanagan, who had known the Krays since she was their mother's young hairdresser, visited the twins in prison, dealing with Ronnie's demands, which included smoked salmon from Harrods and bagels from Brick Lane, plus gifts for the young prisoners who took his fancy. One of Flanagan's roles was to ring the *Daily Mirror* from a phone booth outside Broadmoor after a visit with titbits about Ron. The paper would pay anything from £50 to hundreds of pounds for a story, depending on how big it was, and Flanagan would pass the money to their big brother, Charlie, who would share it with the twins; Flanagan would get a 'finder's fee'. Broadmoor was a secure hospital rather than a prison, and the canteen could be used by inmates to order in expensive items from the outside world, which were put on tick. At one stage, Ron's canteen bill stood at £7,000. Ron's largesse was one of the reasons why the Krays needed to capitalise on their name, and amongst the handy earners was the selling of media rights to his two weddings. In 1985, he wed Elaine Mildener, who had been writing to him in Broadmoor – as did many women – and visited him with Flanagan. Ron had been told that the *Sun* would be the best payers and a fee of £20,000 was agreed – although only £10,000 was eventually paid. This gave the paper access to the wedding in the Broadmoor chapel. His second marriage was to Kate Howard, who ran a strippergram firm and wrote a series of books under her married name, although they divorced in 1994. He died in a hospital in Slough after suddenly becoming unwell. His 100-a-day cigarette habit was seen as a contributory factor, although his family blamed the large quantity of prescription drugs he had taken over the years.

His funeral was a gangland classic. The Order of Service at St Matthew's in Bethnal Green announced that the four pallbearers should be seen as a 'symbol of peace', representing as they did the four corners of London. Thus Johnny Nash of the Nash family, Freddie Foreman, 'Ginger' Dennis and Charlie Kray lowered the coffin into the grave in a Chingford cemetery. The funeral procession was led by six black-plumed horses drawing the coffin and followed by twenty-five limousines driven slowly past crowds of thousands lining the streets, past the old coffee bar Pellici's, where three decades earlier, young East Enders had learned not to blow the froth of their cappuccinos at the twins, and past uniformed police officers resignedly holding the traffic back as if for the passing of some minor royal.

Reg Kray's epitaph for his twin was suitably double-edged: 'Ron had great humour, a vicious temper, was kind and generous.

He did it all his way but above all, he was a man.' Frank Sinatra's 'My Way' and Whitney Houston's 'I Will Always Love You' were played and the W. E. Henley poem, 'Invictus', was read: 'I am the captain of my fate, I am the master of my soul.' Outside the church, young men who looked uncertain whether they were auditioning for *Pulp Fiction* or *The Lavender Hill Mob* provided security for the VIP guests.

Reg was released from prison for the ceremony and it was a sign of how he was now regarded that he was handcuffed to a woman officer, while at his mother's funeral, thirteen years earlier, he had been escorted by two of the tallest prison officers in the service. He was allowed to stroke the undertaker's horses before embracing the gravestone of his late wife, Frances, who had been buried in the same cemetery. Gangland figures then lined up to kiss him on both cheeks – a scene straight out of *The Godfather* – before adjourning to a boozer in Bethnal Green for the wake.

Big brother Charlie, the mildest-mannered of the trio, had not been in trouble since his sentence for being an accessory to the murder of McVitie. He moved to Spain, where Ibiza and Benidorm were his favoured haunts, wrote two books on the family, dabbled in the music business and clubland and kept trim beneath the Spanish sun. His autobiography was entitled *Me and My Brothers*, but in reality, Charlie Kray always knew that it was really My Brothers and, very far behind, Me. If ever there was a man haunted by a famous family name it was the Kray twins' elder brother. It followed him around from the 1950s to his death, like a tightly fitted electronic tag. When he last appeared in court, down in the bleak and characterless wastelands of the top-security Belmarsh complex in Woolwich in 1997, Charlie was already seventy and cut a sad figure. It was no surprise that his defence counsel, Jonathan Goldberg, QC, sought to portray him to the jury as such. He was, said Goldberg, 'an old fool, a pathetic old has-been, an utterly washed-up figure made to appear something he is not at

all'. Charlie had been caught offering cocaine to undercover officers but Goldberg suggested that he was, in fact, 'anti-drugs, anti-
crime and a man with a heart of gold'. He was gaoled for twelve
years but died in 2000 before his sentence was completed.

Reg Kray had concluded his book: 'My eventual aim is to be
recognized first as a man and eventually as author, poet and phi-
losopher.' A far cry from the dustier but more realisable dream of
being Vallance Road's answer to Jimmy Cagney, to be 'top of the
world, ma', that was to land the twins behind bars in the first
place. He died of cancer in 2000 in a Norwich hotel, having been
released a few weeks earlier on compassionate grounds, but interest in the twins continued unabated.

What is remarkable is that more than half a century after the
twins were the most feared – or respected – criminals in London,
there was still such a market for anything to do with them. There
have been four films, a musical called *England, England*, more
than fifty books by or about them, their coshes, knuckledusters
and crossbow are on display in a museum in Gloucestershire and
there is a red plaque commemorating the Cornell murder in the
Blind Beggar pub, which became a popular place for gangsters to
hold launch parties for their memoirs. Memorabilia including
gypsy caravans made by Ronnie out of matchsticks and naif paintings of boxers by Reggie sold for thousands of pounds on eBay.
They achieved the fame they sought but at the cost of spending
half their lives behind bars.

5

GANGLAND

THE RICHARDSONS, MR SMITH'S AND BEYOND

While the Krays had been carving out their empire in east London, another little firm was quietly establishing itself south of the Thames. The Richardsons and the Krays were to clash, most spectacularly with the death of George Cornell, but their methods and style were very different.

'The Richardsons had more charisma than the Krays,' said Eric Mason, who had been at the sharp end of conflicts between the two gangs. 'You had to be tough and prove yourself to be with the Kray twins but the Richardsons were more interested if you had the ability to make money as well as being a tough guy.'

The two gangs had different approaches to people who crossed them, said Mason: 'A guy tucked the twins up over a gold deal and sent them a card from Honolulu saying, "I'm having a lovely time." The twins just wiped their mouths and laughed about it, whereas the Richardsons wouldn't allow anybody to tuck them up because they wanted the world to know – you don't mess us around.'

'Mad' Frankie Fraser, who had been courted by both the Krays and the Richardsons before joining the latter, was in no doubt which was the smarter team: 'Using racing terms, there would be no race, comparing the Richardsons with the Krays. The Richardsons were miles in front, brain power, everything.'

Charlie Richardson had been born in Twickenham in 1934, the son of Charlie, a former prize-fighter and merchant seaman, and Eileen. The family moved soon after his birth to Camberwell, and it was from this south London patch that he was later to build his empire, part legal (through his scrap business and foreign investments) and part illegal (through his frauds and gangsterism). It saw millions of pounds passing through his hands, an international business network and an office in Park Lane. Eventually, it also resulted in thousands of nights behind bars.

He was in trouble as a teenager and was sent away for the first time after he had stolen a car and eluded the police in a wild chase down the Old Kent Road before being collared. An extremely shrewd businessman, he turned his hand to making money as a peripatetic ice-cream salesman on his release from approved school and set up his first scrap-metal business before receiving the dreaded call to do his National Service.

Richardson had no greater desire to bull his boots and press his khaki than any of his predecessors in the underworld. His method of convincing the military authorities in Aldershot of this lack of enthusiasm was straightforward: 'Would you give away information to the Russians?' he was asked by the officer conducting the initial interview. 'Fucking right I would, given half a chance.' Richardson then played mad, cutting up his uniform, giggling crazily, collapsing, making himself ill. Eventually he joined the regiment where he felt most at home: the prisoners serving in Shepton Mallet gaol, where a contingent of men – the Krays, Frank Mitchell, the Nashes – who were later to become names in the underworld were embarking on their apprenticeship.

His younger brother, Eddie, had meanwhile established himself on the outside, winning the local title of 'King of the Teds'.

The Richardsons, like the Krays, acquired an interest in clubs, starting with the Addington in Addington Square, in south London, where they and their cohorts could drink after hours. It was a success. The restrictive licensing laws of the time were a boon to rough-and-ready clubs that could supply a drink in the mid-afternoon or the early hours of the morning. They opened another club, the Shirley Ann, with a local villain called John Bradbury.

One of the policemen sniffing around the clubs was a sergeant called Ken Drury, who was later to be gaoled for corruption. Richardson described his relations with the police thus: 'The most lucrative, powerful and extensive protection racket ever to exist was administered by the Metropolitan Police. As I got older and became involved in more and more dealings, legal or otherwise, I made regular payments to the police. It was a sort of taxation on crime ... Sometimes we would pay people to be "found" committing small crimes so that our friendly local protection racketeer in blue could have somebody to arrest and look like he had been busy.'

Johnny Bradbury, who later moved to Johannesburg, said that initially, the police gave them no problems: 'We just could not put a foot wrong. It didn't matter what police station you went to. There was always someone that our local station knew who could contact someone and straighten things out.'

Clubs now played a major part in the Richardsons' lives, as they did for the Krays, and they won an extra set of spurs when, in the cheekily named Reform Club in the Elephant and Castle, they beat up the men who had beaten up a friend of theirs, Jimmy Brindle, the brother-in-law of Frankie Fraser. This was regarded as rough justice for people who had 'taken a liberty'. As Richardson later described the incident, it had a sound business spin-off to it:

'We worked together like a well-practised team until they lay unconscious at our feet in pools of blood and broken teeth.' It was 'big PR and our soaring reputation would protect us from challenges from ambitious competitors'.

But the police were already becoming aware of Charlie's activities and not all of them could be paid off. Although Richardson had been cleared of involvement in a shooting incident after witnesses failed to give evidence, he was gaoled for six months for a wholesale bacon theft. Facing further proceedings, he fled to Canada with a girlfriend, Jean Goodman, who was to become his common-law wife. On his return, in 1961, he entered a new phase of his career: 'long firm' frauds which he and Eddie operated with greater business acumen than the Krays.

Being a smart operator, Richardson embarked on a variation of the theme in 1962 by setting fire to the warehouse buildings used in the frauds and claiming the insurance money. He would also tell the manufacturers of the goods that had gone up in flames that he was unable to pay them back because he was uninsured. The scheme made a six-figure profit and the Richardson business plan was on course. He had suffered personal tragedy at this time when his younger brother, Alan, was drowned in an accident on the Thames when the speedboat Charlie was piloting capsized.

Onto the scene now came the various conmen and sharp operators whom Charlie saw as his way to a secure business future, but who were in the end to lead to his downfall. Jack 'the Rat' Duval, a portly conman known as 'The Prince of Fraud', seemed to offer the opportunities for investment that Richardson craved. Duval was a club owner who had escaped from Russia in 1919 and been in the French Foreign Legion before joining the RAF in 1940. He was the archetypal wide boy and had flourished in the laissez-faire post-war business world before becoming what Richardson later described as 'a turd that floated down the Thames to my part of London'.

Duval's specialities in the early sixties included the importing of goods in rare supply, like silk stockings, and a travel company to take advantage of the new national desire to see 'the Continent', which was just becoming affordable. He also became chairman of a small bank, but came unstuck and did a runner. When he did see Charlie again it was to be asked, 'Why aren't you a good boy?' and to be given a beating. He was learning, as others soon did, that it did not pay to cross Charlie. Duval apparently still did not digest the lesson. After taking money out of one of the companies in which they had a joint interest, he was summoned on 12 June 1964 with one of his colleagues. They were both punished and a bloodied Duval went briefly into hiding. When Charlie discovered that he had passed dud cheques on to him, he wanted a second appointment.

Unable to find Duval, he settled for Lucien Harris, an associate of Duval, an educated man who also worked as a crossword compiler. Richardson described him as having 'an accent and manner to go with his shop-window-dummy appearance and his fancy name'.

What happened to Harris was to form the cornerstone of the case that was eventually to derail the Richardson express. As far as Richardson was concerned, no more took place in confrontations like the one with Harris than the giving of a few right-handers to people who had taken a liberty or been out of order; their injuries did not even require an aspirin. According to Harris and the others who were to give evidence, what happened was far more brutal and sadistic.

Harris's account went thus: after his summons, he found himself in Richardson's office with Charlie and his associates – Roy Hall, whom Charlie had met when he tried to rob his own scrapyard, John Bradbury and brother Eddie. Charlie demanded to know where Duval was. Harris said he did not know and added that Richardson had been naïve to get involved with him in the first place. Richardson, who had been picking his fingernails with a knife, sent out for some scampi. When the food returned, Charlie shoved a piece of the hot scampi into Harris's eye.

Richardson ascribed this whole scene to imaginative script-writing: 'Cleaning my nails with a knife? What an embarrassing and undignified scene when my nails were always clean and professionally manicured.' But what was to rivet the nation was the presence, always vigorously disputed by Richardson, of the Black Box.

This was a generator or old field telephone which was part of the scrap of the Richardson trade. Harris said he had to take off his shoes and socks and that wires were attached to his toes. Roy Hall, Richardson's long-time associate, was said to have turned the handle and Harris jumped convulsively from his seat. It was suggested that Hall was the Black Box man and was always the one who said, 'Shall I fetch the box?' The rest of Harris's clothes were taken off and further shocks administered. Orange juice was thrown over him, supposedly to make the shocks more painful. Harris said later: 'The leads were attached to my legs, my penis, the anus, the chest, the nostrils and the temples.' He was stabbed in the foot by Bradbury. Then, in what became a routine, a bottle of Scotch was ordered, Harris was allowed to clean up and Charlie even gave him £150 and a clean shirt.

'Our defence, our denial of these events was boring compared with their stories,' wrote Richardson in his memoirs. 'Such down-to-earth inanities seemed insignificant when the minds of the jury were so firmly imprinted with the image of a man with an electric torture box attached to his wedding tackle.'

But Duval was still missing. Another man, Bunny Bridges, who might have known where he was, was brought in. Bradbury described how Bridges was interrogated. Bridges had said that he did not know where Duval was so Charlie instructed Roy Hall and Bradbury to take him upstairs: 'We had what we called the torture box there, an old field telephone. We slung Bunny in a bath of water and then started putting the wires on his nipples and turning the handle and he was springing so high and screaming blue murder. We tied a piece of cloth round his mouth to keep him quiet. You could see he didn't know anything. We kept this up for about an hour and Charlie came running up and said, "What are you two lunatics doing?"' Bridges suggested that Duval might be at his ex-wife's in Manchester and was given some petrol money to go and find him. James Taggart, who was accused of owing money and of being a police informer, was also brought in. He said he was stripped naked and given a beating, after which he had to mop up the blood with his underpants. Cyril Green claimed to have had a pot of boiling tea poured over him.

'You could honestly say that nine times out of ten they didn't know anything in the first place,' said Bradbury. 'They really got tortured for fuck all.' But the troops did not revolt: 'You got orders, you do it. Otherwise you're liable to wind up on the torture box as well. You don't say no to Charlie.'

'We could go and hit a bloke or put him on a torture box or break his toes with a pair of pliers or pull his teeth out, it didn't bother us. And there was no apparent reason for it,' said Bradbury, who played a full part in the violence, often out of his head on purple hearts. 'The things we did, I can't believe it myself sometimes, it was unreal.'

One offender suffered a more basic punishment: 'I said to Charlie, "Have you got any pliers in your drawer?" He said, "Yeah, what are you going to do?" I said, "I'm going to break his fucking toes, he won't tell us what's going on." Charlie gave me the pliers and I got his toes and was bending them this way and that and just snapped them off. There was stuff in his drink so he didn't even feel the pain. So then I got annoyed and I took the knife and cut half his ear off.' The barely conscious victim was dumped near a hospital. With hindsight, Bradbury was still puzzled at his own behaviour: 'It's different to putting a bloke on the torture box, it's just turning the handle, a big joke. But when you get a pair of pliers and break a bloke's toes and just sit there and don't feel a thing, that's when I knew I was going the other way.'

It was tiring work, remembered Bradbury: 'Charlie had a bar at the yard. Whether we had a policeman for a drink or whether someone was tortured, you can't sit there all night dying of thirst. We used to have a whisky or a brandy and a five-minute smoke break and start again. It was like a factory on a tea break. You can't keep going on an empty stomach. We used to send round to the pie shop.

'A bloke could be lying on the floor like that time when we broke his toes and screaming and hollering and Charlie would just carry on with his fish and chips, talking to Frankie Fraser or me. After about fifteen minutes or so he'd say, "Right, carry on," and we'd get back to work again.'

There were also less ambitious but more traditional ways of keeping the money rolling in than big frauds. One involved a Heathrow parking fiddle which the Richardsons heard about. The attendants would adjust the time clocks that marked the parking tickets so that it would appear that the cars had been in the car park for less time than they really had. The extra money which was paid over for the tickets would be split between the members of the team who were involved in the racket and would amount to around £1,000 a week. When the Richardsons became aware of the fiddle, they suggested that the team pay over £500 a week which, since they had little option, they agreed to do. This provided some handy readies while other businesses were being set up.

Brother Eddie's involvement with Atlantic Machines was proving much simpler. People were happy to have him and Frankie Fraser 'minding' their slot machines or, if not, were smart enough not to make a meal of it. Eddie was content to be making a comfortable living and enjoying a laddish life, playing for his Soho

Rangers football team and mixing with show-business figures like the film star Stanley Baker.

The hardmen were cultivated by the up-and-coming gang leaders, who were as anxious to sign up star strikers as any postwar football manager. Fraser had been an obvious target and the young Kray twins had wooed him, taking his sister Eva to Dartmoor or Durham or wherever he was serving his sentence. But the Richardsons won his allegiance. It was a significant move and one that was to have echoes over the next thirty years. Fraser joining the Richardsons was, said one fellow criminal, like China getting the atom bomb.

Fraser already had a reputation as one of the 'staunchest' of villains, a man who would never inform or buckle in gaol, and, despite being only five foot five inches, a package of controlled violence. His position in the underworld was regarded as the more remarkable because he did not come from a known criminal family: 'I'd come up from the ranks, literally fought my way up because I had no help from my family. My mother and father were dead straight so I had to make my own way. If you've got parents who have been to prison they can help you considerably with their contacts and guide you more sensibly.'

Charlie Richardson, meanwhile, had his eyes on the money it seemed possible to make from mining in Africa, in particular the possibilities of exporting perlite from South Africa. It was the beginning of a remarkable phase of his life which was to lead to his involvement with the South African secret service, BOSS, and his glimpse of a fortune. In the mid-sixties he met Gordon Winter, a shadowy creature who combined work for South African intelligence with a job at the *Sunday Express*. Winter introduced Charlie to influential figures, not the least of whom was Winter's own wife, Jean La Grange, with whom Charlie fell in love.

It suited the South Africans to have a man in London who could burgle the offices of groups that were opposing apartheid.

If the security services themselves were caught carrying out such burglaries their government would have been severely damaged; there was less of a risk if the job was done by professional criminals who could always claim they were just stealing equipment or money from an office. In Robert Parker's book on the Richardsons, *Rough Justice*, published in 1981, it is suggested that in March 1966, Charlie organised a break-in at the anti-apartheid movement's headquarters in Charlotte Street and the theft of files and papers that included names and addresses of members. The offices of the *Zimbabwe Review* and of Amnesty International were also burgled and it was only then that the possibility of politically motivated break-ins was taken seriously by the authorities.

Was Richardson also involved in political mischief in Britain? Robert Parker recalled interviewing Charlie in Benidorm. Richardson claimed that he knew of Downing Street shenanigans, of a former Labour minister involved in a sex scandal and a singer having an affair with a Labour politician's wife.

Meanwhile, in South Africa, the wheel was coming off the Richardson machine. There had been the murder of Thomas Waldeck, one of the brothers' associates, and the arrest of Bradbury for the crime. There had also been violent scenes in London involving the cohorts of the Richardsons and the Krays. One of the Krays' men, Eric Mason, remembered, as well he might, one night in the Astor Club in Berkeley Square, a popular meeting place for villains of the era; two gangs would occupy different parts of the club if they happened to be there at the same time. 'There was never any animosity. It was a kind of no-go area for villainy. At that time Jimmy Boyle [a Scottish hardman, later to turn artist and prison reformer] was on the run and they were entertaining him at the bar.' There were some other Scots 'on the bevvy' and one made a remark about Mason's friend's broken nose and asked him facetiously if he had got it falling off a bike: 'My

friend knocked him out. All hell was let loose and so the
Richardsons felt they had to make one against us for the discour-
tesy. So all of a sudden a few knives came out, axes and one thing
and another.' Outside the club, Mason challenged the Richardson
gang and said he would take on any two of them.

'I got in the car and somebody tried to stick a knife in me. We
drove to Tottenham Court Road fighting all the way.' The Richardsons had a one-armed bandit workshop-cum-office there and
Mason was bundled in and hit by Fraser with a chopper, so sav-
agely that his hand was pinned to the top of his head. Fraser was
then stabbed in the stomach and legs. A shotgun was held to
Mason's head. 'I woke up in hospital and I thought I was dead. I
had 370 stitches and three fractures of the skull. After I'd been in
a coma for a few days, I woke up and I saw Ronnie Knight [the
club-owner husband of actress Barbara Windsor]. I thought – this
is me in heaven and the most unlikely angel was there at the end
of the bed.' Revenge attacks were planned and the fire power required – 'enough to start a war' – was obtained, but Mason was
arrested on a robbery charge before vengeance could be wreaked.
The police approached him to give evidence against the Richardsons but he declined.

Then, in March 1966, there was the violent fight at Mr Smith's
nightclub in Rushey Green, Catford, south London. Its full name
was 'Mr Smith and the Witchdoctor' and it provided food, drink,
gaming and a dance floor. It was profitable but for the fact that
some local heavies, led by the Haward brothers, Harry and Billy,
were said to be extracting a tax from it in the form of free drinks
all round for themselves and their associates. Eddie Richardson
was asked to sort things out. On 7 March he went down to Mr
Smith's with Frankie Fraser, Ronnie Jeffrey, Harry Rawlins,
Jimmy Moody and Billy Stayton and found the other group, including Billy Haward, Billy Gardner, Peter Hennessey, Henry
Botton and Richard 'Dickie' Hart, a south London thief known as

'the Catford Fart' by the Richardsons. By the end of the night Hart had been shot dead with a .45 automatic and two men, Eddie Richardson and Frankie Fraser, were badly injured.

One version of what happened is that when the Richardson–Fraser team was about to leave, the club manager asked if they would remove the other group. Eddie Richardson made the request, the Haward gang demurred and Richardson then challenged one of them, Peter Hennessey, who had called him a ponce, to a fight on the dance floor. Richardson forced him to the floor and asked him if he had had enough. Then, according to Fraser, 'Dickie' Hart pulled out a revolver and started firing. One man, Harry Rawlins, was hit in the shoulder. As Fraser described it: 'I said to Hart, "Let's get him out to an ambulance," and we got outside and the next thing you knew there was more gunfire and Hart was lying injured and I was shot in the leg.' Fraser's thighbone was broken by the shot. Hart was fatally wounded. Ronnie Jeffrey was shot in the groin. Billy Haward received serious head wounds. There was blood everywhere.

One of the men who helped the wounded to hospital was Jimmy 'Big Jim' Moody, an enormous man described by a friend as being like 'one filing cabinet piled on top of another' and with geisha girl tattoos on his arm. Years later, he was to come to greater prominence, first when he escaped from Brixton Prison with IRA man Gerard Tuite and later, when he was shot dead in an East End pub.

George Barker, one of the officers who arrived on the scene, remembered finding Fraser: 'I stepped over a wall of a garden and there was a grunting noise. It was Frankie Fraser. I had accidentally trodden on his leg.' He stuffed a handkerchief into the gaping wound. Barker described the mayhem: 'It was like a battle scene. There was a body lying in the gutter and we found a pistol and a big glass bar with a great lump of matted hair on it.' They covered these items of evidence with a dustbin lid and followed a trail of blood to where the wounded Fraser lay. 'Of course, all the combatants had left the scene. We weren't confronted with any-one other than Fraser and the dead body.' He was detailed to guard Fraser in hospital and recalls that his charge was enter-tained by the first portable colour television he had ever seen.

Billy Gardner, one of the Haward team, had his own memories of the incident. For a start, he said, they were not seeking money from Mr Smith's, which was regarded merely as a watering-hole: 'One day we heard that the Richardson mob were going to put some of their men in Mr Smith's. As Bill Haward and I were down at the Ark one evening, we got a phone call saying that they were there and they were going to smack Bill's bum. If they smack his bum, they've got to smack mine and all.' There were, he recalled, about fourteen or fifteen in the Richardson gang and Haward's team was outnumbered two or three to one, although Gardner said that there were only two 'danger men' (of whom Fraser was one) amongst the Richardsons.

'We sent out for some shooters and felt a bit safer. The atmo-sphere changed. It was all nice and cool and then all of a sudden the tension started to rise.' He recalled Eddie Richardson telling the Hawards to drink up and saying that they were no longer wel-come, at which point Peter Hennessey invited Richardson on to the dance floor – but not to tango. Coats came off and a fist fight started, but after five minutes 'all hell broke loose. Two or three geezers gave Bill a clump with a bayonet across the nut. Bill went to the gun in his waistband, got it caught in his braces, but let a couple go and all of a sudden it was off. I thought Bill was dead, the blood was pumping out.' Haward requested, 'If I die, just dump me somewhere and say a prayer for me.' He survived. Gard-ner helped Haward to a doctor who, although 'drunk as a sack', stitched up the head wound impressively and gave him some pills. The team then hid out in the area around the Elephant and Cas-tle while the police search for the combatants continued.

Fraser was charged with Hart's killing on the basis of a statement from one of the Haward team, Henry Botton. He was acquitted of murder but convicted at the Old Bailey of affray in June 1966. The trial itself was the focus of allegations of attempted jury nobbling. One of the jurors had a bottle thrown through his window with a note attached, suggesting that the jury, 'Bring them in guilty or else. A lot more where this came from. You're not alone amongst the twelve.' The apparent intention was to turn the jury the other way or implicate the police. Billy Haward was convicted of affray and gaoled for eight years, Henry Botton for five.

The Haward team disbanded after the battle. Hennessey was later murdered at a boxing match. Botton was shot at his front door – 'over a swindle he was doing with someone and they had the hump and when he opened the door – bosh – they gave it to him double-barrelled', as one colleague recalled.

Two days after the Mr Smith's club shooting, George Cornell was shot dead in the Blind Beggar. The two events and the places where they happened were to become key signposts in the geography of gangland. Some contemporaries believe that taking him out might have been seen by the Krays as a stepping-stone into the Richardsons' territory. Some of the Richardsons believed that Ronnie Kray was taking advantage of the Richardson clan's disarray in South Africa and Mr Smith's.

The violence could have escalated into all-out gang warfare: shortly after the killing, Roy Hall, a good friend of Cornell's and a member of the Richardson team, went round to the Krays' home in Vallance Road and shot the windows out. Violet Kray opened the window and told Hall that her boys were asleep and he should come round at a civilised hour. He departed.

But the police were now on the Richardsons' trail. Gerald McArthur, the Chief Constable of Hertfordshire, who was to be a leading figure in the investigation, said he was horrified by what he discovered. He had embarked on the inquiry after James

Taggart had approached him 'frightened for his life ... he was a man petrified, virtually shivering'. Taggart made a statement in which he said that he had had a dispute over money with another man, but was sorting it out when he was given a severe beating, which had lasted five hours. The doctor who had seen him said that there was not an area of his body that was not damaged and that you could not put a 'penny piece' on any area of flesh that was not bruised. His head had swollen to twice its normal size. McArthur approached John Bliss, then the national co-ordinator of the Regional Crime Squads, and suggested that he contact other people who had fallen foul of the Richardsons. He said that another victim, Benny Coulson, 'really believed that in the end he was likely to die. They wrapped him in a sheet and were talking about taking him to the Thames at Vauxhall and dumping him in the river.' Coulson was told to say he had fallen from a moving car. He was given police protection but this was called off after he said it was an embarrassment in his area of Brixton. But the net was tightening around the Richardsons.

At 5 a.m. on the July morning that England was due to play West Germany in the 1966 World Cup Final, a team of sixty officers was briefed by McArthur. Seven hours later, eleven men were under arrest at West End Central police station. 'Charlie was in bed sound asleep,' said McArthur later. 'But he would insist on shaving before he came away. All the time I could see he was thinking to himself – how am I going to get away from this? I'm sure he still had somewhere in his mind that somehow or other he would beat it.'

The trial began on 4 April 1967, with twenty-six counts, some fraud charges having been dropped, against nine people including both Richardsons, Frank Fraser, Roy Hall, Tommy Clark and Johnny Longman. A strange twist was that Charlie Richardson and Fraser thought they had come across the trial judge, Sir Frederick Lawton, two or three years earlier on Victoria station, when Fraser had 'recognised' him as the son of Governor Lawton of Wandsworth Prison, under whom he had spent part of his unhappy sentence. Fraser had tried to have a pop at the 'judge' but had been dissuaded by Richardson. Sir Frederick said he had no recollection of the incident. The trial drew big crowds to the public gallery, including Cardinal Heenan, the actor Kenneth More and the pianist, Leslie 'Hutch' Hutchinson.

Prosecuting counsel Sebag Shaw opened the case thus: 'The eight men in the dock are part of a gang of thugs under the leadership of Charles Richardson, whose policy and practice over a number of years was to enforce his will and his intentions by violence and intimidation.

'This case is not about dishonesty and fraud, it is about violence and threats of violence, not, let me say at once, casual acts of violence committed in sudden anger or alarm but vicious and brutal violence systematically inflicted deliberately and cold-bloodedly and with utter and callous ruthlessness.'

As the trial unfolded, the two versions of what had happened diverged widely: Taggart claimed to have had a sustained beating and torturing. 'Somebody swore blind I pulled his teeth out,' said Fraser. 'In fairness, he gave me a good due as a dentist. Said it was absolutely painless, it was so fast.' The defence suggested that Taggart drove off afterwards and that the notorious Black Box never existed.

The judge, who had childhood memories of his father's prison occupation, believed the Richardson strategy was to have the case stopped in mid-trial because their chances of ensuring that it never started again were great. 'I thought I was seeing through this ploy and I refused every application,' he said later. The Richardsons were 'two dangerous villains'. Charlie, he believed, was a clever man and a very good businessman; he described Eddie as his brother's 'henchman'. Frank Fraser was 'an unbalanced character. He was just a hoodlum.'

Charlie Richardson was convicted and gaoled for twenty-five years. It was the highest-ever sentence for grievous bodily harm and a double-barrelled shot across the bows of aspiring gangsters, according to the judge: 'I think the signal did go out to the criminal classes that this kind of activity was very dangerous indeed. The description of it as the torture trial was justified. Some very unpleasant things were done to the victims. They were given electric shocks. They were beaten. [The Richardsons] were conceited and of the opinion that they had such a stranglehold over street-traders and others in south London that no one would ever give evidence against them.'

His sentencing speech was a classic of the genre: 'One is ashamed to live in a society with men like you. There is no known penal system to cure you. You must be kept under lock and key. You terrorize those who cross your path and you terrorized them in a way which was vicious, sadistic and a disgrace to society. The only thing that will cure you is the passing of the years. It must be made clear to all those who set themselves up as gang leaders that they will be struck down by the law as you will be struck down.'

The police were commended publicly for their work on behalf of 'every law-abiding citizen in England'. McArthur approved the heavy sentence: 'It was a long period of torture for which there is no real section in the Acts of Parliament. They were getting bigger and bigger and more determined. In the end they could have developed very much as the Mafia developed, except that the Mafia probably developed for better motives than Charles Richardson in that they were looking after their friends in Sicily, who had been ill-treated by the government and were very poor.'

Richardson recalled: 'I wanted to say to everyone I could really sympathize with their need for a bit of colour and excitement. I could understand that they wanted a gangster mythology without relying on American imports. But not me, please, go to the Krays, they liked being gangsters.' He believed conviction was inevitable:

'After all the publicity and lies it would have been like having Caligula, Genghis Khan, Hitler and Stalin all in one box and taking the lid off to let them scuttle away.'

Eddie Richardson acknowledged later that there had indeed been torture: 'the "black box" did exist,' he wrote in his memoir, *The Last Word*, in 2005, 'It wasn't strong ... no stronger than the electrified fences used to keep animals in fields ... That's not to say it wasn't unpleasant, especially as Charlie liked to wire it up to blokes' bollocks.'

Charlie Richardson did not emerge permanently until 1984, after serving eighteen years, to be met by a Rolls-Royce and '100 lobster thermidors and a thousand bottles of champagne'. He wrote his autobiography, *The Last Gangster – My Final Confession*, went into the City – which he claimed was more dishonest than anything he had previously been involved in – and resumed his interest in Africa.

Fraser was gaoled for ten years, as were Eddie Richardson and Roy Hall. Fraser was to feature later in the 1969 Parkhurst riots, which added another five years to his time inside. He was the ringleader and had checked whether other prisoners were agreeable to a riot, which had been long threatened but never put into effect. He received summary punishment from the prison officers, 'a thorough beating' as he put it, and needed sixty stitches in his head.

'Mad' Frankie was the bad boy of the prison system till the end. When he was moved from prison to prison he aggravated the officers by pretending, when the van stopped at traffic lights, that any nearby car containing young men was part of an escape plot, mouthing, 'Not now! Not now!' to the bemused carload as though the escape was almost under way. He had spent around forty years in gaol by the time he reached his seventieth birthday in 1993. He had also been certified insane three times and been in Broadmoor and Cane Hill secure hospitals. 'I was brought up in the thirties era – James Cagney, Humphrey Bogart, Edward G. Robinson – and prison seemed quite comfy in the films, they could all talk to each other through the bars.' When he was finally released, he wrote his bestselling memoirs with the assistance of James Morton, carried out tours of criminal sites in London and had a long relationship with Madeleine Wisbey, daughter of great train robber Tommy. In 2013, he was said to have been issued with an anti-social behaviour order (ASBO) after a confrontation with another resident in his care home. He died in 2014.

Charlie Richardson died of peritonitis in 2012 just before the publication of *My Final Confession,* in which he admitted to 'knocking Taggart about a bit because he owed me £1,200 and he did receive a couple of right-handers', as well as, 'I've nobbled a few juries.' One of the floral tributes at his funeral carried the legend '240DC' – a sly, electronic reference to the Black Box.

Eddie Richardson, who was taught how to play bridge by the gaoled spy, John Vassall, found himself facing another long sentence in 1990 after he was convicted of smuggling 153 kilos of cocaine and two tonnes of cannabis into Britain and was gaoled for 25 years. 'People say I shouldn't have done it, but wouldn't they, if they'd been given the chance to make two million, and sort out all their problems in one go?' was his reaction. 'There's a lot of bollocks talked about morality ... Lord Longford volunteered to speak on my behalf, which I really appreciated but I knew it wouldn't make any difference.' With the Richardsons gone and the Krays to follow them some two years later, what was left of the gangs of the era?

Few of the other 'families' were known beyond the prison grapevine or their local areas. But the Nashs, the Dixons and the Tibbs were all at various stages given, rightly or wrongly, the title of London's major gangsters. The Nashs, an Islington family of brothers – Billy, Johnny, Jimmy, Ronnie, George and Roy, of course – had come to prominence over the Pen Club killing in

1960. In 1961 they were described by the now-defunct *Sunday Pictorial* in a 'We Accuse' series as the 'wickedest brothers in England', in the wake of Jimmy's conviction in connection with the Pen Club fight.

Jimmy was said to be the quietest of the brothers, a teetotal, non-smoking boxer. At the time of his trial, his brother Johnny had eleven convictions, including ones for grievous bodily harm and carrying a gun; he was described as the 'Peacemaker' in that he was reputed to sort out gangland's warring factions. He was the 'chief hoodlum ... a whole menagerie of apes owe him their loyalty'. Roy had done time for manslaughter.

Billy was supposedly the brains of the family and wrote a piece for the *Pictorial*'s series in which he blamed the Street Offences Act of 1959 for 'moving the birds off the streets and into the clubs' and thus causing problems that had not previously existed in club-land. 'Me and my brothers would quit the rackets if we could,' he told readers. 'We have the toughest reputation in London. That means there are fools all over London who would like to take us and make their names.' The article was accompanied by a photograph of Billy holding a wreath in memory of Ronald Marwood, who had been hanged for killing a policeman. He had been hidden by the Nashs before giving himself up.

The Nashs' main interests were in clubs across London, including the Bagatelle and the Embassy in the West End. They did not court publicity in the way of the Krays, nor attract police attention like the Richardsons, and they never impinged on the public consciousness much beyond their brief flurry in the Sunday newspapers.

Even after the Nashs, the Krays and the Richardsons had slipped from prominence, one particular officer was certain that there were organised gangs waiting to be busted. Said Bert 'Gangbuster' Wickstead: 'The first thing I did as a targeting was to look at the whole of the London scene to see who was creating mayhem, where, why and what for. The first two targets were the Dixons [George and Alan], for the simple reason that they were marching around the East End boasting they had taken the place of the Krays: "You will now pay us protection, you will do this, you will do that." The Tibbs were the second because they were creating all sorts of mayhem in the East End, vans being blown up, they had to be looked after.'

George Dixon, who with one of his brothers, Alan, constituted the backbone of the Dixon gang, worked initially with the Krays. As a young boxer, he had been recruited by them after having a tussle with some of their henchmen in an East End drinking club. Dixon later told the *Sun* about their recruitment in the Regal Billiard Hall: 'The man I'd called "Eyebrows" beckoned me over. He growled: "I know you – you're one flash bastard." I said, "Yeah, I know." At that Ronnie Kray broke into a huge grin and laughed. Then he shook my hand. That was my welcome to the Krays.'

The Dixon brothers claimed to have taken over the Poplar and Limehouse areas and became used to what George Dixon referred to as 'the flash of yellow' – guns were kept wrapped in yellow dusters at that time. They took part in the Krays' Monday evening strategy meetings, with business being conducted in a different place every time as a security measure against other gangs and the police. They had their own equivalent of Leslie 'the Brain' Payne – Philip 'Little Caesar' Jacobs, who had been at school with the Krays and who ran three successful pubs. Jacobs liked to drive through the East End in a Rolls-Royce with a 'PJ' number plate and his *Playboy*-bunny girlfriend by his side.

George Dixon would carry out Ronnie Kray's orders: 'He'd look at me and then move his eyes to the person he wanted sorted.' The Krays repaid the favours. When George Dixon faced attempted murder and grievous bodily harm charges over a massive fight in a Stepney pub called Kate Hodders, the Krays saw to it that the case never came to trial.

But George claimed that Ronnie tried to kill him on one occasion in 1966 in the Regency club, shoving a semiautomatic into his mouth and pulling the trigger before Reggie intervened. Luckily, the gun jammed. George reported back to his brothers in Poplar and they suggested an all-out gang war against the Krays. Wiser counsels prevailed on both sides and Charlie Kray was sent as an emissary to say that Ronnie had felt that the young Dixons were becoming too arrogant. A meeting was arranged at which Ronnie handed George Dixon the bullet as a souvenir.

In July 1972, Jacobs and Alan and George Dixon were all gaoled after standing trial for a series of assaults, extortion and conspiracies. Prosecuting counsel Michael Corkery told the jury that the gang had promised, 'We have taken over where the Krays left off.' The sentences of twelve years for Jacobs and twelve and nine for George and Alan nipped in the bud whatever pretensions they might have had. Alan, who had worked as a singer in Jacobs's pubs, shouted from the dock, 'Wickstead's reign is now going to be at an end' and told the policeman he deserved an Oscar for his performance. The mother of Leon Carlton, a club owner and one of the gang's members, shouted from the gallery: 'My poor baby. My son is as innocent as a newborn baby.'

As for the Tibbs, although there had certainly been violent clashes involving the family, few of their associates regarded them as running a 'gang' as such. Rather, they were seen as heavies who had become involved in an increasingly bitter feud. In 1968, Albert Nicholls had attacked George 'Bogey' Tibbs in the Steamship pub and in retribution, Nicholls was attacked with a shotgun outside his minicab office. Johnny and Jimmy Tibbs were gaoled for two years for unlawful wounding. In November 1970, Robert Tibbs had his throat cut outside the Rose of Denmark pub, but survived.

The most fearsome incident came when publican Leonard Kersey was said to have called the Tibbs 'dirty pikey bastards'. His wife, Diane, described what happened shortly afterwards: 'I saw the men hacking at somebody on the ground. Then I saw it was my husband. His face was falling apart.' The Tibbs had been victims themselves of attacks: Jimmy Tibbs's van and their café near their Canning Town scrapyard had been bombed in April 1971.

The last of the major 'gang' trials came in January 1973 when father James Tibbs, known as 'Old Man Tibbs', and three sons – John, Robert and the boxer Jimmy, a one-time middleweight British championship contender – were convicted with two other men, Michael Machin and Stanley Naylor, of a variety of offences including conspiracy to pervert the course of justice, possession of 600 rounds of ammunition, conspiracy to blackmail, wounding, attempted murder and assault on a police officer. Despite much evidence of the family's good works and the local people who appeared in the witness box to affirm that the 'Tibbses are diamonds', they were gaoled for a total of fifty-eight years.

Prosecuting counsel Michael Corkery described the case as 'a sickening story of hatred, violence and severe personal injury on those they disagreed with and on whom they sought to impose their rule'. Charles Whitby, QC, John Tibbs's counsel, told the court in mitigation that there was a tradition of great family solidarity amongst the people in east London: 'It is something the East End might teach the rest of the country about. But if it goes wrong and leads to vengeance and violence, then it goes badly wrong.'

A few hundred miles north, there were people who thought that they could probably teach the Londoners a thing or two about violence and vengeance.

6

GANGLAND

GLASGOW GANGS, PEAKY BLINDERS, MR BIGS AND ONE-ARMED BANDITS: THE UNDERWORLD OUTSIDE LONDON

While London might have been the heart of the underworld, other cities in Britain had their own gangs and godfathers, whether in Glasgow or Liverpool, Birmingham or Newcastle, Manchester or Sheffield. They rarely enjoyed the same notoriety as their southern brethren, not least because the national press and their crime bureaux were concentrated in the capital and also because the received wisdom was that Scotland Yard was the fount of all criminal intelligence and their top detectives did not often venture north. But in the three decades between 1870 and 1900, 'the great cities of the Industrial Revolution became breeding grounds for violent young gangs of a kind never seen before. In Manchester they were known as "scuttlers", in Liverpool "cornermen" and in Birmingham "sloggers" and later "peaky blinders" – for the fringe of hair or cap they typically wore over one eye,' wrote Philip Gooderson in his book, *The Gangs of Birmingham*.

It was in Sheffield in the twenties that two hardmen called George Mooney and Sam Garvin each led a battalion of young heavies who carried out minor acts of terrorism, robbed public houses, ran gambling clubs and generally behaved as they pleased. Mooney, of Irish extraction, was a pioneer of racetrack racketeering in the north and could teach his London counterparts a trick or two. Indeed, he had links for a while with the Sabinis, while Garvin, a self-confident soul, dealt with the Brummagem Boys. Garvin, particularly, presented himself as the archetypal gang leader: smartly dressed and glad-handing, organising a high-profile collection for widows after a local mining disaster in classic 'charitable works' style. Meanwhile, 'junior' gangs, led by younger tearaways armed with stool-legs, coshes and razors, were starting to impose themselves.

It was the Sky Edge tossing ring in Wadsley, a suburb of Sheffield, where games of illegal pitch-and-toss were fought over, that was the focus of the criminality, according to J. P. Bean's history of the Sheffield gangs. When Garvin led a splinter group away from Mooney in 1923, the chief constable of the time, Lieutenant-Colonel John Hall-Dalwood, expressed his concerns that the courts were not dealing harshly enough with such hoodlums.

Percy Sillitoe (later Sir Percy) arrived in Sheffield as Chief Constable of the East Riding in 1926. He was a larger-than-life character, born in 1888, educated at St Paul's School in London and sent out to South Africa as a young man to join first the British South African Police and then the Northern Rhodesian Police. His time in Africa was suitably exotic – hunting elephants, being nearly killed by a wounded lion near the Victoria Falls and being cured of rheumatic fever for £5 by a witchdoctor. His return to England as Chief Constable of Chesterfield must have seemed tame indeed. But he soon found the challenge he sought in Sheffield.

Sillitoe decided to tackle the problem of the Mooney and Garvin gangs head-on by drafting undercover officers into pubs that the gangs regularly robbed or abused by demanding free liquor and behaving riotously. 'I sent for both Sam Garvin and George Mooney and gave them a stern warning: "If any of my officers are put in the dock for hammering you, I shall be in the dock with them."' He was as good as his word. He made a point of attending any trials of the gang members and making a special plea for an exemplary sentence. The magistrates were now happy to oblige. 'If you stand up to [the gangs] and they realize you mean business, they will soon knuckle under,' he told his officers.

Both Mooney and Garvin were eventually gaoled and Sillitoe sought them out after they had served their sentences. He described his armistice meeting with Mooney thus: 'He stood and looked at my proffered hand for a long moment without saying a word. As I was about to withdraw it, he burst suddenly into tears, grasped it and said: "You are the first gentleman I ever had the privilege of shaking hands with, sir."' Mooney thereafter 'knuckled under', but Garvin was less amenable and Sillitoe claims he had to be harassed off the streets of Sheffield; Garvin ended his days stealing fruit and vegetables in the market.

Sillitoe's version of events, however, should be taken with a twist of salt. J. P. Bean describes Sir Percy as an unashamed publicity seeker who inflated his own role in tackling gangland crime. Some of the heroic incidents Sir Percy recounted were, says Bean, 'pure invention'.

Nevertheless, with the Glasgow gangs gaining a fearsome national reputation for violence and mayhem, it was not surprising that it was soon a question of 'send for Sillitoe'. He led the police there from 1931 until 1943. For an Englishman to head Scotland's largest and busiest force was seen as something of a national snub and it was made clear to Sillitoe on his arrival that the defensive senior officers felt they had little to learn from him. He disagreed, and there was a purge not dissimilar to the one that Sir Robert Mark was to bring to the Metropolitan Police some forty years later as Sillitoe attempted to attack the city's legendary heavies.

The Glasgow gangs achieved their public prominence in the twenties and thirties, partly because of the remarkable fictional bestseller, *No Mean City*, the Old Testament of Glasgow's gangland. But organised gangs had been operating there since the 1880s when the Penny Mob, so-called because they levied that sum on their members to pay for inevitable court fines, were active. Protection rackets were run at local racecourses probably well before they became established in the south of England.

The gangs were led first by 'chairmen' and then 'kings', and the prestige attached to the gang leader was enormous. The *People's Journal* of 1916 listed the Beehive Boys, the Bell On Boys, the Death Valley Boys, the Ging Gong and the Kelley Boys and warned readers of the 'hooligan menace' in their midst. The *Glasgow Herald* in the same era reported on the gang that shouted 'We are the Redskins' as they went into battle, and the *Glasgow Evening Citizen* later listed the known gangs of the time as the Billy Boys, the Redskins, the Cowboys, the Beehives and the Calton Entry Mob. There was even the Baltic Fleet from Baltic Street.

There were other exotic names: the Hi-Hi in the north of the city, and the Ping Pong, the San Toy, the Village Boys and the Tim Malloys. Many demanded money from people as they left dance halls and theatres and, like their contemporaries in Sheffield, expected to drink free in the pubs. *No Mean City* painted a vivid picture of the time. Much of it was culled from actual incidents and put the fighting in a social context. The book's authors, Glasgow grocer A. McArthur and writer H. Kingsley Long, observed that 'battles and sex are the only free diversions in slum life'. Young men who wanted prestige in Britain's most over-crowded and insanitary city could achieve it with their fists in the ring, their feet on the dance floor or football pitch, or with a combination of feet and fists and razors on the streets of their neighbourhoods.

The arguments for and against the life are put by the main character, Johnnie Stark, the Razor King, and his hardworking, respectable younger brother, Peter. 'Leave me my weapons and I'll finish far ahead of you,' says the gang leader. His brother retorts: 'A bliddy fine job being razor king – while it lasts. Wi' free holidays in Barlinnie an' aw! Christ! A great job for a gangster!' The Razor King, who would 'whirl his weapons like a drum major', was even given a set of razors as a wedding present. He eventually died in battle.

Sillitoe believed that while many of the gangs were essentially young bucks flexing their muscles, many of them were run by professional criminals and 'older scoundrels' who were happy to employ the muscle for their own ends. Indeed, the 'fly men', the full-time villains, realised that the street kings, with their total fearlessness and the awesome reputations they carried along with their black-handled blades, had a valuable part to play in robberies. No one would dare inform on them or tackle them. But the gangs themselves were not money-spinning operations as they were in London. They might bully their way to free drinks and the like but essentially the wars between them were about territory and pride rather than pound notes and commercial control. This did not stop fierce and bloody battles taking place with hundreds on each side, yelled on by their 'queens' and their supporters.

Evidence of the violent scale of the battles can be gleaned from an *Evening Times* report in 1931 on a gang fight in Kerr Street, where the weapons left behind afterwards included 'the spear of a swordfish and a wicked-looking Gurkha knife ... a piece of copper tubing ... a brass-headed poker ... a cudgel two feet long with a knob of wood as thick as the head of a drumstick ... a wooden baton ... an axe weighing a pound and a half ... a steel file two feet long and a bayonet-like knife ... an iron rod three feet long with a hook at each end'.

By 1935 the *Sunday Express* was confirming that 'the gangsters have come to Britain. Glasgow, second city of the Empire, frankly acknowledges their reign of terror. A thousand young men – not forty are more than thirty-five – rule the poorer-class districts. Their insignia of office are the broken bottle, the razor blade, the "cosh", the knife, and – newest and most effective of all – the bayonet.' There were comparisons then to Chicago – which Sillitoe visited in 1933 to compare notes with J. Edgar Hoover – and dark references to murders committed during gang fights. In truth, they seem to have been small in number, not more than one or two a year. Much more common were the savage and disfiguring woundings that the razors caused; the redeeming feature of this weapon of choice was that it did not cut as deeply or as dangerously as a knife, which later Glasgow gangs were to favour. Razor slashings gave birth to the phrase the 'Glasgow smile' – a head butt was a 'Glasgow kiss' – and to music-hall jokes like: 'Going past a hospital on your way home, pal? Get them to stitch – this!'

There were other criminal sidelines in the Glasgow underworld: good dancers could be legally hired by the dance halls but the practice of 'booking out', whereby a wealthy client would hire dancers of either sex for 'private tuition', was in fact genteel prostitution. The dancers had little choice: if they refused a booking, they would be sacked by the dance hall and lose the few pounds that kept alive their hope of a better life, away from the slums of a city which produced twenty-five of the country's forty most-crowded districts.

There were smart gang leaders such as Peter Williamson, who was from a respectable family and had a reasonable education. He led the Beehives, one of the largest and most ferocious of the gangs, with a heavy named Harry McMenemy as his number two. The leader of the Parlour Boys, James 'Razzle' Dalzell, who was killed in 1924 at his own headquarters, was so self-consciously 'hard' that at gang festivities he would only dance with burly members of his gang because he considered it effeminate to dance with women. Bill Fullerton, leader of the Billy Boys of the era, described a wedding of a gang member: 'The bridegroom stood before the minister with a sword concealed in his morning dress. The best man had a gun in his pocket. I'll never forget the scene as they left the church. The gang waiting outside threw bottles instead of confetti.' Fullerton organised a famous drum-and-flute-band march, which led both Roman Catholics and Protestants into a bloody battle from which one man escaped by hiding in his bass drum.

Before the First World War the Redskins included some women in their number, most famously Aggie Reid, who earned the tribute from Detective Inspector Douglas Grant that 'Aggie was a handful'. Four officers were needed to arrest her. Some of the gang leaders took particular pride in their smart appearance, saying, 'Watch the material, Mac' to enraged constables who collared them. In general, the gangs were not heavily motivated by religious animosity, but in the thirties the Norman Conks, who were Roman Catholic, fought the Billy Boys, who were Protestant, and the Rangers–Celtic football games of the time became a focus for concentrated violence in which gang members would participate. Grant noted: 'Neds have one characteristic in common: a tendency to engage in senseless argument which not infrequently ends in violence.'

Sillitoe realised that it was going to take more than a proffered handshake to get the Clydeside 'Neds' to blub their gratitude and pack in the game. His officers adopted a fairly brisk approach to dealing with these hoodlums and were known as 'Sillitoe's Cossacks' for their periodic heavy-handedness. After the war Sillitoe went on to become head of MI5 in the Attlee administration.

The judiciary fought a losing battle against the violence, which continued regardless. In 1935 Lord Aitchison gaoled one gang fighter, John McNamee, for fifteen years for culpable homicide 'in a dramatic challenge to ruffianism in Glasgow', as the local press described it. But it is fair to say that some of the most organised and pervasive crime of the era was perpetrated by corrupt city councillors and contractors, who became, during Sillitoe's time, the subject of a police investigation that led to the arrest of many of the 'high-heid yins' who were so outspoken in their attacks on the more muscular criminals.

The Second World War drew on the raw aggression of many of the hardmen, recruiting them to Scottish regiments for the battlefields of France and Italy and North Africa. The legendary Billy Fullerton of the Billy Boys, for instance, enlisted in the Royal Navy during the war and returned to work in the 'security' business.

The most remarkable of all the criminals recruited to fight in the war was Johnny Ramensky. Of Lithuanian extraction, he had been born in Glenboig, outside Glasgow, in 1905 and had followed his father into the mines in Lanarkshire. But thieving took him to Polmont Borstal, near Falkirk, and he graduated to safe-cracking, becoming one of the most expert in the field. Unbalanced perhaps by the death of his young bride, Daisy, in 1934, he escaped from Peterhead Prison and thereafter indulged, as his advocate Nicholas Fairbairn, QC, was later to put it, 'a lifelong compulsion to break into whatever he was out of and out of whatever he was inside'.

So skilful with the gelignite was Ramensky that he was dropped behind enemy lines with the commandos, a similar if more active role to that played by Eddie Chapman, his safe-breaking contemporary in England. His part was to break into German safes in captured headquarters, including Goering's, and release the papers and maps. When the Allies marched on Rome he was taken along to blow open the safes in foreign embassies. He cracked fourteen in a day. Having won the Military Medal for his endeavours, he returned to Scotland a hero but was unable to stop breaking into safes – Polar Ammon gelignite was his favourite explosive. His methods became more and more Desperate Dan and less and less steel-nerved pro. On one occasion he overdid the gelignite to such an extent that two patrolling policemen, unaware of his activities at that point, were literally blown off their feet.

At first, judges were lenient because he always pleaded guilty, never attacked his arresting officer except in self-defence, and had a fine war record, but the well of sympathy on the bench gradually dried up and the sentences became heavier. Ramensky never lost the affection of the general public and both the actor Roddy McMillan and the late Labour MP Norman Buchan wrote songs dedicated to him. But he was never able to reorganise his life as had Eddie Chapman. Released from gaol in 1964, he promptly broke into Woolworths in Paisley. He was caught for the last time, a white-haired soul of sixty-six, on the roof of a large store in Ayr. He died in gaol and was buried with gangland's equivalent of full military honours in St Francis Chapel in the Gorbals. The hardmen who survived the war returned home and the level of violent crime rose. In 1948 there were 253 robberies with violence in Glasgow, and the increase in the attacks led to the formation of Glasgow's own Flying Squad in 1952.

By the sixties, the gangs were back in prominence. Some of the old names lingered on, but others sprouted like the pop groups of the era and enjoyed a comparable life expectancy. James Patrick, the pseudonymous author of A Glasgow Gang Observed, listed the names of hundreds. Patrick was a first-year teacher at an approved school who spent weekends in 1966–7 with one of his charges in order to observe the way gangs operated. While he acknowledged that he was merely getting a snapshot of their lives and had to avoid becoming involved in the violence himself, he was able to observe a tightly-knit world with the sort of organisation, structure and sense of loyalty that would have impressed Baden-Powell. By the time Patrick published his exposé in 1973, two of the gang had been murdered and the book and its author's allegations and anonymity infuriated the city elders.

Amongst the best-known gangs of the late sixties were the Gorbals Cumbie and the Calton Tongs (who had supposedly taken their name from the *Terror of the Tongs* film), various Fleets, the Possilpark Uncle (after the television programme *The Man from U.N.C.L.E.*). They now called themselves 'teams', not gangs, and had ever more exotic names, such as CODY (Come On Die Young or, possibly, Cowards Only Die Young). Some, like the Y Y Mods or the Young Young Mods, reflected their era. Patrick recorded that the gang to which he was co-opted dressed in the mod uniform of white cardigans, red polo necks, white trousers, red socks and sandals. They rode on scooters with the 'infantry' in the rear. Some teams had girl members – the Drumchapel Bucks and the Lady Bucks are an example.

There were similar gangs in other major cities and towns; the Jacobites in Edinburgh favoured knives rather than the razors of their grandfathers and would celebrate to the tune of 'Bless 'Em All': 'Stab them aw, Stab them aw, The busies, the judges and aw.'

The Tongs were reckoned to be the biggest team in Glasgow, with a rank structured along strict age lines: the Y Y Tongs or the Young Young Tongs, were under eighteen, the Tiny Tongs were from ten to thirteen and there were even Toddler Tongs and Wee Tiny Tongs, who could run errands or carry out thefts of cigarettes and clothes. Their tender years made them exempt from prosecution. One of Glasgow's best-known criminal solicitors, Joe Beltrami – career criminals in Glasgow were famous for requesting 'get me Beltrami!' on their arrest – recounted one trial where the junior sections of two gangs were represented: the Tiny Bison and the Woodhill Young Team. The Cumbies also had an under-age category. After a sheriff had described the activities of the teams as 'mental', the term was worn as a badge of honour by many gangs such as, in Edinburgh, Young Mental Drylaw.

Court reports of the early seventies contain many a 'stern warning from judge to gangs' and much 'gang law feared'. Lord Cameron was prompted to give one of the sternest of warnings at the end of the trial of members of the Barrowfield Spur on 5 June 1978: 'The streets of Glasgow are not going to be turned into a ring for ill-conditioned gladiators and their followers.'

A major underworld figure, although it was his later activities rather than his actions as a criminal that were to win him public attention, was Jimmy Boyle. Born in 1944, he was the son of a Glasgow hardman: one of his earliest childhood memories was waking to see a man entirely swathed in bandages with blood seeping through – either his father or one of his friends who had been the victim of a gang fight. Jimmy was in the Wild Young Cumbies, which was reckoned a heavier team than Big Cumbie, and in the Skulls, and was both a thief and a respected fighter. His weapons were a bayonet wrapped in a copy of the *Glasgow Herald* and a Walther automatic pistol.

As Boyle himself described the Gorbals gang life in his autobiography, *A Sense of Freedom,* the dominant teams at the time were the two Cumbie gangs, the Beehive, the Stud, the Clatty Dozen and the Dixy. His work with knuckledusters gained him a teenage reputation that he did nothing to disavow. When he slashed another young gangster with a butcher's knife, 'within days I was a force to be reckoned with and some kids were saying I was "mad as a brush". There was a sort of hero-worship about all of this – I was intent on making a name for myself and the only way this could be achieved was by violence. There seemed to be plenty of rewards for the gamest guy and I was intending to be him.' Much of the gang warfare was still about face and territory rather than profit and protection, and bravado played a large part in it.

To escape pressure from the police, Boyle moved briefly to London, hanging around King's Cross and dropping purple hearts, but in 1963 was returned to face charges in Glasgow after he had assaulted a policeman, for which he got six weeks in Wormwood Scrubs. He joined 'the Tallymen', who collected money for the loansharking operation led by Frank 'Tarzan' Wilson. The rate was five shillings (25p) in the pound. If the money was not repaid in a week, another 5s. was added. Sir David McNee, later to become the Commissioner of the Metropolitan Police, was in the Glasgow Flying Squad at the time and took the unusual step of going round Gorbals pubs and addressing the drinkers on this pernicious system. In one pub he stood on a table and said he knew that people who were involved were present and called on others to inform on them: 'They listened in stony silence.' There were some results, however. A Glasgow solicitor was amongst those convicted of loan-sharking and the *Daily Express* reported 'McNee Hammers the Underworld', giving birth to the 'Hammer' nickname that was to follow him to London.

Boyle claimed that non-payers were rarely beaten up and that the 'heavies' gradually took over the running of the businesses from the original moneylenders. He suggested that loan-sharking was the first hint of organised crime in Scotland. The main fights, he said, were with criminals who had borrowed money and refused to pay it back. He also worked as a bouncer – his ferocious reputation was an advantage here – and ran shebeens, basic affairs with one room in which drink was sold and another which was full of mattresses and prostitutes.

Boyle was arrested on a murder charge at the age of twenty but the charge was withdrawn and he did not stand trial. However, as he noted later, the fact that people thought he had done it did no harm to his reputation and so he did not discourage the idea. Ten days later, he was attacked by two men and took out the eye of one of his assailants with a broken bottle. 'I felt much better after this, as though I had somehow "proved" myself.' Following another fight in a house in Govan, during which a near-scalping took place, he faced a fresh murder charge, but again it was dropped. Again, despite the acquittal, he did not discourage the hint of his involvement, which 'added to the myth which continued to grow around [the Tallymen]. Because we all came from different districts and within these districts each of us had reputations, there had never been this sort of gathering by guys in the criminal element in Glasgow before.'

He had met the Krays through Big Pat Connolly, who had acted as emissary for the twins' trip north, and noted the different approaches of the London and Glasgow gangs of the sixties: 'The majority [in London] lived very tough lives but concentrated on cash, whereas we in Scotland were more inclined to weigh things up from the physical side. The English guys realize this, of course, and recognize that Scotland produces good heavies and that is why they have so many in their firms.'

In 1967, when he was on the run after the death of 'Babs' Rooney, he headed for London again. Rooney had died in his Kinning Park home after a visit from Boyle and another man. There had been a heated argument which had ended with Boyle slashing Rooney's bare chest. Rooney was later found dead although Boyle declined to say who had murdered him. When *A Sense of Freedom* was republished in 2016, Boyle explained why: 'The truth is Babs Rooney was killed by my co-accused, William Wilson. The whole dynamics of this sum up the world where I once lived. I kept strictly to the "no grassing" rule. I put myself away for fifteen years for the gangster badge of honour that I wasn't a grass.' Wilson was, by this time, beyond any earthly judgment, having died of cancer.

In London, Boyle was hidden by the Krays. But the police tracked him down and caught him in an East End pub called the British Lion after a car belonging to one of his associates had been spotted outside. Boyle had noticed how the pub had gradually filled up with what appeared to be workers from a local factory, all dressed in their overalls, and was puzzled when the barman unbolted a side door to reveal a large furniture van backing towards it. At a given signal the pub was swamped with police, many of them armed, and Boyle was returned to Scotland to stand trial. He was gaoled for life with a recommendation that he serve a minimum of fifteen years.

In prison, Boyle became a changed man after being involved in riots and receiving beatings so brutal that he would cover himself in his own excrement to avoid further attacks from the officers. Transferred to the Special Unit in Barlinnie, he came under the administration of one of the most enlightened penal projects in the country, which sought to tackle the hardest of the criminals by confronting them with their pasts and making them face their futures. Boyle responded by becoming a successful and admired sculptor and writer.

Boyle was released in 1982 and, with his then wife, the psychotherapist Sara Trevelyan, became a powerful spokesman for penal reform. A television film of his life, *The Hard Man*, was a critical success and he moved into fiction-writing. He became for many an inspirational figure, a sign that it was possible to succeed on the outside despite what had happened on the inside. He also set up a centre in Edinburgh to help rehabilitate addicts and encouraged young artists from the same background as himself. Always the subject of tabloid press harassment, he eventually left Scotland and lived between a house in Antibes, in France, and a studio in Marrakech, while still continuing with his art work. Joe Beltrami reckoned that heavy-duty characters like Boyle were peculiar to Glasgow: 'The "hard man" might well in earlier times have been regarded as a "bonny fechter" and admired – nowadays he is regarded as a hoodlum with a reputation for explosive reactions ... and a high pain threshold.'

But most of Glasgow's 'hard men' would have baulked at the kind of villainous action that erupted in the early hours of 16 April 1984: petrol was thrown on the door of a family home in Bankend Street and a match lit.

Six of the nine members of the Doyle family, the youngest only eighteen months old, died as a result of the ensuing fire. It was the bloodiest indication yet that the Glasgow Ice-Cream Wars had finally spiralled out of control. The notion of ice-cream families fighting it out amongst themselves for pitches seemed faintly comical – film director Bill Forsyth used the wars as the basis for his film *Comfort and Joy* – but the reality was less jokey.

In *Frightener*, their 1992 book on these wars, Douglas Skelton and Lisa Brownlie wrote that the conflicts date back as far as 1978, when police took notice of the feuding over pitches in the Barlanark area. Police took the warring sides to Baillieston police station, where a sort of truce was agreed, but by 1982 the Marchetti brothers were complaining that their drivers in Carntyne were being threatened. One woman who complained was Sadie Campbell, whose brother Tom was a Glasgow heavy in a gang called the Gauchos. When she stopped giving credit, her van was attacked. Tom Campbell located one of the threateners, who set two dogs on him. He stabbed one of the dogs through the heart and attacked the man. Shortly afterwards his sister's grocery van was blown up.

Campbell went into the ice-cream trade in 1983, just after his thirtieth birthday, and in 1984 he was arrested for the murder of the Doyle family. A policeman told him: 'You have spent your life creating the reputation of being a violent monster. Now that monster is going to turn around and bite you.'

In October that year Tom Campbell was sentenced to life imprisonment with the recommendation that he serve a minimum

of twenty years. Co-defendant Joseph Steele was also convicted
and gaoled for life. But the evidence against both men was disputed, Steele arguing that he would never say anything as compromising as 'It wisnae me that lit the match.' On home leave in
April 1993, Steele absconded to London and superglued himself
to the gates of Buckingham Palace to protest his innocence. He
was taken back to gaol but escaped again and only gave himself
up, on a pylon outside Barlinnie, after once again protesting his
and Campbell's innocence. The pair were finally cleared in 2004
after their case had been reviewed by the Scottish Criminal Cases
Review Commission.

After the exotically named gangs drifted from view in the
eighties and the high-profile hardmen were locked away, it did not
take long for a different type of 'team' to emerge with a new leader
of its own.

Arthur Thompson had been born in Glasgow in the thirties
and picked up his first offence for an assault when still in his
teens. From then on his curriculum vitae reads like an application for a place in the British criminals' hall of fame: gaoled for
extortion in 1953; gaoled for bank robbery in 1955; Glasgow
ambassador for the Kray twins in the mid-sixties; mother-in-law
killed in a car bomb meant for him in 1966; cleared of the murder of Arthur Welsh and James Goldie in 1966; manager of a
gambling club; major protection racketeer; gaoled for a £3,000
warehouse burglary in 1968; son Arthur gaoled for drug-dealing
charges in 1985; shot in an attempted murder in 1988 (although
Thompson and his family claimed at the time that he had been
injured by a flying part from a drill); run over in 1990 and suffered a broken leg.

In 1991, Arthur 'Fat Boy' Thompson junior, his son and heir,
was murdered while on a 'training for freedom' weekend leave
from Noranside Prison in Forfar, where he was serving an eleven-
year drug sentence. He was gunned down outside his home at just

after 11 p.m. with three .22 bullets, crying out, 'I've been shot, hen' to his sister, Tracey, as she ran from the house.

But it was the double murder in 1992 which followed the Thompson killing that was to shock Glasgow. Joe 'Bananas' Hanlon, aged twenty-three, and Bobby Glover, aged thirty-one, both members of the Barlanark team, were killed in a car in Darleith Street, Shettleston, near the Cottage Bar, shot in the back of the neck and up the anus. Just thirty-six hours before his death Glover had written to the *Sun* claiming that he had nothing to do with the murder of Arthur Thompson junior. The two dead men were regarded as foot-soldiers in the Barlanark team and had already been warned by the police that they were in danger. At the time of their death, Detective Chief Superintendent John Fleming of the CID specialist services said: 'I had told them a year ago, "Unless you get out of this scene then the next time I see you will be in a mortuary."' They told him to 'get on his bike'.

A young man called Paul Ferris, a friend of both Hanlon and Glover, who had grown up near the Thompsons and had acted as a money-collector for the family, was charged with Arthur junior's murder. He had been aware early on that he might be a suspect and had his lawyer take the unusual step of sending a fax to Glasgow's *Daily Record,* making it clear that his client had 'no connection whatsoever with the murder of Arthur Thompson'. Arthur senior, whom Ferris had also been accused of attempting to kill, gave evidence at a long and lively trial and treated the jury to some colourful language. When it was suggested that he himself had been involved in violence he pointed to the dock and told the advocate: 'That is the dock. This is the witness box.' Questioned about one man whom he blamed for fitting up his son on heroin charges, he said that 'if he was a dog with AIDS' he wouldn't want to know him. Asked if he was well known in Glasgow, he replied: 'I have more cousins than Hitler had an army – everybody claims to know me.'

One of the chief witnesses against Ferris was a supergrass from the north of England called Dennis Wilkinson or Woodman. He had been in Barlinnie with Ferris and claimed in evidence that while there he had heard him confess to the killing of 'Fat Boy' or the 'Mars Bar Kid'. Wilkinson had helped to gaol twenty men for a total of ninety years and gave evidence for five days. The jury were clearly unimpressed and Ferris was cleared. There were some dark Glasgow jokes about his future, such as: 'What's the difference between Elvis Presley and Paul Ferris? Paul Ferris is *definitely* dead.' Ferris survived long enough to do a bizarre interview in 1995 with John McVicar on Channel 4 in which he explained his philosophy of life – answering violence with tenfold violence and trying not to hurt any 'non-combatants' – but said that he was more frightened of being bumped off by the police than any underworld avenger.

Arthur senior died of a heart attack in 1993 at the age of sixty-two and notice of the passing away of a 'treasured grandfather' was published in the *Glasgow Herald*. Even in the grave he did not escape action. There was a bomb scare at his funeral in Riddrie Park cemetery on the edge of Glasgow.

Stories about Arthur were legion. His headquarters, two council houses knocked together, was known as Ponderosa, although some called it Southfork after the *Dallas* soap opera. His advocate, Sir Nicholas Fairbairn, said he was 'the coolest godfather Glasgow had ever seen ... smooth, silken, slow and deadly' and expressed fears that, with his death, Glasgow would turn into a 'criminal Bosnia'. He added: 'he had eyes like a cod. He never blinked and he never stopped licking his lips. He had a very spine-chilling presence. Of all the gangsters I have met, he was the most frightening, the most threatening.' At the end of his days Arthur objected to his image to such an extent that he successfully sued *Scotland on Sunday* for remarks made about his criminal involvement and celebrated the four-figure settlement from the paper with Havana cigars all round: 'Why does nobody believe that I've retired?'

Ferris wrote his memoirs, *The Ferris Conspiracy*, with former social worker, Reg McKay, and suggested that Thompson had started his career by literally crucifying someone who did not pay their debts. Describing his own earliest excursion into violence against a man called John Welsh, Ferris wrote: 'turning abruptly, I drew an open razor from my pocket and silently sliced his throat from ear to ear. As I walked smartly on I didn't look back but could hear him gurgle and rattle before falling to the deck. He almost died that night and never spoke normally again. He would carry the scar for the rest of his life and that was just fine by me.' Although he survived all the death threats and became a very media-friendly ex-con, Ferris was convicted in May 1997 at the Old Bailey of conspiracy to sell weapons. He claimed that he thought he was getting £200,000-worth of forged notes and was surprised to find out that he had actually ended up with a box-load of three MAC-10 submachine guns, some handguns, silencers and ammunition. 'I have no doubt you are a dangerous and ruthless professional criminal,' the judge told him as he gaoled him for ten years. Wrote Ferris: 'I wanted to butt in and say it was all in the past.'

An underworld contemporary was Walter Norval, who died in 2014 at the age of eighty-five and at whose funeral the musical accompaniment was the Clash's song, 'Bankrobber'. He had started shoplifting at the age of eight and 'the myth has him dedicating himself to a life of crime after watching the movie *Dillinger* in a local fleapit,' as journalist Ron McKay recalled. 'In later life he even adopted some of the late US mobster's sartorial taste in pinstripes.' He was sent to Borstal at sixteen after holding up a newsagent with a fake gun and sentenced to eighteen months hard labour for slashing a fellow soldier during his National Service. In 1963, in what became known as The War of Norval's Ear, he lost a piece of it when it was bitten off in a brawl by another criminal, 'Big Mick' Gibson. Norval retaliated by stabbing Gibson eight times, for which he was gaoled for a modest three years.

Norval's money came from protection rackets and armed robbery, but he finally came unstuck because of an informer. He was part of what became known as the XYY Gang because, in 1977, its members were involved in four different trials and, to avoid cross-contamination, the principals were given anonymous identities as Mr X, and Mr Y. Norval was gaoled for fourteen years for his part in the robberies of a bank and hospital. On release, he hankered after the old days when 'gangsters were hard men. They fought in the streets, they fought in the pubs and they made names for themselves – but it was amongst themselves. Nowadays, the people who call themselves gangsters don't do any hard work themselves. They just pay someone a couple of grand to go and hurt people for them.'

Another Glasgow gangster with an equally high profile was Tom 'The Licensee' McGraw. A gang member as a young man, an expert at disabling alarms, he raided post offices with T.C. Campbell and had police on his payroll. McGraw suffered multiple stab wounds in 2002 when he was attacked in his own home. Before he died of a heart attack in 2007, McGraw was accused of being a major importer of cannabis into Scotland from the late 1980s onwards. In 1998, a 'not proven' verdict, which was jokingly referred to in Scotland as 'not guilty but don't do it again', was returned on a drug-smuggling charge and an attempted murder of a policeman twenty years earlier.

Two other Glasgow crime families, the Lyons and the Daniels, were engaged in a long-running feud which resulted in a number of bloody ends. One of the murders, in 2006, described by a witness as 'like a scene from a gangster movie,' involved two masked men in long black coats opening fire with handguns in a car showroom forecourt. It left a twenty-one-year-old Michael Lyons dead and two others wounded. Shortly afterwards, a note was delivered to the home of his uncle, David Lyons, with a demand for £25,000 and a threat: 'I don't want the police, the boys, not even your wife, knowing about it. If you keep them out of this then all your lives can go back to normal.'

The two long-coated gunmen, Raymond Anderson and James McDonald, were each gaoled for thirty-five years, the highest-ever such sentence in Scotland. This was reduced on appeal to thirty years after the advocate, Donald Findlay, QC, for McDonald, told the court, 'the only conclusion a jury could have come to was it was a case of bad men shooting other bad men ... There is in this an element of that old saying that if one flies with the crows, one may expect to be shot.' What sparked the shooting was said to be the drive-by shooting three weeks earlier in Bishopbriggs, of Kevin 'Gerbil' Carroll. Apparently, the Lyons believed that Carroll had vandalised the grave of a young member of their family.

It was not just other members of the underworld who were subjected to attacks. Journalist Russell Findlay, who had written about the Lyons-Daniels feud in his book, *Caught in the Crossfire*, had acid thrown in his face when he was confronted on his doorstep by a man disguised as a postman. He survived to write an account of it in *Acid Attack* and his assailant, William Burns, received a fifteen-year sentence.

Further north, in Aberdeen, Antonio La Torre, a polite Italian with a Scottish wife, who had started two restaurants – Pavarotti's and Sorrento – in the 1980s, turned out to be a member of the Camorra mafia and was extradited and gaoled in Italy in 2006 for extortion and racketeering. 'The Don of the Don', as he inevitably became, was accused of using his businesses to launder money.

On the other side of the border, the Newcastle underworld had been witness to one of the most controversial of murders. The killing in 1967 of Angus Sibbett, a local wide boy, became known as the 'one-armed bandit murder' and continued to make waves into the next century. Dennis Stafford, a flashy London underworld figure, and Michael Luvaglio served time for it but were still protesting their innocence fifty years later. Luvaglio and Stafford had moved from London to Newcastle in the 1960s to work for Luvaglio's brother, Vince Landa, who supplied fruit machines to pubs and clubs, a booming business that served Eddie Richardson so well in the south. Stafford had already served a seven-year sentence for firearms offence, had escaped from Dartmoor and Wandsworth Prisons and had run a gay club in London when homosexuality was still illegal.

Sibbett had the job of emptying the fruit machines for the firm but was suspected of skimming the proceeds to finance a high-rolling lifestyle. Sibbett had been in Newcastle's La Dolce Vita nightclub and was found dead in his Jaguar Mark 10 the following morning in South Hetton, near Durham. He had been shot three times and his body dumped in the back of the car, which had apparently been in a recent crash.

The police suggested that Luvaglio and Stafford had deliberately crashed into Sibbett's car and then murdered him. Supposedly they had then headed off to another club, the Birdcage, in Newcastle, to try to establish an alibi. Luvaglio claimed that he could not have carried out the murder as Sibbett was his best friend, but the trial judge, Mr Justice O'Connor, controversially challenged this defence by drawing the jury's attention to both Judas and Brutus as examples of people prepared to betray or kill those closest to them. At the end of a brief trial, they were gaoled for life and served twelve years. Stafford was gaoled again in 1994 for cheque fraud and published his memoirs, *Fun-Loving Criminal*, in 2007, but Luvaglio went into charity work. Both men continued to claim that they were not involved and Luvaglio was even filmed in a BBC documentary protesting his innocence and visiting Sibbett's grave. All attempts to overturn the verdicts were unsuccessful.

The case is often said to be the inspiration behind the 1971 film, *Get Carter*, starring Michael Caine, but in fact the movie was based on the book, *Jack's Return Home,* by Ted Lewis, which was written before the murder took place and set in the Midlands. Mike Hodges, who both directed *Get Carter* and wrote the screenplay, had independently chosen Newcastle as the location and remembered the killing making headlines three years earlier. 'I did some local research and found that, in some ways, the real story shadowed the fictional one,' he said. 'A hitman from London: fruit machines with false bottoms, working men's clubs, porn films, orgies, etc. This research simply rooted the film, leading me to locations and characters that gave it a certain authenticity ... When talking about the making of the film I mentioned this research and – hey presto! – Jack Carter was shape-shifted into Dennis Stafford.' The film even used Dryderdale Hall, which Vince Landa had once owned, as the home for the fictional villain, Cyril Kinnear, played by John Osborne. A strange postscript to the murder came in 2017 when Luvaglio's own E-type Jaguar, which was supposed to have been used as the murder getaway car, was auctioned for £135,000.

Down in the Midlands, the Brummagem Boys had long since seen off the gang known as the Peaky Blinders, a disorganised crew of brawlers, thieves and protection racketeers, who thrived from the 1890s to the 1920s and would eventually re-emerge in a popular television drama series in 2013. In the wake of the show's success, a 'unisex hoodie' and matching mug inscribed with the words 'by order of the Peaky Fookin' Blinders' were marketed. It was even possible to buy 'Peaky Blinders cufflinks' in the shape of razor blades, as one version of their name came from the suggestion that they stitched blades into the peaks of their caps to attack their enemies, a scenario rubbished by Carl Chinn in his book, *The Real Peaky Blinders.* But real gang warfare remained very much a baleful part of Birmingham life in the new millennium and, as with Britain's other major cities, it would often take a murder to alert the rest of the country as to how such rivalry could too often be fatal.

At the 4 a.m. end of a New Year's Day party held at a hair salon in 2003, two teenagers, Letitia Shakespeare and Charlene Ellis, were caught in the crossfire of a feud between two gangs known as the Johnson Crew and the Burger Bar Boys. Two years later, Charlene's half-brother Marcus Ellis and three others, Michael Gregory, Nathan Martin and Rodrigo Simms, all in their twenties and all said to be members of the Burger Bar Boys gang, were convicted of the murders.

The two gangs had emerged in the 1980s, according to Amardeep Bassey, author of *Homeboys: The Birmingham Gang War and The New Year's Eve Murders*, with 'good intentions' and, in understandable response to the racism and far-right extremism in the area, as a form of self-protection for the black community. But as that threat dissipated, they moved into professional crime through crack cocaine and heroin, a trade that led to a number of inter-gang murders and a 'tit-for-tat spiral of mindless shootings'. The 'Johnnies' and the 'Burgers' became rivals and, when a leading figure in the Burger Boys was charged with the murder of Corey Wayne Allen, another gang member, in 1999, there was finally recognition that there was a deadly side to the rivalry. Two years earlier, members of the Johnson Crew had been arrested after a DJ called Jason Wharton was shot dead in Handsworth. But it was the murders of the teenage girls that were to throw a national spotlight on crime in the city.

In the same way, a decade later, the murder of Paul Massey drew attention to the Manchester underworld, which had acquired the nickname 'Gunchester' in the 1990s. Massey was shot with a sub-machine gun by a man in camouflage fatigues in the driveway of his home in July 2015. The murder was deemed at the time to be a result of feuding between members of what was known in the area as 'the A team'. (No connection to the Adams family in London, who were also known as the 'A team'; there seemed to be no 'B teams' in gangland.)

Described as 'Mr Big' by local councillor Joe Burrows, Massey was short in stature but large in life. With a criminal record from the age of twelve, he was gaoled in 1999 for stabbing a man in the groin but was best known for running 'security' firms that controlled local clubs and music venues. He even ran for Mayor of Salford in 2012 with a promise to rid the streets of drugs and to provide rehab for those in need of it. 'These kids need energy, education and guidance to stop them from being lost souls,' was his pitch. 'When I was a kid there were hardly any drugs around. Now it is different story. Drugs are blighting lives.' He came seventh out of ten with 1995 votes.

His funeral, a month after his murder, was equal to those of the Krays in its pomp, with a pipe band playing 'We're No' Awa' Tae Bide Awa'' while a white coffin on a carriage drawn by plumed white horses took the cortege to the cemetery as bystanders lined the streets and applauded. There was a brawl at the graveside during which a relative of Massey's had chemicals thrown in his face and was battered with the staves used to lower the coffin.

One of the messages left outside Massey's house, which read 'RIP to a true respectful man', was appropriately enough from a member of the Noonan family, who had, over the years, become one of Manchester's best-known gangs and had profited from the drugs scene in the city's clubland, including the legendary Hacienda, as they controlled the security arrangements and took a cut of the drugs business. One brother, Dessie, who proclaimed himself an Irish republican and an anti-fascist, was fatally stabbed in 2004 by a drug dealer, Derek McDuffus, known as 'Yardie Derek'. Another Noonan brother, Damien, died in a motorbike accident on holiday in the Dominican Republic, while a third, Dominic, was gaoled for eleven years in 2018 for sexual offences with boys while already serving time for arson, blackmail and conspiracy to pervert the course of justice.

Three years after Massey's death, in May 2018, John Kinsella, one of Massey's pallbearers, was himself shot dead by a man riding a mountain bike and wearing a high-visibility jacket as he and his partner took his dog for an early-morning walk on a woodland path near the M62. Kinsella, who had served time for robbery, was known as 'Scouse John' and had been on holiday in Wales with Massey just before the latter's murder. In January 2019, Mark Fellows, a career criminal nicknamed 'the Iceman', was given a whole life sentence for the two murders and told by the judge, Mr Justice William Davis, that he was 'a gun for hire prepared to kill whoever you were asked to kill by those that hired you'. His associate, Steven Boyle, was convicted of the Kinsella killing for which he has acted as a 'spotter'. Both murders were described in court as part of a long-running gangland feud.

Until then, the Manchester underworld outfit to attract the most outside attention had been the Quality Street Gang, a loosely-knit crew of artful dodgers who operated from the 1960s through the 1980s and whose exploits were recorded by one of their number, Jimmy 'the Weed' Donelly, in his eponymous memoir. They came to prominence when it was falsely alleged that John Stalker, the Greater Manchester Deputy Chief Constable, had socialised with some of them; Stalker believed he was the victim of a dirty tricks campaign. The QSG started out in the old Smithfield Market and were originally known as the Market Men. Mobs, such as the Gooch and Cheetham Hill gangs, behind many of the shootings that led to the 'Gunchester' label, slipped from prominence after their leaders were either jailed for long terms or killed in the first decade of the millennium.

In Liverpool, it was the murder of eleven-year-old Rhys Jones in 2007 that was to draw national attention to what had been a grim local rivalry. Sean Mercer, aged only sixteen at the time of the killing, was gaoled for a minimum of twenty-two years for the murder that had seen Rhys caught by a stray bullet. Mercer was a member of the Croxteth Crew gang and his intended victims were members of a rival gang assembled in a pub car park. It took the police some weeks before they could charge him as he had made sure his clothes were burned and his body washed down with petrol in the immediate aftermath of the shooting. Mercer had a drugs conviction and only a couple of months previously had ridden on a motorcycle into rival gang territory waving a gun. The trial at Liverpool Crown Court heard that Mercer was in the Croxteth Young Guns, who were involved in a battle with the neighbouring Strand Gang.

Mr Justice Irwin, the judge who sentenced Mercer and his fellow gang-members, who joked and laughed in the dock, was scathing in his disdain: 'this offence arose from the stupid, brutal gang conflict which has struck this part of Liverpool. You were caught up in that from a young age, but it is clear you gloried in it. It is wrong to let anyone glorify or romanticise this kind of gang conflict … You are not soldiers. You have no discipline, no training, no honour. You do not command respect. You may think you do, but that is because you cannot tell the difference between respect and fear. You are selfish, shallow criminals, remarkable only by the danger you pose to others.'

As Eric Allison, the *Guardian*'s prison correspondent, observed: 'Liverpool has traditionally seen a lot more crime families than its neighbour. It was a thriving port long before the industrial revolution put Manchester on the map, and ports bring criminal opportunities ashore, along with cargo and passengers. When established criminals, like the Quality Street Gang, were said to be in control of Manchester's underworld, two brothers from Toxteth, Liverpool, Michael and Delroy Showers, were openly operating in the lucrative drugs market based in Manchester's Moss Side. Their presence did not lead to a turf war; though the brothers almost certainly handed over a few sweeteners to those supposedly running the territory they were trespassing on.'

7

THE ROBBERS

FROM THE GREAT TRAIN ROBBERY TO THE SHOOT-OUTS

Sitting in a convoy of Land Rovers as they sped through the early hours of a Buckinghamshire dawn, one of the robbers fiddled with the radio to try to find the police wavelength. Over the airwaves came the voice of crooner Tony Bennett. He was singing a song called 'The Good Life'.

And for those next few magical days, during which the robbers could not sleep, it must have seemed that the good life had indeed arrived for them all. They had just stolen £2,500,000 from the Royal Mail night train on its way from Glasgow to Euston, in London, and in doing so had carried out Britain's largest-ever robbery and written a chapter in British criminal history.

This was, of course, the Great Train Robbery, the high-water mark for British robbers and one that has endured in the memory even though robberies of more than ten times the value have been carried out since. It occupies a peculiar place in the British psyche, partly because of the daring of its conception and partly because of the strange paths since taken by some of its perpetrators: gaol, escape, flight, kidnap, drugs, murder, revenge.

It was always an ambitious job, although one of the robbers, Tommy Wisbey, said that it was only nine months from conception to execution, during which time a team was assembled that could both handle the physical side of the heist and keep its collective mouth shut until it had taken place. The plan was, in many ways, quite simple. Fix a false signal so that the train stopped, disconnect the van with the money from the rest of the train, steal the mailbags by threatening the mail-workers, hide out in a nearby farmhouse until the initial hue and cry had died down and then quietly launder the stolen money.

The crew eventually assembled was a gallery of south and east London criminality: Buster Edwards, a thief, club owner, former boxer and small-time fraudster; Gordon Goody, a massive man with a reputation as a robber and with 'Hello Ireland' and 'Dear Mother' tattooed on his biceps; Bruce Reynolds, the intellectual of the group, officially an antique dealer, who enjoyed spending the proceeds of his crimes at the Ritz and the Savoy, driving an Aston Martin and holidaying in the south of France; Charlie Wilson, a bookie and well-known 'face'; Jimmy White, an ex-paratrooper who had worked with Reynolds; Bob Welch and Tommy Wisbey, who had an inside man on the railways with whose help they were carrying out some modest robberies on the Brighton line; Roger Cordrey, a train expert; Jimmy Hussey, a big man who had convictions for everything from pickpocketing and theft to attacking the police; two drivers – Roy James, who was involved in crime because he could not find the sponsorship that would enable him to move up a grade to Formula One motor racing; Ronnie Biggs, a carpenter by trade and small-time villain until the robbery, a friend of Reynolds and, more crucially, of a retired train-driver who was co-opted to drive the train the brief distance necessary; Bill Boal, a minor player who worked in air-craft components and whose job it was to get rid of the money; Leonard Field, a florist; John Wheater, the public-school-educated solicitor whose function it was to purchase the farm; and Brian Field, no relation to Leonard, a solicitor's clerk from Oxfordshire, whose job it was to help Wheater. And the ones who were never caught.

Some of the team, such as Wisbey, already had experience of train robbing. One of their stunts was to use a man made up to look like an invalid and seated in a wheelchair, who would be kept in the guard's van with his attendant. When the train stopped at a predetermined spot, the guard would be attacked by the 'invalid' and his companion, who would then make their escape down the line and into a waiting car. Another ploy was for Wisbey and his associates to travel as passengers and one of their number to pre-tend to have an epileptic fit. The van would be raided while the guard assisted. But the sums had been comparatively small.

Once the assembled team had decided to carry out the rob-bery, they looked for a place near enough to London for them to slip back into their normal haunts and yet not too close to any built-up area where people would notice what they were up to. Bridego Bridge near Linslade and Cheddington, and between Leighton Buzzard and Tring, was all they had hoped for: secluded, handy and with the added advantage of an army base nearby, which would allow them to move heavy vans at odd times without necessarily arousing suspicion. Originally, the plan was to carry out the raid in June, but it was thought there would be more money on the train in August because of the holiday fortnight.

Planning was meticulous. The team equipped themselves with blue overalls so that railwaymen would assume that they were working on the line if they were spotted before the robbery. Roy James, who had agreed to find out about uncoupling the engine from the train, posed as a school teacher who wanted to teach his pupils about trains and was able to discover some of the basics of the engine's mechanics.

And so, at 3.03 a.m. on 8 August 1963, the false red signal was activated. 'It's coming down, chaps,' said Bruce Reynolds. 'This is the real thing.'

As the train stopped at Sears Crossing the fireman, David Whitby, went to the telephone at the side of the track to find out the reason for the delay. He saw Buster Edwards and asked him what was happening. Edwards grabbed him and hustled him down the bank to where two of the others were able to hold him. Whitby agreed not to resist, with the remark, 'All right, mate, I'm on your side.'

The driver, Jack Mills, appeared at his cab and realised what was up. After a brief struggle he was coshed and collapsed, bleeding. Who actually hit him has always been a subject of debate, the more so as it was this one act of violence that marred the operation in the eyes of many and certainly led to some of the years in the heavy sentences that were to follow. In Piers Paul Read's *The Train Robbers*, published fifteen years after the event and written with the sometimes mischievous co-operation of the robbers, it is stated that as 'Gordon (Goody) pinned [Jack Mills'] arms to his body, Buster (Edwards) hit Mills twice over the head with the cosh.' But Edwards denied this version. He said that the publishers would only do the book, for which all sides were rewarded, if the robbers would agree to say who had struck the blow. Edwards duly volunteered himself but said that the assailant was one of the men who were never caught. This is the view expounded, too, by Biggs, who in 1993 was quoted in the *Sunday Express* as saying that the wielder of the cosh was a 'heavy villain' who was never caught. Tommy Wisbey said he does not know who struck the blow: 'In the mêlée it could have been anyone.' Truth was, after Jack Mills, a major casualty in the affair.

The robbers tried to get their ex-driver conspirator to move the train but he was unable to set it in motion because he could not 'get the vacuum'. The bleeding Mills was told to take over the controls, and shunted the train to its pre-determined position for the robbery to proceed. Four of the gang burst into the coach where the post-office sorters were going through the mail. There was no resistance and the process of unloading the bags began. The robbers formed a chain down the embankment and whipped the sacks from hand to hand on to the lorry, taking a hundred and twenty and leaving half a dozen behind.

Wisbey says that he and Wilson patched Mills up: 'He said, "I think you're real gentlemen." We sat him on the grass verge and asked did he want a cigarette and, "Do you want any money, we'll leave it on the grass verge for you."' Mills declined the offer. Then, leaving Mills and Whitby handcuffed together with the instruction, 'Don't move for half an hour', the robbers set off in a convoy of Land Rovers and a lorry back to Leatherslade Farm.

Over the police radio came the response of the Buckinghamshire police: 'You won't believe this,' said one officer over the airwaves to his colleagues, 'but they've stolen a train.'

But the robbers were tuned to Tony Bennett. 'We were all singing "The Good Life",' said Wisbey. 'We got the prize. It was a feeling of elation. I think it would have been harder taking sweets off a baby.'

Back at the farm they started counting their haul and found they had around £1,200,000 in £5 notes and £1,300,000 in £1 and 10s. notes. The money was divided up into shares of around £90,000 each. The plan was for the farm to be cleaned and all fingerprints and telltale signs to be removed. But the police were hovering already. The casual warning to Mills and Whitby that they were not to move 'for half an hour' had indicated to the police that their quarry was within a limited circumference, and by 13 August, they found the vehicles and the mail bags at the

farm. Now, because of some simple errors at odds with the profes-
sionalism of the rest of the plot, the game was almost up.

Originally described in the press as the Cheddington Train
Robbery, the heist soon took on the name that was to exemplify
daring crime and the resulting media coverage made arrests
imperative for the police. Flying Squad chief Tommy Butler was
appointed to lead the inquiry from London after some toing and
froing between police from the local and the capital's forces. He
was a veteran of investigations into Jack Spot and Billy Hill and
his full-time hobby – at fifty, he still lived with his mother – was
catching crooks. Assisted by a remarkable number of casual clues
left at the farm and in the vehicles, he was gradually trawling
through known criminals currently on the job and arrests began.

Most of the gang were aware as soon as the enormity of the
robbery became clear they were liable to be picked up for routine
questioning on a 'round up the usual suspects' basis. They had
been counting on the lack of any incriminating evidence either at
the scene or at the farm and on the general reliability of the team
in the pre-supergrass era. But their careful plans were gradually
coming unstitched. Damning fingerprints had already been discovered: Roy James had fed the cats at the farm and his prints
were found on their bowl. Hussey's gloves had shrunk in the heat
and his exposed palm had left its print on the tail of the lorry.
Edwards's prints were on the money-wrappers and those of
Wisbey, Wilson, Daly and Welch were also traced. Goody's mother
was raided, prompting him to write a whimsical letter to the police
expressing his disappointment that he should be regarded as a
suspect – 'more than I can stand'. For this reason, he told them,
he would absent himself until the true villains were apprehended.

Wisbey had set off on holiday after treating his daughter
Marilyn to an *Emergency Ward Ten* nurse's outfit. His mood was
not helped by two friends with him who, completely unaware of
what he had just done, insisted on telling hoteliers that they were,

ho ho, the Great Train Robbers, about whom the papers were then full.

The round-up of the gang was speedy and largely successful. Within five weeks, five members of the gang had been arrested and another five had been identified and were wanted by the police. Thirteen men eventually stood trial on a total of ten charges, the main one, which all faced, being conspiracy to rob the train. Some of the robbers eluded the sweep, either initially or through subsequent escapes, but for the others, as they were driven to court, there was little light at the end of the tunnel.

Roger Cordrey, who had been found with £80,000 of the stolen money (which he returned), pleaded guilty. The trial of the others, in front of Mr Justice Edmund Davies, began on 20 January 1964 in the Aylesbury District Council Chamber, which had been turned into a court-room for the purpose. It had the advantage of being close to the scene of the crime and investigation but, more importantly for the police, it made the chances of jury nobbling more remote than if it had been heard at the Old Bailey. Nonetheless, according to some accounts, attempts were made to extract money from the robbers' wives by people who claimed they could fix the jurors.

The robbers made bold attempts to defend themselves. Wisbey, for instance, explained a palm print found in the bath-room as being a result of him slipping there when he had been delivering a load of fruit to the farm. The trial received acres of coverage and the press benches were packed. 'All the people one knew were there,' observed journalist Peta Fordham, who wrote a book on the case, *The Robber's Tale*, and who was married to Wilfrid Fordham, one of the defence barristers. Her descriptions of the main protagonists reflected some of the ambiguity about the crime felt by press and public alike: 'White is the most ordinary and engaging little man in the world ... Charlie Wilson, the sort of father you see by the hundred in France on Sunday outings ...

Goody, nerves of steel and the wolfish handsomeness of the pack leader ... Edwards, one of the keenest brains in the underworld.' She was to write that 'the events were so vividly in the minds of the actors that they remember, like Henry V's men at Agincourt, with advantages what feats they did that day'. Piers Paul Read was to say in his version of events that 'politically one might describe the train robbers as Saxons still fighting the Normans'.

Mr Justice Edmund Davies took a slightly less breathless view of the defendants. Cordrey was the first to be sentenced and, having pleaded guilty and returned so much money, he might have expected a certain leniency. The judge told him that he was guilty of 'a crime which in its impudence and enormity is the first of its kind in this country. I propose to do all in my power to ensure that it is the last of its kind; for your outrageous conduct constitutes an intolerable menace to the well-being of society. Let us clear out of the way any romantic notions of daredevilry. This is nothing less than a sordid crime of violence inspired by vast greed. As to violence, anybody who has seen that nerve-shattered engine-driver can have no doubt of the terrifying effect on law-abiding citizens of a concerted assault by masked and armed robbers in lonely darkness. To deal with this case leniently would be a positively evil thing.'

While Cordrey must have realised by this stage that he was unlikely to be receiving just a stiff fine and probation, he must still have been shocked at the sentence that the judge announced: twenty years. Although the others had joked through their trials – Goody had drawn cartoons – they now appreciated the fate that awaited those of them who had played larger parts and pleaded not guilty. Their fears were justified. Bill Boal received a twenty-four-year sentence and the Fields twenty-five years each. The mother of Lennie Field shouted out her protest from the public gallery and Field, who was then aged thirty-one, shouted back: 'Don't worry, Mother, I'm still young.' The major players lined up to hear that they were to be gaoled for thirty years. Wilson did manage a final dark joke, kidding the others that he had received a single-figure sentence.

The sentences stunned the men. 'We were thinking in terms of ten to eighteen,' said Wisbey, who eventually served twelve and a half. 'I thought the judge was off his head. It was like he was at a bingo hall – three oh – thirty.' One of the policemen cheerfully told him he would be in a wheelchair when he came out.

What happened to Jack Mills has often been cited as a reason why the crime should not be considered glamorous. In his autobiography, Bruce Reynolds dealt with the issue thus: 'I regret what happened to Mills but I believe it was exaggerated out of all proportion ... Although I wasn't there [on the train itself], I do know it wasn't planned. The last thing we wanted to do was injure the train driver. By the same token, none of us was overly concerned with what had happened ... There is no doubt that the authorities used the attack on Mills to brand the Great Train Robbers as brutal, murderous gangsters who had to be hunted down and punished severely, scotching perceptions that we were in any way glamorous figures who had pulled off a film-script plot. Mills was awarded compensation of £250 by the Post Office and returned to work on less onerous duties. For the record, when he died of leukaemia seven years later, aged sixty-four, the coroner felt impelled to add that it had nothing to do with the bang on the head. Yet the belief always persisted that it did.'

The robbers were distributed around maximum-security gaols. Some measure of how seriously their prowess was taken can be gleaned from the fact that one northern chief constable speculated about the possibility that atomic weapons might be used to effect their escape and also raised the possibility of tanks coming through the streets of Durham to free them. The Chief Constable of Leicester, Robert Mark, was even summoned to see the Home Secretary, Sir Frank Soskice, who suggested that the prevention of the escape of the robbers was a matter for the army rather than the police. Mark dissuaded him and was given a dozen new automatic rifles for his force.

But the authorities still had to follow the recipe for successful punishment: first, catch your robber. Still on the run, Reynolds and Edwards waited until the Court of Appeal turned down their colleagues' pleas in the summer of 1964 before deciding to leave England. Mexico was the chosen destination and the escape route was via the south of France with the aid of false passports. Reynolds made it there first with his wife and booked Edwards and his wife into the Hilton Hotel. Reynolds, the most cosmopolitan of the robbers, was at ease in their retreat but it was not exactly Edwards's glass of Corona and his family missed home (as later portrayed in the film *Buster*, in which Edwards was played by singer Phil Collins).

White, who had also fled, was recaptured and received an eighteen-year sentence, a stiff penalty but a large reduction from the trial sentences. Edwards decided to give himself up, having learned that Detective Superintendent Frank Williams would treat him fairly if he did so. Although Tommy Butler of the Flying Squad thought at first that the surrender must be a joke, Buster Edwards was taken back into custody on 19 September 1966. At his subsequent trial he was gaoled for fifteen years.

Wilson, whose reticence during the trial had earned him the title of the 'silent man', had meanwhile escaped from Winson Green Prison in Birmingham and made it, complete with beard and bogus passport, by ferry to Calais and ultimately, to Montreal. Here, he was joined eventually by his family and by Reynolds, who had found out that he could not make a living in Mexico. Reynolds was restless and moved on to the south of France. Wilson seemed to have blended successfully into Canadian life but on 25 January 1968, Tommy Butler and fifty Royal Canadian Mounted Police officers arrived at his door as he was about to take his daughter to school. He was soon on a plane back to England and a cell in Parkhurst.

Reynolds quit France and moved first to London and then to Torquay where, on 8 November 1968, Tommy Butler, who had stayed on at the Yard to track the remaining train robbers, arrived on his doorstep with the words: 'Hello, Bruce, it's been a long time.' To which Reynolds, ever the cavalier, replied: 'C'est la vie.'

And then there was one. Ronnie Biggs had escaped from Wandsworth Prison in July 1965 through the ingenious use of a rope ladder and a pantechnicon lorry with a specially constructed turret that had been parked outside the gaol. Two getaway cars waited nearby. Biggs made it first to Paris, where a plastic surgeon changed his features, and then to Australia, to Adelaide and then Melbourne, where he led a suburban life as Terry Cook, the carpenter. But when an illustrated article about the train robbers appeared in Australia, a previous acquaintance recognised him, told the police and his photograph was broadcast on television. Biggs decided he had to move on again and sailed for Brazil, which had no extradition treaty with Britain.

In 1974 he was nearly hoisted back to England after a *Daily Express* journalist, Colin Mackenzie, had met up with him in Rio de Janeiro. The *Express* had tipped off the police about the meeting and Chief Superintendent Jack Slipper appeared at the hotel where the interview was due to take place with the standard, 'It's been a long time' greeting. But Biggs did not come quietly. His Brazilian girlfriend, Raimunda, was pregnant and, as the father of a Brazilian child, Biggs was immune from deportation. In 1981 a ham-fisted attempt was made by three seedy English ex-soldiers to kidnap him and bring him back to England via Barbados. This also failed. Bob Welch emerged in June 1976 as the last of those gaoled at Aylesbury to be released. Hussey and Wisbey were to be gaoled for cocaine dealing in 1989.

Jack Slipper was sanguine on the robbery: 'I have to respect them for some aspects of it and I admit it was bold and daring, but they were no Robin Hoods and I've always been convinced that it was only by chance that there wasn't more violence.'

What happened to all the money has never been completely explained. Certainly, the robbers on the run found themselves having to pay out vast sums for false passports and escape routes. Those inside saw their 'investments' being frittered away by former friends, who assured them that the businesses in which the money had been placed had failed. Later, the robbers would emerge to find that some of the moneyminders had acquired fine houses or even hotels.

The main lesson to be learned from their capture was that too many crooks – at least fifteen here – left too many clues. The underworld had known of the job for too long and the likely suspects were too easy to round up. Young up-and-coming robbers learned that there was safety in lack of numbers and, accordingly, the most successful teams of the sixties and early seventies were four-handed or five-handed and did not share too widely the knowledge of jobs which were planned.

The massive sentences handed out to the train robbers had little deterrent effect – some members of the underworld felt that they might as well carry guns since they could hardly face a stiffer penalty than thirty years – and by the early seventies the armed bank robber was in his balaclava-ed pomp. Robberies were happening every few days and the police seemed unable to catch any of the figures who sped off from banks and security vans in stolen cars.

Bank robbers were the new criminal aristocracy, 'the faces', admired by the young villains, fancied by the prettiest of the young women who enjoyed the clubs and the clothes and the racing weekends at Longchamps. They saw the Krays as old-fashioned and mocked them with the nicknames 'Gert and Daisy', chumps who had been caught because they stuck their necks out, dinosaurs who liked Matt Monroe while the new boys played The Doors and T. Rex on their newly-discovered car tape decks as they slung their 'happy-bags' stuffed with sawn-off shotgun, masks and gloves into the back seat. They also realised that provincial robberies were easier to carry out because of laxer security arrangements and the distance from the knowing eyes of the London detective.

They were mainly from the London area and a large number were from around Hornsey Rise – 'Hungry Hill' as the young hoodlums liked to call it – and the patch that spanned Holloway and Finsbury Park, the Angel and Hoxton. They fancied themselves. A bunch of them were photographed posing moodily in Finsbury Park by Don McCullin, one of their schoolmates who had gone straight, for a 1958 *Observer* colour supplement feature entitled 'The Guv'nors'.

Eric Mason, who worked in the sixties and early seventies and served a total of seventeen years for robberies, initially met up with other robbers in the two main robbery centres of higher education: Dartmoor and Parkhurst. As a former safe-cracker, he realised early on that bank robbery was the coming thing: 'Peters weren't worth it. People weren't keeping money in them anymore. You found it easier to pull up at a bank, one minute later you would walk out with everything that was on show.' Monday morning was a good time, when banks held large sums neatly packaged behind their counters waiting for the security to take them to the feeder banks.

'You'd walk in on a Monday morning, jump over the bank counter, two or three of you, hold the staff at bay with a shotgun, let one go in the air ... and take the bag that was waiting for Securicor plus all the night-safe bags plus the money in the tills. You were guaranteed twenty or thirty grand in every bank. It took you one minute.' Mason's timing was accurate and the press duly christened the team 'The Minute Men'.

The shotgun was used partly for show, according to Mason. 'We'd take the shot out of the shells and replace them with ordinary household rice. It would make a noise and the only stuff that would come out would be rice.' While this might have made matters safer all round, it had an unfortunate side effect for Mason. When he was arrested in Cardiff, detectives realised that the same *modus operandi* had been used by robbers in Nottingham and London – four bank robberies had left enough rice to start a curry-house chain splattered over tills and counters.

Mason reckoned that there was an almost psychological barrier against robbing banks and post offices: 'In the old days, you had this thing, you don't do it because it's establishment. In the sixties, people began to realize that anything was fair game in the days of Profumo, people realized that politicians, people we looked up to, were fragile and people lost respect. People began to realize this was a big con. The barriers started coming down.'

The normal method for Mason and his colleagues was to smash the glass of the inside doors of the bank: 'That would be the first effect and we'd fire a shot into the roof. There'd be no opposition. The one thing you never did was lay a hand on anybody. I did once and it stuck with me for many years. We went into a place and a woman was standing by the wall, absolutely petrified, and I tried to reassure her by putting my hand on her and saying, "Just sit down, don't worry, luv, nothing will happen to you." The mere fact of me touching her absolutely broke her completely. She went into hysterics. I learned from that that you never touch anybody. You just cajole them into sitting on the floor and don't worry about things.'

Some robbers used ammonia sprays, after which security guards wore glass shields over their faces; the robbers merely switched tactics and carried black spray-paint cans to spray over the visors. But the really heavy-duty villains were not discouraged.

The speciality of the Crash-Bang Gang, operating from 1969 to 1972, was to park about a hundred yards away so that their get-away car could not be blocked. The normal procedure then was for one or two quick changes of the stolen vehicles before a 'meet' to share out the spoils.

One reason for the high success rate of the robberies was that sophisticated alarm systems connected to police stations and video cameras, which would become regular features by the nineties, did not yet exist. There were few time-worked safes, it was still easy to recycle money through the system via bookies or casinos, and bullet-proof grilles had still to become standard.

Robbers were clearly not much affected by the recommended normal sentence of fifteen years for bank robbery laid down by the Court of Appeal in 1965, and the increasingly heavy sentences that followed. These double-figure sentences were very much a post-war phenomenon. Sir Frederick Lawton recalled: 'My father (former governor of Wandsworth Prison) told me in his early days in the prison service that anybody who got a sentence of more than five years was looked on with pity, as it was regarded as a very cruel sentence indeed. In my early days at the Bar, the standard sentence for robbery with violence in the streets was twelve months' imprisonment and twelve strokes of the cat.' (Eric Mason, the recipient of such a beating in the presence of Governor Lawton: 'He was as bad as any prisoner I ever met. He took great pleasure in watching me be flogged.') Sir Frederick, who had gaoled Charlie Richardson for twenty-five years, also expressed the concerns of some members of the judiciary that the long sentences for armed robbery might lead robbers to kill a potential eyewitness as the difference between the sentences for murder and robbery was slight.

The issue was brought into grim focus on 12 August 1966 when three police officers in an unmarked police 'Q' car were shot dead after checking on a suspicious-looking vehicle with three men in it at Shepherd's Bush. One of the men, John Witney, was swiftly traced and after his alibi had crumbled named the other two as John Duddy and Harry Roberts, who was known as a robber of post offices. Duddy was caught in Glasgow but Roberts, a former soldier with decorations for service in dangerous terrain in the Far East, bought himself camping equipment and hid out in thick woodland in Hertfordshire. Home Secretary Roy Jenkins described the killings as 'a threat to the whole fabric of society'. An enormous manhunt was launched and Harry Roberts's face was everywhere, provoking a macabre football terraces taunt: 'Harry Roberts, he's our man, He shoots policemen, Bang Bang Bang.' Roberts was eventually caught on 11 November after a local Gypsy, who had been wrongly accused of stealing, pointed out smoke coming from a campfire in the forest near Bishop's Stortford.

All three men were gaoled for life. Duddy died in gaol. Witney, who had not fired the fatal shots and who said that Roberts's policy was 'leave no witnesses', was freed in 1992 and beaten to death by his heroin addict housemate in 1999. Roberts remained in Dartmoor and told the *Guardian* in 1993: 'We shot them because they were going to nick us and we didn't want to go to gaol for fifteen years. We were professional criminals. We don't react the same way as ordinary people. The police aren't like real people to us. They're strangers, they're the enemy. And you don't feel remorse for killing a stranger. I do feel sorry for what we did to their families. I do. But it's like people I killed in Malaya when I was in the army. You don't feel remorse.' He was released after serving forty-eight years in 2014, to the dismay of the Police Federation.

Perhaps the paradigm of the robbery era was the Wembley bank job. This was planned at a meeting in the Thatched Barn Hotel in Borehamwood, north of London, at which one of London's most active robbers, Bertie Smalls, selected the wines. It took place on 10 August 1972 and £138,000 was stolen. Six raiders blasted shots into the ceiling and then ran from the bank in single file, carrying bags of money and looking so ponderous that one witness described it as 'like something out of a *Carry On* film'. The raid had been timed to coincide with the arrival of Security Express at the bank and a spokesman said, almost admiringly, that it was 'spot on'. The robbers were gone within ninety seconds.

Another typical job was the Ralli Brothers robbery in Hatton Garden, in London, on 26 March 1969. An inside man let in the robbers, led by Bertie Smalls, at 6.30 a.m. They then hid in the ladies' lavatory until the rest of the staff arrived, tying them all up, including their inside man. By threats, they overcame the two-key system whereby one staff member had one key and the combination number and the other had one key but no number. They met to share the spoils at a house in Finchley, in north London.

Some jobs required larger teams. Here is how bank robber Bobby King described the robbery of Barclays Bank in Ilford in February 1970: 'There were nine of us. The planning was five to six weeks. I had to go in the bank dressed in a suit looking like a travelling salesman writing a moody cheque out, mingling.' They had been tipped off about the run from a local Tesco supermarket by a friend of a friend of a relative of a security van driver, and knew that a red Mini arriving at the bank in advance of the delivery was an indication that big money was around: the Mini was meant to check out whether there were suspicious characters in the vicinity. King's colleagues, some dressed as painters, held up the driver, who dropped the bags and ran. The robbers piled into a white transit van and fled, turning right, left, right, left until they reached their next fleet of stolen cars for the second stage of the getaway.

'We used to put salt instead of pellets in the shotgun cartridges,' said King, who took an Open University degree in prison, with the novels of Virginia Woolf as his specialist subject, then became a chef on the outside. 'This meant that if one of those rugby-tackling types tried to stop us we could shoot and he would think he had been hit. The theory was that this would give us time to get away and if we were caught it was less serious because we hadn't actually shot anyone. We were quite a liberal gang.'

Insiders were often crucial to some of the more spectacular heists. Never more so than at 6 p.m. on the evening of 24 April 1975, when eight smartly suited men entered the Bank of America in Mayfair and departed three hours and around £8 million later. The key to their success was a feckless young petty criminal and electrician called Stuart Buckley who was, amazingly enough, employed by the bank despite the fact that he had only just emerged from prison for handling stolen goods. Buckley's job had won him the attention of some more experienced criminals who discussed his access to the vaults in meetings in the Crooked Billet pub in Wimbledon. He took Leonard Wilde, known as 'King of the Twirlers' because of his expertise with keys and locks, Johnny the Boche, so-called because of his slightly Germanic appearance, and other members of the gang, posing as fellow electricians, on conducted tours of the premises under his employers' noses. The bank's computer room, in the same building, was in use sometimes twenty-four hours a day and gave an excuse for movement at odd hours.

After Buckley had turned up the in-house muzak to give some added sound cover, Wilde was shown the complex twin dials that opened up the vaults. Buckley even removed the lock from a back door to the bank so that the gang could have a key made to fit it.

On 26 October 1974 the gang made their first attempt to break through. They had discovered that the alarm worked much like an old-fashioned record player, coming down on a disc which was immediately relayed through to the nearest police station; by removing the needle they were able to de-activate the alarm. But the other aspects of the robbery were less simple. The drills first started to overheat – they had to be cooled with ice-cold Cokes from the building's soft-drinks dispenser – and then snapped. Billy Gear, the look-out man, spotted computer workers but his shouted warnings could not be heard above the drilling so he disconnected the power. The attempt was a failure and the gang had to abandon the pieces of broken drill as they departed.

Amazingly enough, this attempt, with its clear hints of inside involvement, did not alert the bank to the role of Buckley, who was actually asked to assist in strengthening the electronic security. It was while working in a false ceiling above the vault that he 'accidentally' shoved his electric screwdriver through the ceiling and, to his surprise, saw the manager and chief cashier carrying out a routine opening of the twin-locked vault, each with knowledge of one lock's combination number. Buckley, perched above them, was able to witness each man dialling the four key numbers per lock. This was, if the word can be used for such a break-in, dynamite for the robbers. But to ensure that Buckley had correctly observed the numbers he was asked to go back and hide out again, this time with a pocket spy-glass. Concealed with two bottles, one of orange juice and the other for him to urinate in, he was able to check and record the vital numbers.

As he left the bank on the day of the robbery, he flashed his car lights twice to let the team know the coast was clear. The game was on. Ninety-four of the 550 safe-deposit boxes were broken into and cash, jewels, rare books and works of art were scooped out and split between the gang above a greengrocer's shop in Lambeth. They might have escaped with more had not a member of the computer bureau staff, who was working upstairs, come down to use the office telephone to make a dial-a-disc call. He was tied up along with his colleagues and the robbers decided to make a speedy departure, taking Sir Winston Churchill's old Mauser pistol, which he had used as a subaltern in the 21st Lancers during the cavalry charge at Omdurman in the Sudan, but leaving behind an Enid Blyton first edition and a Picasso.

The police, led by Detective Superintendent Bob Robinson, had been watching Buckley since the earlier aborted attempt and he was arrested the next day. His share of the loot was found in a wood in Brenchley, in Kent. Others in the team were already under suspicion: Billy Gear, who had taken his son to the dentist before the robbery, had used his wife's car because he was late and it had been ticketed nearby by a traffic warden; Jimmy O'Loughlin had been seen entering his house with a heavy suitcase. Buckley decided to give evidence for the prosecution, which resulted in a smaller sentence, a third of what the other main players received.

At the end of an often bad-tempered ninety-one-day trial, Wilde was gaoled for twenty-three years, Billy Gear for eighteen years, Peter Colson for twenty-one, Jimmy O'Loughlin for seventeen, Micky Gervaise (later to become a supergrass) for eighteen months, Henry Jeffery for twelve years and Henry Taylor for three. O'Loughlin had escaped briefly by pretending to be a solicitor's clerk during an appearance in a magistrate's court. Mr Justice King Hamilton, no friend of the criminal, said that between £2.5 million and £8 million had been stolen but only £485,982 recovered and said he was giving them stiff sentences so that 'what has been salted away will remain salted away as far as you are concerned'. He described Colson as 'slippery as quicksilver' and said he was 'beneath contempt' for making allegations about police corruption.

This was one of the Robbery Squad's successes. It had been brought under one command with the Flying Squad and Number 9 Regional Crime Squad in 1973 and during that year there had been twenty-six bank robberies compared with sixty-five the previous year. By the following year the figure had dropped to seventeen. In 1974, 150 people were arrested for robberies going back to 1965, for sums totalling around £3 million, and twenty-seven of them were gaoled for a total of 315 years. But this was partly because the robbers were shifting their tactics. The rise of the robbers seemed unaffected. There were 380 robberies in 1972 in London and no fewer than 1,772 ten years later.

So what made a bank robber? John Ball, Lewis Chester and Roy Perrott, the authors of *Cops and Robbers*, suggested that, 'There was a marked gap between the status they could achieve in straight society and what their aspirations encouraged them to feel they deserved.' And they noted, too, the 'sense of the casual' in the approach to crime, with the robbers scoffing at what the public imagined went on – the Mr Big, the detailed planning and so on – when much of it was quite casually planned and executed, done at speed to avoid leakage from the growing number of informers.

John McVicar, an armed robber who became famous mainly through a daring escape from Durham gaol in 1968, had his own theory: 'The professional criminal wants respect, prestige and the recognition of those who subscribe to his own need of machismo. The field in which he tries to achieve this is one in which profit, crime and gangsterism overlap.' His mother put it more bluntly when she described her son's and his friends' apparent fascination with prison life: 'I think you must all like it in there, you're always talking about it when you come out.'

McVicar was a bright war baby who had drifted into crime as a boy and picked up sentences for riotous assault, robbery with violence and possession of offensive weapons and had spent time in Wandsworth, the 'Hate Factory'. In 1966 he and a group of Parkhurst prisoners engineered a court case in Winchester so that they could escape from the coach on the way back. Nine, including Roy Nash, tried to escape, but only two, including McVicar, succeeded and he was at large for the summer. In 1967, he was gaoled for fifteen years for firing at a police car after an attempted robbery.

His escape in October 1968 from Durham, accomplished with the assistance of the man who was the unofficial chairman of the prison escapologists society, Wally Probyn, brought him to prominence partly because Durham was such a difficult prison to break out of and partly because he was described in the press, American-fashion, as 'public enemy number one'. He remained on the run for two years before being recaptured in November 1970 after an informant, encouraged by a £10,000 reward, had tipped off the police. His own assessment in his autobiography paints a less glamorous picture perhaps than the one given him when Roger Daltrey played him in the film *McVicar*: 'As a criminal I have been a lamentable failure. Whatever money I earned by crime, I could have earned as a labourer in half the time I have spent in prison ... Money has always been a secondary goal; crime has always been directed to more powerful objectives.'

But McVicar was able to turn his reputation and an education he acquired inside, including a degree in sociology, to his advantage. He emerged to take a postgraduate degree at Leicester University and became something of a media pundit on crime, fashioning a successful career as a freelance journalist for the likes of *Esquire*, the *New Statesman* and the *Guardian*, clubbing at Groucho's and playing tennis to keep in trim.

For his part, Probyn was caught during the Durham escape but emerged to write *Angel Face*. He had had this nickname since his youth, which had been spent almost entirely in custody for petty offences. He had also escaped from Dartmoor and numerous young offenders' institutions and almost made it out of Parkhurst on the Isle of Wight with Harry Roberts, whom he reckoned did not really want to make the final jump: 'He was pitting his wits against the screws to find ways but it was only in theory; he didn't want to do it in practice.' Probyn went on to careers in the antique business and as a photographer. He settled in Hoxton with his rare fish collection and became a father in his fifties. He was portrayed by Adam Faith in the McVicar film but never really felt at home in the limelight and has never followed the gold-chain 'diamond geezer' school of ex-villains.

To a certain extent Probyn took on the mantle of another 'great escaper': the late Alfie Hinds, a safe-breaker and burglar whose spectacular escapes in the fifties captured the public imagination. A member of Mensa, Hinds protested his innocence of the 1953 break-in at Maples department store in Tottenham Court Road, for which he was gaoled for twelve years. He used his escapes to publicise his claims of innocence and his time inside to become a barrack-room lawyer. He successfully sued Herbert Sparks, who had arrested him, when the detective wrote about his great cases and named Hinds. A libel jury awarded Hinds £1,300.

One robber who came to prominence in the seventies was George Davis, who had been convicted of robbing the London Electricity Board offices in Ilford in March 1975. An enormous campaign, spearheaded by his wife Rose and friends and with the oft-graffitied slogan 'George Davis is Innocent OK' was launched to prove his innocence. Its most public activity was digging up the pitch at Headingley cricket ground in Leeds in the middle of the Ashes Test. He was pardoned and released but on 23 September 1977, he took part in a raid on the Bank of Cyprus in Holloway, north London, and was caught in the act and gaoled. It was a blow to his loyal wife. As she recounted in *The Wars of Rosie,* published just before her death in 2009, this time there was no question about his guilt and no campaign. 'I was ashamed,' she wrote. 'I felt gutted for all those people who had helped us.' When Davis told her once again that he had been fitted up by the police, she replied: 'And I'm the Queen of Sheba.' His behaviour created a general cynicism about miscarriage-of-justice campaigns for the next few years.

Many other 'faces' also lost out: Billy Tobin, one of the best-known bank robbers of the seventies, was gaoled in September 1981. And not all the 'faces' survived: Adgie Pitts, brother of Shirley 'Queen of the Shoplifters' Pitts, died young in a car crash in the sixties. Two years earlier, he had been the getaway driver in an attempted springing of another villain, Freddy Sampson, driving on the pavements through the streets of Tooting in a spiffy red Jaguar car.

Other robbers met more brutal, untimely ends. The Torso Murder case in 1977 involved two of the most controversial deaths: Billy Moseley was cut up into pieces and dumped in the Thames without his head, and Micky Cornwall, who was known as 'the Laughing Bank Robber' because of a permanent grin, was shot in the head and buried in the traditional shallow grave in Hertfordshire. Reg Dudley, who had a long criminal record and had worked at the Krays' El Morocco club, and 'Fat Bob' Maynard were convicted of their murder after what was then the Old Bailey's longest murder trial.

It was claimed that Dudley and Maynard formed part of a gang called Legal and General, which held sway in north London. In fact, there was no such gang and this was just a joke name given to the pair because they looked, on one occasion in a pub, like the two characters in a Legal and General television commercial. At their trial it was claimed that such traditional gangland motives as pursuit of loot, jealousy or informing had been involved. But the evidence against the two men was always shaky. In a macabre gesture that indicated that the wrong men had indeed been gaoled, Moseley's slowly defrosting head was left in a public lavatory in Islington shortly after the trial ended in June 1977. The supergrass Tony Wild, who claimed that the men confessed to him, became a born-again Christian in prison and recanted his evidence, which he admitted he had made up. Dudley and Maynard were finally cleared by the Court of Appeal in 2002, after Wild had been given immunity from prosecution for perjury. The two men were given hundreds of thousands of pounds in compensation for their two decades inside.

Some robbers became prominent for reasons not entirely connected with their profession. On 2 May 1970, silver bullion worth

£400,000 was stolen from a security van in Mountnessing, in Essex. One of the men arrested for this was George Ince, who received a fifteen-year gaol sentence for the crime. But he became better known as the man wrongly accused of the murder of Muriel Patience at the Barn restaurant in Braintree, Essex. He had been picked out on an identity parade. Ince had the embarrassing alibi that he had been with Dolly, the wife of Charlie Kray, and he was eventually acquitted. The case became a *cause célèbre* for those seeking a change in the identification rules of evidence.

David Martin achieved possibly the highest profile of all the robbers who made a reputation for reasons other than their hauls or escapes. He was a remarkable character, much more complex than the image of the 'transvestite bank robber' with which he was later saddled. He was a risk-taker: he used to enjoy stealing unmarked police cars from outside police stations, zooming across the English Channel to France for the weekend and calling the police station from Charles de Gaulle airport in Paris to tell them where they could pick up their Rover. He was a small man and could pass for a woman when he effected escapes in drag. He had been to Borstal for assaulting an off-duty policeman, served a long sentence for cheque frauds and had been part of a team that used a dust-cart as a battering-ram to escape from Brixton Prison in 1974.

In August 1982, Martin had been spotted posing as a security man called David Demain in a West End building. Asked to empty his pockets by PC Nicholas Carr, he had opened fire and wounded the officer in the groin. 'Demain' was traced to Crawford Place in Paddington, where police saw a woman at the entrance. The 'woman' turned out to be Martin, who first pulled a semi-automatic pistol from his handbag and then a Smith & Wesson .38 revolver from his waistband. The police fired back and Martin was shot in the head and shoulder and captured. A search of his flat suggested his involvement in a series of robberies and thefts. But before he could come to trial, Martin, using a duplicate key, had managed to escape from Marlborough Street Magistrates Court, where he was attending a remand hearing. The hunt was on. A tip-off led police to a yellow Mini in Earls Court on 14 January 1983.

The police, believing that Martin was a passenger in the car, opened fire. They hit their target five times and pistol-whipped him in the street as he spilled out of the Mini. It was the wrong man. The innocent passenger was a film technician called Stephen Waldorf, who was later paid £120,000 in compensation and departed to France to write a fictionalised account of the event. He felt no bitterness: 'I could never muster it. I hate wasting time hating people.'

A fortnight after the event, police had found out that Martin would be dining at the Milk Churn in Hampstead. They were plotting his movements through tapping the telephones of his friends. Just before they were about to pounce, Martin realised that a trap awaited him and ran for the underground station, sped down below, leapt on to the electrified line and headed for Belsize Park. There, in an alcove, Martin was found. He had a tiny penknife stuck to the roof of his mouth with chewing gum.

In October 1983 he was sentenced at the Old Bailey to twenty-five years. He had not expected such a heavy sentence and could not face the tedium and the fear of becoming a prisoner with 'the 100-yard stare'. He hanged himself in his cell. Even the policeman he had shot expressed his regrets. (Robbing in drag is not quite as popular as films might suggest, but bank robber Bobby King recalled an occasion when an attempt was made to approach a security van by using a robber who had been dressed in his girlfriend's clothes. The robber, a small but quick-tempered man, had to push a pram in which a sawn-off shotgun was hidden towards the security men and then hold them up. Unfortunately for the gang, the blagger in drag had to pass a building site and was subjected to a few 'get yer tits out, darlin'' remarks from that direction. For a moment it appeared that he was about to lean into the pram and grab the gun to teach the builders a lesson. The other robbers panicked and intercepted him. The robbery was abandoned, thus jettisoning a few thousand pounds and a potential hammer-blow for the women's movement.

Bank robbery was mainly a white profession. One outspoken exception was Trevor Hercules. As a sixteen-year-old in the 1970s, he had been arrested after a fight and had his head bashed against the side of the police van. 'I had been brought up to believe the police was my friend so it was a real shock to be racially abused, not just by one but by all of them.' He was soon running with a team of armed robbers and arrested again. He gave a Black Power salute from the dock as he was sentenced, and served time in Wormwood Scrubs, Wandsworth, Parkhurst and Gartree. When he came out after seven years, he wrote a well-received book, *Labelled a Black Villain*, but was still an angry man. 'I was obnoxious, unforgiving and frightening. I didn't see myself as part of society.' He was soon back inside but on his last release, in 2000, he decided he had had enough of prison and worked with young people at risk to try to steer them away from prison.

In the nineties, bank robberies were an almost daily occurrence in London – there were 291 in 1992 – but within a couple of decades they seemed almost as old-fashioned as an edition of *The Sweeney*, the TV series that celebrated the Flying Squad and flared trousers. There were only twenty-six such robberies in the UK capital in 2012 and the figures nationally show the same decline, from 847 down to 108 in the twenty years from 1992. Jackie Malton, a former flying squad officer and the model for the TV series, *Prime Suspect*'s Jane Tennison, reckoned there were a number of factors to the decline. 'It's just too risky nowadays,' said Malton, whose new role was working with addicts in prison and as a TV programme consultant. 'Because of all the increased security they have a much higher chance of being caught and a heavy sentence – sixteen or seventeen years – is a reality. Crime is going online now.'

Another reason for the decline in the robbery teams is that they found themselves facing not only the narksmen but the marksmen: police ready to shoot armed robbers caught in the act. In November 1990 Kenny 'Big Head' Baker was shot dead by a police marksman near Reigate, in Surrey, during an attempted raid on a Securicor van, with members of the Arif family. He was the seventh robber in four years to be shot dead on the job.

Bucking the trend were the Arifs, a family of Turkish-Cypriot origin who finally emerged from the shadows of the Old Kent Road in the nineties, when brothers Dennis and Mehmet were gaoled for the same attempted armed robbery in Reigate.

Dogan Arif, the oldest of the six brothers, had already been gaoled for an £8.5-million cannabis-smuggling plot – he had dabbled in football, briefly owning the non-league Fisher Athletic club – and Dennis and Bekir also had convictions. But it was the Reigate shoot-out that was to lift the veil on the family, whom police had been pursuing for more than a decade.

The team that did the job had an impressive array of fire power, enough 'to start a small war', as was said during their trial: a 12-bore Browning self-loading rifle, a Brazilian-made pistol, a 1922 Browning pistol and a US Army self-loading pistol. The robbers had disguised themselves in Ronald Reagan and 'old man' masks and were hoping for a haul of around £800,000, which police believed could have been used to finance drug dealing. But armed police were waiting for them and Kenny Baker, a veteran bank robber, was shot dead, his Reagan mask still covering his face.

In December 1991 Dennis and Mehmet Arif and their brother-in-law, Tony Downer, were gaoled for twenty-two, eighteen and eighteen years respectively. Dennis ran the imaginative defence that Baker had forced him to take part because he owed him money from gambling debts, but the jury was unconvinced. The judge, Heather Steel, whose looks and forthright manner had won her a reputation in the Old Bailey for making the hearts of barristers beat faster, was unimpressed by the defence's references to the Great Train Robbers: 'In comparison with this case, the train robbers seem like gentlemen.'

On 23 November 1987, Tony Ash was shot dead in the process of a wages snatch at the Bejam supermarket in Woolwich, south London. The police had been tipped off by informer Seamus Ray. Ash was a larger-than-life character who had never had the best of luck: he had once offered some stolen Scotch to a pleasant woman he met at a hotel dance in Ramsgate only to find out that she was an off-duty policewoman. Ronnie Easterbrook, another of the fifty-something robbers on the job, was also shot but survived. Ash's was a very public death: a Thames Television crew had been in the process of filming the Flying Squad at work. A wreath sent to his Camberwell funeral read: 'May your executioners and Seamus Ray live long and suffer every day.'

Eighteen months later, Jimmy Farrell and Terry Dewsnap were shot dead when they tried to rob a post office in North Harrow on 13 April 1989. Police, who included the Yard's PT17 marksmen, had been tailing the team. Farrell had only been back on the street for eight months after serving a sentence for robbing the National Westminster Bank in Isleworth in 1977, a crime he claimed he had not committed. Dewsnap was one of the men whose name had been mentioned as the real murderer of Micky Cornwall.

The Great Train Robbers slipped in and out of the national consciousness still. Bill Boal died while still inside, despite his fellow-defendants' claims that he was the one innocent man amongst them. Field died in a car crash in 1977, his in-laws unaware of his notoriety until after his death. Charlie Wilson was to suffer a violent death at the hands of a hitman in Spain. Buster

Edwards hanged himself at the age of sixty-three on 29 November 1994 in a lock-up garage near the flower stall he had run at Waterloo station; he had a serious drinking problem and was suffering from depression. His coffin arrived at Streatham Vale crematorium for the funeral with a train made out of flowers above it, and the Krays sent a wreath. Bruce Reynolds turned his hand to writing and his *Autobiography of a Thief* – a title chosen in homage to Jean Genet's *Diary of a Thief* – was published in 1995. He died in 2013 and at his funeral, his son, Nick, an artist, musician and former Royal Navy diver, said that with the looming fiftieth anniversary of the robbery, his father had not been looking forward to all the bother from the media. 'So, as he had so often done before when wanted for questioning, he chose to split the scene.' His ashes are now in Highgate Cemetery, beneath a death's head mask made by Nick.

Ronnie Biggs, still cheerfully on the run in Brazil, brought out his own book, *Odd Man Out,* and popped up at the Earth Summit in Rio de Janeiro in 1992, advising delegates on how to avoid being mugged. Ex-Superintendent Jack Slipper, the man who tried unsuccessfully to extradite him from Brazil, even went out for a reunion in 1993, courtesy of the *Sunday Express.* Slipper told Biggs that if he came back, he would probably only face four or five years inside, but Biggs said that while he might miss his jellied eels, he felt no great nostalgia for the dank, dark cells of Wandsworth. Having suffered a major stroke, he returned to England in 2001 with his son, Michael, after making a deal with the *Sun*; during his thirty-six years at large, there was never a shortage of a reporter with a chequebook to hand. Despite his frailty, he was held in prison until 2009, emerging to launch an updated version of his memoirs at a fashionable Shoreditch club and died in 2013. His funeral was spectacular: a wicker coffin, draped in the flags of Great Britain and Brazil, and an Arsenal scarf was accompanied by an escort of Hells Angels and the

London Dixieland jazz band playing 'Just a Closer Walk with Thee' and departed at the end of a ceremony, in which Shakespeare, Dylan Thomas and Oscar Wilde all received a mention, to the strains of 'The Stripper'. 'This is,' said the Revd. Dave Tomlinson, with priestly understatement, 'unlike any funeral I've ever taken.'

Roy James died in 1997, after serving another sentence for wounding his father-in-law. Goody died in Spain in 2016 and Tommy Wisbey in London in 2017. At a time when robbers pour petrol over their victims or threaten to rape their wives, a rosy hue now suffused the men of the Great Train Robbery. Even Sir Robert Mark wrote of Biggs in his autobiography that his escape had 'added a rare and welcome touch of humour to the history of crime'. Sir Robert observed drily that Biggs's retreat to Brazil made him the most memorable figure to undergo the punishment of banishment since Henry IV in 1398. Robbery in any case was becoming less enticing for criminals. In his 2005 memoir, *A Few Kind Words and a Loaded Gun,* the veteran armed robber Noel 'Razor' Smith ruefully recalled his botched jobs, including one where he tried to hold up a newsagent's with a Luger pistol only to be told by its Ugandan-Asian proprietor, with commendable sang-froid, 'Your gun is unloaded – you are minus the magazine. And you swear far too much for such a young man.' An abashed Smith bought a Mars bar instead. He reflected: 'When you're young and strong and you can afford to throw away a decade or two in some pisshole prison and still have plenty of life left to live, it's all a big laugh. Then you wake up one morning and see a strange face staring back at you from the shaving mirror. Some old geezer with bitter, weary eyes, where there used to be a devil-may-care twinkle.'

And the arrival on the scene of a beefed-up version of the old snitch, nark, canary or squealer was already changing the face of robbery. The supergrass had arrived.

8

THE SUPERGRASSES

BERTIE, 'KING SQUEALER' AND THE REST

The supergrass is a modern phenomenon, distinguished from the old-fashioned nark, who has been known as long as there has been a notion of crime and punishment. Jack Wild in *The Beggar's Opera* was an informer and Dick Turpin himself was tracked down by officers who used the promise of favours to his fellow criminals. Scotland Yard has long operated its Information Fund and by the end of the Second World War the informer in a case of stolen goods was entitled to 10 per cent of the value of the property.

But although they have always been a feature of criminal life, the men who broke the eleventh commandment of the underworld, 'Thou shalt not grass', have always had to suffer the penalties. The 'snitchers' in the fifties were sometimes punished with the 'mark of the nark', a razor slash from cheekbone to the corner of the mouth. 'Snitches get stitches,' as the popular prison graffiti had it. A man with an obvious scar and without a Clydeside accent was often thought to be an informer.

The title of the first 'supergrass' – someone who gives evidence against many of his former colleagues in exchange for a lenient sentence and protection – is usually bestowed on Bertie Smalls, the London bank robber who helped the police in 1973, but there is debate on this. Leonard 'Nipper' Read, who investigated the Krays, claims that Leslie Payne, adviser to the twins, who gave evidence against them at their Old Bailey trial in 1969, was the first genuine supergrass.

The use of supergrasses in Britain was to mirror what was happening in the United States, where the first major cracks in the underworld's code of loyalty were appearing: Joseph Valachi, a veteran Mafia man, became in 1963 the first member of the organisation to become an informer. His move led to the setting-up of the Witness Security Programme, a less formalised version of which now operates in the United Kingdom.

By 1974 the policy was starting to work in Britain. Sir Robert Mark noted of a number of criminals that, 'faced with honest and trustworthy detectives for the first time in their experience, they began to sing'. But a sentencing policy which had more than doubled the standard term for robbery is as likely a reason for the ending of the concept of 'honour among thieves'. While a robber might accept with equanimity the six- or seven-year sentence that was normal in the fifties, knowing that his family, hair and libido would probably still be intact by the time he came out, the notion of a dozen or more years behind bars concentrates the minds of even the 'staunchest' criminal.

Smalls was a short, squat man who looked like the film actor Bob Hoskins and held ferociously right-wing views. Bobby King, one of the bank robbers on whom he informed, said, 'He loved violence. He couldn't handle straight company, he liked to be with "one of his own", an expression he used all of the time.' Before being a robber, Smalls had worked as a ponce, which some of his victims hinted was an indication of the decadence of character that would lead him to inform.

In 1973, faced with the possibility of a daunting sentence for his part in the Wembley bank job, and tracked down at a hide-out in Northampton through his au pair, he co-operated with the police and started on a process which would help to gaol many of his colleagues. Detective Jack Slipper believed that a key factor in the final turning of Smalls came when he first had to face the men who were then his colleagues at the committal hearings. Smalls was heavily hung-over, having downed his regular bottle of vodka the previous day, and Danny Allpress, one of his seven co-defendants, taunted him by asking him who would be having his wife while he was away.

An agreement was drawn up with the Director of Public Prosecutions, Sir Norman Skelhorn, granting him immunity in return for complete co-operation. He, his wife and two children were hidden at a guarded address. By September 1974 he had helped to gaol twenty-one former associates for a total of 308 years. As he concluded his evidence in the committal proceedings, King and Danny Allpress sang, 'We'll meet again, Don't know where, Don't know when ...' This scene was later used by screenwriter Peter Prince in *The Hit*, which starred Terence Stamp as a supergrass hiding out in Spain. Allpress even taught his prison budgie – long-term prisoners were allowed pet birds and 'Do not enter, budgie loose' was a not-uncommon cell-door sign – to say 'Bert is a fucking grass'. Diane Smalls was sympathetic to her husband's victims: 'I wept all night because I considered the sentences (between sixteen and nineteen years) were inhuman,' she said of the gaolings of Allpress, King and five others. 'People may find it difficult to understand but my heart goes out to their wives, families and friends.'

The deal which gave Smalls immunity did not meet with universal judicial approval. In the words of former judge Sir

Frederick Lawton: 'He was undoubtedly a villain. He would only turn Queen's Evidence if he was given a complete immunity from prosecution and wanted that in writing, which seemed the quintessence of impertinence. There was this criminal saying "I've committed a large number of offences and I don't believe a word you say about not prosecuting me, unless you put it in writing." It was outrageous.'

Some unexpected embarrassments for the authorities resulted from Smalls's co-operation. One man, Jimmy Saunders, who had been convicted of a robbery on the evidence of a supposed verbal admission to the police, was cleared on appeal when Smalls explained that Saunders could not have taken part in it. Remarkably, Smalls survived to die peacefully at his home in Croydon in 2008. 'There will certainly be a few glasses raised in celebration at the news,' said one former bank robber at the time. 'In fact, I might nip out and buy a bottle of champagne myself.'

Other grasses sprouted. The old habit of honour amongst thieves became dishonour amongst robbers: George du Burriatte, Billy Williams, Jimmy Trusty, Freddie Sinfield, Roger Denhardt, Billy Amies, Tony Wild, Colin Francis, Charlie Lowe, Maurice O'Mahoney, Chrissie Wren, Dave Smith, George Piggott, Billy Young, Roy Garner and Micky 'Skinny' Gervaise all sang for their supper.

The tariff for telling tales became five years. Reducing Lowe's sentence from eleven and a half to five years, Mr Justice Roskill said: 'It is in the public interest that a person such as this should be encouraged to give information to police in order that others may be brought to justice.'

O'Mahoney, or 'King Squealer' as he called himself in his autobiography (complete with foreword by musician Rick Wakeman), was born in 1947 into a large Irish Catholic family and was involved in a wide range of crime – robbery, burglary, extortion, blackmail, hijacking – from an early age. He was a violent man who had once bitten a diamond off the ring on a victim's hand and swallowed it. On his own admission, he took real pleasure from battering and cutting up his enemies or victims, beating them in the face with a hammer or smashing their kneecaps. He took contracts to wound people – £1,000 for shooting a man in the legs, for instance – and acted as a debt-collecting heavy who would beat adebtor about the head with a hammer until he came up with the money. He boasted of having plotted to kidnap both Elton John and Elizabeth Taylor and of having robbed the actress Dinah Sheridan.

On 11 June 1974 O'Mahoney was arrested at gunpoint in London. His girlfriend, Susan Norville, had already made a statement to the police about a Securicor robbery with which he was charged. Some of his associates had also started to talk, he said later, and that was what persuaded him to go QE – Queen's Evidence. He claimed that they had threatened his lover and had suggested that they would gouge his eyes out with a toothbrush. 'I've had enough,' he said. 'Give me a high-ranking officer from Scotland Yard. I want to confess.' Confess he did. He admitted 102 offences, including thirteen armed robberies and sixty-five burglaries, involving £197,000 in cash. He dealt with Deputy Assistant Commissioner Ernest Bond, Commander John Lock and Jack Slipper.

O'Mahoney enjoyed the good life of the grass in Chiswick police station. The 'grass-house', as it became known, was itself to provoke controversy: his girlfriend was allowed in to see him, he was granted a television and an eight-track stereo system and smuggled in whisky, brandy and beer. He celebrated major events with champagne and whiled away the time between making statements with games of Ludo with his girlfriend, Scrabble with fellow-informers, fishing and snooker with the officers and trips to the golf course. Slipper defended the use of some facilities: 'Prisoners in a normal prison watch TV in the television room and supergrasses have to have the same facility in their cell or they would go bonkers.'

On 19 September 1974, O'Mahoney appeared at the Old Bailey and pleaded guilty to his 102 crimes. Prosecutor Michael Hill described him as the most guarded man in Britain. His assistance to the police had been 'incalculable'. His own barrister, Kenneth Machin, told the court that 'by his action he may have already signed his own death warrant'. O'Mahoney was then allowed to address the court himself: 'I know that what I have done in the past is wrong and I believe that what I am doing now is right ... I want to hit right at the heart of the criminal underworld.'

The judge, Sir Carl Aarvold, gave him the lenient sentence of five years and O'Mahoney wept with relief before being taken to a solitary cell in Oxford gaol. Word soon spread as to who the new guest was and cheery cries of 'You're going to be poisoned, you grass,' greeted him and notes threatening damage to himself and his family were shoved under the door.

He returned to court for the 111-day trial on 4 June 1975. Thirteen people faced charges of armed robbery, conspiracy to rob, receiving stolen property and conspiracy to pervert the course of justice. It was heard in front of Mr Justice Bernard Gillis, a genial and mild-mannered 'cove from Hove', whose slightly more lenient than average sentences had earned him the affectionate nickname 'Gillis-is-good-for-you'. O'Mahoney's evidence was convincing and a further seven people were convicted and given gaol sentences of up to fifteen years.

O'Mahoney finally refused to give any further evidence. He claims that this was because there was an increasing likelihood that juries would be nobbled and he did not want to risk himself without reason: 'That was it. King Squealer would sing no more.' His armed protection abruptly ceased, to his dismay, and he called the *Guardian* to complain: 'They've dropped me flat, the canary that fell from its cage. They've told me to go out and get a decent job. The only trade I know is how to break into banks. I'm in a terrible state. I could go round the corner and cry.'

But he dried his eyes and re-emerged as a security man on Rick Wakeman and David Bowie tours, selling dodgy jewellery and carrying out electrical work at the homes of his police minders. Amazingly, he was back at the Old Bailey in July 1993, charged with robbery and possession of firearms over the snatch of a money bag outside a post office in Shepherd's Bush, during which police had fired four shots.

Appearing under his new name of Peter Davies, he offered a fantastical defence: that the police had themselves asked him to carry out the robbery so that they could frame another man with the stolen bag. Now grey-haired and pony-tailed, he told the court that he believed the police had been planning to kill him because he had hinted that he would do a second volume of memoirs in which he would expose police corruption. He said that he had often lied on the instructions of his handlers in order to convict men and named a former detective constable who ran a south London wine bar as one of his middlemen. He was acquitted and immediately attempted to sell his story to the *Sun*.

Many other criminals followed O'Mahoney's example, although whether this was from the high motive of striking 'at the heart of the criminal underworld' or for the sake of a hefty sentence reduction is less certain.

Billy Williams also made the jump in 1974. He claimed that he turned when PC David Clements was shot at the wheel of a panda car by robbers escaping from a bank raid in July that year. He saw Clements flinch as the bullet struck him yet still managed to carry on the chase. This was his conversion on the road to Chiswick police station. He pleaded guilty to three armed raids and asked for thirty-six other offences, mainly robbery and conspiracy, to be taken into consideration. Williams became so nervous about giving evidence that he would vomit before appearing in the witness box. He was sentenced to five years. Like O'Mahoney, he had to contend with threats – cyanide in his orange juice was one – and scalding water was thrown at him, a hazard for informers and sex offenders in gaol.

Williams was allowed out of his cell to marry his fiancée, Barbara Stanikowski, and the *News of the World* featured a photograph of him celebrating, wearing a policeman's helmet and apparently living the life of Riley inside. Philip Trusty, who shot the constable, was gaoled for twenty years for a series of robberies, while Trusty's brother Jimmy, by now an informer, too, received a sentence of two years and nine months.

One of the most enigmatic of the informers was Roy Garner, a former meat porter and property developer turned cocaine dealer, whose prominence came from his relationship with Detective Superintendent Tony Lundy. Lundy described him as the most useful informer in the history of Scotland Yard and there is no doubt that Garner provided much vital information to the police without ever serving much time in gaol himself, at least initially. Lundy and Garner's association ran for fourteen years, during which Garner picked up around £200,000 in payments for information leading to the recovery of goods or money.

Garner prospered because, although his friends had suspicions, he was not yet known as an informer and was able to tap information through his clubland associations; he owned a north London villains' hang-out called Elton's and his financial success helped him to run stables for trotting horses in Britain and Florida. Garner's charmed life ended when Customs and Excise nailed him for VAT fraud. Like many criminals, he had moved into a simple and lucrative fiddle: gold krugerrands were flown in from Holland and sold on without the VAT on gold being paid but with the VAT price added to them, representing a 15 per cent profit. Since shipments worth £1 million each were being brought in, the sums to be made were significant. Garner was gaoled for four years for his part in the game.

The relationship between Lundy and Garner was to attract greater attention than Garner's informing activities. The pair were shown together in a photograph at a 1974 charity function given by the Lady Ratlings (the women's branch of the Grand Order of Water Rats) at the Dorchester Hotel. Lundy's detractors suggested that there was something less than healthy about the relationship and queried how Garner had been able to collect so many lucrative rewards for robberies solved.

The robbery that was to spark the greatest controversy about the Lundy–Garner axis was the hijacking of £3.5-million worth of silver bullion on 24 March 1980 after Micky Gervaise, dressed as a policeman, had waved the lorry driver into a lay-by for a bogus road test. Most of the ingots were recovered but twelve were missing, fuelling speculation about dirty dealings. Lenny Gibson and Dolph and Ron Aguda were gaoled for ten years for the robbery. Micky Gervaise received a shorter sentence because of his cooperation and the inside man, Bill Parker, got seven years.

Garner now wanted his reward and felt entitled to the 10 per cent that he might have anticipated. According to Martin Short's book on Lundy, £180,000 was eventually paid out. But Garner appeared to believe he was untouchable and was caught smuggling nearly 400 kilograms of cocaine into Cornwall by Customs in what was called Operation Redskin. In March 1989 he was gaoled for twenty-two years, which was reduced to sixteen on appeal, and retired, furious, to prison threatening to spill beans. Nikolaus Chrastny, the German crook believed to be behind this enormous cocaine deal, was also arrested in the sweep. But on 4 October 1987, Chrastny escaped from the cell where he was being held for security reasons in Dewsbury, West Yorkshire. Because he was being so co-operative, he had been allowed model-making equipment, which he used to effect his escape.

Lundy's successes were undeniable and Martin Short in his biography of the detective describes him as the Yard's equivalent of Andrew Lloyd Webber: six trials involving him were on at the Old Bailey simultaneously. During a five-year period up to 1982 around fifty 'resident informants' (RIs) gave information that led to 451 people being charged, of whom 262 were convicted.

But the character of some of the supergrasses was starting to make the whole exercise less palatable. It emerged that one, Dave Smith, who admitted to around seventy robberies, had also been responsible for the death of Kurt Hess, a handbag manufacturer, who had died a month after Smith had coshed him and robbed him of £782. The charge was dropped to manslaughter because Hess had a thin skull, but there was unease that a man such as Smith could escape the normal penalties of his crimes. In October 1986, arrested and locked up after an attack on a Securicor vehicle, Smith did to himself what countless of his former colleagues would happily have done: slit his throat.

The Liverpudlian Billy 'The Queer' Amies was another supergrass whose conduct was less than saintly: he had been involved in one robbery where a man had been tied up and his teenage daughter stripped and threatened with rape unless the victim revealed the whereabouts of his money.

For his part, Lundy took early retirement on health grounds, blaming a combination of Masonic officers at the Yard, embittered criminals and gullible journalists for his demise. He went to Spain, where he ended up in the same neck of the woods as some of the men, like the Agudas who watched him on his morning runs, whom he had helped to gaol.

By the mid-eighties the tide was beginning to turn against the supergrasses. Some, like Tony Wild, who had given evidence in robbery and murder trials, had been reconvicted and had admitted to inventing evidence. Others decided against co-operation once they reached the witness box, most notably in the trial of

John 'The Face' Goodwin and Brian Reader in April 1982 for £1,250,000 worth of burglaries, when supergrass Gervaise indicated his unhappiness in mid-trial and a re-trial was ordered. Goodwin was cleared but was then charged with jury nobbling and gaoled for seven years. His conviction was overturned on appeal in 1984.

Goodwin was as wily as the rare birds of prey he used to keep in his country home: he tape-recorded drunken detectives discussing his case with him, using a bug hidden in a Christmas tree at a mutual friend's house. The detectives were eventually charged with corruption offences and ran a 'cut-throat' defence, in which they told mutually contradictory stories. One claimed he had never been in the house at all and that the voice on the tape was not his; the other claimed they had both indeed been there but that the £1,000 Goodwin had offered them was merely so they would tell the truth in his trial and hence no corruption had taken place. The jury accepted this explanation. Goodwin's problems were not over; his wife, Shirley, was kidnapped while he was in prison and held for a ransom of £50,000. Charlie Pitts, the brother of 'Queen of the Shoplifters' Shirley and bank robber Adgie, was convicted of the kidnapping in June 1984 and gaoled for eighteen years.

There was now a growing feeling that there was something inherently cynical about violent men who had profited from crime parleying their way out of a long sentence by informing on their colleagues. Juries started to find them unpersuasive and they ceased to form a major part of the police's armoury. There were a few exceptions, such as the major Triad trial at the Old Bailey in 1992, where the chief witness was the first Chinese supergrass in Britain, but his evidence failed to convince.

A dark joke that floated around prisons in the eighties went thus: a Jewish criminal who hated Arabs had decided to join the French Foreign Legion, so that he could shoot as many of them as he wanted. On his first night on duty he was on guard on the battlements of a desert fort when the sentry tiptoed towards him and whispered: 'See, out there behind that dune, four Arabs hiding.' The sentry tiptoed away and the criminal took his rifle out and fired – and shot the sentry in the back. 'Why did you do that?' another legionnaire asked him, 'I thought you hated Arabs.' 'Yeah,' replied the criminal, 'but I hate a grass even more.'

Although remarkably few informers have suffered retribution despite frequent reports of prices on their heads, some of them did suffer violent ends. Johnny Darke was stabbed to death with a machete at the Ranelagh Yacht Club in Fulham in November 1978 after rumours that he had been helping the police. Johnny Bindon, an actor who played opposite Carol White in the film *Poor Cow*, and who was famous in the press for the anatomically remarkable way in which he could lift beer mugs, was charged with the murder but acquitted.

By the nineties it had become clear that the old *laissez-faire* attitude of letting bygones be bygones had passed and that unwary informers whose faces had not already been altered by plastic surgeons could expect to have a slightly cruder job done for them by their former associates.

In 1989 the body of Alan 'Chalky' White, a small-time criminal and drug dealer who had been giving information to the police about his associates, was found wrapped in tarpaulin in a lake at the Cotswold Water Park. He had been picked up from his home in the idyllic village of Minchinhampton, in Gloucestershire, 19 kilometres away, stabbed to death and dispatched to a watery grave. One of the men against whom he was due to give evidence, Danny Gardiner, was convicted of his murder.

Dave Norris, a police informer, was shot dead outside his front door in Belvedere, south-east London, by two men wearing crash helmets on 28 April 1991. The trial of two men accused of murdering him was abandoned halfway through. Three other men who were believed to have been informers were also killed.

There are other risks, highlighted by a case in 1995 when it transpired that a Jamaican criminal convicted of an armed robbery in Nottingham was, in fact, one of Scotland Yard's most active informers. Eaton 'Leon' Green had been recruited as an informer in 1991 when he was arrested on a minor traffic offence in Brixton and threw in his lot with the police. He was given a code-name and a cash advance; had he not co-operated, he would have been deported to Jamaica, where he faced firearms charges. During the course of the next two years he provided Scotland Yard with high-level intelligence, meeting his handler in a Sainsbury's car park or a Home Office building and passing on the names of Yardies involved in murder, shootings and drug dealing. He also informed the police when key Yardies arrived in the country and the aliases under which they were operating. For a police force that had always had difficulty in infiltrating serious black crime, Green was dynamite.

The twist was that Green was cheerfully committing crimes himself while he was informing. He was also able to assist in the arrival in Britain of another Jamaican criminal, Rohan 'Colonel Bumpy' Thomas. In May 1993, the pair were involved in an audacious robbery at a blues party in Nottingham, where they were part of a five-man team who held up 150 party-goers and stole their money, credit cards, mobile phones and jewellery. Green even announced that 'We are the SAD Squad – Seek and Destroy' while firing some shots into the ceiling and some into the leg of one of the guests.

When Nottingham detectives finally tracked him down in London they were completely unaware of the fact that their gunman was a top Scotland Yard informer. This was, of course, deeply embarrassing for Scotland Yard. When the case eventually came to court in 1995, Green received a reasonably lenient sentence of six years to be followed by deportation, which happened in 1999. His former friends on whom he had informed were confident of what awaited him if he was ever sent home: 'He's dead,' said one, 'he'll never get off the plane.' That was soon to become a reality, although his death may not have been connected to his role as an informer.

Perhaps the most controversial supergrass since Smalls was the Liverpudlian, Paul Grimes. A violent criminal in his own right, making his money from hijacking lorries, stealing construction equipment and 'enforcement' – essentially, whacking anyone who got in his way – Grimes claimed that his decision to inform, mainly to Customs and Excise officers, was prompted by the death from a heroin overdose of his son, Jason, at the age of twenty-one. His biggest coups were the major drugs dealers John Haase and 'Cocky' Warren. Haase worked with Turkish heroin dealers and was gaoled for eighteen years in 1993, but bluffed his way out of gaol by arranging for the importation of firearms and Semtex, towards which he then helpfully pointed the authorities, winning a pardon from a gullible home secretary, Michael Howard, for this smart stunt. Grimes, whose code-name was 'Oscar Wilde', justified his informing, even when it led to the arrest of another of his sons, Heath, who had worked with Haase.

'I am a real-life dead man walking,' he told Graham Johnson for the book, *Powder Wars*, in 2005 and suggested that there was a £100,000 bounty on his head and there had been at least six attempts to finish him off. He was moved by his handlers to an old people's home and supposedly turned down the offer of a Hampstead safe house. 'Every car that pulls up, every knock on the door creates a ball of stress in my shoulders.'

Sometimes it was the 'inside man' who would turn supergrass, as happened in the wake of an old-fashioned armed robbery at Heathrow airport in 2004. Darren Brockwell, who worked as a supervisor at the airport's Menzies warehouse, had been feeding information to a team of professional robbers about how much currency would be held in the warehouse vault. After being arrested, Brockwell agreed to give evidence against the rest of the gang in exchange for a short sentence of six years and a new identity for himself and his family. The trial of the four robbers, John Twomey, Peter Blake, Glenn Cameron and Barry Hibberd, was, in addition, of great legal significance as the first such trial in 400 years to be held without a jury. After three previous trials had collapsed amidst claims of jury nobbling, the four were tried, convicted and sentenced by Mr Justice Treacy. The principle of trial by jury was set aside under controversial powers introduced by the 2003 Criminal Justice Act.

The supergrass, like crime itself, will be always with us. 'The police like the image of a sort of Sherlock Holmes figure solving crimes, whereas the truth is that eight out of ten people get nicked because someone grasses them,' said James Saunders, one of the lawyers most experienced in representing members of the underworld. 'It's cheaper to come up with 200 quid than have coppers on the streets for long periods of time. Grassing is alive and well.'

Some informers, equipped with a new identity, have slipped away to the United States, Canada or Australia. It is a complex business: bogus documents for bank accounts, educational qualifications and medical records have to be obtained and the men are sometimes guarded for years afterwards. Others, apparently undismayed by the prospect of encountering some of the old lags they helped to gaol, took off to the sun.

9

COSTA DEL CRIME

SPANISH KNIGHTS, THE 'SILENT MAN' AND 'OPERATION CAPTURA'

Wrapped in white plastic and bound in black duct tape, the body of twenty-five-year-old Liverpudlian Francis Brennan was washed up on the beach of La Zenia in Alicante, Spain, in April 2014. He had last been seen being stopped by three men dressed as members of the Spanish Guardia Civil in the nearby town of Javea, which was popular with British expats. Brennan was on the run, having skipped bail in England where he was about to be sentenced for stabbing a man at a Swedish House Mafia concert in Milton Keynes. He had been tortured before being killed and dumped at sea; a concrete block had apparently come loose from his body otherwise he would have forever been lost in muddy waters. His death and the manner of it was a reminder of the part that Spanish coastal resorts had played in providing a home-from-home for runaway British villains for the past decades.

A quarter of a century earlier, Charlie Wilson, the Great Train Robber, by now fifty-seven, was slicing tomatoes and cucumbers for a salad at his home in Llanos de Nagueles near Marbella, in Spain, at around 7 p.m. on 23 April 1990 when the bell rang. A tall young man in a grey tracksuit and a baseball cap was standing there. He had arrived on a yellow mountain bike. He told Pat Wilson, who answered the door, that he wanted to see her husband and mentioned the name Eamonn. Wilson beckoned him in and they went to the patio, where Charlie had built a barbecue and where he had been entertaining guests earlier that day to celebrate his wedding anniversary.

A few moments later there was the sound of voices raised in argument, then two loud bangs. Charlie Wilson staggered dying towards the pool, blood streaming from a wound in the neck where his carotid artery had been severed. Nearby, the Wilsons' husky–Alsatian cross-breed, Bobo, also lay dying. Charlie had been kicked in the testicles, punched so hard in the face that his nose was broken and then shot with a Smith & Wesson revolver. The young killer fled by vaulting the back wall. An accomplice had probably been waiting nearby in a getaway car. The 'Silent Man', as he had been called during the Great Train Robbery trial, was silent for ever.

Charlie Wilson had bought his Spanish retreat in 1987 for the reasonable price of £25,000 and had spent lavishly to refurbish it, with pink Portuguese marble for the bathrooms and a turret inlaid with coloured glass. He called it Chequers. Apart from that one gesture of braggadocio, he kept a low profile. In the evenings he painted still-lifes rather than clubbing like many of his contemporaries. The local Spanish police had been unaware that he was even living on their patch when he was murdered.

His funeral was attended by many of his old colleagues: Bruce Reynolds, Buster Edwards, Roy James and Robert Welch paid their respects while Charlie's favourite song, Frank Sinatra's 'My

Way', was played. Ron and Reg Kray sent floral tributes. Many of the mourners wanted to know why Charlie had been killed. The likeliest explanation involved drugs. Although Pat Wilson was adamant that her husband had never been involved in trafficking, it is inevitable that Wilson mixed with those who were, but the specific reason for his death was said to be connected with a south London drugs dealer called James Rose.

Rose had found his niche in criminal history by being a member of the first gang to be arrested after a co-operation agreement had been signed in 1988 between the then Foreign Secretary, Sir Geoffrey Howe, and his Soviet counterpart, Eduard Shevardnadze. He had been smuggling highly prized Afghan black, which had increased in value in the eighties as the result of the Afghan war, into Britain via Moscow and St Petersburg, hidden in sacks of liquorice. He realised that he might receive a lighter sentence if he named the gang leader, one Roy Adkins, who at the time was out of harm's way in Amsterdam. Rose apparently wanted Wilson's approval to name Adkins.

Whether Wilson ever contemplated such approval is not known and Rose had been gaoled in January 1990 at Chelmsford Crown Court for his part in the ring. When Wilson was last in London before his death, a man called Eamonn, acting as a middleman, had delivered a message from Adkins in Amsterdam censuring him for supposedly okaying his name. Wilson denied any involvement and his friends believed him. They say that naming another man was not his style.

Adkins was not to be reassured. It would seem that he brooded and one theory was that he got two young hoodlums to kill Wilson. Not everyone buys this theory. Gordon Goody, another Great Train Robber who retired to Spain, told the *Sunday Times*: 'Charlie would never have given no one no names ... the young villains of today – for a couple of grand, a few lines of coke, they'll get a gun and use it.'

The police were not the only people who were anxious to find out who had disposed of Charlie. Norman Radford, a holidaying cousin of Charlie who had seen the gunman sitting nonchalantly by the side of the road earlier in the day, told reporters, 'His murder has upset a lot of big names out here. They are not happy men.'

In September 1990 two men walked into the Nightwatch bar of the American Hotel in Amsterdam and fired six bullets into Roy Adkins. But whether his death was a result of a feud with Wilson is another matter. The police believed not, saying that on the night he died he had met two Colombians with whom he was involved in selling smuggled emeralds. One of Adkins's associates had been robbed of part of the emerald consignment and the Colombians had arranged the meeting with Adkins who, as the middleman, was being held responsible for the loss. (Adkins's death was followed by another fatal shooting in Amsterdam, that of Micky Blackmore, a south London gangland figure who was owed money by Adkins.)

The news of the Adkins shooting caused fresh ripples in the bars of the Costa del Sol. At Charlie Wilson's inquest in Horse-ferry Road coroner's court in London, coroner Paul Knapman remarked: 'It is ironic that Charles Wilson should end his day, being gunned down in the barbecue area of his retirement home in Spain.'

The notion of the 'Costa del Crime', the part of Spain that 'fell off the back of a lorry', was already a cliché, but the shooting blew a hole in the idea of a villains' nirvana, where the chaps could still enjoy all the pleasures of 'home' – satellite football, Carling Black Label, bacon and the *Daily Express* – with none of the pain – rain, taxes and the Regional Crime Squad.

It was the collapse in the summer of 1978 of the extradition agreement between Spain and Great Britain, originally drawn up by Benjamin Disraeli a hundred years earlier, that had made Spain so attractive to men who, if not on the run, were at least travelling at jogging pace. The extradition arrangements had broken down because Spain felt that Britain was not playing the game and was making it too difficult for the Spanish to retrieve their fugitives from the United Kingdom. The British authorities had not realised at the time what their lack of co-operation would cost them. Spain became a safe haven for criminals: close enough for the family to come out and visit yet far enough away to avoid the attentions of the police. By the mid-eighties, British detectives reckoned there were between seventy-five and a hundred men on the Costa whom they would like to interview in connection with serious crimes.

The early pioneering villains wondered to themselves why they had not thought of the move earlier. The area had been chic in the late fifties and early sixties before the big hotels and apartment blocks were built, and even in the seventies it suited many of the new immigrants perfectly: across the Mediterranean was Morocco and a plentiful supply of cannabis resin for which many had acquired a taste while in prison. Up in Morocco's Rif mountains, locals waved packets of the stuff at tourists driving through villages. A kilogram of cannabis resin in the late eighties, at the height of the trade, cost as little as £200 and was fetching £700 in Marbella and around £2,000 in England.

Gradually the Costa del Sol became a sort of European Miami – sunny, spoiled, decadent and dangerous. The chaps didn't mind. They were free and the only bars they were behind had names like Sinatra's, Roxy's and El Bandito. They were joined by other, less spectacular, criminals: the bent businessmen with bad debts, the spivs offering time-shares to gullible tourists, the sort of blokes who liked to be judges in Miss Wet T-shirt competitions and couldn't be bothered to learn Spanish. They merged with the 100,000 other Britons who had already moved south.

Then in 1985, after negotiations between the British and Spanish governments and a thaw in the traditionally chilly relationship between the two countries, the extradition decision was reversed. Spain's Justice Minister, Fernando Ledesma, announced that 'no Briton can escape the justice of his country'. The door was closed but the new agreement was not retroactive. Those who did not commit an offence in Spain could stay.

One who did return was Freddie Foreman, the Krays' old henchman. He was wanted for a Security Express robbery in Shoreditch in 1983 and was hoisted back to Heathrow on 28 July 1989, still in his beach mufti, to stand trial and be gaoled for nine years. Foreman had happily moved to Spain, invested in property there and started the successful Eagles country club in Nueva Andalusia. 'I knew Jack the Hat's boys when I was living in Spain and we were quite pals together, they used to have a drink with me in the club,' he recalled in 2018. Others managed to avoid the attention of the Guardia Civil. One of these was Ronald Knight.

If the underworld had its own aristocracy and its court jesters, then the man who was its ambassador to Spain was undoubtedly Ronnie Knight, known more or less equally for his bad-boy status in London and his marriage to the actress Barbara Windsor, star of many *Carry On* films and rated very highly by director Joan Littlewood, who had spotted her talents early on.

Ronnie, born in Hoxton, east London, in 1934, was known to villains – and inevitably the law – as the man who ran the Artistes and Repertoire Club in Charing Cross Road. This club was to the criminal fraternity what Groucho's was to television executives and the Travellers Club to spies: a place for gossiping, drinking too much and being recognised. Knight, after a youth spent committing a few minor offences and lying in hospital with a leg-bone disease, became mine host to London's gangsters and the many actors and singers who liked rubbing padded shoulders with them. Like many criminals of the sixties, he was fascinated by celebrity. In his autobiography, *Black Knight*, his memories of a party at Danny La Rue's were made of this: 'Noel Coward, tinkling away on the ivories for all he was worth ... That Russian ballet bloke, Nureyev, ponced around ... Roger Moore drew the girls like horse-flies to a cow-pat.' Over the years the A & R attracted them all, from the young Rolling Stones through to Freddie Mercury and Queen. But the more regular visitors were villains. One of the functions of the A & R and Knight's later club, the Tin Pan Alley, was that of alibi: many villains would claim they had been there at the time of a robbery or piece of mayhem. Knight's other business, with his partner Micky Regan, was pool tables, which were just starting to take over from bar billiards as a major moneymaker in pubs. Freddie Foreman, later to acquire the title 'the Mean Machine', acted as collector.

What was to become part of the spiral that eventually took Knight off to Spain was the killing in 1970 of his brother David. David had been beaten up in a pub in the Angel by a group that included a man called Johnny Isaacs. Ronnie and his older brother, Johnny, became obsessed with vengeance or extracting an apology for the episode and in May 1970 they set off with David to the Latin Quarter Club in Soho to find Isaacs. Isaacs was not there but a fight broke out nonetheless, during which young David was stabbed through the heart with a carving knife by Alfredo 'Italian Tony' Zomparelli. Zomparelli pleaded self-defence at the subsequent Old Bailey trial, was convicted of manslaughter and gaoled for four years.

On his release he started running a Soho bucket-shop travel agency while Knight, by his own admission, went hunting for him 'like a lion after a wart hog'. On 4 September 1974, while playing pinball on the Wild Life table in the Golden Goose amusement arcade in Old Compton Street in Soho, Zomparelli was shot four times with a .38. Knight celebrated the news of the death with a bottle of champagne. He had no idea who had done it, he said, but was delighted they had.

Nearly six years later, Knight was arrested for the murder. George 'Maxie' Bradshaw, also known as Maxwell Piggott, a long-haired gangland hitman with a droopy moustache and a beard, had told the police that Knight had paid him £1,000 to carry out the killing. To prove his own involvement, Bradshaw described in detail the spot by a golf course near Winchester where he had hidden the murder weapon. He said that he had knocked back several large brandies, put on a false beard, which he had later discarded because it looked so ridiculous, and had then, with an accomplice, shot Zomparelli, fleeing on the underground. He was remanded in custody in Brixton. Bradshaw, who had taken part in between thirty and forty robberies, was gaoled for life for murder and duly gave evidence against Knight.

Knight's trial, with Barbara Windsor making an appearance despite the fact that the marriage was nearly over, was a high-profile one. Knight and Nicky Gerrard, who was accused of being Piggott's accomplice, were cleared and Knight ran from the Old Bailey, his exit impeded only by a *Sun* reporter who foresightedly jammed the revolving door to stop him making a quick getaway with the newspaper that had actually bought his story. (Gerrard was shot dead in south London in 1982 after being seized by masked men who beat him around the head. His cousin, Tommy Hole, was charged with the murder but cleared.)

Knight sold his clubs and received an £80,000 pay-off for money that he had invested in Soho peep-show clubs. He had already made around £3,000 a week from these establishments, where young women took off their clothes and did improbable things with rubber snakes for the entertainment of lonely men who shovelled coins into the slot machine that kept the peep-hole open. His more puritanical colleague, Micky Regan, was disgusted.

A silk-shirt-with-embossed-initials man, Knight had spotted the potential of Spain in the early seventies and, with brother Johnny, had bought 1,600 square metres of land in the hills beyond Fuengirola. An American architect designed his four-bedroomed house, with pool and gym, and in 1975, after spending £40,000, Knight moved in. He took a share in the local Wyn's Bar and a supermarket and went into property and a car-hire company. 'It was Paradise found,' he said. Knight told his mates about the glories of the Costa del Sol and soon they were all buying plots of land. He extolled its advantages: 'Restaurants where there's only roast beef and Yorkshire pudding on the menu – and English mustard.' (He started the Mumtaz in Fuengirola because he missed a decent curry.) Los Boliches, one of the *barrios* of Fuengirola, popular with what the Spanish police called 'The Mafia Inglesa', was nicknamed 'Bethnal Green in the Sun'.

Knight married Sue Haylock in June 1987 at Fuengirola town hall, with a blessing and reception at El Oceano, a restaurant-cum-club and sports centre on the beach. Sue wore a £3,000 dress of ivory silk and satin and carried a bouquet of orchids and salmon roses. The press loved it and some fanciful stories about the cake being in the shape of Wandsworth Prison and £10,000 being spent on a fireworks display were telephoned back to news desks. Years later, the vicar who had officiated at the wedding appeared as himself in *Eldorado*, the ill-fated BBC soap opera. 'If I'd got a commission for every Londoner I'd introduced to the delights of the Costa del Sol,' Knight wrote in *Blood and Revenge*, one of his two ghosted memoirs, 'I would have earned fortunes.'

The one nagging problem was the British police. They had hinted that they wanted to see Knight in connection with the 1983 Shoreditch Security Express job for which his brothers Johnny and Jimmy were gaoled for twenty-two and eight years respectively.

During the trial *The Times* had recorded that amongst those sought for questioning were five men: Ronnie Knight; Freddie Foreman, who by then had a penthouse apartment in Marbella's Alcazaba complex; Ronald 'Big Ronnie' Everett, a mate of Foreman's; John James Mason, a former company director who had been cleared of the £8-million Bank of America robbery in

Mayfair in 1976; and Clifford Saxe, former landlord of the Fox in Kingsland Road, Hackney, where it was alleged that the Security Express robberies were planned. The quintet soon became known to tabloid readers as the Famous Five. Ronnie always said that robbery was not his game and blamed the attention he has attracted on the fact that he was 'a West End face ... the police had me marked down as a gangster, a thief'. However, reports suggested that Knight ran a criminal outfit in Spain called The Office, which planned big robberies, and he and the other members of the quintet became irritated with the tales and innuendo. He blamed the press, for whom a trip to see what Ronnie was up to was a popular mid-winter jolly, and his own outgoing personality: 'If there's one thing the press love it's a colourful charismatic character to play around with ... I worried they might extradite me from Spain for stealing the limelight from the monarch.' The worry gave him a burst ulcer with the Fleet Street 'reptiles descending like a plague of blood-sucking locusts'.

By 1989 the Famous Five had become the Nasty Nine as far as the *Daily Mirror* was concerned. The four other unfortunates supposedly being hunted by the British police were Keith Cottingham, wanted in connection with a murder inquiry; Jimmy Jeffrey, an amiable north Londoner who was later to be sentenced to four years in Madrid for drugs offences; Micky Green, an outgoing former north London nightclub owner, who had been wanted in connection with an alleged VAT fraud; and John Corscadden, a liquidator (of the financial sort) from Manchester, wanted in connection with major fraud.

The sun did not shine so brightly any more. Eight drunken Welsh rugby players planned to kidnap Knight for a mythical £60,000 reward – they were supposedly going to abseil into his house and smuggle him across to Gibraltar. Others tried different approaches: a policeman who had pursued him even invited him to his own wedding in Loughton in 1989, on the grounds that detectives had attended Ronnie's in Spain. The Knights regretfully declined. They had a prior engagement. For Ronnie, at least, Spain still provided the safety that had eluded Freddie Foreman and Charlie Wilson. He told people he would go back to England if the police gave him a guarantee of bail. In the end, however, he gave himself up and in 1994 flew back to England, under the auspices of the *Sun* newspaper and Sky television, to stand trial. While he claimed that he came back because he wanted to see his ailing old mum, most of his erstwhile colleagues believed that life was too hot on the Costa and he was about to become a victim of some of the more violent new boys there because of bad debts. In January 1995, he pleaded guilty to handling £314,813 from the Security Express robbery and was gaoled for seven years at the Old Bailey. His counsel, Richard Ferguson, QC, told the judge that his client's image of a 'swashbuckling figure basking in the sun in Spain' was at odds with reality.

Back in England, Knight set up a website called 'Crooks Reunited' to enable ex-cons to get in touch with each other for a £10 registration fee; in true 'ODC' (ordinary decent criminal) style, he said that sex-offenders and paedophiles would not be welcome. Ill-health took him eventually to sheltered accommodation in Cambridge.

Another arrival was Derek Maughan, an ex-con and former boy soldier from north-east England, who went out to Spain in the eighties with the idea of opening a pub. But through the ex-prisoners' grapevine, he met up with hash smugglers who offered him a chance to join the lucrative market. 'When I first came down to Alicante, I didn't know anybody there. I rang a friend in England and he said he had a friend in Marbella and that he might be able to put me on to something. I didn't like the Marbella atmosphere too much, it was too flashy. It was dangerous, there were too many villains milling around, gold chains, cock of the walk kind of thing, so I moved out of town.'

London fraudsters with large amounts of capital were bank-rolling drug-smuggling trips but they wanted people with 'pedigree' at a middle-management level to be in charge of operations. This would involve going out in Zodiac dinghies, meeting the mother-ships loaded with hash from Morocco and bringing the cargo back to a safe beach in Spain. The Moroccan authorities were paid off so the main problem was ensuring a safe arrival in Spain. 'They'd pick a beach which was isolated or near a town and have a car with a radio three or four kilometres along the road,' said Maughan. 'There would be another car on the other stretch of road in constant contact – "the road is clear, the road is clear" – and they'd do the same with the dinghy: "Come in now." We were rarely caught on the beach. I thoroughly enjoyed it, it was very exciting and it gets the adrenalin pumping.'

The hash would be stored in a safe house until it could be loaded into a container lorry bound for Holland or Germany or England. But the problem was the quality of the personnel. 'If you do a big job in England, you check people's pedigree and you certainly wouldn't rob a bank with people you hardly knew. But in Spain you'd meet people one day and they'd be on the boat with you next day. When trouble arose, they weren't reliable. They didn't have any loyalty.' Maughan spoke from experience: he was gaoled in Spain for three years for his part in a major operation.

As a drug smuggler he was chased by a helicopter on one occasion and shot at on another. But the money was good: 500 kilograms of cannabis, an average load, was worth £1 million, and Maughan would make on average £25,000 a trip in the late eighties. The big sums involved made dishonesty tempting. On one occasion, a bogus 300-kilogram load was sold from Morocco: 'There were serious repercussions. People went to Morocco to look for the people who did that. I understand a couple of people got killed down there.' There were other casualties.

'One man whose firm kept losing load after load was pin-pointed as the source of the leak and they told him to go to Morocco to operate from that end. From there he was asked to go on the boat and was put in a sleeping-bag and dropped over the side,' said Maughan. 'There's been some terrible hidings for stealing small parts of loads.'

Unusually, Maughan himself was not a drug user, although he saw no harm in it. He married a Spanish woman and started a family. He also learned Spanish, which few of the other ex-pat ex-cons did: 'It's unpleasant to sit in a bar and listen to them, and the Spanish look at them with disgust ... getting drunk all day and driving big cars, open-top BMWs, Range Rovers, on the pavement. Most of them don't even let their kids go to Spanish schools.' The film, *Sexy Beast*, directed by Jonathan Glazer and starring Ray Winstone and Ben Kingsley, reflected this world.

In 2013, Mark Lilley, aka 'Fatboy', 'Mandy' and 'Big Vern', a forty-one-year-old drug dealer from Merseyside, was arrested after more than twelve years on the run. The whole operation, from the scaling of the front gates of his villa in Alhaurín de la Torre near Málaga, to the exposure of his en-suite lair, was captured on film by Spanish police, who were more than happy to co-operate with their British colleagues to get rid of ex-pat crims; the European Arrest Warrant, brought in for all EU countries in 2004, had significantly streamlined the extradition process. Although trained in the Brazilian martial art of *vale tudo* (which means 'anything goes'), and guarded by three large dogs, Lilley went quietly and was returned to England to serve a twenty-three-year gaol sentence for drug-trafficking.

The arrest came two months after another Briton on the run, Andrew Moran, was grabbed by his pool in Calpe, on the Costa Blanca. He had escaped four years earlier from Burnley Crown Court, where he was convicted in his absence of conspiring to commit armed robbery. Lilley was the fifty-first criminal on the eighty-six-strong Operation Captura wanted list to have his collar felt on the Costas; the operation, run by Crimestoppers, sought anonymous information on criminals on a list drawn up by the National Crime Agency.

'The attraction for Spain is still there, as there is a huge ex-pat British population,' said Dave Allen, the head of the international crime bureau at the NCA. But there were other European options. 'The language is not too much of an issue in the Netherlands either – the Dutch speak very good English and are culturally similar to the British, so it's easy to fit in.' But some are now looking further afield: 'The places we're seeing them go to now are Thailand, certainly, South Africa, and the United Arab Emirates.'

Jason Coghlan, a former armed robber from Manchester who served time with Lilley as a Category A prisoner in Strangeways, started a Marbella law firm, JaCogLaw, which advised ex-pats in trouble with the authorities. Its website boasted an impressive series of quotations from Aristotle to Gladstone, although the one probably most likely to catch the eye of potential clients was from eighteenth-century jurist William Blackstone: 'Better that ten guilty men escape justice than that one innocent man goes to prison.' Coghlan thought that Spain was a daft place to hide. 'If you're a villain on the run in Spain, you're just in a queue waiting to get nicked. What a lot of them don't realise is that the Spanish police can even trace where your emails are coming from. Being on the run is no life – and it's no life for the family of someone on the run. Some of them think that, with the passage of time, their sentences will be reduced. But the sentences don't go away.' He said that if he were on the run himself, he would probably head for eastern Europe, either Albania or Romania. 'A lot of the armed robbers come to Spain because they can go into drug smuggling – it's the number one place, not just because of the hashish from Morocco, but because of cocaine coming in from Mexico.' Coghlan

said he thought the tip-offs that led to the arrests of Britons generally came not from sharp-eyed members of the public spotting a
chap with a dodgy tattoo but from other members of the underworld: 'If someone throws their weight around and makes a nuisance of themselves, that might lead to a tip-off.' By 2018,
seventy-four of the eighty-six wanted villains had been caught.

It was also clear that there were other refuges: the National
Crime Agency website's 'most wanted' list in 2018 had a special
section for Spain, of course, but also for the Netherlands and
Cyprus. And Turkish-occupied Northern Cyprus, which had no
extradition treaty with the United Kingdom, became a popular
bolt-hole for people on the run from the 1980s onwards. One of
the best-known fugitives was Brian Wright, one of Britain's most
active cocaine smugglers, who was nicknamed 'The Milkman' –
because he always delivered. In 1998 he was alleged to have
imported almost two tonnes of the drug, with the result, according to one Customs investigator, that 'the cocaine was coming in
faster than people could snort it.' The Dublin-born Wright owned
a villa near Cádiz which he named *El Lechero* – the Spanish for
milkman. He had a box at Ascot, a flat in Chelsea's King's Quay
and used some of his proceeds to fix races on which he then bet,
thus laundering his drugs profits. Finally arrested in Spain, he
was brought back to England and, in 2007, at the age of sixty,
found guilty at Woolwich Crown Court of conspiracy to supply
drugs and gaoled for thirty years.

Another fugitive on the island was Gary Robb, a former Tees-
side nightclub owner who skipped bail on drugs conspiracy
charges in 1997 and enjoyed the island's hospitality for a decade
before being eventually extradited back to Britain and gaol. 'I
came here because I knew I wouldn't get a fair trial in Britain,'
said Robb, over a coffee in the bar of the Mercure Hotel in 2008.
'I explained to the government here that I wasn't guilty. It's a fan-
tastic place to live. There's no violence and the police here are

very respectful, nothing like the police in England. I've got young children and they love it here. It's very safe and you can literally leave your door open.' Robb knew Wright, Kenneth Noye and Asil Nadir, the Polly Peck tycoon who had also holed up in Cyprus for many years before returning to Britain, standing trial for theft from the company and being gaoled for ten years.

But any notion that Spain might still be a safe haven for ex-pat criminals was dispelled in 2018 when Brian Charrington, the close associate of major drug trafficker Curtis Warren and regarded as one of the major international drug dealers of his generation, was gaoled for fifteen years for trafficking and money laundering in Alicante in 2018. Described in the Spanish press as 'el narco que escribía en Wikipedia', because of his reputation for updating and correcting his Wikipedia entry, the former car-dealer from Middlesbrough had been arrested in 2013 at his villa in Calpe, on the Costa Blanca, an area where some estate agents offer 'bullet-proof glass' as a special feature along with the spa bath and barbecue area. Disappointingly, the police found no crocodiles in his swimming pool, despite wild rumours of their existence. Charrington was alleged to have brought vast quantities of drugs into the country via a yacht docking in Altea, north of Benidorm. He claimed his money came legitimately. 'I buy and sell villas and I pay my taxes,' he told the court, but was still fined nearly £30 million. Following a lengthy investigation involving Spanish, British, Venezuelan and French police, his assets, including a dozen houses and his cars and boats, were impounded. After his sentence, his Wikipedia entry was speedily updated.

10

VICE

THE MESSINAS, TOMMY SMITHSON, SILVER AND MIFSUD AND SOHO

'He dresses in a semi-flashy style and oozes a lubricious self-satisfaction,' wrote Rhoda Lee Finmore in the introduction to her book on the trial in 1951 of Alfredo Messina for living off immoral earnings. 'A gross exterior was married to practical illiteracy but with a shrewd organizing brain.'

The Messina brothers were perfectly cast in the role of purveyors of vice to post-war Britain. They had lived in Italy and Malta and Egypt. They had avoided fighting in the war because of their 'reserved occupation'. They even looked, with their little moustaches and their fancy suits, suitably foreign and spiv-like.

But the Messinas did not quite invent the vice trade in Britain. The various Acts of Parliament still in force in the second half of the twentieth century give testament to the fact that if prostitution was not the oldest profession, it had not exactly escaped the notice of the English legislators: the 1751 and 1818 Disorderly Houses Act and the 1824 Vagrancy Act and 1847 Town Police Clauses Act had all been in operation for more than a century before the Messinas had their camel-hair collars felt.

In the twenties, vice prosecutions were frequent and more than 5,000 arrests for street offences were recorded in 1922, with 2,231 in London alone. But the police faced criticism for their zealous interpretation of the law and the number of arrests in the capital in 1923 dropped to 595 as a result of successful appeals which showed that, in many cases, it had not been proved that the person accosted had been 'annoyed'.

The Second World War saw the arrival of the 'Piccadilly Commandos', prostitutes who catered to the free-spending American GIs in London. Much of this activity was disorganised and self-regulating, epitomised by the naughty war-time song sung by Florence Desmond: 'I've Got the Deepest Shelter in Town'.

By 1953 there was even a boom in the demand for prostitutes' services, which peaked at the time of the coronation of Elizabeth II as thousands of men, many visitors from overseas, expressed their monarchist enthusiasms in a less obvious way than waving Union Jacks or buying mugs imprinted with the faces of the new queen and her consort. Police estimated that around 150 prostitutes began work in the West End in the period leading up to the crowning.

Nor was organised prostitution a twentieth-century innovation. In 1885, in a series of famous articles, the *Pall Mall Gazette*, under the editorship of W. T. Stead, had exposed a trade in child prostitutes from England to the Continent, in particular Belgium. Stead was gaoled for his pains; to prove his point, he had nominally purchased a young girl whose father was then persuaded to make an official complaint, but his campaigning led to the change in the legal age of consent from thirteen to sixteen.

Lurid tales of a burgeoning 'white slave' traffic circulated in the twenties, but were much exaggerated. In Britain, according to

'Nutty' Sharpe, former head of the Flying Squad, it was 'a sordid, small-time affair – there is more rot written about white slavery than any other subject in crime'. The biggest racket, he claimed, was importing Frenchwomen and marrying them off to down-and-outs under the protection of a ponce: 'A new girl appearing in London without a "protector" would be torn to bits like a tame canary amongst a bunch of hawks. When the word goes round that "she's Johnny the Basher's new girl" the other women leave her alone.'

Europeans and North Africans were the most high-profile members of the vice business in the years between the two world wars, and of these the Algerian Casimir Micheletti and the French Juan Antonio Castanar were the most active. The former had a reputation for ruthlessness when crossed and the latter was a tango teacher who used his job to recruit prostitutes. Both controlled dozens of girls and both were deported to France in 1929. Their feud continued and in 1930 Castanar shot and killed Micheletti. Violent trouble had been connected with their enterprises and a French pimp, 'Charles the Acrobat', had been murdered at the Cochon Club in Frith Street. French involvement in prostitution continued to claim victims. Emile Allard, whose cover was diamond dealing, and Michel Vernon were rivals in the field, a rivalry that ended in January 1936 when Allard, who was also known as 'Red Max' Kassel, was found shot dead in St Albans, in Hertfordshire, although he had actually been killed in Vernon's Soho flat. Vernon was convicted of the murder in France, whither he had fled, and sent to a penal colony. The home-grown queen was Kate Meyrick, who had come under scrutiny when Freda Kempton, who was one of her dancers, had died of a supposed overdose. Born in County Clare and famed as the first woman in Ireland to ride a bicycle, she entered the entertainments industry in 1919 after her husband abandoned her, leaving her to support two sons at Harrow and four daughters at Roedean. She co-managed

Dalton's in Leicester Square, which was known as a pickup place for cheerful prostitutes and was frequently raided by the police, who went in wearing nightclub mufti of top hat and white tie.

One of the officers in charge of the West End raids was Sergeant George Goddard, who topped up his meagre police salary so heavily with bribes that he was charged with corruptly receiving money and gaoled for eighteen months in 1929. Goddard, whose imagination had clearly been enriched by so much exposure to the heady life, claimed in court that the £18,000 savings he had acquired were the result of successful betting at the races, the sale of rock at the Wembley Exhibition and astute foreign exchange dealing.

Kate Meyrick also ran the '43' in Gerrard Street, the Folies Bergère, the Manhattan, the Little Club and, most famously, the Silver Slipper in Regent Street. The '43' saw the mix of gangsterism – Ruby Sparks was a regular – and show business that was to become the pattern of such clubs until the seventies. 'Nutty Sharpe described the raids: 'I went to the Manhattan Club in evening dress and opera hat with a friend who was a man about town. We gained admittance without difficulty and at the same moment a colleague similarly attired found his way into the "43", where the licensing laws were being flouted. The main body of the raiding party, thirty or forty members of the squad, waited in cars on the Embankment, near the Tate Gallery ... The music stopped as the cry went up "It's a raid" ... I think the majority of them regarded it more as a lark, for it gave them a thrill, but they changed their views when they appeared before the beak.'

Although Mrs Meyrick was gaoled for six months in 1924 she continued to run the clubs through her daughters. But the law pursued her. She was sentenced to a further eighteen months' hard labour and additional small sentences eventually drove her from the game. Having made and lost a small fortune from her clubs, she died in 1933. Sharpe, who had helped to gaol her, reminisced affectionately about her clubland days: 'Personally, I can't see that much harm was done.'

'The extent of the evil is often exaggerated,' said the first post-Second-World-War Metropolitan Police Commissioner, Sir Harold Scott, of the gaming dens that often co-existed with the brothels. 'It is mostly confined to lower-class establishments in the West End and East End and the promoters and players are largely Cypriots, Maltese or coloured people.' Not that Sir Harold subscribed to the view that immigrants were largely responsible for vice: 'Most of our criminals are home grown.' But in the period's climate of moral hypocrisy, it was perhaps not surprising that outsiders seemed best equipped to cater to the tastes of a nation more repressed in sexual matters than its European neighbours.

Prostitution was dangerous work. In the forties prostitutes working Shepherd Market in Mayfair paid as much as £20 a week for protection. Detective Robert Fabian was impressed with their toughness: 'Strong as a young bullock with legs like marble – she does so much standing about. She would ask £5 and take £3.' He had his own psychological interpretation of the women: 'The greater majority of London's prostitutes are very much under-sexed, almost at zero, by contrast with an ordinary respectable housewife, and that is a professional asset to them.'

John Gosling, head of the Vice Squad for two years in the fifties, offered similar bromides: 'Their faces go before their time, their skin coarsens, their speech turns foul until at last it is true to say that they are almost completely de-womanized in every gentle aspect of that word. This, like the mark of Cain on the brow of the murderer, is the stigmata of prostitution which none can escape.' Another Yard detective, Superintendent Arthur Thorp, said that the British women, rather than the French and Germans, caused the police most trouble: 'Unlike the foreigners, they seem to let go of themselves, to lose every shred of self-respect and decency when they go on the streets. Perhaps that is because they are more conscious of the depths to which they have sunk.'

By 1952 clubs were raided on a regular basis, about every fortnight, by plainclothes men and 'zombies', the police slang of the time for policewomen, posing as revellers. Gosling felt that the London of the fifties had become as shamefully amoral as 'Marseille and Port Said'. The prostitutes 'lie in ambush like brigands, along the defiles through which money passes'. He noted the arrival of the 'car prostitutes', young women who cruised the West End to pick up clients. By the late forties, the area of operation had extended from the West End to take in the main-line stations such as King's Cross, Euston and Victoria, the previously respectable area of Maida Vale, and Stepney, which the police believed was coping with 'the demand from the City'.

The police reckoned that by 1950 there were around 3,000 prostitutes. When the evangelist Billy Graham visited London at the time he found so much sex in Hyde Park that he said: 'It looked as though your parks had been turned into bedrooms, with people lying all over the place.' His remarks provoked questions in the House of Commons and the Home Secretary, 'Rab' Butler, defensively reported that the police were actively making arrests in the park with half a dozen prosecutions a day.

Eddie Chapman, the safe-cracker, noted that one of the remarkable aspects of the boom in prostitution was that so many of the women were living in Church of England property – 'they [the Church] were the greatest ponces of God's earth'.

The Messinas had entered this world in the mid-thirties. The paterfamilias, Giuseppe, a furniture repairer, had been born at the foot of Mount Etna in Sicily in the 1860s. He moved to Malta, where he married a Maltese woman and where the two oldest boys, Salvatore and Alfredo, were born. In 1905 the family moved to Alexandria, in Egypt, where Giuseppe opened a brothel and where Eugenio, Attilio and Carmelo were born. The brothels expanded to the extent that the Egyptian authorities became concerned. Salvatore was gaoled and the family was expelled in 1932. Two years later, Eugenio, by now married to Colette, a French prostitute, came to England to assess the market.

His brothers followed him and over the next decade the family vice business expanded in the centre of London, using women from the Continent who were often married off for a small fee to local ne'er-do-wells. Each prostitute was given her own maid, whose role was to ensure that clients did not stay any longer than was physically necessary, under what became known as the 'ten-minute rule'. The brothers also provided legal services and paid the frequent fines incurred by the women at the local magistrates courts.

Other criminals had meanwhile noted the profits being made and another gang of 'Epsom Salts' (Malts), led by Carmelo Vassalo, demanded protection money from the women, who went to the police. As a result four of the Vassalo mob were sentenced to penal servitude for up to four years. Violence had already broken out between the Messina and Vassalo gangs and in 1947 Eugenio was gaoled for three years for cutting the tips off two of Vassalo's fingers. His brother Carmelo was gaoled for bribery. The burgeoning gang warfare became public and the Norwich Member of Parliament, John Foster, asked the Home Secretary, Chuter Ede, to set up a commission to look into organised vice in London. Ede declined to do so.

The Messina brothers were classic vice kings from the tips of their manicured fingers to the toes of their two-tone shoes but all had sensibly adopted solid-sounding English names: Attilio became Raymond Maynard, Salvatore chose Arthur Evans, Eugenio was Edward Marshall, Carmelo was Charles Maitland and Alfredo selected Alfred Martin. All of them played the part of the respectable, if somewhat flashy, businessman. Eugenio drove a yellow Rolls-Royce.

Their operation was finally exposed in the *People* by Duncan Webb, a classic crime reporter who was a confidant of gangster Billy Hill. Webb, who had come to the *People* via the *South London Press*, the *Daily Express* and the *Evening Standard*, was an intriguing enough character in his own right. He had become the lover of Cynthia Hume, a nightclub hostess and the wife of Donald Hume, who had been gaoled in connection with the killing of a car dealer. Webb was one of a breed of larger-than-life crime reporters who were in their heyday in the fifties when papers had crime bureaux rather than a single correspondent. Their number included Percy Hoskyns, Tom Tullett, Ted Sandrock and Stanley Firmin. Jimmy 'the Prince of Darkness' Nicholson, who worked for the *Daily Sketch*, the *Daily Express* and the *News of the World*, was the only one of the genre still reporting in the nineties. The fifties was also the time when it could be fairly said that the *News of the World* was 'the judge's trade paper' because it published long and detailed reports of criminal trials.

Webb did not sell himself short. 'The reason the underworld chaps talk to me is because they trust me. They know I cannot be bought or sold, nor is there a lot of which I am afraid.' And he reported in *Dead Line for Crime*: 'There was a distinct dearth in the vice trade in London after I exposed the notorious Messina brothers.'

Not that the Messinas were his only target. Antonio Rossi, or Tony Ross, who had been born in Corsica but claimed Scottish ancestry, was another. Webb invented the rather awkward nickname of 'the Hyena of Soho' for him, although it seems unlikely that anyone ever referred to him as such. Webb bearded him in the estate agent's shop he had in Soho with the immortal lines: 'I am Duncan Webb. The last I heard of you was that you were going to cut my throat. Here is my throat. Cut it.' Rossi resisted the temptation.

Webb had started his investigations into the Messinas with a prostitute called Ellen. He wrote in his memoirs: 'When she knew I was a newspaper reporter, she offered me one night's hospitality if I would persuade a certain well-known male film star to use his influence to get her an actress's job.' He recorded that, as he continued his inquiries, someone attempted to run him down in Old Compton Street in Soho: 'A streetwalker came up to me. With a sneer on her lips, she said, "That was meant for you, dearie."'

Reckoning day for the Messinas came on 3 September 1950 when Webb named the 'four debased men with an empire of vice which is a disgrace to London'. At that stage the brothers owned properties that operated as brothels in Shepherd Market, Stafford Street, Bruton Place and New Bond Street, all in the West End. Webb catalogued their connections with prostitutes and exposed their cover addresses before passing his dossier on to a grateful Scotland Yard, who later said they had already been aware of much of what was happening. The following week, Webb reported that he had been attacked in the street and that his assailant had informed him: 'The Messinas are pals of mine. It's about time you journalists were done proper.'

Scotland Yard set up a task force to deal with the ring and all the brothers, with the exception of Alfredo who had not featured in the *People* exposé, decamped to France. Alfredo did not have long to wait for his comeuppance. Detective Superintendent Guy Mahon and his officers paid a visit to his home in Wembley, north London, and arrested him for living on the immoral earnings of Hermione Hindin, with whom he shared the house. Remarking, 'Let's be friends, we are men of the world,' Messina hospitably offered the officers champagne, whisky, tea and turkey and, if they would drop the charges, a £200 bribe. While some tea and Haig whisky was consumed – leading Superintendent Mahon to venture the information that he had led the hunt for the acid-bath murderer, Haigh – the rest was resisted.

Mrs Hindin had 104 convictions for soliciting around the West End. She was one of the most loyal and hardworking of the Messina prostitutes, along with Cissy Cohen, Georgette Borg, Blanche Costarki, Marthe Watts and Jean Gilson. Watts wrote about the brothers in her memoirs, *The Men in My Life*, and had 'Gino le Maltais, homme de ma vie' tattooed on her left breast. Watts hated Webb and once attacked him ferociously in a pub.

The charge against Alfredo Messina was, effectively, that he dropped Hindin off in the West End of an evening and financed his comfortable lifestyle on her earnings. He denied even knowing that she was a prostitute, although they had lived together for eight years, saying that he imagined she went to see her mother or to the cinema on the nights she was not in Wembley.

Alfredo was tried at the Old Bailey in May 1951, prosecuted by Christmas Humphreys and Mervyn Griffiths-Jones, both later to become judges, in front of Mr Justice Cassels. Enough emerged about his financial arrangements to give an idea of the scope of the Messina operation. He had bank accounts with the Bank Italo Egyptiano, the Banque de Commerce in Brussels, Barclays Bank in Gibraltar and Barclays Bank in Paris, as well as money held in a safe-deposit box in Selfridges department store. He also had accounts in Casablanca and Tangier. Much was made of the fact that he had paid £987 10s. for a mink coat for Mrs Hindin in 1945.

Messina's version of events was that Mahon saw the 'money' in his safe – with three diamond rings, a champagne swizzle stick and a gold fountain pen – and called his assistant Bert Foster into the room and announced that he was going to charge Messina with bribery. The jury did not believe him. Mr Justice Cassels was equally disapproving. He summed up, allowing himself the indulgence of some judicial wordplay but making it plain what he thought of the defendant: 'It is perfectly right and proper that you should be invited to let pass through your minds the reflection that it would be unlikely that a police officer, who could have no other interest in this case other than discharging his duty, would stoop so low – as well as stooping low to get money out of the safe – as to pull out of the safe £200 and then round and say to this man, "I am now going to charge you with bribery".' Before sentence, the judge delivered a stern rebuke: 'You thought that so far as the police of this country were concerned, you could do anything. You are an evil man.' Alfredo was gaoled for two years on each charge, to run concurrently, and fined £500.

Attilio meanwhile slipped back into the country and set up home in Chalfont St Giles, in Buckinghamshire, with one of the leading members of their team, Robena Torrance, who was a prostitute. He was gaoled briefly in 1959 under the Sexual Offences Act, but escaped deportation to Italy when the Italian government refused to accept him. John du Rose, one of the detectives on the case who later became a Deputy Assistant Commissioner at the Yard, recalled searching Attilio's flat and finding a book called *The Road to Buenos Aires*, which gave details of how procurement and prostitution functioned. Sentencing him, the recorder, Gerald Dibson, said: 'You made a sumptuous but revolting living from the suffering bodies of the women you trapped, seduced and reduced to a form of slavery. You caused great suffering and it is only right that you should suffer.'

Eugenio and Carmelo shifted their operation to Brussels, where they recruited Belgian women, but were arrested there in 1955 in possession of loaded revolvers and stood trial in Tournai in 1956. Eugenio was gaoled for seven years but Carmelo, now in poor health, was deported and moved to Ireland before finding his way back to England under a false name, Carlos Marino, and with a Cuban passport. He was arrested, gaoled and deported to Rome, where he died six months later at the age of forty-three. Attilio managed to lie low in Bourne End, Buckinghamshire, where he had a house called, appropriately enough, Hideaway, and affected the manner of an English country gent in tweeds and cap, but he was eventually deported to Italy. Salvatore moved to Switzerland and only Alfredo remained in England. He died in Brentford in 1963.

Remarkably, the Messinas' operation survived some of these upheavals. The brothers controlled it from France and the prostitutes travelled to Paris to make their payments. Initially, Marthe Watts assisted but, as she wrote, 'I could not help feeling a sense of pity and remorse as I thought of my own young days and saw these foolish young creatures deceived into a new way of life that could only bring them unhappiness.'

Messina relatives took on some of the business. Anthony Micalleff, who operated from a boarding-house in Earls Court, was targeted by both the police and the press. In 1958 he was found guilty of allowing the Norfolk Hotel to be used as a brothel and also of permitting his children to be there while it was so used. He was fined £100. That year there were no fewer than 16,900 arrests for prostitution in London.

The Maltese connection survived well. Joe 'Mantini' Spiteri, who came to London as a young man in 1952 and was gaoled with the Messinas, was so innocent that when he first saw prostitutes in the West End he thought they were well-dressed beggars for why else would they be approaching people in the street? The women stayed willingly with the Maltese men, he said, preferring them to the less hot-blooded Englishmen.

The vice world also became more overtly violent as people like Tommy Smithson arrived on the scene. Smithson, a rangy Liverpudlian, ex-boxer and ex-stoker in the merchant navy, first emerged as a force to be reckoned with in 1953. He had protected one of the main Maltese vice operators, George Caruana, a handsome man said to look like Tony Curtis, from an attack by a heavy called Slip Sullivan, organised, so one version has it, by Gypsy Hill, Billy Hill's partner. Sullivan was badly slashed about the arm and throat and Smithson was summoned to the Black Cat factory in Camden Town, according to his old ally Jim Barnett, who told this dramatic version of the attack: 'There was Moshe Blueboy, "Billy Hill, Jackie Spot and they said, "Look, Tommy, you know you're carrying a gun, give us the gun." He gave them the gun and Billy Hill hit him over the head with it.'

At that stage, said Barnett, a furniture van arrived and eight to ten men poured out, including Sonny Sullivan, Slip's brother. Smithson nearly lost, literally, an arm and a leg as the attackers slashed and cut him: 'You could put fingers in the scars in his arms and legs, where they tried to cut it off. Then they threw him over a railway embankment.' One account suggests he was dumped outside the National Temperance Hospital, another that a small child spotted him and summoned help. Spot, for whom Smithson ran a Soho club, made financial amends for the attack and for Smithson's refusal to help the police.

Known for his fearlessness, his scarred face and his padded shoulders, for a while Smithson ran the deceptively named Publishers' Club and a bookies in Soho. His main money, however, came from protection rackets and his practice was to cream a shilling in the pound off all bets in the spielers under his control. The protection was double-sided: no other villains attacked the premises and the police would only raid by appointment. As Jim Barnett, his partner, recalled: 'The police would tell us when they were going to come so we would arrange to have a few friends round, a little money on the table, next to nothing. Somebody would be carrying the rent book and he would be the one who went in front of the magistrate. After he'd been pinched a couple of times, someone else would carry the book.'

Some of the magistrates were clearly well aware of the charade played out in front of them. One, Roland Thomas at Marlborough Street court, responded to one rent-book carrier who wished him a happy Christmas in court: 'Merry Christmas to you, too, but it's still

£90 and nine guineas costs – but don't worry, there's a man at the back of the court who'll be only too pleased to pay the fine for you.'

Smithson's punishment for offenders was less gentle and many of the Maltese lived in fear of him. Although guns were rarely used, Jim Barnett explained that there was no shortage of alternatives: 'A wall is a marvellous weapon. You ram someone's head into a wall, that's a pretty heavy thing to hit them with. Tables, heavy ashtrays, chairs, your hands, your feet. And another good weapon is to drive yourself raving mad.'

The 'mad' act was invariably successful and the owners of clubs and brothels paid up regularly. The enforcers lived a crazy life of little sleep, purple hearts and black coffee, breakfast at the corner shop, visits to the Turkish baths, where they would throw away their dirty underwear and shirts and then plunge back into the day. Money changed hands swiftly in Soho in those days: clients paid prostitutes who paid pimps who gambled the money and paid protection and would be out hunting for more money all within a few hours. Smithson's cut, often as much as £500 a night from the clubs, was also squandered on fast living and, according to Barnett, through his generosity to those down on their luck. Smithson was not above taking money from people to beat others up and then splitting the money with his intended victim and organising a bogus fight to satisfy all sides. On one occasion he 'beat up' Barnett for £200 on the instructions of a bent Flying Squad officer.

According to Barnett, Smithson grew jealous of Hill's power, started pressuring people too heavily and demanding too much money, upsetting many people. In June 1956, ten days after Fraser, Warren and Co. had been gaoled for the attack on Spot, Smithson was shot dead in a lodging house in Carlton Vale in Maida Vale, West London. As the *Daily Mirror* had it, he was 'murdered Chicago-style, in broad daylight … the crêpe-soled killers walked in Indian file. In the upstairs room at Number 88, there were two dull "plops".' An indication of the importance with which such events were treated at the time is the fact that it was reported by no fewer than nine members of the *Daily Express* Crime Bureau.

Smithson's widow, Jessie, who had left him when he joined the gangs, said: 'His wasted life should be a warning to others ... the time for tears was many years ago.' In Leytonstone, in east London, Smithson was given what was then becoming the ritual criminal's funeral, complete with limousines, wreaths inscribed 'To a Gentleman' and dark glasses for the mourners.

Zoe Progl, who called herself the 'Queen of the Underworld', recalled Smithson's demise: 'Tommy's death seemed to have a peculiarly stultifying effect upon all the prominent members of the underworld and so many of his friends, including me, for some time lost the urge to graft and tended to live on the proceeds of past jobs while we drank in various groups and mourned the passing of a friend.'

There were almost as many theories as to why Smithson died as there were scars on his body. Barnett believed that the Maltese had become tired of paying Smithson off and organised his murder, which Barnett did not approve but accepted: 'If you were having rows with Tommy Smithson, you had to kill him. He was somebody that had had so much damage to him, nothing stopped him any more.' He believed that the message for the British gangsters was: 'Watch out for the Malts, they will retaliate.' Joe 'Mantini' Spiteri agreed: 'Everyone was pleased about it, they felt more relaxed.'

Certainly Smithson had had an argument with Caruana, from whom he wanted money, possibly for his friend Fay Sadler, of Pen Club fame, who had been arrested because of his bouncing cheques. There had been a row and Caruana had been slashed with a pair of scissors. The police theory was that Smithson was becoming an irritation to two new vice organisers, Frank Mifsud and Bernie Silver, possibly blackmailing them, and that they wanted him off the scene, with the added advantage of having Caruana implicated; Caruana was believed to be branching out on his own, against the wishes of Silver and Mifsud. The murder was, according to detective Bert Wickstead, 'A landmark inasmuch as it let every other contender for the vice position in the West End know that the Syndicate [Silver and Mifsud] were in pole position and would brook no interference to thwart their powers.'

But the real reason for the murder was much more mundane, according to the man who actually pulled the trigger, Phillip Ellul. Smithson had previously tried to recruit Ellul to his protection team but had been rebuffed. Ellul, who moved to San Francisco, remembered Smithson having a fight with Caruana after which Ellul and he had squared up to each other with knives. The moment passed, but Ellul then heard that Smithson had been looking for him with a gun.

'So I thought to myself – mmm – and went and got me a gun,' said Ellul. He lay in wait for Smithson to appear at his normal gambling haunts but saw no sign of him for ten days. With his colleagues he set off for Maida Vale, looking for Caruana and not expecting to find Smithson: 'I knocked on the door. It was nothing like they said in court. I didn't go there to kill him, I didn't know he was there.' A woman opened the door and told them that Smithson was upstairs.

'He was sitting on a chair with a little pair of scissors,' recalled Ellul. 'I said he had a pair of scissors that big, but that wasn't true. I was going to let it go at that because sometimes I'm looking for somebody and I'm mad, ready to explode inside and then the next minute I might be buying them coffee.

'I said – "Listen, Tom, you carry a gun, you use it. I'm carrying one and I'm going to use it." And I just – BANG – shot him in the shoulder. He said, "Phillip!" So I cocked it and it jammed. So I hit him and he went right over the bed.' Ellul left the room to try and fix the gun and Smithson locked the door and shouted, "That man's crazy!"'

Victor Spampinato, Ellul's confederate, and another Maltese heavy, tried to calm things but Ellul kicked the door in – 'One kick, you get the strength. I just walked in, put the gun to his neck and BANG. I said, "Let's go."

'Smithson's behind me, he's bleeding. I said, "Now you're satisfied. It had to come to this." I never had any qualms about what happened there.' He believed his dignity required him to use his gun once he had produced it. He borrowed £2,000 from Caruana who, according to Ellul, knew nothing about it and fled with Spampinato to Manchester. They read the newspaper reports of the killing over breakfast the following day in a Maltese café on Trafford Road.

'We were busy looking at all those papers. It said that Scotland Yard knows who did it. They said "He died in his shoes" and all that carry on. So I thought to myself, well, Smithson's dead now.'

A hunt was launched for Ellul and Spampinato. Both were lured back to London apparently on the understanding that a deal had been done and that they would face only a manslaughter charge and a probable five-year maximum sentence. But, after they had given themselves up, murder charges were placed against them. At their trial prosecuting counsel Reginald Seaton, QC, warned the jury that many of the characters they would encounter were 'by no means admirable persons or useful citizens'.

Ellul, who had told Smithson to 'say your last prayers' before he executed him, was convicted and sentenced to death, being reprieved forty-eight hours before the hangman was due to arrive and eventually serving eleven years. Spampinato was cleared. Spiteri, who was meant to be part of the hit team, had a lucky escape: he had been chatting up an old girlfriend called Sharon when the other two set off from a Cable Street café on their errand and was too late for the kill. But more attention was focused on the two men eventually to be charged with plotting the murder and paying for it: Silver and Mifsud, who were credited with filling the vacuum left by the Messinas.

Silver, who had been born in Stoke Newington, in north-east London, had been in the Parachute Regiment during the war until he was discharged on medical grounds in 1943, and had worked as a market trader and jobbing builder before moving into vice, where he was one of the Messinas' apprentices. Initially in the fifties he had a brothel in Brick Lane, in east London, and a strip club in Soho's Brewer Street, but he was expanding speedily. He had expensive tastes and was in the process of buying a £27,000 yacht at the time of his arrest on vice charges in 1973. He claimed to be an 'estate agent and art dealer'. Mifsud was an aggressive and erratic former traffic policeman from Malta. Spiteri says he was a generous soul, forever buying drinks, although he 'used to dress like a bum, loaded with money but always dressed like a bum. Torn shirt, maybe even torn trousers.'

In the sixties the two men virtually controlled Soho's vice rackets. They owned around twenty strip clubs between them and made a fortune on the backs of the young women who rented their properties. They used strong-arm tactics to move people out of their properties if it interfered with their 'flat farming' and were said to have set fire to the staircase of one flat they wanted vacated.

There were hiccoughs. Mifsud and Caruana were prosecuted under the Metropolitan Police Act for running an unlicensed theatre, namely the Stripperama in Greek Street, but were rescued by the Lord Chamberlain, whose decision that stripping could not be classified as a 'stage play or dramatic entertainment' may well have been true in the rather joyless establishments run by the men. For more than fifteen years the Syndicate flourished, making what the police claimed was as much as £100,000 a week and becoming the 'Rolls-Royces of the criminal fraternity'.

The vice world had its ear to the ground and in October 1973, before Bert Wickstead's first planned raid in response to new intelligence, Mifsud and Silver and their associates fled, tipped off by a policeman. 'I then enlisted the aid of the press,' wrote Wickstead later. He persuaded them to print stories with head-lines like 'The Raid That Never Was' and to give the impression that the operation had been abandoned. This ruse appeared to work because the crew drifted back from abroad and were mostly in their old haunts when the real raid took place in December 1973 and 170 people were held.

Five of them were found in the Scheherazade Club, which was in full swing and where, as Wickstead recalled, a 'buxom blonde' was singing. Guests, staff and band were rounded up and taken in buses for questioning at Limehouse police station: 'I put them all in the charge room and they were thoroughly enjoying them-selves, the band was playing and everybody was singing.' Mifsud was not among them. He was later arrested in a tent on the Switzerland–Austria border and booked into a private Swiss psychiatric hospital, where he claimed to be suffering from a mental condition that would make travel back to England unwise.

However, the vice charges did stick and in September 1974 Silver and Mifsud found themselves at the Old Bailey, accused of running what was described as the 'Soho Vice Syndicate' and of making £100,000 from their 'slaughter-houses of love', as Henry Miller called brothels.

In what was the biggest vice trial since the Messina days, it was claimed by Michael Corkery for the prosecution that this was a 'vicious empire ... an unsavoury world of prostitutes, ponces and pimps' that rented out flats to prostitutes at what were then seen as exorbitant rates – £100 a week for a little room above a strip club. Witnesses reeled off the exotic names of the clubs alleged to have housed prostitution: the Perfumed Garden and the Taboo, the Casbah and the Gigi. One of the prosecution witnesses, Frank

Dyer, Maltese despite his name, claimed that when police raids became a problem, 'a man at the Home Office was fixed to have it stopped'. Dyer said that he himself had been threatened, beaten up and offered £20,000 to disappear and not give evidence. Joe 'Mantini', who also gave colourful evidence, accusing defence counsel Michael Havers of being a 'ponce', claimed that he was offered £10,000 not to go into the witness box and threatened with death if he did. Years later, he was still carrying a knife, spike and hammer for self-protection.

On 19 December 1974, after a sixty-three-day trial, Silver and six other Maltese men were gaoled, Silver for six years with a fine of £30,000. The judge, Lord Justice Geoffrey Lane, told them: 'The profits you reaped were enormous ... the only mitigating fact I can see is that there is no suggestion that you drove any girl into prostitution. You employed every device and artifice which your considerable intelligence enabled you to use in order to try and escape detection and to avoid conviction.' The court appeared not to have been moved by Silver's claim that he had once organised prostitutes to cheer up the British troops in Northern Ireland, and that he had been allowed to run a brothel there in the hope that it would lead to information about the IRA.

Smaller fry, Anthony Mangion and Emmanuel Bartolo, were each gaoled for five years with Mangion's loyal sister shouting from the public gallery, 'Don't push him, he's a good man,' before being hustled out, screaming abuse. Frank Melito, Frank's younger brother Joseph and Romeo Saliba were also gaoled for acting as frontmen. Reports of the time claimed that £50 million had passed through the Syndicate's hands to be stashed in Swiss banks, but little evidence was advanced for such vast sums.

Bert Wickstead had meanwhile been re-investigating the Smithson case and decided that Mifsud and Silver must have ordered it. Both men were to face murder charges. Silver was convicted on 8 July 1975, a conviction quashed on appeal on

18 October 1976. It is fair to Silver to say that he was also exonerated both by Ellul, the killer, and by contemporaries who had no axe to grind on his behalf and who believe he was wrongly charged.

Spampinato was traced to Malta and gave powerful evidence against Silver and Mifsud at the Old Street committal hearing. He arrived straight from the airport and cut a dramatic figure, dressed all in black and with a Fu Manchu moustache. He said that he had been given the message that 'this punk [Smithson] has got to be exterminated' and described in detail how Ellul had shot Smithson. He recalled the sight of 'thick blood like liver from his mouth'.

Wickstead had been to the United States in pursuit of Ellul, who had served his sentence for Smithson's murder, and found him, remarkably enough, after making a television appeal. A 'true crime' magazine had printed Ellul's photograph and he was spotted by a diligent reader, in a hostel in San Francisco. Eventually, he was brought back to England and asked to give evidence.

But the time awaiting the big drop had made him a nervous customer and, although the police let him go to a betting shop every day to calm his nerves, he said that he wished to return to the States for medical reasons, because of his ulcers. He never came back to give evidence and Silver in the end walked free, as did Mifsud.

Silver's troubles were not over. In 1978 he was deported from Malta, then a popular watering-hole for criminals. Back in England, reporters from the *People* were still on his case – they had described him as a 'human vulture' as early as 1953 – and announced in August 1979 that 'Godfather Bernie Is Back in Business', citing half a dozen clubs with Silver connections and suitably exotic names. He suffered personal unhappiness when his wife, Albertine Falzon, a French former prostitute, committed suicide by jumping from her room in Soho.

Mifsud faced other charges but was cleared of conspiracy to murder Smithson, convicted (but on appeal cleared) of attempting to rig an Old Bailey trial by suborning a Soho hot-dog seller to give false evidence, and had his five-year sentence and £50,000 fine set aside. In the original trial Mifsud was alleged to have approached a man to implicate Anthony Cauchi, a club rival in Soho, in an explosion at one of Mifsud's Greek Street clubs.

Mifsud and Spampinato retired to Malta, where the former berated those curious about his past with threats of legal action and the latter looked after his elderly mother.

The years when the Syndicate was all-powerful had seen the vice world changing for reasons other than arrests and gaoling. Public attitudes had shifted. 'In the late forties and fifties, the ordinary member of the public regarded vice as something which ought to be put down,' says former judge Sir Frederick Lawton. 'But later many people took the view that the kind of activities which I used to have to prosecute ought not to be prosecuted at all.' He cited the 1967 legislation concerning homosexuality as an example of this change in attitude.

The arrival of the Street Offences Act on 16 August 1959 had driven many prostitutes off the streets, the police remarking that it was like a 'vacuum cleaner'. Instead of the £2 fine for soliciting there was £25 for a first offence, and double that for a second. The sentence for a third offence was gaol. Prosecutions for soliciting in the first quarter after the Act came into effect were down by a remarkable 90 per cent, from more than 4,000 to just 464. But the trade – and there were estimated to be 5,000 prostitutes work-ing in London at the time – moved speedily elsewhere. A euphe-mistically named *Ladies Directory* appeared with photographs and telephone numbers of prostitutes. Its publisher was convicted of conspiring to corrupt public morals.

'Near-beer' joints, which were not licensed, acted as pick-up places for prostitutes. Advertisements rich in *double entendre* started appearing in newsagents and in telephone booths. Many strip clubs were able to offer prostitution services, and establishments that charged enormous sums for bottles of bogus bubbly, on the often false understanding that a woman would be provided, also flourished.

New figures emerged on the scene and disappeared: 'Big Jeff' Phillips became a millionaire through the porn trade and survived by paying substantial backhanders to the police. But in 1975, after serving a brief prison sentence and naming corrupt officers, he killed himself because of an unrequited love affair.

Others made their profits from renting out parts of property empires for prostitution. One of these was John Gaul, gaoled and fined £25,000 in 1962 for living off the earnings of prostitutes. He was later to become better known when his wife was killed by hit-men. After Gaul's imprisonment Alec 'The Count' Kostanda took over some of his properties until he himself was convicted and gaoled for six months. In west London, one of the people who profited from the climate was racketeer landlord Peter Rachman. There was male prostitution, too, but on a tiny scale, although the police believed that Hungarian refugees in the late fifties found it an easy way to make money.

Soho remained an area of vice up to the eighties, when the police, in co-operation with the local Westminster Council, clamped down on the many peep-shows and porn clubs. By this time, prostitution had moved off the streets of the West End. The top end of the market worked as 'escorts' for hundreds of pounds a night, catering to high-rolling and often foreign businessmen, while the bottom end moved to Finsbury Park, Streatham and King's Cross, the place where, in 1991, the Director of Public Prosecutions, Sir Alan Green, was stopped for kerb-crawling.

But a development had already taken place which was to change the face of vice in London. Working hand in sweaty glove with corrupt police officers, one of the main pornographers of the seventies, one Jimmy Humphreys, was emerging.

Humphreys, a crook but not a major one, was amongst the first to profit from the sixties' boom in pornography. He moved into Soho clubland with his wife Rusty, an attractive and self-willed stripper. He had his early brushes with the police, paying over money, he complained later, to a detective called Harry Challenor. The policeman, for his part, denied taking the bribes but was to reappear in the annals of the underworld soon enough. Humphreys' neighbour in his Soho club was Silver and it was Silver who was to be helpful when he ran into problems with expanding his empire, helping out with advice on the necessary bribes that had to be paid.

Prostitution and the clubs provided a combination of illegality and cash that was to prove too tempting to the very people whose task it was to control them, who soon found themselves swimming with the tide rather than against it. A vice that was to be as corrosive as any being offered by strip clubs or pimps turned out to be a corruption at the very heart of the police themselves.

11

GOOD EGGS AND BAD APPLES

POLICE CORRUPTION AND THE UNDERWORLD

Detective Sergeant Harold 'Tanky' Challenor was a resourceful man. He had served in the Special Air Service with distinction during the Second World War and played an active role in the Flying Squad before being moved to West End Central at the heart of London's crime in the early sixties. Always imaginative, on one occasion he persuaded a small-time crook to take him to a criminals' pub so that working villains could be pointed out to him. Since the man was not prepared to be seen with a policeman, Challenor 'got hold of a woman's wig, borrowed one of Doris's [his wife's] longest skirts, a roll-neck sweater, high-heeled shoes, nylon stockings and a cloak-like coat and handbag'. Heavily made-up, he sat nursing his gin and tonic while the villain nodded at the professional heisters and hoisters present. Challenor's cover was nearly blown when he entered the gents by mistake and told a startled drinker: 'I've recently had a miscarriage and must still be a bit light-headed.' He was even propositioned, and rescued by his 'boyfriend' for the night, who kept up the deception and called him a 'silly old cow'.

By the time he had established himself in the West End, Challenor was being called worse things than a silly old cow. He already had a reputation in the Soho patch in which he worked for what could be euphemistically described as eccentric behaviour. He had for some years been suffering from a mental disorder which had been noted by his colleagues but never confronted. In July 1963 there was a demonstration against Queen Frederika, who was staying at Claridge's Hotel and who was seen as symbolic of the repressive right-wing regime then in power in Greece. Challenor, furious at what he saw as impertinent anti-royal activities, arrested a number of the participants, gave them some whacks and planted half-bricks on them with the words: 'There you are, me old darling. Carrying an offensive weapon can get you two years.'

One man he arrested, Donald Rooum, who was a member of the National Council for Civil Liberties (now Liberty), was able to prove that since there was no brick dust in his pockets he could not have concealed a brick there and he was cleared. Challenor was suspended and eventually stood trial in June 1964 with three young detectives. He observed later: 'The whores danced outside the Old Bailey when Oscar Wilde was gaoled, glad to see a menace to their profession out of the way. I'm pretty certain that though there may not have been quite such an exuberant display of relief when I was publicly disgraced, a few glasses were raised in the clip-joints and strip clubs by the men who controlled organized crime and prostitution in the West End.' His three colleagues were convicted of conspiring to pervert the course of justice and gaoled for a total of eleven years. Challenor was found unfit to plead.

He was clearly not the full sovereign. He had convinced himself and his wife that he was being prepared for a secret mission by being hypnotised and brainwashed and as he travelled to Brixton in the prison van during his trial he would chant to himself, mantra-like, 'Who Dares Wins', the SAS motto.

In his memoirs, Challenor says that he has no recollection of planting the bricks and fabricating evidence and is adamant that corruption was not his practice when dealing with vice in Soho. Plenty of the area's denizens claimed otherwise. Challenor said that these were the sort of men who, when on trial, would suffer from what was called in the Met a 'fit of dock asthma', during which they would fix their gaze on the jury and roll their eyes while a police officer was giving evidence, to convey the impression that the officer was lying. All too often they may have been right. Challenor admits that he was not averse to delivering a right-hander when he felt one was merited and, when he felt someone was due for a prison sentence, he would brush their lapel and say genially, 'I thought I saw some porridge on your suit.'

Although psychiatrist William Sargent agreed that Challenor was 'mad as a hatter', others took a more cynical view and for a while pretending to be mad in court was known as 'doing a Challenor'.

The bent detective was hardly a new phenomenon. In 1877, the country had been transfixed by the 'Trial of the Detectives', which led to three officers being gaoled after a forty-eight-day Old Bailey case in which they had been found guilty of tipping off a team of con-men who were defrauding wealthy gamblers through a bogus 'fail-safe' betting method. And, as we have seen, one of the officers in charge of the raids on West End clubs, George Goddard, was gaoled in 1929. But Goddard's and Challenor's manic dishonesties were as nothing compared with a much-greater cancer that had grown inside the detective force of the Metropolitan Police by the early sixties. Bribery had long been endemic. Safe-breaker Eddie Chapman reckoned that bail and adjusted evidence could always be bought at a price and said he

once paid a policeman £30,000 to say in a pre-trial statement
that he would be available to give evidence on his behalf. The
case was duly dropped. Criminals of Chapman's era who wanted
the same favours used a middleman, often a taxi-driver called
Jack the Liar, who would arrange the handovers.

The judge who was to gaol Charlie Richardson, Sir Frederick
Lawton, also had his theories about corrupt officers. He believed
that the rot set in because of wartime regulations which exposed
the police to bribery when businessmen and industrialists were
able to buy their way out of trouble if they had committed
offences.

Eric Mason, a major gangland figure from the fifties through
to the seventies, recalled: 'I've paid the police plenty of money
over the years to get bail or lessen the charge or even knock a few
of my previous off before sentencing. There's hundreds of ways
they elicit money from you and that was part and parcel of your
business and you accepted that.' He remembered a local superintendent in Cardiff, where he was held for a bank robbery, remarking on the London detectives and how they could afford
500-guinea suits and double Scotches. 'The Cardiff top coppers
knew that every copper in London was bent.' Sir Frederick also
recalled a man who had made a 'confession' full of Cockney slang
and Yiddish expressions, but who was a well-educated Pole. The
case fell and led to a successful action for malicious prosecution.

'The practice of police putting words into the mouth of a suspect they're arresting started in the fifties,' said Sir Frederick. He
remembered one sergeant whose suspects would, on arrest, always
say: 'Blimey, who's grassed me this time?' This was regarded as a
classic verbal in that the statement immediately suggested that
the man was a member of the criminal classes because he knew
the word 'grass', and that he had been in trouble before.

The Yard hierarchy took the Nelsonian view. When, in 1955,
Superintendent Bert Hannam produced a report on corruption,

particularly in West End Central police station, the Metropolitan Commissioner, Sir John Nott-Bower, not only ignored its findings but went personally to the station to stand on a chair and reassure the troops that he did not believe a word of it.

While the payment of bribes to detectives may have been routine in the sixties and seventies for career criminals, it was in the specialised areas of drugs and pornography that the most systematic forms of police corruption emerged. Both fields offered enormous profits to their protagonists, who were happy to pay a percentage if it ensured that they were not bothered by the law. Public ambivalence as to whether drugs, in particular cannabis, and pornography should have been illegal anyway further confused the issue because the police could reassure themselves that they were essentially condoning what many saw as 'victimless' crimes.

It was in this climate that on 29 November 1969 *The Times* published a remarkable story, by reporters Julian Mounter and Garry Lloyd, about police corruption. It stated baldly: 'We have, we believe, proved that at least three detectives are taking large sums of money in exchange for dropping charges, for being lenient with evidence offered in court, for allowing a criminal to work unhindered.'

The article named three officers: Sergeant John Symonds, Detective Inspector Bernard Robson and Detective Sergeant Gordon Harris. *The Times* reporters had tape-recorded and photographed the officers' meetings with a small-time criminal. One of the telling remarks in the taped conversations was Symonds saying: 'We've got more villains in our game than you've got in yours, you know.' But the most memorable snippet was when Symonds said reassuringly: 'Always let me know straight away if you need anything because I know people everywhere. Because I'm in a little firm in a firm. Don't matter where, anywhere in London I can get on the phone to someone I know I can trust, that talks the same as me. And if he's not the right person that can do it, he'll know the person that can.'

It was this theme of a 'firm within a firm' that was to send tremors through the Yard over the next three years as a tale of cynical and pervasive corruption was slowly and painfully revealed. By the end of this time, a number of policemen were behind bars, the work of three major squads had been mightily damaged and the reputation of the police had been severely dented.

The initial inquiry into *The Times*'s allegations was entrusted at an operational level to Detective Chief Superintendent Bill Moody. With hindsight, it was a breathtaking appointment: Moody was himself one of the Yard's most corrupt officers and would follow the men he was investigating to the dock of the Old Bailey within five years. The flashy Moody, who drove a Lancia purchased from a porn-dealer friend, must have enjoyed the irony of investigating officers whose dishonesty was almost amateurish in comparison with his own.

The task of overall head of the inquiry was given to Frank Williamson, one of the inspectors of constabulary, Home Office-appointed officials whose duty it is to oversee the police. A former chief constable from Cumbria, Williamson had made no secret of his distrust of some of the Met's habits. The Home Secretary, James Callaghan, indicated that he should report either directly to him or to the Commissioner of Scotland Yard, Sir John Waldron. Williamson later said that he found his inquiries frustrated through 'a misguided loyalty to the Criminal Investigation Department, arising from a deep-rooted desire to avoid publicity from prosecution of police officers.' He said that he believed there were three types of officers at the Yard: those who were corrupt, those who were honest but did nothing and those who were too stupid to realise that there was any corruption in the first place.

The cornered Symonds tried his best shots: first, he threatened libel actions against *The Times*, then he concocted a story that the

whole tale had been fabricated by the Richardson gang as a way
of settling scores over his (minimal) role in their demise. But
despite attempts to impugn the honesty of the reporters and a
battery of sound experts who sought to cast doubt on the taped
evidence, Robson and Harris were gaoled on 3 March 1972 for
seven and six years respectively. Symonds went, in the argot of the
underworld, 'on his toes' and fled the country, reputedly to southern Africa, but gave himself up seven years later and was gaoled
for eighteen months.

The seven-week trial cost around £500,000 and the bribes the
men were convicted of taking totalled a mere £275. But the story
of what prosecuting counsel John Mathew called 'complete and
utter corruption' was a pebble thrown into a pool of dishonesty
and the ripples were about to wash through the Yard. Indeed,
they were already lapping at the edges of the Drugs Squad.

A London heroin addict, facing a cannabis charge in Oxford,
had been recruited as an informer and encouraged to set up a
large LSD deal. However, he felt uneasy about the police's methods; he had been part-paid with some of the drugs seized. He
reported his misgivings to the Oxford police, who relayed the
story to the Home Office. The first official concerns about
the work of the squad were now being privately aired.

The informer had come into contact with the man who was in
effective charge of the growing squad, Detective Chief Inspector
Vic Kelaher, who after time in the Flying Squad had become the
youngest DCI in the Yard's history. He and his loyal deputy,
Detective Sergeant 'Nobby' Pilcher, relied heavily on informants
and were making a mark for themselves as a new can-do team
who provided high-profile convictions. Pilcher was known as
someone who loved carrying out raids on the famous, most notably John Lennon and Yoko Ono, who were raided in 1968 in an
over-the-top operation in which officers burst in through the windows in SAS style. The team's methods were well known to the

hippie dealers of Notting Hill but complaints from that direction could be safely ignored.

At the time, relations between Customs and Excise and the police were at a low ebb; the former regarded the latter as being, at best, flash and superficial in their approach and at worst, dishonest and corrupt. It was no accident that the game started to unravel for Kelaher when Customs targeted Basil Sands, a cannabis dealer, who was gaoled for seven years but who claimed loudly that he had been acting with Kelaher's knowledge and agreement in order to snare the main dealers in the operation. Kelaher was not prosecuted at this stage but was moved to desk duties, which he carried out until he left the force three years later.

But he had not escaped. On 5 November 1972, the *Sunday Times* published a detailed exposé of the Drugs Squad and two days later, Kelaher was charged with conspiring to pervert the course of justice, along with officers Prichard, Lilley, Acworth and McGibbon. Prichard and Lilley were gaoled for eighteen months, Pilcher, who had initially fled to Australia, for four years and Kelaher was allowed to resign from the police on medical grounds. Mr Justice Melford Stevenson made what was to become a famous sentencing speech in which he told the shamed officers: 'You poisoned the wells of criminal justice and set about it deliberately. What is equally bad is that you have betrayed your comrades in the Metropolitan Police Force which enjoys the respect of the civilized world – what remains of it – and not the least grave aspect of what you have done is provide material for the crooks, cranks and do-gooders who unite to attack the police whenever opportunity occurs.'

One of the most active bent officers from the 1950s to the 1970s was Detective Inspector Alec Eist. Said Reg Dudley, the north London career criminal wrongly convicted in the 'torso murder' case: 'I had a close relationship with Alec. My friends knew that if they were in trouble, for a few grand channelled through me, Alec would do what he could to make evidence "disappear".' Eist tended to work alone, rather than within a 'firm' of bent coppers and was said to have profited from the proceeds of the 1972 Baker Street bank job. He was returned to uniform in 1975, and retired on 'health' grounds in 1976. He was eventually charged with corruption and conspiracy to pervert the course of justice but was acquitted and went on to run a pub in Six Mile Bottom near Newmarket. He had an odd, unrelated claim to fame in that he interviewed the fugitive James Ray, the assassin of Martin Luther King, when he was arrested in Britain in 1968.

Another maverick officer of the period was Detective Sergeant Derek Ridgewell of the British Transport Police, who made a name for himself in the early 1970s by arresting young black men on the London underground at the time of a panic over 'muggings'. After doubts were raised in one trial about his honesty, he was quietly – and amazingly, in retrospect – moved from the London underground to handling mailbag security, where he joined forces with two professional thieves, with whom he shared the proceeds of their joint crimes. He was gaoled in 1980 for conspiracy to steal mail-bags and died in Ford Prison in 1982. Asked by the governor of the prison shortly before he died why he had become involved with criminals, he replied: 'I just went bent.' The full extent of his involvement only came to light in 2018 when a businessman, Steve Simmons, whom Ridgewell had fitted up for a mail-bag robbery more than forty years earlier, in 1975, managed to get his case re-investigated by the Criminal Cases Review Commission and finally have his conviction quashed. 'One of the hardest things for me was that my parents did not believe me because they were of the generation that believed that the police could not lie,' said Simmons after his name was cleared. But if the revelations about the Drugs Squad were messy and the Eists and Ridgewells were able to ply their trade with ease, what was to happen to the Obscene Publications Squad – the Dirty Squad as it was presciently known – was muckier still.

The scandal arose from the corrupt associations between the leading Soho pornographers, who in the sixties were starting to reap the harvest of blue films and dirty magazines, and senior officers who were paid to cast a blind eye to the activities, tip off the dealers when raids were imminent or eliminate competitors in a cynical abuse of power.

At the heart of the relationship which was eventually to fell the Dirty Squad was Jimmy Humphreys, who had seen the opportunities on offer from the vice world of Soho and was now, with the help of his wife Rusty, firmly establishing himself in that world. The couple's timing was impeccable and they were soon profiting heavily from three clubs, which they ran with as much flair as was possible in the seedy backwaters of Soho.

Humphreys had arrived on a scene in which vice racketeers Bernie Silver and Frank Mifsud were already operating success-fully with the knowledge of the police. He and Silver used to vie with each other as to who could provide detectives with the best tables at charity boxing events at the Grosvenor House hotel in Park Lane.

Jimmy Humphreys was a south Londoner from the Old Kent Road who had spent time for minor villainy in approved schools, Borstals and prisons, where he became friendly with people like Bruce Reynolds and Buster Edwards, later two of the Great Train Robbers, and other south London 'faces', such as Jimmy Brindle and 'Mad' Frankie Fraser.

But while the others went for the more conventional types of crime, he had spotted a gap in the market for pornography at a time when post-austerity Britain was unbuttoning itself. He went into the club business with Johnny Nash of the Nash family and the strip trade with the Maltese Tony Micallef. At the same time, one June Packard who had renamed herself Rusty Gaynor – Rusty

after the colour of her hair and Gaynor after the film star Mitzi –
was becoming the Queen of the Soho strippers. From the family
of a respectable Kent master-builder, she had been encouraged to
learn tap-dancing and singing by a mother who dreamed of
another Shirley Temple. Rusty had started as a chorus girl but,
when music hall faded from fashion, found herself working as a
Soho stripper. She decided to make herself one of the best, choosing her own musical arrangements, hiring Shirley Bassey's
choreographer of the time, flying to Paris to see what they were
doing at the Crazy Horse and the Folies Bergère, and stripping to
torch songs and 'Rhapsody in Blue'.

Humphreys and Rusty fell in love and married in 1964 and a
new Soho dynasty seemed assured. They ran one club at Walker's
Court with twelve strippers dancing to taped music, and another
called Queens. Norma Levy, whose activities as a call girl later led
to the resignation and downfall of Lord Lambton, the Conservative minister, was one of the strippers.

It was the good life, with a flat in Soho and a manor house with
fourteen bedrooms in Kent, where the champagne flowed and the
parties lasted all weekend. Amongst the first people to notice this
lavish lifestyle were the detectives responsible for the patch. At
first they would pop into the clubs and be happy enough with a
few free drinks, but they gradually became greedier.

At the outset the sums of money paid over were small, but
there was a lot of 'hospitality'. A detective would 'invite' Jimmy
Humphreys to a do at an expensive restaurant and tell him to
'bring the wife'. To the detectives, with their matronly spouses,
Rusty was an exotic and they loved being in her company. It was
always clear that Jimmy was meant to pay for the evenings. Rusty
found these occasions awkward and would take along a well-
educated friend, Sheila, who could make conversation with the
wives. Rusty preferred to be at the men's end of the table where
the laughs were. The wives started to ask for jewellery for

themselves and there was some embarrassment when Humphreys bought a necklace for one wife and the detective asked for a replacement because his wife's neck was too thick for it. Corruption was endemic. On one occasion a detective arrived at Rusty's flat with a load of stolen jewellery which he had taken off a burglar and tried unsuccessfully to sell it to her.

Commander Wally Virgo of the CID and Bill Moody, head of the Obscene Publications Squad, were soon on the payroll. The detectives demanded the best restaurants, places like the Caprice or the Savoy. When Ken Drury, head of the Flying Squad, came aboard the gravy train some of his junior officers were worried about the weight he was putting on, so Humphreys bought him an exercise bicycle and a rowing machine.

The Humphreys would attend Flying Squad functions, often being expected to buy hundreds of pounds' worth of raffle tickets. On one occasion they won a holiday to Spain but they already had their own villa in Ibiza, where Jimmy would take detectives with some of the girls from the clubs for weekend breaks.

The marriage had its explosive moments. Rusty was gaoled for three months in Holloway Prison after an incident in which Jimmy was supposedly threatened with a gun. Jimmy said that if she was not released on appeal he would 'bomb' central London with pornography – he even investigated the hiring of a small private plane, a DC4, with which he could dive-bomb Shaftesbury Avenue and the Haymarket.

It was because of Commander Drury's indiscretion that the racket ended. He and his wife had been treated to a holiday in Cyprus, where holiday snaps had been taken – Rusty got on well with the Commander and had even beaten him in a challenge champagne-drinking competition, drinking him under the table. But in February 1972, a photo of Drury on holiday in Cyprus with Humphreys was published in the *Sunday People* and this meant that the Met could no longer dodge the issue. Drury's comeuppance turned out to be the work of a gangland figure, Joey Pyle: he had been raided by police searching for Freddie Sewell, who had murdered a Blackpool policeman, and charged with a firearms offence. He was acquitted but apparently 'got the hump' with the Met sufficiently to tip off the press about the Drury–Humphreys relationship. No one believed Drury's excuse that he was attempting to find Ronnie Biggs, the escaped Great Train Robber. A squad was set up to investigate.

Then Peter Garfarth, a hotel thief and conman with whom Rusty had lived before she met Jimmy, was attacked in the toilet of the Dauphin Club in Mayfair. He was later given a severe slashing on New Year's Eve. Although he always professed his innocence, Humphreys was charged with the attack. He fled to Amsterdam but was arrested and held in prison there. Rusty tried to arrange his escape, but the plot was thwarted and he was brought back to stand trial at the Old Bailey. He was gaoled for eight years. Garfarth gave evidence against him and committed suicide a year later.

But all the while Jimmy had kept his diaries meticulously. All the names of the officers were there, a ticking time-bomb. The diaries themselves were stored in a safe-deposit box. Assistant Commissioner Gilbert Kelland, the clean officer brought in to hose out the Augean stables, took his tape-recorder to Wandsworth Prison and for three months listened as Humphreys described the depth of the corruption.

Finally, the police acted. In February 1976, a series of dawn raids netted those same officers who had so often and so cynically raided others. Drury was taken from his home with a blanket over his head. It was the biggest police scandal of the century and the highest number of officers charged since the great detective scandal of 1877. Kelland wrote later: 'We strongly believed that, for the eventual benefit of the force, the crow of corruption had to be nailed to the barn door to convince and remind everyone of the need for positive action and eternal vigilance.' Of the seventy-four officers investigated, twelve resigned, twenty-eight retired, eight were dismissed and thirteen were gaoled. Jimmy Humphreys's evidence played a crucial part.

In 1978, having been given a royal pardon for his help to the police, Jimmy was released. Rusty had been running a guest-house in Westcliff-on-Sea. They left the country because of un-welcome police attention. Jimmy went into the racehorse and greyhound business in Tijuana, in Mexico, and in Florida, but Rusty was homesick and returned to England. Jimmy eventually joined her and by the nineties they had moved into a different area of vice on a much smaller scale, renting out properties to prostitutes in flats in the Marble Arch and Paddington areas of London, with Rusty occasionally acting as a 'maid' for the women.

The women advertised their services through cards, often with elaborate illustrations, stuck up in phone booths around central London. The trade created a whole new profession, that of 'card boy', the men who for sometimes as much as £100 a day would stick up the cards faster than British Telecom or the local council could take them down. The prostitutes preferred this method of attracting trade as it meant that clients had to come to their flats, where they could arrange their own protection. A high proportion of the services advertised were for discipline and bondage, with many offers to punish 'naughty boys' with canes and whips – something that puzzled foreign tourists in search of more conven-tional services. Another sign of the changing times was the nationalities of the women advertising, with Russians and Brazilians replacing Swedish and French girls, the former favourites.

But if the Humphreys thought that their new low-profile part in the business would mean a quiet life, they were mistaken. In November 1993, the police swooped at the conclusion of a major surveillance operation. The following summer, both were gaoled for eight months. The vice world had moved on since the Messinas' days, with no one family and no one nationality controlling the market. The risks of both random violence and AIDS had taken many of the prostitutes off the streets and into flats from where they could advertise their services through cards or employment by escort agencies and unlicensed massage parlours.

Sir Robert Mark had been appointed Commissioner in 1972. It was a bold move because essentially he was an outsider. He had started as a policeman in his native Manchester and had been Chief Constable of Leicester for ten years before being brought to the Met in March 1967 as an assistant commissioner, the 'Lone Ranger from Leicester'. To say he was made unwelcome would be an understatement: 'I felt rather like the representative of a leper colony attending the annual garden party of a colonial governor.' When he was elevated to the top job with an aim of 'making virtue fashionable', there were still plenty of officers, mainly detectives, who greeted his appointment with dismay. 'I had served in two provincial forces for thirty years and though I had known wrongdoing, I had never experienced institutionalized wrongdoing, blindness, arrogance and prejudice on anything like the scale accepted as routine at the Met,' was his assessment of his task. In his autobiography, *In the Office of Constable*, he was moved to quote Hamlet:

> The time is out of joint: O cursed spite
> That ever I was born to set it right.

Partly because of Sir Robert's strategy of going public with his reforms, the era just prior to his clean-out has been seen as one of the most corrupt in the history of the British police. Certainly, it was a time when policemen appear to have been at their most cynical; but their underworld reputation for routine dishonesty was longstanding, as was public cynicism about police honesty: 'If you want to know the time, ask a policeman' comes from an old music-hall song based on the widely held view that officers stole the watches of drunken toffs they found in the streets.

Sir Robert had already made some changes in his role as Assistant Commissioner, immediately sacking officers who were convicted of criminal offences. (Incredibly, they had previously been allowed to remain on the payroll until their appeal, invariably unsuccessful, was heard months or even years later.) He also returned to uniform any detective whose disciplinary record suggested that he was unfit to work unsupervised, a source of mild enjoyment to the uniformed officers who, for a number of years, had mistrusted their plainclothes colleagues. During Mark's five years as Commissioner, 478 men left the force following, or in anticipation of, disciplinary procedures. Of these, fifty were prosecuted. The vast majority retired in advance of events. The annual rate of departure was around six times higher under Mark than in the immediately preceding years.

Mark identified three main forms of corruption on a sliding scale: the first was charging for bail, suppressing previous convictions and dropping more serious charges; the second affected the more senior officers who were involved in crimes like bank robbery, drugs and obscene publications; and the third applied to officers who believed the system of justice was weighted against them and felt justified in bending the rules. The ranks themselves had a snappier classification: 'Bent for yourself' (taking bribes) or 'bent for the job' (fitting up people who were believed to be guilty but could not be proved so). Paul Condon, who took over as Commissioner of the Metropolitan Police in 1993, was later to describe, without condoning, 'noble cause' corruption, whereby a police officer massaged evidence to ensure the conviction of someone he was sure was guilty.

A newly-created body to investigate allegations of police corruption was set up in 1971, first called A10, then CIB2. It was initially headed by a uniformed commander, the hand-picked

Ray Anning, thus breaking some of the power of the detective side of the force. Service was limited to two years and all allegations of corruption had to go directly to A10 to prevent the old problem of CID men at the Yard tipping off colleagues in the field. By the new millennium, the name had changed to the Directorate of Professional Standards. Other forces also have their own Professional Standards Departments, although smaller, provincial forces may pool their resources. The nicknames for these units have changed, too. Once they were the 'Untouchables' and their detectives known as the 'rubber heels' because of its members' supposed habit of creeping up silently on their prey. In their less effective days, some were dismissed by cynical detectives as 'the muppets'.

Mark meanwhile had summoned the representatives of the CID to what they thought would be a placatory discussion. 'I told them that they represented what had long been the most routinely corrupt organization in London, that nothing and no one would prevent me from putting an end to it and that, if necessary, I would put the whole of the CID back into uniform and make a fresh start.' One of the detectives clandestinely taped the chat and leaked it to the press, but this strengthened rather than weakened Mark's hand. As far as he was concerned, 'the century-old autonomy of the CID had ended'. Home Secretary James Callaghan wrote him a note: 'Dear Commissioner, Quick, decisive, right. All I hoped you would do. Congratulations!'

The next time the notion of police corruption received a wide public airing was in 1978 with Operation Countryman, in which officers from the Dorset police force were brought in to investigate allegations of corruption within the detective branches of the City of London and the Metropolitan police. It was the biggest ever external corruption inquiry into the Met.

It was sparked by allegations made by a supergrass, Geoff Simms, who had been gaoled for ten years for a wages snatch and was facing further trials. He told Regional Crime Squad police in

Hertfordshire that police officers had helped to plan robberies in the City of London and that criminals were routinely paying officers for bail and assistance in their trials. Simms, a strange young man who kept his cricket gear and his guns in the boot of his car, suggested that bribed police deliberately stayed away from areas when they knew a robbery was about to take place.

The allegations coincided with rumours circulating in police and underworld circles that officers in London had been indirectly involved in the 1978 robbery of the *Daily Mirror*, in which a guard was killed and £200,000 stolen, in the 1976 payroll snatch at the *Daily Express*, in which £175,000 was stolen and in the 1977 robbery at Williams & Glyn's Bank in the City, in which £225,000 was taken.

More than a hundred officers worked on the inquiry, interviewing criminals, police officers and journalists in a bid to establish the truth of the rumours. Led by Arthur Hambleton, Chief Constable of Dorset, under the operational control of Leonard Burt, his Assistant Chief Constable, Operation Countryman started in a prefabricated building at the back of a Met police station in Camberwell, in south London, before moving to a more secure headquarters in Godalming, in Surrey.

After six months, the team had a list of seventy-eight officers from the Met and eighteen from the City of London against whom there were allegations of corruption, perjury and conspiracy. One officer was said to have profited by £40,000 from a bank raid, others had arranged for early parole, it was claimed. Others had been paid thousands for information that would lead to robberies. Even given that some of the allegations might have been malicious or score-settling, they were deeply disturbing.

Alf Sheppard, who acted as a go-between for police and villains, provided the startling information that £80,000 had passed through the hands of Detective Chief Inspector Philip Cuthbert, much of it handed over in a restaurant opposite Bishopsgate police station. He described Cuthbert as 'a criminal who chose to be a policeman' and said that the officer had told him of potential places to rob, including the Post Office headquarters, where Cuthbert claimed to 'know the form'. Said Sheppard: 'He told me he wanted to be rich and very quickly so he could retire and live off the proceeds.' A secret tape-recording showed Cuthbert talking about the extent of corruption and discussing which senior officers he used to 'bung' (bribe).

Cuthbert was the chief catch of the inquiry, along with the man described in court as his 'cheerful assistant', John Goldbourn, a former detective sergeant. Cuthbert, an arrogant man and a master of a Freemasons' Lodge from Brentwood, in Essex, was told at his trial on 20 July 1982 by the recorder of London, James Miskin, QC: 'Each of you has tried unsuccessfully to pull the wool over these sensible jurors' eyes. You failed.'

But the investigating team, dismissively nicknamed 'the Swedey' by the Met because of its rural origins, had started to encounter problems early in the inquiry. Files would mysteriously disappear and the investigators took to requesting whole batches of documents so that it was unclear which ones they sought. They were not taken over-seriously by many of the Metropolitan wide boys who did not believe – correctly, as it transpired – that they would be able to penetrate the tightly-knit lodge mentality of the Met. By 1980 the inquiry was in difficulties. Two senior Scotland Yard men were appointed to the team and the provincial officers, seething at what they saw as a further sidelining of their work, departed. The souvenir tie designed for the Countryman officers told its own story: it shows a fluttering eagle (the symbol of the Flying Squad) and, beneath it, a little country mouse making a V-sign. (Such ties are often made to commemorate a major investigation, but usually of a more traditional crime.)

By the end of the inquiry in 1982, £4 million and four years after it had been established in 1978, there was a feeling that the nettle remained ungrasped. Operation Countryman had investigated a total of 200 corruption allegations and submitted forty-one reports to the Director of Public Prosecutions but only four prosecutions were sanctioned. A total of 2,000 statements was taken. After it was all over Hambleton publicly attacked the obstruction he encountered. He claimed that an earlier statement he had made in 1979, suggesting all was well, had been signed to save the inquiry. 'Basically, you may say that we were stopped from cleaning up the Yard,' he said.

In October 1982, the Attorney-General, Sir Michael Havers, suggested that the officers had got 'carried away on a wave of optimism' in their investigation. In his memoirs, Sir David McNee, who had been Commissioner during the inquiry, is scathing about it. Of Hambleton's complaints, he says: 'If they thought their inquiry was being obstructed, all they had to do was tell me. Neither of them ever did.' He also had little respect for the inquiry: 'All sorts of tittle-tattle by criminals, by associates of criminals or by disgruntled complainants was listened to and acted upon ... I was not impressed. Wholly innocent officers were going into the pool of suspects often only on the word of rogues.'

But in 2018, documents retained by one of Countryman's most senior officers, Detective Chief Superintendent Steve Whitby, shed new light on the investigation; he had held on to the papers to demonstrate how he felt his team's efforts were thwarted. He died in 1999, but his daughter, Lynne Kerley, who kept the papers, said: 'he felt peeved that individuals were allowed to go scot-free.' The papers show that in July 1979, Whitby told Burt: 'the information we now have clearly shows that corrupt police officers have permitted criminals who are guilty of serious offences, i.e. armed robbery, to be released and not prosecuted.'

At the start of the operation, Whitby interviewed Cuthbert, who 'explained that he first became involved in corrupt deals during his secondment to the Regional Crime Squad. He said that it was a way of life and involved deals, informants, money and recovered property. Any reluctance to participate resulted in the officer leaving the squad.' Whitby's papers added that Cuthbert had said 'he was not going to be the patsy if things went wrong and he would put Mr Moore [Commander Hugh Moore of City of London police] in it as well'. He claimed Moore had received £20,000 for allowing bail during the *Daily Express* investigation. Moore, who died in 1993, strenuously denied the claim and Cuthbert said at his trial that he had been drunk when he made the accusation. In memos in 1982, Whitby wrote that Cuthbert, who was awaiting trial, initially appeared to seek help from Dorset police, but within weeks retracted the request. This suggested that Cuthbert had been offered a deal by others whereby, if he did not implicate anyone else, he would be looked after at the end of his sentence.

Home Office documents held in the National Archives underline the level of frustration felt by the Countryman officers. One document refers to Burt and his team being 'in a very depressed state. They felt that unless they were able to offer the immunities which the Director of Public Prosecutions had not, up till now, been disposed to grant, their inquiry would not succeed.' In his book, *Operation Countryman*, the former Flying Squad officer, Dick Kirby, was highly critical of the 'inept and inexperienced country policemen' but also of Moore, who, he suggested, had warned Cuthbert of the impending inquiry, 'championed the cause of officers who were thought to be crooked, denigrated those who were straight' and was 'found to be less than truthful.'

Some of the most significant inquiries into police malpractice since Operation Countryman concerned the West Midlands serious crime squad based in Birmingham and the Stoke Newington police. The former, carried out between 1989 and 1992, ended with more than a dozen cases brought by the West Midlands police being thrown out on appeal, but no officers convicted of any offences.

The focal allegation of Operation Jackpot, the Stoke Newington inquiry, between 1991 and 1993, was that officers had been involved in recycling crack cocaine and other drugs seized from dealers on Sandringham Road, north London's 'front line'. Police were also accused of fabricating and planting evidence on locals, mainly those of Jamaican origin. At the centre of the corruption was Detective Constable Roy Lewandowski, a long-haired Liverpudlian wide boy. He was arrested for stealing goods worth more than £2,000 from the victim of a brutal killing. A recluse, David Berman, had been tied up and left to die by burglars. Lewandowski, as the exhibits officer in the case, had access to the rare books in the house and had helped himself. He was gaoled for eighteen months. The Met Commissioner, Sir Paul Condon, told a House of Commons select committee that there could still be more than 200 wrong 'uns on the payroll. 'I honestly believe I command the most honourable large city police service in the world,' he said. 'However, I do have a minority of officers who are corrupt, dishonest, unethical... They commit crimes, they neutralise evidence in important cases and they betray police operations and techniques to criminals... they are very difficult to target and prosecute.'

In 1997, another of the Stoke Newington officers, Detective Constable Ronald Palumbo, was described by Judge Giles Rooke as a 'lieutenant' in a smuggling ring which operated between England and Spain and involved his father-in-law, Kenneth Harris. A large quantity of cannabis was found hidden in the trailer of a lorry owned by Harris and stopped at Dover Docks in November 1995. Palumbo said: 'I agreed to go on the trips for a break. I have been used by Harris. I had nothing to do with the drugs. If I had known about the drugs, I would have told someone.' Judge Rooke told him: 'You are what's known as a "bent copper" in an otherwise honourable force.' He was gaoled for ten years. He had previously launched an unsuccessful action for

libel against the *Guardian*, which he claimed had wrongly suggested he was corrupt.

One of the most striking cases was that of John Donald, a
detective constable with the South East Regional Crime Squad.
He was exposed by BBC's *Panorama* in 1993 after a wheeler-
dealer called Kevin Cressey, who was awaiting trial for cannabis
dealing, named him for accepting £18,000 for arranging bail and
agreeing to sabotage the case against him. Donald was gaoled for
eleven years in 1996 for corruption which his senior officer, Commander Roy Clark, described as 'acts of treachery beyond belief...
he became part of the criminal underworld which the public had
paid him to combat.' Donald emerged from prison to start a new
career as a self-employed chauffeur and pub musician.

Then in 1999, a former detective called Duncan Hanrahan,
who acted as a conduit between the underworld and corrupt officers, was gaoled for eight years after it emerged that he had
ordered drugs, stolen and resold them, arranged bribes and
plotted robberies. Initially, Hanrahan, who served in the Met for
four years before retiring on health grounds, had blown the
whistle on former colleagues when he was first arrested for trying
to bribe an officer.

'Drunken Duncan', as he was nicknamed, was regarded as the
Met's first supergrass but he lied to the anti-corruption officers
about his own continuing role. He pleaded guilty to conspiracy to
rob, steal, supply drugs and pervert the course of justice. Hanrahan, a Freemason, as were a number of other corrupt officers
within the Met, had even been part of a plot with serving officers
to rob a Lebanese businessman who was known to bring in as
much as £1 million in cash in briefcases at Heathrow airport. As
the cases of corruption had shown, one criminal commodity was
now creating temptations beyond belief.

12

DRUGS

FROM THE BRILLIANT CHANG AND FABIAN TO HOWARD MARKS AND 'COCKY' WARREN

During the First World War the Mayfair chemists Savory & Moore advertised cases containing sheets impregnated with morphine and cocaine in *The Times* as 'a useful present for friends at the front'. Barely a decade later the same drugs, 'fear-banishers' as some of the troops called them, were to provoke one of the biggest scares of the twenties. The ensuing panic led to a fear that would never be banished again.

What has been suggested as 'London's first drug bust' involved a young man called Willy Johnson, who had convictions for theft, lived with a prostitute and was arrested in 1916 for selling boxes of cocaine for 2s. 6d in the West End. There was at the time no specific drugs legislation and he was charged under the Poisons and Pharmacy Act, which only made it an offence to sell. Since he had been unsuccessful in the actual sale, he was acquitted. The law was soon to change. From 28 July 1916, under the Defence of the Realm Act, possession of cocaine and opium without prescription became a criminal offence.

The Dangerous Drugs Act was passed in 1920, but the scares began before then. As was to happen so often in the future, the involvement of a celebrity focused attention on the issue. A chorus girl called Billie Carleton, who had graduated to the lead role in *Watch Your Step* at the Empire in Leicester Square, had supposedly been introduced to opium by the club owner Jack May, who ran Murray's in Beak Street, in Soho. She soon also acquired a taste for cocaine and was supplied by a costume designer called Reggie de Veulle, who got his drugs from Lau Ping You, a Chinese man in Limehouse, and his Scottish wife, Ada.

On the night of 27 November 1918, after she had performed in *The Freedom of the Seas* and attended the Victory Ball at the Albert Hall – an event of patriotic kitsch with Lady Diana Manners playing Britannia and other celebrities playing the parts of other loyal nations from the colonies – Billie Carleton retired to her bed. Her maid went in to wake her the next day and found her dead, a little gold box half-full of cocaine on the dressing table. Arrests followed: Ada Lau Ping, described as 'the high priestess of unholy rites' by the Marlborough Street magistrate Frederick Mead, was sentenced to five months' hard labour. Lau Ping himself was only fined £10 in the belief that opium was a national vice of the Chinese and therefore understandable.

Reggie de Veulle stood trial at the Old Bailey in front of Mr Justice Salter on charges of manslaughter and conspiracy to supply cocaine. The jury cleared him of the former charge and he pleaded guilty to the latter. He was sentenced to eight months' hard labour and dispatched to Wormwood Scrubs. Marek Kohn, in *Dope Girls*, questions whether Carleton really did die of a cocaine overdose, which is extremely rare, and suggests that a more likely scenario is that she took a depressant and choked.

No matter. Following her death there was a series of newspaper articles of the sort that have now become familiar whenever the offspring of a famous person dies of drug abuse. The *Daily Express* series was a classic: 'You will find the woman dope fiend in Chelsea, in Mayfair and Maida Vale. An obscure traffic is pursued in certain doubtful teashops . . .' The *Daily Mail* told its readers: 'Men do not as a rule take to drugs, unless there is a hereditary influence, but women are more temperamentally attracted.' Voices in Parliament called for the flogging of dealers and the deportation of all Chinese.

The member of the Chinese community on whom the greatest attention focused was the man who had given evidence at the Carleton inquest: the Brilliant Chang – his real name was the less exotic Chan Nan. Born in Canton in 1887 to a merchant family, he originally worked in England as a marine contractor before opening a Chinese restaurant in Regent Street where, according to the *World Pictorial News*, he 'dispensed Chinese delicacies and the drugs and vices of the Orient'. The same paper, in a series of articles about Chang, noted that his 'obsession' with white women led him to demand to be paid for his drugs in kind. When he discovered that the women would oblige, 'the flame of evil passion burned more brightly within and he hugged himself with unholy glee'. The story, told by a 'Special Commissioner' of the paper, commended women who retained 'sufficient decency and pride of race' to turn down this fellow with 'lips thin and cruel tightly drawn across even yellow teeth'.

Chang, a short, elegant, self-confident figure who dressed in fur-collared coats and grey suede shoes, became a marked man. He was linked with the drug-related death of Freda Kempton, a young dancing teacher, and abandoned his Regent Street restaurant for the Palm Court Club in Gerrard Street, before opening the Shanghai Restaurant in Limehouse. But his Limehouse warehouse was raided, cocaine was found and he was gaoled for eighteen months in 1924. At his trial the Recorder of London told him sternly: 'It is you and men like you who are corrupting the womanhood of this country.' After he had served his time, he was deported. He was escorted by taxi from Wormwood Scrubs to Fenchurch Street station and then by train to the Royal Albert docks, where he was seen off, according to one report, by 'unhappy girls ... with dope-sunken eyes and pallid cheeks'.

Legend followed him abroad and there was a choice of stories to believe: he jumped ship in Port Said, set up a drug business in Zurich, moved to Antwerp or died blind and disgraced in Shanghai. According to the *Daily Telegraph*'s crime reporter, Stanley Firmin: 'A strange Nemesis overtook him. He went blind and ended his days not in luxury and rich silks but as a sightless worker in a little kitchen garden.'

Politicians and journalists were happy to add to the general xenophobia surrounding Chang, although not all police were convinced. 'Nutty' Sharpe described him as the most libelled of men. 'The Chinaman,' he concluded, 'is a pretty honourable fellow.' Marek Kohn suggests: 'If the ultimate menace of drugs had to be summarized in a single proposition, it would be that they facilitated the seduction of young white women by men of other races.'

The trade was essentially associated with foreigners. In 1922, Sitaram Sampatrao Gaikwar, the nephew of the Maharaja of Baroda, was arrested after he had collected a package of cocaine at Lyons Tea Shop in Waterloo, and his case was seen to symbolise both the weakness of foreigners and their involvement in the trade. Germans had been arrested importing cocaine via Newport in Wales but it was the Chinese who were suspected of bringing opium up the Thames. In 1922, the *Empire News* warned: 'Mothers would be well advised to keep their daughters as far away as they can from Chinese laundries and other places where the yellow men congregate.'

There was, however, a general uncertainty about the drugs and their effects. *The Times*, for instance, felt the need to put its readers straight on cocaine: 'Most cocainomaniacs carry revolvers to protect themselves from imaginary enemies.'

Besides the Brilliant Chang, the other main demonic figure was Edgar 'Eddie' Manning, known as 'the Villain' by police and press. Born in about 1888 in Jamaica, one story suggests that he was christened Alfred Mullin and was the son of two former slaves. The version he himself told was that his real name was Freddie Simpson. He had worked in Britain during the war in a munitions factory and played in the band at Ciro's nightclub. In 1920, he shot three men in the legs with a Colt revolver in Shaftesbury Avenue, in London's West End, after one of them had punched and insulted an actress friend, Molly O'Brien. For this he was gaoled for sixteen months. He was also damaged by association: a man called Eric Goodwin, an ex-serviceman with a drug habit, overdosed on heroin at Manning's house in 1922, which drew more attention to the Jamaican. He was eventually arrested in Primrose Hill, in north London, in possession of cocaine and opium, and a silver-topped cane that had a secret compartment for hiding drugs. He received a six-month sentence, the maximum under the 1920 Dangerous Drugs Act, and one month for possession of a firearm. The spiral had begun: in 1923, he was arrested again and gaoled this time for three years after being caught with opium and cocaine. The *News of the World* recorded the event with the headline 'Evil Negro Caught'.

In 1926, he wrote a highly fanciful account of his life in *World Pictorial News*. In this, his humble background was transformed and he claimed that he had actually come to England to study for the bar rather than work in a factory and had been seduced and corrupted by a woman he had met in a nightclub. Gaoled for three years in 1929 for possession of goods stolen from Lady Diana Cooper's car, he was described by Detective Sergeant

Powell as possibly 'the worst man in London'. He became ill in Parkhurst and was taken to the prison hospital, where he died from acute myelitis, toxaemia and heart failure on 8 February 1931.

In 1928, Britain had ratified an international agreement controlling cannabis which the Egyptian government had proposed three years earlier. However, marijuana was not considered a major issue and it was 1950 before the annual number of cannabis arrests passed the hundred mark and 1951 before the Dangerous Drugs Act, which regularised the various statutes on narcotics in a major piece of legislation, became law.

In their report on drugs to the League of Nations in 1928 the government noted that there were 620 drug addicts in Britain, 320 of them women. More than a hundred of the total were doctors. Imported drugs were carefully monitored, said the report, which recorded that 211,969 pounds (96,150 kilograms) of raw opium had been imported legally, with more than 90,000 pounds (40,800 kilograms) of raw coca leaves, 8,000 pounds (3,600 kilograms) of Indian hemp and 16,000 pounds (7,200 kilograms) of crude morphine.

The year 1928 also saw the remarkable, if exaggerated, posthumous intervention of Major Cyril McNeile, 'Sapper', the creator of Bulldog Drummond, into the world of drugs. As the *News of the World* reported it, Sapper, 'disgusted by the degenerate parasites of the West End against whom the police were powerless', had suggested in an army mess shortly before his death that 'any young man of energy' should take a tip from Bulldog and form a 'black gang' to deal with the low-lifes. These energetic young men were reported to have pounced on miscreant 'dope peddlers and other crooks' in the West End and to have taken them to a garage off the Great West Road, where they flogged them with dog whips until they promised to mend their ways. The paper reported the extent of the menace with the story of a young officer whose engagement had been broken off because his fiancée had become addicted to marijuana: 'She has been going to these cigarette orgies. It will be years before she is well.'

By the thirties attention had begun to shift to marijuana, 'the vicious drug which causes men to lose all sense of responsibility and perform the most reckless acts', as the *News of the World* described it in 1938. The case which promoted this assessment was that of a soldier, Andrew Vanderberg, who was gaoled for ten years for a series of crimes, culminating in a gun battle with the police, which he said were carried out under the influence of marijuana. A drugs squad was set up but disbanded not long after, and by 1950, the police were satisfied that drugs had practically ceased to exist except amongst foreign seamen and the new Caribbean immigrants.

It was clear how these 'coloured fellows' were regarded in some quarters: Superintendent Robert Fabian describes them in *London After Dark*, published in 1954, as 'like schoolboys ... simple folk, believe me, but they so often get bad names through the young trollopes who become their "camp followers" ... they have the brains of children, can only dimly know the cruel harm they do these teenage girls who dance with them and try thrilled puffs at those harmless-looking marijuana cigarettes'.

Fabian noted the shift from cocaine and opium to marijuana and found its market amongst the 'jazz-crazy youngsters – there is, I believe, some scientific foundation for the claim that marijuana addiction can help a musician for this drug has some effect upon that part of the brain which responds to rhythmical vibrations'. He warned the innocent of the dangers of underestimating the drug. 'Chelsea drug addicts! You wouldn't think them glamorous if you could see them as I have,' wrote Fabian. 'That pale dull young man in the frayed grey suit and duffle coat is not enjoying his beer. The middle-aged woman with dyed hair streaky with grey. She wears black corduroy trousers and a purple utility box jacket.'

Chapman Pincher of the *Daily Express* took up the theme: 'Coloured men who peddle reefers can meet susceptible teenagers at the jazz clubs.' And in 1957 *The Times* agreed that 'White girls who become friendly with West Indians are from time to time enticed to hemp smoking ... this is an aspect of the hemp problem – the possibility of its spreading among irresponsible white people – that causes greatest concern to the authorities. The potential moral danger is significant, since a principal motive of the coloured man in smoking hemp is to stimulate his sexual desire.'

The authorities did not see drugs as a major problem at this stage. Former Flying Squad Commander Frank Cater recalled that in 1959, the Drugs Squad had one car at its disposal – provided it was booked well in advance. In 1961, Sir Ronald Howe, the post-war head of the CID at Scotland Yard, wrote without irony: 'In this country drug trafficking presents a very small problem. Englishmen don't take drugs, they prefer Scotch whisky.'

Although it is easy with hindsight to smile now at the notion of drugs being virtually obsolete in Britain by the fifties, it was certainly a minor business as far as the underworld was concerned. It was left to others to supply the chaps in frayed grey suits and the gels in their black corduroy trousers. The organised criminal was still far removed from the trade.

But all that was soon to change. A new breed, who had a more romantic vision of drug smuggling than Messrs Fabian and Pincher, had arrived.

'It was a summery sort of night, very warm and balmy. There was incredible phosphorescence in the water. It was actually magical, coupled with the nervous tension of waiting and wondering whether the opposition was going to emerge from the hedgerows and bushes, whether the boat was actually going to get there. Romantic is the right word for it. It seemed to have a timeless quality. The classic scene – a deserted estuary, a sailing boat, moonlight, secrecy and I felt that I was part of a long, long tradition that stretched back for years and years, the brandy smugglers of the eighteenth century and so on. It was like something out of a Robert Louis Stevenson novel.'

Thus Charlie Radcliffe, drug smuggler. With the sixties had come the sea change for trafficking. A generation that did not get its travelling experience from National Service in Cyprus or Aden had, for the first time, the money and the time to take advantage of cheap foreign travel in Morocco or India or Peru or Thailand. Many young people tried their first joint in Tangier or their first chillum in Benares and some found it easy enough to bring small supplies back into Britain, where sniffer dogs and a drugs-alert Customs force were not yet in place.

From these young men – and a few women – came the first of the new generation of drug dealers. Many were university educated, bright, trusting and without links, at that stage, in the criminal world. For a while they could operate with apparent impunity, in the same ways as new immigrant teams of criminals; the police had no entrée into their world and did not speak their language. Their methods at first were fairly crude. The simplest hiding-place was the space below the side window of a van; drugs could be packed there without distorting the shape of the vehicle. But Customs officers soon grew wise to drivers who had difficulty in winding down their window. Dealers in Asia and North Africa used mechanics and technicians to construct an array of ingenious devices for smuggling – model elephants that were hollowed out and filled with hash, entire buses stripped down and packed with it, false-bottomed boots, tubes of toothpaste, packs of tea, delicately carved chess sets.

The growth of travel on the hippie trail, through Greece and Turkey and Afghanistan to Pakistan, India and Nepal or through Spain to Morocco, meant a constant flow of buses, which could be packed and loaded during a stopover and driven profitably home.

Cocaine was lighter and easier to carry than marijuana. Some could be coloured pink and brought in as mouthwash – although the British market proved to be as conservative about its white coke as about its white sliced bread. Mixed with distilled water, it could come in as white wine. It could be smuggled in hairbrushes and eventually, and sometimes fatally, wrapped in condoms or plastic bags and swallowed by the 'mules' who were fired at Europe from bases in Colombia, Venezuela, Nigeria, Jamaica and Peru.

There were highly publicised arrests, of Keith Richards and Mick Jagger of the Rolling Stones, who were sentenced initially to a year and three months respectively on benzedrine and cannabis charges, provoking *The Times*, only a decade after they had warned of the dangerous race-mixing effects of the drugs, to ask in an editorial by William Rees-Mogg: 'Who breaks a butterfly upon a wheel?' There was talk, too, of legalising or at least decriminalising cannabis, and in 1969, a committee under the chairmanship of Baroness Wootton recommended reducing the penalties for cannabis possession. But the establishment was not to be persuaded. The drug remained illegal and the subject of a massively expanding trade.

Radcliffe was a typical smuggler. The son of an army officer and product of a military public school, where he had smoked his first joint, he had planned a career in publishing or journalism when the opportunity to become a cannabis smuggler gradually presented itself. At that time, dealers chose different ways of operating: 'Some people took so many precautions that their lives weren't really worth living. They'd move address every few days and emerge wearing dark glasses and behaving as if they were part of some spy movie. Others were recklessly upfront. I suppose we saw ourselves in the vein of Robin Hood.'

In the late sixties the ounce price of drugs was based on a tenth of the pound price: a £100 pound of cannabis would split into sixteen £10 ounces. Lebanese drugs used to come in 200-gram sacks, muslin- or cotton-wrapped, with stamps of the Syrian army, the Palestine Liberation Organisation or the Christian Militia, depending on who controlled the passes. Army involvement was standard; the Moroccan army and police often assisted dealers to their boats with their loads.

'There was a phenomenal level of trust and comradeship across rival companies,' said Radcliffe. 'It's like antique dealers. They work together, they co-operate over certain things and other times they are fiercely competitive. When Bob Dylan sang "If you live outside the law you must be honest", it struck a very resonant chord.'

There was some heaviness, however. In the seventies a Glasgow gang descended with shotguns on a deal in Ladbroke Grove and took all the hash and money. The apocryphal tale was that retribution followed and the Lebanese importers involved cut off the robbers' hands in symbolic punishment. Smuggling by sea gradually came to seem a more sensible option than running drugs through points where there were always Customs officers. The drugs were offloaded on the shore and driven up to London in hired camper vans. The drugs would be hidden in the garage of a house in which a homeless and unsuspecting friend had been installed.

The money was good although nothing like the 'street value' given by Customs and police in court. 'The street valuation has always been a bone of contention between the forces of law and order and the forces of unlaw and disorder,' said Radcliffe. 'When you appear in court the assumption is that you bring in a ton of dope and you then cut it up into one-pound deals and sell it at your local pub and you amass this huge fortune. In reality, it is all about margins. For every one you invest, you get three back.'

As Radcliffe described it, there was a chairman of the board and shareholders who put up the money. He acted as managing director and personnel officer. The team required was around eleven people: four on the main boat doing the fortnight-long trip from Morocco using British Admiralty charts from the Second World War, two on the landing craft, one in Spain, one in Morocco, two to drive the shipment to London and one to guard it. On one occasion there was a panic when the boat went missing. 'It never occurred to me that I'd ever have the kind of embarrassing situation of ringing wives and girlfriends and saying, "I hate to tell you this, but I've a feeling your old man isn't coming home."' But although the boat had sunk, the crew survived and even managed to save some of the cargo, which was remarkable in the circumstances: 'Two were non-swimmers, they were all Londoners and I think their combined nautical experience was half an hour on the Serpentine.' Eventually, Radcliffe decided to get out but was persuaded to back that one final run. It ended like many a 'one last big job'.

'At about two o'clock in the morning there was a noise like a sledge-hammer and I said, "Who the fuck is that at this time of the morning?" A big deep voice came back: "This is the fucking Customs and Excise and if you don't come down and open this fucking door, we'll fucking knock it down with a fucking sledge-hammer." My hair was standing on end. It was Nemesis. Customs officers produced, with some pride, a scroll, a "writ of assistance", their equivalent of a search warrant. It was a scroll which began rather alarmingly "In the name of Her Majesty the Queen, greetings", which I thought was somewhat inappropriate at the time, but I was delighted to have her greetings anyway.' The Customs officers, in bulletproof vests, asked for his gun and did not believe him when he told them he was a pacifist who would not allow his children to play with guns.

The evidence compiled by what had been called 'Operation Yashmak' was enough: notes with figures, drugs hidden in the garden in screw-up drainage tubes, £10,000 in small boxes and

£40,000 stashed in a safe under the stove along with safe-deposit box keys. It was a thorough search: 'Customs showed me a photograph of one of their officers holding a goat, which belonged to a neighbour and which used to graze in our garden, by the tail with its backside slightly raised and shining a torch at it. Written on the back was "We've looked everywhere".'

Customs told Radcliffe that their arrest-conviction rate was 90 per cent and that his wife had been arrested: 'Initially, they were making, it would be unfair to call them threats, but they were saying, "The council looks after children pretty well these days, it's not so bad being in care as it used to be in Victorian times."' He agreed to make a statement if charges against his wife were dropped. On 22 October 1980, barely six months after his arrest, Radcliffe found himself confronting a different type of Victorian institution. 'I got a five-year prison sentence from a civilized sort of judge from an academic background who clearly didn't have a big thing about cannabis being the source of all evil. I think he referred to us as gentlemen smugglers, and at the time it was like something out of *Boy's Own Paper*, the sort of thing Biggles did. It had a kind of schoolboy feel about it.'

Prison followed and he met old villains who would say '"Come here, son, I want to pick your brains ..." I didn't see it as a progressive step, having a lot of people prepared to use firearms.' These were the new drug dealers, heavy-duty men who were more Jimmy Hoffa than Jimi Hendrix. 'While we were on remand they'd found a handless corpse in a quarry and I thought – God, this isn't like the Round House '66. And there were Customs officers getting shot. It seemed a different world.' So he quit. Took, as he put it, voluntary redundancy from Customs and Excise, and he concluded: 'I have a lot of regrets but then, on the other hand, I had a more interesting life than I would have had if I had stayed on the straight and narrow. It's been an adventure.' He did not go back to smuggling, working instead for twenty years in education with troubled youngsters in Dorset and as a cab driver before moving in 2000 to Valencia, in Spain, far from the recognised Costa del Crime. 'It got violent and I didn't want to be involved in that,' he said. He wrote about his life in a book called *Don't Start Me Talking – the Story of a Sixties Scapegrace.*

Another major smuggler was Surya 'Chris' Krishnarma, an Indian who owned a casino and restaurant on the Isle of Wight that were in financial difficulties. He entered the business in the early seventies because he saw cannabis smuggling as a swift way out of his problems. A married man with four children, he did not believe the drug should be illegal anyway. 'Cannabis had been used throughout history. Only the other day I was reading about an archaeological find in Israel which suggested that it was being used for pre-menstrual tension in the fourth century. I was breaking a law I believed to be bad. There were 100,000 tobacco-related illnesses and 100,000 alcohol-related illnesses, but there had not been one single cannabis-related death.'

Krishnarma started modestly enough in Morocco, buying cannabis at £40 a kilo. 'I thought of it as a great adventure. We had code words and signs, we didn't consider the dangers.' He and his associates would load a car and take the ferry from Tangier to Southampton: 'It became a well which wouldn't run dry, you just went and dipped in, your lifestyle expanded.' By now they were buying for £35–£40 a kilo in Morocco and selling for £200 a kilo in England. But they realised that there were greater profits to be made. They set up a trekking company offering cheap holidays to young people in North Africa, drove the coaches down, deposited the holidaymakers in thatched huts on the beach and then loaded the cannabis into the coach at a villa. The drugs were hidden in side-panels that could only be reached by removing all the seats, an operation that took around an hour and a half.

Krishnarma learned a lesson which might have been useful to him when, on his return from a non-drug-smuggling trip, he asked a Customs man why he was always stopped. 'He told me it was because I looked as though I had just very recently come into money. I didn't have money built into me. They could see that I wasn't quite happy with money, that I was still flashing it about.'

But cannabis smuggling was still a relatively gentle trade: 'The violence and the business, the professionality, all that came later.' An indication of this was the occasion when Krishnarma's driver telephoned to say that a London gang had broken into their hotel and had stolen the diesel van. Later, he heard that his driver was selling the supposedly stolen haul in Brighton.

'This guy said, "Do you want me to get it back?" and I said, "Well, of course we do." He said it would cost 20 kilos of canna-bis, no money. He said, "We'll just go and threaten the man." I got a call much later that same night to say, "We've got the load back, we've got the driver, do you want us to break his legs?" And I said, "No, no, no, let him go."' The gang had held the driver's girlfriend hostage and when he returned, he had agreed to take them to the stolen drugs. 'I thought – now I am well and truly in the criminal underworld.'

Arrest was not long in coming. 'Customs and Excise wanted to bring the case and they would say, "Chris, answer these questions and we will handle this, we are much better than the police." And the police would say, "Have nothing to do with Customs and Excise, we'll look after you." There was this rivalry between them.' Nineteen of the team were arrested and two turned Queen's Evidence. Arrested on 5 June 1973, Krishnarma was gaoled on 11 July the following year for ten years, one of the longest sentences of the early seventies and one of the first major police–Customs joint operations. He was to face two fur-ther sentences. 'In prison in Winchester, we were stars. We were pointed out in the exercise yard.'

Krishnarma met many armed robbers who were realising that bank robberies were increasingly hazardous and were becoming interested in the prospects of bringing 'puff' in from Morocco. The old, slightly puritanical, underworld attitude to drugs was changing – with results that could scarcely have been foreseen – and in Spain some of the ex-robbers, who knew little about the quality of drugs, tried to enlist him as an adviser. He had met Great Train Robber Charlie Wilson in Long Lartin gaol and visited him for breakfast at his villa. 'If you belong to the same club somewhere, it's likely that when you move on to some other place and you hear an old club member is there, you go and see him.' A month later, Wilson was shot dead. Krishnarma later recounted his exploits in *The Ballad of the Lazy L*. The book closed with his release as he emerged in the August sunlight at the end of the country lane on which the gaol stood: 'I did not know whether to turn left or right. What I did know was that I was not going straight.'

But the man who epitomised this era of drug smuggling in the seventies was Howard Marks, an effortlessly charming, Welsh-born Oxford physics graduate who won over everyone he met, with the eventual exception of some of the officers of the United States Drug Enforcement Administration (DEA) and a judge in a Florida court-house. In Oxford he had lived in a house that was later to be rented by an American student who had also smoked cannabis but famously 'did not inhale': Bill Clinton, who became the President of the United States.

Born in 1945 to a merchant navy father and a schoolteacher mother in Kenfig Hill, near Port Talbot steelworks in Wales, Marks had done well enough at Garw Grammar School to be accepted for Balliol College, Oxford. After graduating he drifted into drug dealing and set up an Oxford boutique called Annabe-linda's as a front for laundering his funds. Around thirty or forty friends were employed in the network. He started by bringing a ton of cannabis in a car from Frankfurt to Switzerland on behalf of an American group, for which he was paid £3,000. There was a clear attraction and, for someone who would not have objected to being a rock star, there was the compensation of being able to live like one. Marks also enjoyed the ingenuity required in working out routes from, say, Karachi to Switzerland so that cases could be shifted from plane to plane.

With an eccentric and devious Irishman called Jim McCann, who had told key people at Shannon airport that he was smuggling guns for the IRA, Marks managed to set up a new bridgehead in Ireland, placing the drugs in an industrial estate that was used for export goods and avoiding Irish Customs. The drugs were driven out piece by piece and taken to a lonely farmhouse, where they were redistributed into cars to be driven via ferry to London. The driver would be paid £2,000–£3,000 to take more than 90 kilograms of cannabis. There was no shortage of volunteers.

Marks's entrée into the world of drugs had coincided with a strange twist in his life. At the end of his university career, he was briefly recruited by MI6 through a Balliol contemporary, Hamilton 'Mac' McMillan, who thought that his friend could find out what was happening in the twilight worlds that his Bohemian charm opened to him. The intelligence service link was to have a remarkable side effect.

All went smoothly until, in 1973, Marks was arrested. 'I'd got too big for my boots, I was very arrogant.' The team had been smuggling into the United States, using sound systems for major British bands and the special Customs licences which meant that they were not subject to the usual search. A smart sniffer dog nipped at the ankles of this burgeoning enterprise: 380 kilograms of hash came into New York en route for Las Vegas, one of the speaker cabinets got left behind and was spotted by the dog on a routine patrol. The DEA moved into action. At the end of an international operation, Marks was arrested in Holland, accused of involvement in dealing in England, Holland, Italy and the United States.

For the first time he was able to play his MI6 card, telling the Customs men who came to interview him in detention that he had been asked to infiltrate IRA drugs-smuggling operations. Nonetheless, he was extradited to England and held in Brixton Prison for three weeks before being granted £20,000 bail.

The already confused saga was further complicated by the role of McCann, who lived in a netherworld between reality and fantasy, and whose claims to be an IRA man were drawing attention to the operation. Marks had meanwhile rented a house in north Oxford as he prepared for his trial. One morning in April 1974, a large man in a raincoat came to the door and asked for him. Marks emerged carrying his baby daughter and the man introduced himself in front of the landlady as being from 'Customs and Excise'. 'You'd better come with us,' he said. Marks gave the baby to the landlady and, looking shaken, departed. The forces of law and order were not to see him again for six years. Speculation about what had happened was rife: he had been abducted by the Mafia and assassinated by their hitmen, he had staged his own disappearance, he had been spirited away by MI6.

Detective Superintendent Phil Fairweather of Thames Valley police was aware of the security aspect and contacted MI6 in London. The cannabis, as a saying of the time had it, was about to hit the air-conditioner. The press, naturally enough, were intrigued. Eddie Laxton of the *Daily Mirror* was to pursue the Marks tale across the years and his first effort appeared on the front page of his paper in May 1974: 'Where Is Mr Marks? A man who vanished before an Old Bailey drug-running trial has been named to detectives as a link between an American drugs ring, the IRA Provisional and MI6 – the British secret service.'

Marks read the various newspaper reports in a hide-out on the Isle of Dogs in east London, where he was trying to grow a moustache. He was about to embark on a marathon stretch on the run. Travelling with a false passport, as a geography teacher called

McKenna, he went via Harwich to Denmark then flew to Italy and holed up in the resort of Pineta de Arenzano, a few miles north of Genoa. Streams of friends and hangers-on drifted out to visit the always hospitable Marks. But Eddie Laxton, that old sniffer dog of a reporter, was still curious. In October 1974, the *Mirror* splashed again: 'HE'S ALIVE! WHY THE MAFIA HID MARKS.'

Over the next seven years, Marks slipped in and out of Britain, disguised and running under the *nom de guerre* of Albi, sometimes Albion, Jennings. The surname was in honour of the American country singer Waylon Jennings, who was one of the 'outlaw' breed of singers taking on the conservative Nashville establishment, and also of an old scallywag called Albert in Kenfig Hill. Marks lay low, spending a summer in camping-sites, where he always pitched his tent near the toilets so as to be close to the telephone.

The drug-smuggling machine soon started moving again. He set up a 315-kilogram deal for Pakistani hash to be brought by sea from Karachi to Dubai and thence to Rome. The money flowed in. Marks travelled the world with three different identities, setting up nine deals over the next eighteen months – the largest a 5-ton shipment – and keeping one or two moves ahead of the authorities. He returned to Britain, under the name of Albert Lane, for the birth of his second daughter in Wimbledon in October 1977. He seemed untouchable. He would pop up at parties and even sing Elvis Presley songs in the Nashville pub in Hammersmith. He was the bubbles in the champagne of many a media party and enjoyed playing the part of the Velvet Pimpernel. He went to Thailand to invest in the newly-profitable Thai sticks, which were stronger than hashish and had been a favourite with American servicemen enjoying rest and recreation from the Vietnam War in Bangkok hotels.

'I was a fugitive for six and a half years, and I smuggled as much cannabis as I could. I felt that this was my destiny, this was my karma. I suppose I felt like a prizefighter. One day, one's going to get knocked out on the canvas. You have to carry on until you're beaten.' The quantities smuggled were enormous, Marks taking the view that a car was as likely to be stopped by police as a container lorry.

Meanwhile the dealing and smuggling world was changing. People from the supplier countries like the Lebanon, Pakistan and Morocco wanted a greater involvement in Europe by taking part in the whole operation. Diplomats were able to use their immunity to act as smugglers, almost untouched. Marks was ready for the big one, a job that was to make him £1 million and involved shipping drugs from Aruba Island off Colombia over to Scotland's Western Isles on New Year's Eve, 1979.

The front on this occasion was to be a film company called Worldwide Entertainments, which provided a good excuse for large vehicles and odd movements. It was going to make a 'semi-documentary film located in the Western Isles and set in the latter half of the last century'. It was about Freud and had all the necessary props in terms of cameras, lights, even a genuine film director.

In truth, Marks and his associates were enacting a far more remarkable tale than any nineteenth-century yarn they could have dreamed up. New York heavies, ex-CIA men, were waiting to offload what would make the team's fortunes from two 12-metre yachts, *Bagheera* and *Salambo*. The engines of the three-ton lorry were cut so that it would not attract attention before it hit the main road. There was a police car on the road and an officer emerged. Marks approached him and said he was a film-maker checking the light for a dawn shoot. The policeman amiably inquired if he had any petrol he could borrow and Marks obliged.

The operation was immaculately planned. Black rubber Zodiac dinghies shipped the drugs from the mother vessels to the Scottish shore on Loch Linnhe. Fifteen tons came ashore and the team of fifteen or sixteen, all furiously smoking dope, unloaded in forty-five minutes. The cannabis was stored at four different warehouses – two in Scotland, one in Essex and one in Northamptonshire.

One of the hauls had to be jettisoned in Scotland after a panic over a message heard on the radio. Bales of marijuana surfaced off Kerrera in Scotland and were washed up on the shore, provoking apocryphal tales along the lines of Sir Compton Mackenzie's *Whisky Galore*, in which a consignment of whisky is shipwrecked off the island of Barra. There were stories of cannabis galore, including one of farmers feeding their hens the strange substance and of the resultant laidback hens.

But the Colombian and American ends of the operation were becoming anxious that their shipment was not moving fast enough, certainly not at the rate of American shipments. They started to make their own inquiries: 'This was simply mad,' according to Marks. 'In the end they approached a man who turned out to be a Customs informant and that is how it all got discovered. Just impatience really.'

In 1980, Customs searched the room in the Dorchester hotel in London, where the syndicate pair – the American end of the operation – were staying and found a Knightsbridge number for 'Albi'. Arrest and the seizure of around ten tons of cannabis followed. When Marks booked himself and his girlfriend, Judy Lane, into the Swan in Lavenham, in East Anglia, he noticed that there were two young men at the bar. As he ordered a sherry, one of the young men, Higher Executive Officer of Customs and Excise, Nicholas Baker, leaned over. 'He said, "Can I have a look at your watch?" and he was putting handcuffs on me at the same time.'

The following day the newspapers reported the arrests of those alleged to have been involved in Britain's largest-ever cannabis haul. But Howard Marks was not dead yet. He still had his MI6 card to play. It might be tattered, it might be rough round the edges, but it might still be an ace.

The trial started in 1981 with Marks and his colleagues in the dock in Court Six of the Old Bailey. It was reported in the *Sun* under the headline: 'Eggheads Ran £20 million Drug Ring'. The *Daily Mail* recorded that 'An Oxford graduate was the master-mind in a brainy gang.' The case seemed so overwhelming that Marks had been prepared to plead guilty for a seven- or eight-year sentence, something the judiciary would not contemplate, stating that the matter was so serious it would have to go to full trial.

Howard's charm spilled over the dock and into the jury benches. One of the jurors even drew a heart as she doodled her way through the evidence. When he was asked by the stern judge, Mr Justice Peter 'Penal Pete' Mason, why he was smiling, Marks replied: 'I still try to smile although I have spent the last eighteen months in prison. It is the only way of dealing with adversity and is in no way smugness or contempt.'

When it looked as though the case was slipping away from Marks, there arrived to give evidence a mysterious Latin Ameri-can. He claimed to be a member of the Mexican security police involved in anti-terrorism and his mission and his work were so secret that the court had to be cleared of press and public. He told the jury that he had paid Marks $150,000 for his help in setting up a contraband and drugs deal that would assist Mexico's anti-terrorist work. He could not give his name or further details of his work 'for security reasons'. It worked. Marks was acquitted despite Crown Counsel John Rogers's entreaties to the jury to dismiss the tale as rubbish. The joker had proved to be the ace.

'It was obviously such a nonsensical story,' said Marks. 'I'm sure the jury didn't believe it really, they were just looking for an ex-cuse not to consign me to years and years in prison. I had to some-how link up MI6 with the Mexican secret service if such a thing exists, a really bizarre story. Someone came over from Mexico who was a genuine government employee, to do with law enforce-ment, and confirmed that I had indeed worked for the Mexican secret service but that he wasn't allowed to give any details. As far as I know, they don't exist.'

He pleaded guilty to the earlier charge for which he had fled and was given a three-year sentence, which meant that he was free again in a matter of months because of the amount of time he had spent on remand.

Eventually, however, he was tracked down on 25 July 1988 in Palma, Majorca, by a team led by the Drug Enforcement Administration man Craig Lovato, who had become obsessed with the case, possibly after reading Howard's indiscreet account of events in David Leigh's book, *High Times*. The British, American, Spanish and Canadian police and Customs forces combined to snare him.

One of his Judases was the unlikely figure of a *louche* remittance man, Lord Moynihan, the half-brother of the former Conservative Party minister Colin Moynihan. Marks and the peer had discussed setting up a cannabis plantation on an island off the Philippines, where Lord Moynihan worked as a sort of corporate pimp, running massage parlours staffed by young Filipinas. Faced with the possibility of imprisonment, Lord Moynihan made a deal with the authorities to tape-record conversations with Marks which would establish the latter's drug-dealing intentions. He died not long afterwards.

Marks was faced with the choice of fighting the case and running the risk of a gaol sentence of sixty years to life, or pleading guilty and receiving a shorter term. His wife was held in custody mainly, he believed, to put pressure on him to plead guilty as their three young children were at that stage deprived of both their parents. Extradited to the US, he duly pleaded to cannabis importation charges at Palm Beach Federal Court in Florida and was sentenced to twenty-five years. He was moved to serve his term at the high-security federal penitentiary in Terre Haute, Indiana, where he taught English grammar to the inmates and philosophy in evening classes to Mafia men, members of the Colombian cartels and the Corsican Laurent Fiocconi, one of the surviving players of the real-life French Connection team.

His sentence was reduced on appeal to twenty years and, to his surprise, he was released in 1995 after completing a third of his time and bundled at gunpoint on to a plane back to England. Just before he left the penitentiary, he heard the noise of the construction work on a death cell being prepared in which not only murderers but also drug smugglers who had imported more than a hundred tonnes of cannabis could be lethally injected. He returned to Spain in time to celebrate his fiftieth birthday and to begin work on his memoirs. Back in Palma with his family, he told anyone who could trace the missing millions that he was said to have stashed away that if they found the money, they could keep it.

He reckoned to have made and spent $2–$3 million during his smuggling years. 'For a long time I conned myself into thinking that I was only breaking the law because the law was foolish,' he said after his release. 'I do sincerely believe that the law is foolish but I do think I would have gone that way anyway ... If I was living in Saudi Arabia, I would have opened up a bar.'

He set about writing *Mr Nice,* a frank autobiography which sold more than a million copies. He also did one-man shows, telling anecdotes, joint in hand, to sell-out theatre audiences, many of whom had not been born when he was arrested. More books, both factual and fiction, followed. In 2010, *Mr Nice* became a film, directed by Bernard Rose and starring Marks's friend, Rhys Ifans, in the title role. After being diagnosed with inoperable cancer, he gave what was effectively a farewell performance to a packed house at the Forum in London in 2015 and the supporting cast included Ifans, singer Cerys Matthews and the Alabama Three, whose song, 'Woke Up This Morning' was the theme tune for *The Sopranos* television series and whose band members included train robber Bruce Reynolds's son, Nick. Marks died the following year.

While Marks's cannabis enterprise was taking off, an equally complex and ambitious effort was being put into the production of LSD – acid. It came to an end when one of the conspirators, Henry Todd, walked to his front door, which was quivering under a barrage of blows. He unlocked it and stepped back to dodge a swinging sledge-hammer wielded by a plainclothes police officer: 'I suppose you've come about the television licence,' he said.

Alas for Mr Todd, no. On 26 March 1977, Inspector Dick Lee and his team discovered six million tablets of acid and carried out a series of arrests of the team that was manufacturing and distributing them. It was the largest such police operation ever mounted in Europe. Code-named 'Operation Julie' after Sergeant Julie Taylor, one of the officers on the case, it had involved hundreds of police, many acting undercover.

The conspirators were a diverse crew. Dick Kemp, who was producing some of the purest acid ever manufactured, had been educated at Bedford Grammar School, St Andrews University and Liverpool University, where he gained his Bachelor of Science degree in 1966. He had moved in with Christine Bott, who had graduated in medicine at Liverpool University. Brian Cuthbertson was the son of a civil servant. A Reading University mathematics drop-out, his travels throughout the world had given him a wide range of contacts if no visible means of support. Henry Todd brought his entrepreneurial and organisational skills to the operation. The son of an RAF squadron leader, Todd had two A-levels and a theft and false pretences conviction; he was a keen mountain climber, played rugby for a London Scottish side, and had worked as an accountant. (Todd found himself back in court in 2006 in a bizarre private prosecution case for manslaughter brought against him by the wealthy father of a young City trader who died on an Everest expedition, for which Todd had supplied the oxygen. The judge dismissed the case, saying 'If ever a criminal charge should be emphatically dismissed, this is it.') The

American in the group, David Solomon, had come to Britain in 1967 and had met Kemp two years later.

The main point was that these people and their associates were not from what was normally seen as the criminal underworld. They had only one previous conviction between them, they were brains not muscle, and there was no fire power. When arrested, many made full, detailed confessions, far removed from the world of 'no comment until I've seen my brief'. They shared a common interest in the properties of drugs and the operation was never set up solely as a commercial enterprise. Kemp started producing LSD in about 1971 in flats rented in London. Todd brought in a group of friends centred around Reading University, including Brian Cuthbertson, Russell Spenceley and Nigel Fielding. Internal problems caused a split in the team and Kemp and Bott moved to Plas Llysin, in Wales, in 1974.

Nigel 'Leaf' Fielding, who produced and distributed the tablets, recalled their original motivation: 'We began as idealists who had seen much wrong in human affairs. We thought we had found a non-violent means of effecting great changes in the world – changes that would, we believed, be of lasting benefit to the human race. As psychic guerrillas, we willingly risked our liberty in the pursuit of a global expansion in consciousness.' This was not exactly how Mr Justice Park was eventually to see it when he sat in judgement on them.

The operation had some strange side effects. In the course of searching the London laboratory where spillage had saturated a carpet, three of the officers had ingested LSD. Their depositions indicated their puzzlement, amusement and fear at what happened: in the pub after the search one of them thought his pint was too heavy to lift, another became fascinated with the foam on his glass and a third hid behind a pillar. Unable to reverse their car out of the pub parking lot, they walked back to the laboratory pointing out to each other, as Fielding says, 'the thousand mysteries of the southwestern suburbs'. They were found collapsed with hysterical laughter watching *Jesus of Nazareth* on television and taken to Kingston hospital.

Kemp and Todd were gaoled for thirteen years, Cuthbertson for eleven, David Solomon and Russell Spenceley for ten, Christine Bott for nine, Fielding for eight and others for sentences that in all totalled 124 years. They were released during the eighties and disappeared into more normal occupations – in the City, computing, publishing. One became a police surgeon.

Both Dick Lee, who led the 'Operation Julie' inquiry, and Craig Lovato, who hunted Howard Marks, expressed a grudging admiration for their quarry. Lee described the gaoling of Kemp as a 'waste of genius ... where might he have gone but for his warped ideals'.

But by the late seventies the business of drug dealing was already changing. There was too much money for it to be left to people who liked playing Grateful Dead music and reading Hermann Hesse. The headbands were giving way to the head-cases. Drugs were to become the major criminal currency and to bring with them much violence, a period that was to see violent deaths and shootings.

One dealer who made his money in the seventies and early eighties recalls the moment when he and his team realised that the game was changing: 'A Customs guy stopped a lorry, opened the door and got shot. It was a great shock. We thought: "Who are these guys? What's happening? We'd better all look for another way of earning a living."'

It was 19 October 1979 and the man shot dead was Customs investigator Peter Bennett, who was attempting to arrest Leonard 'Teddy Bear' Watkins on the Commercial Road in Stepney, east London. He was the first Customs officer to be killed on duty in 182 years. It was the culmination of 'Operation Wrecker' which, with a force of 120 officers, was targeted at a major cannabis-smuggling scheme that brought 'Paki black' in from Karachi.

Bennett was shot with a Beretta and his colleague Detective Sergeant John Harvey of the Hampshire drug squad was wounded as Watkins attempted to escape before being felled with the aid of a pensioner who hit him about the head with a walking stick.

The architect of the scheme was said to have been Colin 'The Duke' Osbourne, a flash dresser who had met Watkins, along with two other drug smugglers, in Maidstone Prison. In fact, Osbourne's role was probably no larger than that of his colleagues. Watkins, who had been serving a three-year sentence for a supermarket robbery, ran a straight transport operation after his release under the name of Edward Bear Motors – which gave him his 'Teddy Bear' nickname – in Fareham, Hampshire. Container lorries were fitted with false floors and dispatched to the Indian subcontinent ostensibly with sanitary goods for sale in Pakistan, returning with cheap sports shoes for sale in Britain. After each operation, the lorries were cut up and disposed of. By the time they were caught the team had, police estimated, made about £10 million, although this seems almost certainly an exaggeration. The quality of their cannabis was high, however, and they embossed it with the Rolls-Royce emblem and a gilded treble seven motif, the international gambling symbol for the jackpot.

On what Customs believed was the fifth such trip, Watkins was driving a lorry from Felixstowe docks and was being shadowed by Bennett. He was unable to throw him off and was in London's Docklands, attempting to hide the load, when he stopped to make a check call to his colleagues and was told that an orange van would arrive to guide him to a hide-out. At this moment, Bennett approached him and was fatally shot. Inside the lorry were two sawn-off shotguns and some ammunition, which Watkins unsuccessfully claimed was there merely as a means for him to commit suicide, if caught. His defence was that he thought Bennett and Harvey were part of a rival gang.

Gaoled for life at Winchester Crown Court in November 1980 with a recommendation that he serve a minimum of twenty-five years, 'Teddy Bear' cheerily told the judge and police: 'You win the battle but you won't win the war. I hope you die screaming of cancer.' Lesser members of the gang – Brian Bird who had been the 'overseas manager', Graeme Green and James Johnson – were gaoled for six, six and five years respectively for their part in the smuggling. Osbourne was never caught. Six weeks after the shooting, he was found dead on Hackney Marshes. An inquest recorded an open verdict but former associates say he died of a heart attack and was kept in a deep-freeze while his colleagues decided what to do with him.

The quantities seized by police and Customs grew ever larger and the smuggling methods more ingenious. In January 1991, a van supposedly carrying inert nuclear waste samples from the Dounreay power station was stopped by a policeman in Newtonmore, in Scotland. Inside, in cellophane and Gucci wrappers, was 500 kilograms of cocaine worth, it was said in court later, £101 million. So ended 'Operation Klondyke'.

For more than a year Scottish Customs officers posing as fish farmers, tourists and film crews had been following the smugglers, who were mainly young Scots who had met while working on the oil rigs. The smugglers had taken their work seriously and had memorised the faces of all the officers who appeared in a documentary series on Customs work called *The Duty Men*. To no avail. The four men who were caught were gaoled for a total of fifty-seven years. Chris Howarth, a Yorkshireman who lived in Ullapool, received twenty-five years. The case demonstrated that the Scottish Highlands and Islands, with 4,000 miles of coast and 700 separate islands, offered fabulous opportunities for sea-smugglers.

One Highland cannabis smuggler, Boyd Keen, gaoled for eight years in the mid-eighties, described the experience in almost lyrical terms: 'I took my old harmonica out and gave the distant Africa coast a burst of "Leaving Port Askaig" and followed it with the jaunty air of "John D. Burgess of Coll". Both tunes written by men leaving old familiar places, men going out into the unknown to face their future.' Keen soon discovered that one of the disadvantages of taking the high road was the heavy sentencing policy of Scottish judges.

In England, barely a month seemed to pass without new record seizures or record gaol sentences passed, although neither seizure nor sentence seemed to dent the market, whether for the old (cannabis) or the new (Ecstasy).

On 28 May 1993, the country's largest Ecstasy trial concluded with sentences of ten years for Thomas Slater, eight and a half for his son Zachary and six for Gary Eales. Slater senior was ordered to pay £600,000 of his profits under the Drugs Trafficking Offences Act in a trial that had lasted twenty weeks and had itself run into millions of pounds. A new generation of drugs trials had started. As cannabis smuggler Derek Maughan said: 'A lot of younger guys come up today who didn't come up the way the older criminal did, by being a thief or a fence or whatever. Now all of a sudden, they're buying three or four thousand Ecstasy pills in Holland and getting £15 or £20 a time for them. They're making bundles of money. They're millionaires at twenty-three.'

But more significantly, perhaps, the old robbers had already moved emphatically into the game. In August 1989, the Great Train Robbers Tommy Wisbey and Jimmy Hussey were both gaoled for cocaine dealing. Mr Justice Robert Sanders, sentencing them at Snaresbrook Crown Court in east London, said: 'You are both old enough and experienced enough to know exactly what you were doing and your motive was greed.'

Wisbey explained: 'We were against drugs all our lives but as the years went on, towards the seventies, it became more and more the "in" thing. Being involved in the Train Robbery, our name was good. They knew we had never grassed anyone, we had done our time without putting anyone in the frame ... But it's another ten years out of my life.'

Frank Simms, a robber from Stratford, in east London, who had been gaoled for fifteen years for the 1972 £400,000 silver bullion robbery at Mountnessing, in Essex, was one 'face' who saw the attractions of drugs. He financed one of Britain's largest amphetamine operations from a Hertfordshire cottage and was gaoled for thirteen years after a police raid in November 1990 uncovered the laboratory.

'In the sixties if you were a drug-taker, you could never be a proper thief,' said Simms, who became a keep-fit fanatic in gaol. 'It wasn't accepted.' But that had all changed by the time Simms saw the chance of fast profits in the speed business. He was accused of supplying 40 per cent of the amphetamines in the country and running a £200-million operation, a proposition he dismissed as ridiculous, citing the tendency of the authorities to exaggerate the worth of drugs hauls. But he agreed he was fairly caught, attributing to the police 'more strokes than a cat o' nine tails' and ruing a cocaine habit which he thought made him nastier and affected his judgement.

He said that some of the team he was financing were taking advantage of him, making money behind his back: 'It's all going to pot. There's no loyalty. The youngsters are probably looking at us saying "Look at that silly old sod." We're like the old Dad's Army.'

Other underworld names have been weighed off in the nineties. In October 1990, Eddie Richardson was gaoled for twenty-five years for his part in a multi-million-pound cocaine- and cannabis-smuggling operation. The judge, Mr Justice Schiemann, at Winchester Crown Court, told him: 'It was a terrible crime. It would not be fanciful to liken it to spraying bullets into a crowd.' Under the Drugs Trafficking Offences Act a confiscation order for £356,979 was slapped on him. Richardson and his colleagues were alleged to have tried to bring in 153 kilograms of cocaine and two tons of cannabis worth £6 million in a balsawood container shipped to Southampton. His sentence did not surpass the longest in a drug-smuggling case – that given to Paul Dye, who was gaoled for twenty-eight years in 1986 for heroin smuggling.

In October 1992, Joey Pyle, the enigmatic figure who had popped up in the history of the underworld so many times, found himself in the Old Bailey on a drugs charge. The man who had been present during the Pen Club killing in 1960, who had shared drinks and jokes with Charlie Richardson, who had acted for the Krays, but who had walked free from many cases, was caught on a heroin and morphine sulphate charge. At the age of fifty-six, he was gaoled for fourteen years after being caught in a classic sting in which undercover officers infiltrated his own office staff.

One of his co-defendants was Pete Gillett, the adopted son of Reg Kray, whom Gillett had met in Parkhurst. Gillett had been hoping for a career as a pop singer and had even recorded a song called 'Masquerade' that Reg had written for him. Pyle, who had show-business connections and an office at Pinewood Studios, was helping to relaunch his career.

In April 1993, Robert Tibbs of the Tibbs family, described in court as a company director now based in Suffolk, was gaoled for eight years for a one-and-a-quarter-ton cannabis shipment that had made its way from Morocco to Oban on the west coast of Scotland. He was ordered to pay £200,000 under the DTOA or alternatively face another three years inside.

The person who was to rewrite the underworld's rule book on drug dealing was a street-smart Liverpudlian called Curtis Warren, better known by his nicknames 'Cocky' or 'the Cocky Watchman'. Born in 1963, his criminal career started at the age of twelve with a conviction for car theft and by sixteen he was on his way to Borstal for assaulting the police. Other offences followed but it was only when he moved into the drugs business that he established his reputation as one of the most prolific traffickers of modern times, Interpol's 'Target One' and the subject of a joint British–Dutch investigation code-named Operation Crayfish. This led, in October 1996, to the seizure in the Netherlands of 400 kilos of cocaine, 60 kilos of heroin, 1,500 kilos of cannabis, handguns and false passports. Nine Britons and a Colombian were arrested and Warren was soon portrayed as the biggest fish in the net.

While Warren's move to Amsterdam, where fellow-dealers had also established themselves, seemed like a smart idea in that he was less exposed to the British police, it was also a weakness, because the Dutch authorities were able to tap his phone without restriction and secure the evidence they needed. (Although they also required English help in translating 'Liverpudlian' for them.) He was gaoled for twelve years for a conspiracy to import what was claimed to be £125 million of drugs into Britain. The *Observer* suggested he was 'the richest and most successful British criminal who has ever been caught' and he was the only drugs dealer to make it onto the *Sunday Times* Rich List. T-shirts with an old mug-shot of Warren on them were still for sale in Liverpool twenty years after Crayfish.

Held in Nieuw Vosseveld gaol, which had been a Nazi prisoner-of-war camp, Warren found himself facing further charges in 1999 after he kicked to death a Turkish inmate who attacked him. The dead man, Cemal Guclu, serving time for killing a woman, had supposedly hurled unprovoked abuse at Warren in the prison yard and tried to punch him. Warren pleaded self-defence, was convicted of manslaughter and had four years added to his sentence.

After his release from gaol in the Netherlands in June 2007, Warren was only a free man for five weeks. He followed a girl-friend to Jersey but was under constant surveillance and soon arrested. In 2009, he was convicted of conspiring to import

£1 million of cannabis into Jersey and gaoled for thirteen years. A Jersey court then ordered him to pay £198 million after he failed to prove he had not earned that amount from his cocaine trafficking in the 1990s; Warren was alleged to have invested his wealth in everything from petrol stations to vineyards, football clubs to hotels. Detectives had secretly recorded him boasting during a 2004 prison visit of funnelling huge amounts of cash via a money launderer. 'Fuckin' 'ell, mate, sometimes we'd do about £10 million or £15 million in a week,' he told some of his visitors. 'I was bragging like an idiot and just big-talking in front of them,' was Warren's explanation later. The Jersey attorney general, Timothy Le Cocq, QC, described him as 'one of Europe's most notorious organised criminals.' His failure to pay the money resulted in a further ten years' gaol time.

He told *Guardian* journalist Helen Pidd, when she interviewed him in gaol in Jersey, that he disapproved of drugs: 'I've never had a cigarette in my life, or a drink. I've never tasted alcohol or anything. No interest.' His ambition after he was freed was to leave England – 'and never come back.' He added: 'I just wish I'd not been such a worry to me mum ... I've had a great mother and father – not known much of him – but a great mother, intelligent, educated. My sister's been to university, brother used to play chess for Wales, sister's got a degree in maths, physics and statistics.' And he would have liked, in another life, to have been a lawyer.

Few people were better qualified to comment on Warren than Tony Saggers, the former head of Drugs Threat and Intelligence for the NCA and an expert witness in Warren's trial and proceeds hearing. 'Curtis Warren was a forerunner,' he said. 'You get people like him who come from a tough background, a council house environment, and he had a sort of bare-faced courage in some respects to put himself in places like Venezuela and Colombia, which were probably even more dangerous then than they are now. He put himself at the other end of the supply chain and in a way established that pattern for the elite drug trafficker. But nowadays high-level, high-profile criminals play less and less of a role and make use of others below them in a detached way.'

Whereas twenty years ago only half a dozen nationalities might have been involved in major drug trafficking into the UK, that had now changed. 'At the last count at least thirty nationalities were involved in cocaine trafficking alone and, if you include synthetic drugs being produced in the Netherlands and China, for instance, the figure is much higher.' The fact that many nationalities – and their criminals – spoke English as a second language was a key factor. English was now the *lingua franca* of the international underworld. 'We're lazy in languages and the world speaks English and that correlates across organised crime which, in turn, allows them to have access to the UK,' said Saggers.

Regarding cybercrime and the part that the internet now played in drug trafficking, he said: 'There is a danger that there is too much concentration on the dark net. There is a generational aspect to it in that the young user, who is used to eBay and Amazon, uses it but a snapshot would indicate that no more than 1 per cent is bought on the internet – which is still quite a big figure. But the culture in Britain is that people still like to see the people they buy from. It is a dealer-to-user society, they like that platform of trust.'

As to the level of violence within the drugs world, he said: 'At the low levels it is much more violent than before. It is now extremely rare to execute a search warrant for drugs and not find guns or knives.' The majority of the violence was in London and the larger cities. 'Often mindless tit-for-tat incidents and often over almost nothing but there are also many incidents where the drug trade and competition play a part.'

Perhaps the most publicised development in drug dealing within Britain in the new millennium was that of the so-called 'County lines' phenomenon, a phrase that, like so much of the drugs jargon, had come from the United States. Said Saggers: 'The business model exports these drugs from saturated competitive urban city hubs – starting from London – into county towns and smaller cities. The method is predominantly used by gangs, with adult members often grooming and recruiting children and young people to run the drugs and cash in and out of the new markets.' He said that the system exploited mainly the young and vulnerable by offering them more money than they would get in low-paid jobs.

By the new millennium, the United Kingdom had established itself as second only to the US as a drugs market and by 2007, Home Office research concluded that there were 300 major traffickers, 3,000 middle market wholesalers and 70,000 street dealers in action. As Max Daly and Steve Sampson put it in their book, *Narcomania*, the market was by now dominated by 'Mr Middles' rather than 'Mr Bigs', the old pyramid of supply having changed. With an end of apprenticeships and high youth unemployment for people without qualifications, drug dealing became, for some, a logical career choice.

Gary Sutton, of the drugs advice organisation Release, founded in Notting Hill in 1968 by Caroline Coon and Rufus Harris because so many young people were being arrested, said that the rules of the drug-dealing game had changed. 'In the past, if a deal disappeared it would be written off as a business expense, but now if you lose it, you're responsible. It would once have been wiped out as a loss, now you've got to pay for it.' He said that rival gangs now monitored each others' couriers with tracking devices.

The home-grown cannabis market, whether through organised, Vietnamese-run farms or discreet amateurs, had mushroomed. 'There are so many tutorials online that explain how to grow cannabis that it is quite easy to do,' said Sutton. 'There are now 33 different varieties or grades of cannabis and the same sort of snobbery about the quality as there is in the wine market.' He was unconvinced by the notion of 'County lines': 'You would think suppliers from the major metropolises and ports had never shifted out of their postcodes before!' he said. 'I'm sceptical about the Dickensian aspect of using kids as couriers/sex slaves. A glance around the estates of lower-income areas will reveal no shortage of poorly parented kids involved at the lowest end of the supply chain.'

Symbolic perhaps of the significance of the illicit drugs trade was the appointment in 2018 of Max Daly as the global drugs editor of *Vice*, the online magazine, the first but surely not the last such appointment. (In the 1970s, the underground paper, *International Times*, had a drugs correspondent called 'Maybelle', whose column was so well-informed and accurate that the police who periodically raided the paper's Soho offices were always curious as to who the author might be and how he or she knew so much. It was, in fact, Peter Mond, better known as Lord Melchett, the free-spirited one-time Labour minister, who died in 2018.)

Daly pointed out how the whole structure of drugs dealing had changed from the days of the underworld's first involvement, not least through the internet. 'Synthetics is the new kid on the block,' said Daly. 'You don't need old-school contacts if you have contacts with the Chinese labs. You can be a student at Leeds University and become an international drugs trafficker.' His words were borne out by the conviction in 2010 of an unlikely underworld figure in the shape of the enigmatic David Wain. He was gaoled for twelve years at Reading Crown Court as the first wholesale chemical supplier to be convicted of encouraging offences under the 2007 Serious Crime Act. A west Londoner and an accountant by profession, Wain ran his business from his flat and his unknowing mother's garage and imported tonnes of the chemicals, such as the anaesthetic benzocaine, used by dealers to mix with cocaine and increase their profit margins. He supplied dealers in Bournemouth, Sheffield, Liverpool, Cardiff and Glasgow and was thought to have made around £400,000 a year. The judge who sentenced him described the quantities of chemicals supplied as 'mind-boggling'.

The underworld had diversified in other ways, too, with extensive networks throughout the whole of the British Isles. For instance, Mohammed Qasim in his book *Young, Muslim and Criminal* examined the existence of British Pakistani men arrested for drug dealing in the wake of a Bradford-based network of thirty-five men being gaoled for a total of nearly 200 years for smuggling heroin. In one of the related trials, the judge Roger Thomas, QC, said that 'street dealing in heroin and crack cocaine was so commonplace in parts of Bradford it was almost considered the "social norm".' Qasim reported how the younger dealers – 'the Kids' – 'saw eastern Europeans who were moving into the area as potential customers, conversing with them, asking them if they wanted to buy any drugs – "I got dobra (Polish for good thing) for you" – whenever they recognised any of them.' Yorkshire had come to prominence through the gaoling for nine years for drugs conspiracy in 2014 of Mohammed Azam Yaqoob of Dewsbury, who was known as 'Mr Sparkles' because of his carwash business. Heroin was being smuggled to Yorkshire from Pakistan in everything from Afghan rugs to baby powder and chapatti ovens.

The old adage that the only certainties in life are death and taxes was particularly true of the drugs trade. Just as the gangsters of the mid-twentieth century made much of their money from extortion, so did some of their successors enrich themselves by 'taxing' drug dealers, knowing that their victims would be unlikely to go to the police. One of the most violent of those was Stephen French, a kick-boxing champion and associate of Warren's, who rejoiced under the title 'the Devil'. His eponymous memoir opens with a description of how he tortured one dealer with a red-hot iron applied to his genitals in order to 'tax' him for £320,000 and 20 kilos of cocaine.

French eventually went into legitimate debt-collecting and the book ended with a claim that he was now a reformed character who sought only to bring peace to Liverpool. A few years later, however, in 2013, he was gaoled for three years for pistol-whipping a businessman with a replica gun, which he then dumped in the Mersey along with a machete. He apologised for this lapse with an open letter to 'the whole of Merseyside' signed 'ST French, formally the Devil, now the Fighting Preacher'.

Prisons became an increasingly profitable market for drugs sales with some even being delivered by drone. In 2018, seven members of a gang that used drones to airlift £500,000 worth of drugs into prisons were gaoled at Birmingham Crown Court. They had managed to fly drugs into seven different gaols, including HMP Birmingham and HMP Liverpool. *Vice* reported that such was the value of the prison market that some offenders out on licence were 'deliberately committing crime so they can go back to gaol with Kinder Egg capsules full of the stuff hidden up their arses.' Particularly popular was the synthetic cannabinoid, Spice, also known as Mamba, Smeg or Bird Killer, which had gained its initial popularity in young offenders' institutions before spreading throughout the country. Such was the proliferation of the drug in some provincial cities that the vehicle frequently despatched to aid its discombobulated victims became known as the 'Mambulance'.

The old criminal families and gangs were now linked to the new world of drugs. For many of them, the real money was no longer in safes or security vans with all the attendant risks of capture. Drugs could provide a far steadier, if less spectacular, income. But for some the old lure of that one massive job lingered on.

13

BIG HITS

BULLION AND SAFE DEPOSITS

The young radio enthusiast sitting by his equipment in Wimpole Street, in London's West End, one weekend in September 1971 pricked up his ears. Robert Rowlands was tuned in to a group of men and a woman talking about what appeared to be a major bank robbery in which they were, improbably, engaged as they spoke. 'We have all got 300 grand to cut up when we come back in the morning,' said one voice. Another, apparently that of the look-out man, complained that he was tired. 'My eyes are like organ stops, mate,' he said. What was under way was the theft of the Baker Street branch of Lloyds Bank and Rowlands had a front row seat to what was unfolding.

The thieves had taken over a neighbouring handbag shop, tunnelled their way through the dividing walls and broken into the bank's safety deposit boxes. The gang's look-out man, using a walkie-talkie, was perched on the roof of the building opposite, ready to alert his colleagues if the police appeared. Rowlands tried his best to contact the police to tell them what was happening but found it hard to convince them. When uniformed officers eventually arrived, according to Rowlands, 'They were grinning. It was like a scene from a Peter Sellers' film.'

This was to become known as the Baker Street Bank Job, later to become a film, *The Bank Job*, starring Jason Statham and Saffron Burrows. Four of the gang were eventually gaoled in 1973 for a total of forty-eight years and £231,000 was recovered but, since much of the loot was in safety deposit boxes, the true scale of the theft would never be known. Many a wild rumour accompanied the heist. One tale was that it had been carried out at the behest of MI5, who wanted to get hold of compromising photos of Princess Margaret frolicking in the Caribbean which were supposedly held in one of the boxes; it was also claimed that the press were banned via a 'D Notice' from reporting any of this. This was all cheerful nonsense; if MI5 had really wanted access they would merely have told the bank manager what they needed, walked in and helped themselves. But it was nonetheless a spectacular burglary and an example of the carefully planned 'project crime' that would pop up roughly once a decade and require detailed plotting, teamwork and trust.

There was a filmic element, too, a decade later when the leader of the raid on the headquarters of Security Express in Shoreditch, east London, on 2 April 1983 was described as a 'Jack Hawkins figure'. This was a reference to the 1960 film, *The League of Gentlemen,* in which Hawkins played an ex-army officer who led a team of disillusioned ex-servicemen in a meticulously planned robbery which was to make their fortunes. In the original version of the film the robbers escaped, but the rules of censorship of the day demanded that crime should not be seen to pay and the team were all caught in the final reel. Although most of the men who robbed Security Express of £5,961,097 were also rounded up, others were never found.

The robbers, around fifteen men all dressed in black, broke into the Curtain Road building known locally as 'Fort Knox', captured the supervisor, Greg Counsel, and forced him to admit the unsuspecting staff, who were tied up as they arrived. The robbers obtained the combinations of the vaults where the money was held by pouring petrol over one of the staff and threatening to set fire to him. They spoke in bogus Irish accents – as had the team in *The League of Gentlemen* – and were clearly well briefed, knowing that one member of staff smoked a pipe and another owned a dog. They also told staff, 'If you have to go on an ID parade, you'll recognise no one. We know where you live.' As they left, they warned: 'We've got a man upstairs. He's going to be there for 20 minutes just watching out for you. He's got a shooter and he's as fucking mad as they come.' It was the largest haul since the Great Train Robbery and the stolen goods weighed five tons. Security Express offered a £500,000 reward.

It was nine months before there was a breakthrough. In January 1984, Johnny Knight, brother of Spanish exile Ronnie, was arrested. He had deposited around £250,000 in bank and building society accounts around north London and had bought a villa on the Costa del Sol. Another ring-leader, Terry Perkins, had invested in property in Portugal, having shown up at his accountant's office with £50,000 in his anorak pockets. Both received twenty-two years at the Old Bailey in June 1985 after being told by Mr Justice Richard Lowry that they were ruthless and evil men. 'Your aim was to live in luxury,' he admonished them. Knight's brother Jimmy, John Horsely and William Hickson were given shorter sentences but the police accepted that many of the gang, including whoever had the vital inside knowledge, had not been found.

Nearly five years later Freddie Foreman, famous for his old associations with the Krays, was gaoled for nine years after being brought back from Spain to stand trial. The claim was that

Foreman had boasted to Spanish police that he had taken part in the robbery, a scenario that, given Foreman's criminal background, seemed highly unlikely.

Foreman was cleared of taking part in the robbery but found guilty on the lesser offences of handling its proceeds. His barrister, John Mathew, QC, said: 'There has been a suggestion that he was leading the life not only of Riley but of a very rich Riley. He was not. He was certainly not doing a nine-to-five job in Spain but it was not a life of luxury or ostentation.' No matter. The 'Mean Machine', as the press liked to call him, had been disconnected. But the capture and sentencing of the Shoreditch team did not have the desired deterrent effect as another group of security men were to discover.

'Get on the floor or you're fucking dead,' were the straightforward if unoriginal words that first alerted the guards at the Heathrow International Trading Estate that they were about to be the victims of what was, for a while, the largest robbery in British history. The instructions were delivered just before seven on the morning of Saturday 26 November 1983, and were the start of a heist and an investigation that would end in the death of an undercover officer, the recycling of tens of millions of pounds' worth of stolen bullion and gaol sentences that totalled more than 200 years. This was the robbery that was to become known in both police and criminal circles simply as 'Brink's-Mat'.

As with so many major robberies, both the strength and the weakness of the operation was an inside man, in this case security guard Tony Black. He was the brother-in-law of career criminal Brian 'The Colonel' Robinson. Black was already working for Brink's-Mat in 1980 and had supplied Polaroid snaps of the insides of the security vans for Robinson, who courted him on weekend fishing trips. Black was promised that something would be put away for him in a Swiss bank account if the job succeeded, but told that he would have to continue working there for at least a further five years to allay suspicion. He was given plasticine and cuttlefish so that he could make impressions of the warehouse keys, which he then passed back to the team that had been assembled by Robinson.

On the morning of the robbery Black overslept – he had been too nervous to enjoy a normal night's rest – and his criminal colleagues thought that, in the elegant vernacular, 'his arsehole had dropped out'. But he fulfilled his part of the bargain, at least initially. Excusing himself to go to the toilet, he managed to give a wave to the waiting robbers, who crashed in, fully armed, to tie up the security guards.

As Black lay bound on the floor one of the robbers, the hot-headed Micky McAvoy, whispered encouragingly to him: 'It's all right, we've got the lot.' Indeed they had, a far greater haul than they had imagined. They had expected to get between £1 million and £2 million, which was the normal amount of cash deposited on a Friday night. But a large consignment of gold for onward transit on the Saturday had arrived late the previous night and when one of the guards failed to remember his part of the combination-lock number of the safe containing the cash the team settled on the gold bullion. Its enormous value inevitably provoked a massive investigation.

But if Tony Black had facilitated the entry of the robbers, he was soon to facilitate their discovery. It was not long before the Flying Squad found the weak link – there was surprise in their ranks that Robinson would have used someone so identifiably close to him. Black had no criminal pedigree and was soon making statements and identifying the robbers. Robinson, McAvoy and a man called Tony White were arrested. On 17 February 1984 Black pleaded guilty and was sentenced to six years, after the court had been told that he would assist in the prosecution of the main conspirators. The judge, Mr Justice David Tudor-Price, told him solemnly: 'You and your family will for ever be fugitives from those you so stupidly and so wickedly helped.' Robinson, McAvoy and White, the men Black had named, offered alibi evidence in their defence at their Old Bailey trial and challenged his evidence. White was cleared but both the other two men were gaoled for twenty-five years after a trial during which the jurors were given police protection and had their telephone calls intercepted.

But if the robbers were now inside facing long sentences, what had happened to the bullion? The police had their suspicions but little hard evidence. It was some time before they targeted Kenneth Noye. A businessman in his mid-thirties, Noye lived in a mansion in the village of West Kingsdown, in Kent, with his wife, Brenda, and their two children. He was a bright and ambitious man, who had established lucrative haulage and property companies and had worked hard to capitalise on his successes, which gave him an entrée into an affluent Kentish world of charity dinners, Freemasonry and squash clubs. He had, however, a number of minor offences to his name. These were for receiving stolen property and evasion of duty on importation of a firearm.

Noye was observed shifting large sums of money and purchasing gold bars in St Helier, Jersey. The police also took an interest in a visitor to his home, an unassuming man called Brian Reader who had gone on the run while awaiting trial in a case in which supergrass Micky 'Skinny' Gervaise was due to give evidence; he had convictions for store-breaking and burglary. By the beginning of 1985, following information from London gold dealers, the pair were under heavy surveillance. The police were also particularly interested in a bullion company in Bristol – Scadlynn Ltd – whose managing director was Garth Chappell. There was evidence that it had experienced an upsurge in its activities not long after the robbery.

It was decided that Noye's home should be staked out by two undercover officers, so in January 1985 Detective Constables John Fordham and Neil Murphy hid in the grounds in camouflage gear.

The Noye home was guarded by two Rottweilers and the suspicious animals scented the men's presence and started barking. Murphy tried to feed them the yeast tablets which had been recommended as a way of keeping them quiet, but to no effect. He beat a retreat, gesturing to Fordham, who he imagined would follow suit.

The Noyes and Reader, who was visiting them, had been alerted by the barking and Kenneth, taking a torch and a knife from the garage, went to investigate. As he was later to tell it, he saw a figure in a balaclava: 'I thought that was my lot. I thought I was going to be a dead man ... As far as I was concerned, I was fighting for my life.' He said that Fordham had struck him and that he had lashed out with his knife, stabbing the officer ten times. He demanded to know who the wounded figure was and Fordham gasped out 'SAS – on manoeuvres', which was presumably his final attempt to maintain the secrecy of the operation. In the meantime, Reader had fled the house.

Brenda Noye had come to her husband's aid and, on discovering what had happened, had returned to the house to call an ambulance and fetch a camera to record Fordham's appearance. 'You see a man in a balaclava and a camouflage suit, you don't say "Excuse me, before I hit you, are you a police officer?",' said Brenda Noye later.

Murphy could tell that something had gone terribly wrong and was already radioing his concerns to the control point. Soon the Flying Squad was arriving in numbers. Fordham was pronounced dead later that night and Noye was arrested. Reader, who had tried to hitch a lift away from the area, was also held and both men were accused of murder and stood trial at the Old Bailey in 1986. It was a highly charged affair: Murphy had difficulty giving his evidence. Noye's defence was straightforwardly put by John Mathew, QC, best known as a devastating prosecutor: that Noye had been alerted by the dogs, that he had seen a man in camouflage, that the man had attacked him and he had defended himself. To the anger of the police, the jury acquitted both men. But Noye was now a marked man and official determination to convict him for connection with Brink's-Mat hardened.

Five months later, Noye and Reader were back in court again, with five others, including Garth Chappell, charged with disposing of the proceeds of the robbery and accused of handling stolen goods and evading VAT. Noye, Reader and Chappell were convicted of handling. Noye was given the maximum sentence of fourteen years, Chappell received ten and Reader nine. The case was described as 'the worst case of handling stolen goods that we have encountered' and the robbery itself as 'astounding in its audaciousness' by an unsympathetic Lord Justice Watkins when it eventually reached the Court of Appeal.

Solicitor Michael Relton, who handled much of the laundering through foreign banks, was also convicted for his part and gaoled for twelve years, later reduced on appeal. Relton was the archetypal bent lawyer so hated by the police – or most of the police, since he did defend large numbers of officers charged with corruption offences and ran a wine bar called Briefs, which he later sold to three of the officers he had successfully defended. His success in laundering and investing the money had been such that he was virtually able to give up his law practice.

But the saga was not over. The police were still searching for people they believed had been involved. John Palmer, a Birmingham-born man who had picked up the nickname 'Goldfinger', was arrested in July 1986 on his return from Brazil, where he had flown after being expelled from Spain. He stood trial on charges of handling the proceeds of the robbery and was acquitted. Having left school at fifteen, Palmer made his first money selling paraffin off the back of a lorry, but he was soon on his way to more profitable work as a dealer in jewellery and director of a small bullion firm on the outskirts of Bristol. It was this involvement with smelting that gave his nickname and led police to him. Nearly three decades later, he was to come to a sticky end. The case trickled on. In September 1992, following an eight-month trial, four more members of the team – Gordon Parry, Brian Perry, Jean Savage and Patrick Clark – were gaoled for a total of thirty years for laundering £14.5 million of the money. Some of the loot had been invested in Docklands during its eight-ies boom and the rest moved through banks in the Channel Islands, the Isle of Man, Ireland, Switzerland and Liechtenstein. It was the ninth trial related to the robbery and raised the cost of the prosecution high into the millions.

Having served his sentence, Kenneth Noye was to resurface in different circumstances. In May 1996, he was in an altercation with another motorist, Stephen Cameron, on the M25 in Kent, which resulted in the latter being stabbed to death. Noye fled to Spain, where he was tracked down two years later in the village of Barbate, near Cádiz, and eventually extradited to Britain. In April, 2000, despite once again pleading self-defence, he was con-victed and gaoled for a minimum of sixteen years. But while Brink's-Mat was wending its way through the courts another, even more spectacular, robbery was being planned and executed. When it too finally came unstuck, even the trial judge seemed mildly impressed.

'The stakes were colossal,' Mr Justice Robert Lymbery told the immaculately dressed young man in the dock in front of him on 30 January 1989. 'Having lost, you have to pay the price accord-ingly. In this court I have seen a man of charm and courtesy, a man of substantial abilities. But these qualities, combined with others, serve to make you a very dangerous man.'

It was probably an assessment with which the man at whom it was directed, Valerio Viccei, would have broadly agreed. The Ital-ian, who had just been convicted of the multi-million-pound rob-bery of the Knightsbridge Safe Deposit Centre in July 1987, was never one for false modesty or, indeed, any other kind of modesty. He had, in the words of one detective, 'an ego the size of the Old Bailey.' Had he decided to leave London speedily after the heist, rather than cruising its more expensive streets in a Ferrari Testarossa, he might have remained free instead of facing a twenty-two-year sentence.

The robbery itself was one of the largest ever to take place in the United Kingdom, although it is still unclear exactly how much was stolen. Many holders of the safe deposit boxes declined to say how much they lost and Viccei claimed that cocaine and laundered money were contained in them. At the time of the trial the police estimate it was £40 million. The cover of Viccei's autobiography, *Knightsbridge, the Robbery of the Century*, tells of 'How I escaped with £60 million', although nowhere in the book itself is the figure mentioned.

The robbery was significant in more ways than just the sum that was stolen. Viccei had assembled what was essentially an international team to carry out the job, breaking the fairly traditional English mode of such operations, where only tried-and-tested 'staunch' allies were entrusted with such a major robbery. To carry out the spectacular crime the Italian recruited an Israeli, a Russian, a Pakistani and some home-grown English heavies.

Viccei himself came from Ascoli Piceno, on Italy's Adriatic coast, the son of a lawyer father and a furrier mother. He had studied law briefly, then joined up with a group of neo-fascists in 1972 and had blown up the cables of a television station he considered too left-wing. Claiming Nietzsche as his inspiration, he burned out the offices of left-wing political parties but was eventually arrested and gaoled. In his memoir, he recorded his transformation from teenage neo-fascist fire-bomber to mature career criminal: 'I have abandoned the rarefied pure air of my idealized forest and travelled all the way down to the polluted town. I switched targets and instead of destabilizing society, I long to make money just like its most respected citizens do.'

He arrived in Britain in the mid-eighties on the run from the police in Italy, linked up with members of the underworld and carried out a robbery of a branch of Coutts bank with one English colleague, despite being tackled by a game woman clerk who bit his fingers. The profits helped him move into a smart flat in St John's Wood, in north London, and he undertook a further bank robbery, netting £50,000 and escaping on a motorcycle. But in January 1987, the police tracked him down with an extradition warrant and he only escaped by kicking his way out of a car and hiding out briefly in Lord's cricket ground, dressed as a hard-hat workman. After a holiday in Colombia, where he was able to indulge his appetite for pure cocaine, he returned to England. He was still undeterred in his desire to carry out the mythical 'one big job', and to fund it he and another robber stole around £70,000 in travellers' cheques from the Mayfair branch of American Express.

Viccei had meanwhile met Parvez Latif, the Pakistani manager of the Knightsbridge Safe Deposit Centre, where Viccei was storing his ill-gotten gains. Latif had impressed him with his discretion over what were clearly illicit dealings, and when Viccei found that a friend in London's night-club circuit also knew him, he realised that the centre could be the big job he was waiting for. He approached Latif and, over several dinners and champagne at Tramp's nightclub, gradually massaged him with flattery, promises of amazing wealth and some of the purest Colombian cocaine. Viccei also started an affair with Latif's glamorous girlfriend; he later repaid her friendship with a lubriciously soft-porn description of their liaison in his memoirs.

Viccei's strategy was simple: Latif would arrange to have the Centre closed for a brief period; he would then allow Viccei and his team, posing as potential clients, to enter. Latif would continue his act as he and his colleagues – a supervisor and two guards – were tied up and the boxes robbed. With the inside knowledge from Latif, Viccei would be able to break into the most profitable boxes and make an escape with enough time to throw off the police.

On Sunday 12 July 1987, armed with a Beretta and a sawn-off shotgun, Viccei led his team to the building. It had been closed and a note of explanation left on the door: 'We apologise to all our customers for any inconvenience caused to them during the improvements to our security system. Business as usual from tomorrow. Thank you'. Dressed in Armani (suit), Hermès (tie) and Ferragamo (loafers), Viccei and a colleague rang the bell and were greeted by Latif. They pretended they were ordinary customers who had telephoned a few minutes earlier asking for an appointment. This exchange was watched by the guards, who were not in on the plot and therefore had to be misled.

Viccei was then taken on a phoney tour of the premises during which he pulled a gun on Latif and 'forced' him to call the guards. He made an overt homosexual overture to one of the Centre's employees, which so upset the man that he was offguard when Viccei pulled a gun and subdued him. The robbers were then able to let in two colleagues to help with the attack on the boxes. With power drills, crowbars, sledge-hammers and screwdrivers, the team prised open the steel boxes and grabbed the banknotes, jewels and drugs inside them. But in his eagerness to whack open the doors, Viccei did not notice that he had torn his glove and cut his finger, leaving blood and fingerprints all over the vaults.

As the team left, Viccei warned the Centre's employees, who were tied up, handcuffed and fearful, that he was leaving one member of the gang behind for a period and that if any of them attempted to escape, the man had instructions to shoot. The team loaded the haul into a white Renault van and sped off. As Viccei remembered: 'The atmosphere was one of pure ecstasy: we had

written a page of criminal history. We had just pulled off the bold-
est, largest and most spectacular robbery in recent times.' To
celebrate, he fulfilled an old fantasy and filled the bathtub of the
hide-out flat with money and jewels.

The reaction of the media was not dissimilar to the way they
had reacted to the Great Train Robbery. Here was a daring robbery in which no one had been killed and in which the financial
victims, either fairly or unfairly, elicited little sympathy. There was
even an element of schadenfreude in watching the damp-eyed
souls who gathered outside the Centre to find out if their boxes
had been emptied.

But the bloody fingerprints, coupled with weak links in his
team, were to prove Viccei's undoing. In addition, his self-
confidence got the better of him and instead of fleeing the
country, he stayed and played. His arrogance was his undoing.

Inspector Fred Leach soon realised that Viccei was a part of
the operation and knew that he had been associated with an
Israeli called Israel Pinkas when he had slipped away from the
police earlier in the year. The police put Pinkas under observation
and noted that he was using White's Hotel just north of Hyde Park
as a base. They decided to check on White's other guests and
found that one was a man called 'Raiman' (Viccei's alias) and, the
key factor for them, that he was Italian. The police now realised
that the man who had just left the hotel in his Ferrari was the
man they sought.

Viccei was finally cornered in a traffic jam at Marble Arch
and dragged out through the windscreen of his beloved car with,
according to the arresting police, the words, 'Right, chaps, the
game is up now and you have no need to be nasty. You are the
winners, so calm down and everything is going to be fine.'

The trial was in many ways a formality for Viccei. One of his
team, Steve Mann, decided to co-operate with the police and received five years. Peter O'Donohue was gaoled for eleven years,

David Poole for sixteen and Eric Rubin for twelve. Israel 'Izzy'
Pinkas got ten years, later reduced to nine. Parvez Latif, who had
betrayed the trust of his employers, received the heavier sentence
of eighteen years. His girlfriend was given a suspended sentence.
Viccei's twenty-two years was the heaviest sentence and he was
soon in Parkhurst, knocking out his story with the help of Jimmy
Nicholson, the crime reporter known as the 'Prince of Darkness'.
In 1993 he was, as he had predicted, transferred to an Italian gaol.

In *The League of Gentlemen*, as the police close in one of the
robbers tells another: 'Give them their money's worth at the trial
and then flog your memoirs to the Sunday papers.' After the
Knightsbridge trial *News of the World* readers were to discover
that on one occasion Viccei's girlfriend 'lay naked on her lover's
bed and felt her skin crawl as she looked down at the £4-million
plum-sized diamond nestling in her navel. It was part of the treasure Italian stallion Valerio Viccei had stolen ...' More purple
prose was to follow. While in prison, Viccei wrote *Too Fast To
Live* and, in 2000, the title became reality.

On day release from his open prison in Pescara, supposedly so
that he could work at a publishers before returning every night to
gaol, he was shot dead in a confrontation with traffic police not far
from his home town of Ascoli Piceno. The officers had spotted a
stolen Lancia parked suspiciously and Viccei opened fire rather
than be captured. His companion, Antonio Malatesta, a Puglia
Mafia man and fellow-prisoner, was caught. Police reckoned that
they had been planning a kidnap or robbery.

What had the potential to be the biggest hit of them all took
place in the City of London in 1990 and at first looked like a random mugging rather than a massive sting. A small-time criminal
called Patrick Thomas pulled a knife on an elderly messenger for
the money-broking firm, Sheppards, in an alleyway and stole
£292 million in bearer bonds. The reports the next day suggested
that it was almost certainly a random mugging and the thief

would have had no idea of the value of what he had stolen. In fact, it was a carefully planned international operation and Thomas had been deliberately chosen because he was black and this would fit people's preconceptions that this was just 'another black mugging'. The plan had been to launder the bonds in America, but it fell apart when the team was infiltrated by an American undercover FBI agent and when more than £150 million of the bonds were recovered at Heathrow and in Cyprus. Thomas, who had become increasingly nervous about his involvement, was found shot dead in his flat. The detectives investigating the case came to the conclusion that he had killed himself.

With the new millennium came the – well, the new millennium robbery. It appeared to have everything: the highly appropriate celebrated site, a priceless collection of diamonds and an escape route via a powerboat down the River Thames. There was only one thing wrong with it: the robbers were all caught red-handed.

It was October 2000 when four men wearing gasmasks and body armour broke through the perimeter fence of the Millennium Dome with a mechanical digger and lobbed smoke bombs as they headed towards a display of diamonds worth around £350 million. Waiting to take the robbers and their stolen diamonds away was their getaway powerboat moored by the Queen Elizabeth jetty nearby. But also waiting for them were Flying Squad officers and armed response units posing as cleaners, their guns hidden in bin liners; an operation involving 100 officers and code-named 'Magician' had been under way for months, thanks to a tip-off. No shots were fired and the quartet surrendered without a struggle. 'Only 12 inches from payday,' said Robert Adams, one of the frustrated robbers. 'It would have been a blinding Christmas.'

The main object was to capture the De Beers Millennium Star diamond, although the robbers had been unaware that it had been replaced the previous day by a replica in anticipation of their arrival, which would have made their Christmas rather less than blinding. As they bashed the reinforced glass cases with hammers and electric nailguns, the police surrounded them. Another man was arrested in the powerboat and a suspected look-out man believed to be monitoring police messages was grabbed on the north side of the river. A total of twelve were held.

Detective Superintendent Jon Shatford defended the decision to allow the attempt to evolve. 'The biggest danger would have been to let them escape or frustrate them before they could commit the offence. We have to produce the best evidence. If we fail to do that, we are letting the public down because we are saying it is too difficult for us and we will let them go and commit crime elsewhere.' What the robbers were planning to do with what was, almost literally, the jewel in the crown – the Millennium Star – remained unclear. Cut it up or sell to a collector? Andrew Lamont, a spokesman for De Beers, said that 'cutting up the Millennium Star would be like cutting up a Van Gogh or Monet. It would only be worth a tiny fraction of the whole.'

In 2002, members of the gang were sentenced at the Old Bailey: Raymond Betson, William Cockram, Robert Adams and Aldo Ciarrocchi all admitted conspiracy to steal. Gaoling Betson and Cockram for eighteen years, Judge Coombe told them: 'This was a very well-planned and premeditated attempt to rob De Beers of what would have been the most gigantic sum in English or any other legal history. You played for very high stakes and you must have known perfectly well what the penalty would be if your enterprise didn't succeed.' (The late armed robber Bobby King used to say that if he had a quid for every time a judge told him he had 'played for very high stakes', he would have been able to cash in and retire.)

Colin Dixon, the manager of the Securitas depot in Tonbridge, Kent, was driving home one late February afternoon in 2006 when he saw the flashing blue light of what he believed was a police car. He had just texted his wife, Lynn, to say he was on his way and was looking forward to seeing her and their young child. Pulled over to the side of the road for what he presumed was a routine check, he was told by two men dressed in police uniforms that he was being arrested for a number of speeding offences, bundled into the back of their car and handcuffed. His puzzlement at being detained so roughly for a minor offence increased with the realisation that BBC Radio 1 was playing on the car radio and by the erratic way in which the driver set off. He asked to see their ID but was told that it was 'back at the station'. Puzzlement turned to panic when one of the 'policemen' told him: 'You'll guess we're not policemen. Don't do anything silly and nobody will be hurt.' The bogus officer pulled a gun out and pointed it at Dixon, assuring him: 'We are not fucking about – this is a 9mm.'

Months of planning had gone into the operation that was to culminate that February night in Tonbridge. Back at Colin Dixon's family home, his wife and son were kidnapped by two more men dressed as policemen and taken to a farm. Dixon was taken to his Securitas depot and forced to use his swipe card to gain entry. 'Just do whatever the bloke says,' Dixon told his staff and they, mindful perhaps of the poster on the wall that advised employees 'Don't be a hero', did as they were told and all of the fourteen Securitas employees were tied up as the robbers went to work. They only realised it was over when one of the robbers shouted 'Come on, let's rock and roll!' as they fled, taking £53 million with them and only leaving behind £150 million because they could not fit it into the lorry.

The robbers' triumph was short-lived. A tip-off took the police, within twenty-four hours of the robbery, to the door of Michelle Hogg, a young hairdresser who had created the latex masks worn by the gang as disguises. She had left some material, with DNA traces of the robbers, in her rubbish bin, which had not been cleared.

Initially, Hogg claimed she had thought she was making the masks for use in a music video and refused to identify the men but her mobile phone showed she had been in touch with an Albanian, Jetmir Bucpapa, twelve times on the day of the kidnapping. She was charged with conspiracy and started the trial as a defendant before being acquitted and becoming a crown witness. The police soon realised that another young Albanian, Emir Hysenaj, a friend of Bucpapa's who had briefly been employed at the depot, was the inside man.

The main man, a mixed martial arts fighter called Lee Brahim Murray-Lamrani, was now being hunted but fled to Morocco where, because his father was Moroccan, he was able to avoid extradition. This would turn out to be a mixed blessing as he was eventually gaoled in Morocco for twenty-five years in tougher conditions than English prisons.

A very different but equally audacious crime took place over the Easter weekend in 2015 when Hatton Garden, the centre of London's jewellery trade, was fast asleep. Except for a team of burglars who were busily drilling their way into a safe deposit centre and then departing with the loot. How much stolen? £100 million? £200 million? Think of a number and double it. But whodunnit? Imaginative theories were rife, as were movie references. The headline of the *Sunday Express* read: 'Police Hunt Pink Panthers over jewel heist'; the story suggested that 'the gem thieves may be part of the infamous Balkans-based Pink Panther gang (who got their name from the Peter Sellers *Pink Panther* film)'. The *Daily Express* asked, 'Did £35m gem gang use a contortionist?,' speculating that there must have been someone similar to the Amazing Yen, played by Shaobo Quin in the film *Ocean's Eleven*. The *Daily Mirror* reported that 'An expert has revealed how a Mr Big is likely to have hired elite thieves from eastern Europe and Israel to pull off the operation'. The BBC carried an interview with media gangster Dave Courtney, who suggested that the stolen jewels might have been smuggled out of the country stuffed 'up a racehorse's arse'.

Then came the arrests of Brian Reader, seventy-six, Terry Perkins, sixty-seven, Danny Jones, sixty, and John 'Kenny' Collins, seventy-four – four career criminals from north and east London. You could almost hear the collective sighs of relief: not only was this whole thing home-made, but it was carried out by a bunch of distinctly grey rather than pink panthers.

It was a complex operation. Five of the gang, including the ghostly figure of 'Basil', gained access to the Hatton Garden Safe Deposit company and disconnected the CCTV and alarms. They tried to drill their way through the inside 50-cm wall while Collins acted as look-out man from a building opposite. They hit problems, which meant that they needed different equipment, so they left the building to get new tools. At this stage Reader and Carl Wood, another member of the team, decided that they'd had enough: the risks were too great. The others continued, grabbed around £14 million in jewels, gold and cash and bailed out. With the help of a friend, William 'Billy the Fish' Lincoln, they got the goods to Enfield, where they were split up. Now the media saw them as 'The Diamond Wheezers', 'The Old Blaggers' or, in the French press, *'le gang des papys'* (the grandads' gang).

Perkins and Reader already had form, through the Security Express and Brink's-Mat robberies respectively and by now were neither in great health: Perkins had a dicky heart and Reader had prostate cancer and neutropenia, a blood condition that makes the sufferer susceptible to infections. He had lost his beloved wife, Lyn, to cancer and perhaps he felt he had nothing to lose.

Danny Jones, a mere boy at sixty but an experienced robber, was a fitness expert and someone who often spoke about how much he would have liked to have been in the SAS. Having pleaded guilty, Jones decided to tell the police where he had hidden his loot, in Edmonton cemetery. Jones wrote to Martin Brunt, the crime correspondent at Sky News, and told him: 'Whatever I get on Judgment Day, I will stand tall, but I want to make amends to all my loved ones and show I'm trying to change. I no [know] it seems a bit late in my life, but I'm trying.' And try he did. The police went with him to the place where he had hidden his loot, in an in-law's plot. Alas for Jones, they found more of his ill-gotten gains in another plot he had perhaps forgotten to mention. The fourth of the main conspirators, Kenny Collins from Islington, was a break-in expert who had made money from football ticket sales and was, according to one former fellow inmate, 'the man with the hardest head and the biggest heart in London'. He was always accompanied by his Staffordshire terrier, Dempsey.

In *The League of Gentlemen*, the thieves are caught because a diligent schoolboy notes their car registration. The fact that Collins's Mercedes was spotted via the Automatic Number-Plate Recognition (ANPR) technology and led the police to him was another indication that these were 'analogue criminals in a digital age' as the judge would note in his summing-up. All four of the ring-leaders pleaded guilty and were gaoled for up to seven years. (You get a third off your sentence if you plead guilty immediately and the maximum for a commercial burglary is ten years; crucially, this was a burglary not a robbery, which requires force or the threat of force and can carry a life sentence.) Also arrested and given a suspended sentence, although he would always plead that he did not know why his mates wanted to use his premises, was Hugh Doyle, a sprightly, bearded Dubliner of a mere forty-eight, and a plumber who knew the main protagonists as drinking mates from an Islington pub. While awaiting trial in Belmarsh Prison, Doyle read Christopher Hitchens's *God Is Not Great*, which he found helpful in discussions about religion with some of the al-Qaeda inmates, who were more responsive to debate than he had imagined. The four Ringleaders – Perkins, Reader, Jones and

Collins – were later ordered to pay back more than £6 million each or face another seven years inside, a sentence both men challenged on legal grounds.

Much of what was known about the burglary was garnered from taped conversations between Jones and Perkins, in whose cars police had hidden bugs once the men became suspects. 'The biggest robbery in the fucking world we was on,' they chuckle as they discuss how to dispose of the goods. 'The biggest tom [jewellery] robbery in the fucking history of the world.' There was also a clue in the tapes as to what made them embark on it all: 'If we get nicked, at least we can hold our heads up that we had a last go.' Ah, that last job. And a prescient comment, too, from Jones, as they reflect on past glories: 'It's a young man's game.' After Jones was arrested, his computer indicated that he had been looking at 'drilling online' and 'drilltec' sites as far back as April 2012. And he had a book, *Forensics For Dummies*, which promised that 'now everyone can get the lowdown on the science behind crime scene investigations.'

The burglary prompted three films, the most successful of which was *King of Thieves*, directed by James Marsh and starring three knights (none of them Ronnie): Michael Caine, Tom Courtenay and Michael Gambon, not to mention Ray Winstone and Jim Broadbent. There was also a four-part television series, four books and a catchy ska song, 'It's The Hatton Garden Job', on an album by Arthur Kay and the Clerks which contains the lines: 'Wonder what they're thinking/If they ever get out again/Will they buy us a decent striker?/Or a villa down in Spain?'

It was not until March 2018 that 'Basil' was arrested in the shape of 58-year-old Michael Seed, in whose Islington council flat no fewer than 789 items of the stolen jewels and gold were found. His background was far removed from those of his confederates. The son of a Cambridge bio-chemist, as a bright schoolboy he had been fascinated by electronics, a subject he studied at Nottingham

University, where he embarked on another key phase of his life: using and selling recreational drugs. In 1984, he was jailed for three years for dealing in LSD, his only previous criminal conviction.

At his trial in 2019, Seed cheerfully denied being Basil but a forensic gait specialist gave evidence that there was a 'strong' possibility that the bewigged character caught on CCTV leaving the scene was indeed Seed who, it was suggested, walked a little like Charlie Chaplin. Seed claimed that the chaotic treasure trove of electronic gadgetry – blockers, jammers, drills, sensors, alarms – that detectives found in his flat was just an eccentric hobby, but it was his skill with alarms and communications that had been vital to the enterprise. Whippet-thin, he was also one of the two burglars who slipped through the hole in the vault; he was described by an admiring associate as 'game as a bagel'. He was jailed for ten years after the jury had deliberated for more than a week, the longest sentence of any of the burglars.

The Hatton Garden job must, like so many of those foiled or failed project crimes, have seemed irresistible. Other underworld crimes that were causing alarm had a less sophisticated air to them.

14

THE HITMEN – AND HITWOMEN

THE CONTRACT KILLERS

When John 'Goldfinger' Palmer was acquitted at the Old Bailey in 1987 of conspiracy to handle stolen gold bullion in the wake of the Brink's-Mat robbery, he blew a kiss to the jury that had found him not guilty – and gave two fingers to the detectives who had arrested him – as he left the court. He was soon on a plane back to his crooked time-share business in Tenerife and must have thought that he had also kissed goodbye to the high-risk end of criminal life. But in Sandpit Lane, near Brentwood, in Essex, on 24 June 2015, he became the latest in a long and bloody roll call of those involved in that robbery who suffered violent ends.

Remarkably, it took the police six days to realise that Palmer had actually been murdered; the wounds on his body caused by six bullets shot at close range from a .32 revolver were initially thought to have been the result of recent key-hole surgery. But once it became clear that he had been shot there was immediate talk of a 'hitman', the almost mythical hired hand who is often blamed for the unsolved killings of underworld figures.

There was no shortage of people who had good reason to wish Palmer ill. In Tenerife, he was a ruthless operator, taking advantage of thousands of gullible souls, many of them elderly holidaymakers, who believed his spiel about the fortunes they could make by investing in time-share apartments that were never built; no one ever accused Palmer of only hurting 'his own'. He had a large staff working on commission and malcontents who claimed they had not been properly paid were rewarded with a smack in the mouth. Outwardly, he appeared to have it all: the *Brave Goose* yacht, the cars with the personalised number plates, the dozens of properties, the glamorous blonde wife, Marnie. He even made it to No. 105 in the *Sunday Times* Rich List. 'Remember the golden rule,' was the motto he loved to quote, 'he who has the gold makes the rules.'

But he could not resist boasting to undercover reporters from *The Cook Report* in 1994 about his abilities to launder money, which led to a programme called *The Laundry Man* and in 2001, he was back at the Old Bailey charged with a massive time-share fraud. This time the tanned Palmer cut a less dashing figure and there were no kisses for the jury; he gave his watch to his lawyer before he went down to the cells. The prosecuting counsel, David Farrer, QC, told the court that he was 'the largest shark in the time-share water' and had callously exploited his clients. Gaoled for eight years, he served four and was also ordered to repay £2.3 million of his ill-gotten gains. 'He was a very tight little fellow and hated parting with any money in spite of the fact that he had millions,' said Jason Coghlan, who served time with him in Long Lartin prison.

Palmer was also under investigation in Spain where, in 2007, Baltasar Garzón, the Spanish judge who pursued the Chilean dictator General Pinochet through the courts, suggested that he was

involved in a little more than '*el time-sharing*' and was responsible
for money laundering, fraud and firearms offences. Palmer was
arrested, held in gaol in Spain for three years but later released.
According to Marnie, in her memoir, *Goldfinger and Me*, a
cocaine habit had damaged him and made him unpredictable. On
one occasion he had pulled a gun on her and said 'Die, you bitch'
before cackling, 'Not loaded, see!'

Three years after his death, with no arrests in sight, his new
partner, Christina Ketley – he and Marnie had parted on bad
terms – offered a reward of £100,000 for information leading to
his killer, whom police now believed was a professional who had
been spying on his prey through a hole drilled in the fence and
watching Palmer as he burned documents in the garden. Theories
as to why he had been killed included the suspicion that he might
have been about to inform on associates to the Spanish police in
order to avoid another gaol sentence, that there was a Hatton
Garden burglary connection and that his death might have been
connected with the very grim murders in 2006 in Tenerife of two
former associates, Billy and Flo Robinson.

Compared to most parts of the world, such underworld murders are rare in Britain, which is why whenever there is an unsolved hit, speculation about a mystery 'hitman' is rife. One of
the strangest such cases emerged after the disappearance in
1974 of a businessman called Terence 'Teddy Bear' Eve from
Dagenham, in Essex. Two months later, not far away in Upmin-
ster, a transport contractor called George Brett and his ten-year-
old son Terry also went missing. Brett's wife, Mavis, told police
that a man who called himself Jennings had visited and asked
Brett to come and inspect some goods. Brett had gone to do so
and taken his son along for the ride. His Mercedes was found in
King's Cross but, despite a massive police hunt, neither father
nor son were ever seen again. There were other puzzling disap-
pearances: of Robert Brown, a criminal and wrestler, in 1975; of

Fred Sherwood, a nursing-home proprietor from Herne Bay, in Kent, in 1978; of Robert Andrews, a roofing contractor from Barkingside, in Essex, in 1978. But there was little indication that they were connected.

Then in June 1979, following an armed robbery on a Security Express van in Hertford, police arrested a strange character called John Childs, a small, scruffy man with a wispy beard and spectacles who gradually recounted an extraordinary story of his involvement in six contract killings. Interviewed in Oxford Prison by Detective Chief Superintendent Frank Cater, Childs slowly embarked on a chilling series of confessions. 'Those hours were among the most horrific of my entire police career,' said Cater.

The victims had either been strangled or shot in the head and their bodies supposedly burned in the fireplace at Childs's home in Poplar, east London, and the ashes thrown in the river at Wanstead Park. Childs claimed that he had embarked on his killing spree after starting a small business with a former fellow prisoner, Terry Pinfold, and a man called Harry 'Big H' MacKenney, a six-foot six-inches tall engineer and diver with convictions for causing actual bodily harm and car and lorry theft. They had a small factory in Dagenham, shared with Terence Eve, where they were planning to produce diving jackets designed by MacKenney.

Childs claimed that they had decided to get rid of Eve so that they could take over his soft-toy business. He said that they had killed him with a hammer and attempted to mangle his body through an industrial mincer bought through *Exchange & Mart* for £25. This failed, as did efforts to flush it in chunks down the lavatory. The remains were eventually burned in the fireplace. Childs also claimed that the three of them had worked together and that Pinfold had offered to act as an agent, finding clients for them, while they carried out other executions.

The unfortunate George Brett was an early victim: £2,000 was the price offered by a man with a grudge against him. Childs tricked Brett into coming to the factory to discuss a possible deal and had not anticipated that the boy would come along for the ride, but his presence did not seem to be a deterrent. This double killing presented a dilemma. The factory's handyman, Robert Brown, was on the run from prison and might have suspected something. If caught, he could implicate them. He was told that the authorities were onto him and was offered a safe house as a hideaway, where he too was murdered.

A £4,000 price had been offered meanwhile for the killing of Fred Sherwood in 1978. Chillingly, by the time he confessed, Childs had even forgotten the actual motive. Sherwood had a Rover for sale and Childs pretended to be a potential buyer, asking Sherwood to drive him to his brother's house in Dagenham to pick up the money to pay for it. After this amazing unburdening by Childs, who appeared to have made a total of only £3,180 for all the killings, the hunt was on for 'Big H', who was tracked down to a maisonette in Plaistow, east London, the house surrounded by armed police. MacKenney gave himself up in the glare of spotlights and under the gaze of the marksmen.

In October 1980, MacKenney, who always denied any involvement, stood trial. It was an ugly affair. MacKenney attacked the evidence of Childs, who had already pleaded guilty, calling him 'ill-mannered and crude in the extreme' and attacking his 'frightful' attitude to women, but he and Pinfold were both gaoled for life. Relatives of the victims and the guilty screamed insults in the public gallery.

It would take more than two decades before MacKenney and Pinfold could prove their innocence, after a successful appeal in 2003. It was by this time accepted by the court that Childs suffered from a serious mental disorder which compelled him to lie repeatedly in a way that would not have been detectable to a jury. Said MacKenney after he was cleared: 'This has been a long time coming. The case should never have got to court.'

Another 'hit' that had attracted great attention was carried out on model Barbara Gaul, the flamboyant fourth wife of property millionaire John Gaul, who made his fortune by renting his Soho flats out to prostitutes. In 1976, Mrs Gaul, who was in the process of divorcing her husband, was shot in the car park of the Black Lion hotel in Brighton by two brothers, Keith and Roy 'Micky' Edgeler. She died later in hospital. Gaul fled to Malta and successfully resisted extradition by Sussex police. The brothers were both gaoled for life. 'Micky' Edgeler admitted he had carried out the shooting for £5,000 but resolutely declined to name his paymaster. However, there is little doubt that Gaul hired him, wanting to be rid of his wife, either because she had potentially embarrassing information that she was threatening to disclose or because he wanted to avoid the expense of divorce. Gaul died of a heart attack in 1989 without ever standing trial.

The hitman re-emerged with a vengeance, sometimes literally, in the nineties. One of the victims was Ahmet 'Abbi' Abdullah, a member of the Arif south London gangster family, who was shot dead in March 1991 in a betting shop in Walworth, south London. Two brothers, Patrick and Tony Brindle, were cleared of his murder after a trial in which witnesses were allowed to give evidence from behind a screen. Then the Brindles' brother, David, was shot dead on 3 August 1991 in The Bell in Walworth by two men whose random blasting also killed a bystander, Stanley Silk.

In January 1993, Robert Urquhart, the wealthy owner of the Elstree Golf Club, was walking in Marylebone with his Thai girlfriend when a man on a Yamaha motorcycle, dressed in black leather and wearing a crash helmet, shot him three times in the head. Urquhart's shocked family offered a £100,000 reward for information that would lead to the people behind his killing. The hitman, Graeme West, a former bouncer and debt collector from south London, was gaoled for life at the Old Bailey at the end of 1994 but refused to tell the police who hired him, although he could not resist bragging about the shooting to friends. It seemed most likely that the murder resulted from a business argument.

In the same year, a massively built character, known to the regulars at the Royal Hotel in Hackney, east London, as 'Mick' and often employed locally as a bouncer, was having a quiet pint of bitter in the pub on a June evening. A stranger wandered in and ordered a pint of Foster's lager, which he left on the counter. Then the man reached inside his jacket, pulled out a Webley .38 revolver and shot 'Mick' four times, cursing as he did so, before disappearing in a stolen Ford Fiesta parked outside.

'Mick' was, in fact, Jimmy Moody, the man who had helped wounded gang members escape from the Mr Smith's shoot-out back in 1966, the man who had stood trial with the Richardson gang, the man who had been a member of the 'Chainsaw Gang' of robbers who broke into security vans in the seventies using chainsaws, the man who had escaped from Brixton Prison with IRA man Gerard Tuite thirteen years earlier. Remarkably, he had been on the run ever since before surfacing under a pseudonym in east London. More significantly, some people believed he was himself a hitman and the person behind the double murder of David Brindle and Stanley Silk.

The most controversial 'hitman' case of the last few decades was the murder of Robert Magill in Chorleywood, Hertfordshire, in October 1994. Magill, a car dealer with a criminal background and many enemies, who lived nearby in a house known locally as 'Fort Knox' because of its elaborate security system, was shot dead by two men as he walked his Weimaraner one morning. Two men, Roger Vincent and David Smith, were said on the grapevine to have been responsible for the murder, but it was Vincent and another man called Kevin Lane who stood trial and the latter who was eventually convicted and gaoled for life. He was duly described in some of the press as 'the Executioner' and countless unsolved murders attributed to him.

Lane, an amateur boxer known as 'Lights Out' Lane, was running a security company by the age of eighteen, supplying bouncers to pubs and clubs. He had convictions for handling stolen goods, actual bodily harm and criminal damage. After his release from a gaol sentence, Lane embarked on various business ventures, including organising raves, selling vacuum cleaners and working for a while in Tenerife. So how did find himself under arrest for murdering Magill?

The BMW car used as the getaway vehicle by the two gunmen was traced, and one of Lane's fingerprints was found on a bin liner in the boot. Lane said that the car had been loaned to him by a relative the previous weekend, and he used it to drive his family around; his five-year-old son's fingerprints were also found in it. Shortly after the murder, Lane bought a car for £5,400, which could have been seen as part of the payment for the hit. 'If I had killed Magill, I would have got out of the country immediately,' he said. 'I wouldn't have hung around and bought a new car.' Then, long after his conviction, came two remarkable twists to the story. In 2003, one of the officers in the case, Detective Inspector Chris Spackman, was gaoled at the Old Bailey for plotting to steal £160,000 from Hertfordshire police, money that had been seized from criminals. Spackman, who admitted conspiracy to steal, theft and misconduct in office, had a major role as the officer handling disclosure information in Lane's case and had contact with other suspects and informers.

Then in October 2003, David King, thirty-two, was hit by five of a burst of twenty-six bullets fired from an AK-47 assault rifle as he emerged from the Physical Limit gym in Hoddesdon, in Hertfordshire. The two men originally suspected of Magill's murder, Vincent and Smith, were arrested and later gaoled for life for the murder. It was thought that King, a massively built man, might have become a police informer because he had been arrested in connection with a 14-kilo shipment of heroin but later released.

Vincent was told he would serve a life sentence of at least thirty years and Smith, who acted as getaway driver, was sentenced to a minimum of 25 years. It was the first time the AK-47 had been used in Britain in automatic mode. Gaoling the pair, Mr Justice Wilkie said: 'This was a thoroughly planned, ruthless and brutally executed assassination.'

Kevin Lane, who served twenty years before being released, hoped that the revelations about Spackman, Vincent and Smith would lead to a successful appeal in 2015, at which he was represented by Joel Bennathan, QC. There was a 'compelling picture', Bennathan told the court, that Smith and Vincent also carried out the Magill murder and had acted as a two-man team. 'The court must have disquiet about what is going on here,' he said, referring to the fact that Spackman was a corrupt officer with access to the case's exhibits and had links to both Vincent and Smith. But the court of appeal, less responsive now to allegations of miscarriages of justice than in the 1980s and 1990s, turned Lane down. He became a successful building contractor in Kent and continued to campaign against his conviction, backed by fresh revelations in a BBC *Panorama* programme. A book he wrote about his experience, *Fitted Up But Fighting Back*, opens with a quote from Arthur Schopenhauer: 'Fate shuffles the cards and we play.'

But while the Magill case may have been the most controversial, the one that caused most astonishment at the time took place in Rettendon, in Essex, and this was no game of cards. On an icy December morning in 1995, the two men sitting slumped in the front seat of their Range Rover in the icy Essex country lane appeared to have no faces. They had been blown away by a hitman. Their companion in the back seat also lay dead, his blood splattered against the interior of the car. The discovery by a couple of locals on their way to feed their pheasants at Whitehouse Farm was certainly a grim one.

Three professional criminals shot dead with a pump-action shotgun in the space of a few seconds. Tony Tucker, who had been a bodyguard for the boxer Nigel Benn, Patrick Tate, a bodybuilder and career criminal, and Craig Rolfe, the owner of the Range Rover, were all involved in the drugs business in the south-east. Tate, who had recently been released from prison and an armed robbery sentence, had survived an attempt on his life the previous year: a brick had been thrown through his window at his Basildon home and he had been shot as he peered out to investigate. On the night before his death he had beaten up the manager of a local restaurant after being told that he could not have the topping he wanted on his pizza. What was remarkable about the killings was that they seemed to have been carried out without the three men, all proven heavies, putting up any resistance. It indicated a level of ruthlessness and planning that was becoming increasingly common in the underworld. It became known as the 'Essex Boys' murders, particularly after a 2000 film of the same name starring Sean Bean.

It was not until 1998 that Michael Steele, of Great Bentley, and Jack Whomes, of Brockford, Suffolk, were found guilty of the murders at the Old Bailey, although they, too, like Lane, protested their innocence. Two appeals, in 2006 and 2013, failed, and a third was mounted in 2018.

Bumping off members of the underworld has not been an entirely male pursuit. In 1990 Linda Calvey, nicknamed 'the Black Widow', was gaoled for the murder of her boyfriend, armed robber Ron Cook. He was supposedly killed because she had spent all his money while he was inside and was worried about his reaction. She persuaded another criminal, Daniel Reece, who had become her lover while Cook was inside, to act as a hitman when Cook was on a day release from Maidstone Prison. But Reece panicked and Mrs Calvey fired the fatal shot herself. She was the widow of bank robber Micky Calvey, who had been shot dead by police during a robbery. Linda, who signed her name with a drawing of a black spider, emerged after serving eighteen years and married a former ski instructor.

The Royal Free Hospital in Hampstead, in north London, was the unlikely site for what is believed to be the only murder carried out by a hitwoman. In 1992, Graeme Woodhatch, a man with many business enemies because of his sharp practices, was in hospital to have his haemorrhoids treated when he was shot dead. What was more remarkable was the identity of his killer: a twenty-seven-year-old Maori woman called Te Rangimaria Ngarimu, nicknamed 'Sparky', who had represented New Zealand at surfing and was a trained shot. She had been recruited by two of Woodhatch's aggrieved business partners, Paul Tubbs and Deith Bridges, who accused Woodhatch of having defrauded them. Bridges had worked in a Camden pub with Ngarimu and supplied her with the weapon. She fled to New Zealand after the murder, for which she was paid only £1,500 of the £7,000 she was promised and which she had planned to use to buy a mobile home. She returned voluntarily to Britain after 'finding God' and gave evidence against Bridges and Tubbs after pleading guilty herself. All three were gaoled for life. Ngarimu was deported to New Zealand in 2005 after serving twelve years.

Then in 2010 came the arrival of the 'hitboy': Santre Gayle, aged only fifteen, was hired for £2,000 – although he received only £200 – to kill a young Turkish woman, Gulistan Subasi, at a flat in Hackney for what the prosecution suggested was a domestic dispute. He had been recruited to carry out the attack because he had no connections with the Turkish community, although he had already been in trouble, with a conviction at fourteen for attempted robbery. The officer who headed the inquiry, DCI Jackie Sebire, found that 'the frightening thing is his confidence and his lack of remorse. Even though he is only fifteen, he knew what he was doing.' He was told he must serve at least twenty years for the murder, which was carried out with a sawn-off shotgun. Gayle's gang nickname was 'Riot' and he had boasted casually of the crime which led in part to his conviction. The man who recruited him, Izak Billy, twenty-two, was also found guilty of murder, and given a life sentence with a minimum term of twenty-two years. Judge Stephen Kramer told Gayle: 'It was an efficient, ruthless and calculated execution... You shot and killed Gulistan for money, and at the bidding of an older man who you were trying to impress.'

The new millennium inevitably introduced Britain to the notion of the 'online hitman'. In a trial at Winchester Crown Court in July 2018, a retired GP was accused and acquitted of trying to hire a hitman via a very dodgy-looking website supposedly run by 'the Chechen mob', which offered to carry out a murder for $5,000 on selection of the 'kill the bastard' option. For a further $4,000, they would obligingly 'make it look like an accident'. The GP denied planning to make use of the site and was convicted only of sending malicious communications to a former financial adviser.

There has been relatively little research conducted on this phenomenon but a study entitled 'The British Hitman: 1974–2013', published in the *Howard Journal of Criminal Justice*, by Donal MacIntyre, Professor David Wilson and colleagues from Birmingham City University, examined a list of 27 cases of contract killings, involving 36 hitmen (and the one woman) – a lower figure than found in previous research. It came to the conclusion that the reality of the hired assassin in Britain is very far from the cinematic image of the cool, ruthlessly efficient killer casually blowing the smoke from the barrel of his revolver, and much more likely to be a bumbling inadequate leaving countless clues behind him. The average cost of a hit in their sample was £15,180, the lowest was £200. Motives for a hit were mundane: 'Husbands and wives fell out with each other or wanted to gain early access to life insurance policies; business partners decided to go or wanted to go their separate ways; business deals fell apart and young gang members wanted to impress other older gang members with their bravado. All of this is far removed from the media portrayal of the fictional hitman who, on the evidence presented here, has little or no connection to his British reality.' Four different types of hit-men were identified: 'novices' or first-timers; 'dilettantes', solving a personal crisis; 'journeymen' considered capable and experienced, and 'masters', who might come from a military or para-military background.

15

THE MILLENNIAL GANGS

POSTCODES AND STABBINGS

The Old Bailey, September 2018. Five separate murder trials were under way. All the accused in each of the cases were young men, many of them too young to be named because they were under eighteen. All the victims were also young men. Each one had been stabbed to death. In every case there was the claim of gang or theft involvement. There could, perhaps, have been no sharper snapshot of how 'gang life' had evolved in Britain in the twenty-first century.

There were other common factors in most of the cases. There were multiple defendants in almost all of the trials. There was incriminating CCTV evidence of the violence, as though the perpetrators were unaware that Britain was the most observed country in the world, with one camera per fourteen people. The press benches for most of the trials were empty and the cases went largely unreported; the days when newspapers, both local and national, could afford to cover murder trials in detail had long passed. Perhaps the most noticeable aspect was, in many of the cases, the presence of the parents of the victims: solemn, puzzled souls, some holding hands, listening to accounts of how their young sons had died – and lived.

These were very different gang members from what constituted those fifty years earlier. They were not interested in wearing snappy, tailor-made suits, shirts and ties. Instead their wardrobes included anti-stab vests that they had bought on the internet and cardio-masks and hoodies to hide their faces. The retailer, Blade-runner, reported that in the previous month of that year, their sales were up by 22 per cent, thanks to people buying anti-stab hoodies and anti-slash gloves.

In one of the courts, concerning the murder of a seventeen-year-old student called Mohammed Hassan, from Wandsworth in south London, prosecuting counsel Anthony Orchard, QC, spelled out the case: 'The evidence points to the conclusion that this was gang-related violence. Tooting Trap Stars and 417 are gangs based in Tooting, south London. All 'Bout Money – also known as ABM or Team Raw – are a gang based in Stockwell, south London. Stick 'em Up Kids – SUK, also known as Block 10 – are a gang based in Wandsworth, south London… TTS and SUK were engaged in a long-running feud. This feud has resulted in a number of violent offences and at least two deaths.'

The jury heard how Tyriq Aboagye, Ralique Young and Kishon Allen of the Tooting-based gangs and Donald Gaote from Stockwell, South London had hunted their victim down and stabbed him to death. They also heard how, just before the murder, a young couple had been spotted by the gang as they cruised past in their Mercedes. 'Yo,' said one of the gang, 'where are you from?' To which the young man had replied, 'I'm from round here.' 'What do you mean "round here" …Who do you bang for?' One gang member asked the young woman in the couple how old she was and when she said 'Sixteen', replied 'All right, darling' before telling the young man, 'You are lucky this time' and driving on and murdering Hassan.

A moment's stroll away, in Court 8, one could have heard how a group of teenagers 'celebrated' after carrying out a fatal knife attack on another teenager called Lewis Blackman, who gatecrashed a girl's sixteenth birthday party in Kensington, west London. The court heard that the girl had circulated invitations on Snapchat and was careful only to invite people from Hackney to the flat, rented through the Airbnb website. She knew that the 'Hackney Boys' would not welcome the presence of the 'Camden Boys'. 'I knew there was some sort of history between the boys,' she told the court. Blackman, nicknamed 'Dotty', was one of the Camden Boys and arrived with his knife and his friends, one of whom had a gun. He was killed after being chased from the flat. The six accused, none as old as eighteen and now in white shirts and striped ties, looked like schoolboys.

Prosecutor Oliver Glasgow, QC, described Blackman's death: 'The brutality of the attack, which saw him stabbed a total of fourteen times as he lay defenceless on the ground, is truly shocking. What is perhaps even more disturbing is the apparent celebration that his killers enjoyed after he had been fatally wounded and the calm and carefree manner in which they walked away ... They chased him, they caught him, they butchered him, and then they walked away without a care in the world.' Three teenagers were convicted of murder and a fourth of manslaughter.

In Court 10, where Tyrone Farquharson was convicted of the murder of Kelva Smith, supposedly over the issue of a stolen bike, a neighbour of the dead man giving evidence from behind a screen – as did many of the witnesses in all the cases – described how he had seen an axe amongst the weaponry. He blurted out, 'I couldn't sleep that night!' before being overcome and unable to continue.

In Court 7, the jury was told how a young Romanian, Benia-min Pieknyi, who had just arrived in Britain, was knifed to death as he and a friend tried to escape from a confrontation at the Stratford shopping centre, in east London. Prosecutor Duncan Atkinson, QC, said the pair had been targeted after two of the accused 'shouted words to the effect "this is our area" – a phrase in keeping with the proprietorial approach the group adopted at the shopping mall.' Police knew the assailants as part of a loose-knit group who called themselves 'the Portuguese mafia'. One of the accused, giving evidence, said that Pieknyi 'showed no respect'. He had been pinned to a Subway restaurant window and stabbed to death. Kevin Duarte and Moses Kasule were convicted of manslaughter and the ring-leader, a young Ukrainian, Vladyslav Yakymchuk, pleaded guilty to murder. All three were gaoled, Yakymchuck, who was identified by a bluebird tattoo on his cheek, for a minimum of twenty-two years.

As the other trials unfolded, it became clear that a lack of 'respect' was sufficient justification for murder.

Nothing spelled out the nature of the attacks better than this series of boasts left on the phone of Duke Quainoo, a twenty-one-year-old gang member convicted in another of the trials, helpfully translated in brackets by the prosecution for the jury: '*I done told these opps it ain't safe on they block I turn tapped on the pagan blocks.* (It is not safe on the estate for the opposition and the author has spilled blood on enemy territory.) And, celebrating the death: '*I bored up a pussy and bored up his friend/And one them niggas turned ghost.*' (Boring is a slang term for stabbing.) Quainoo and fellow gang member, Bilkan Bilkaner, twenty, were both jailed for life in January 2019 for the murder of a student, Russell Jones, who was not the 'opposition' or a gang member at all but just happened to be with a group of friends in the area of Enfield, north London, where Quainoo's rivals sometimes hung out. He was attacked at random.

Journeys to Court 2 of the Old Bailey go past the statue of prison reformer Elizabeth Fry, beneath which are the words of her admirer, Robert Browning: 'One who never turned her back but marched breast forward, never doubted clouds would break, never dreamed, though right were worsted, wrong would triumph.' For all the prison reforms that she and others pioneered over the years, most of the young men on trial that September would not emerge from their sentences until middle age and would serve their time in a world in many ways as hopeless as the old Newgate gaol.

So what was the motivation for the new millennial gangsters? They may be generations removed from the Krays and Richardsons but many of the motives for membership – territory, status, bravado, dosh – were all too similar.

'Everyone wants to be a gangster,' said BX, as he calls himself, who is from north-west London and who knew all too well that world. 'Everyone's seen it on TV and that's what they want to be. They look at music videos and it looks like the people in them are making hundreds of thousands of pounds although the reality is that they are still living at their mum's house.

'Most of them come from estates and they see their parents going to work, struggling to pay the bills. They come home, their mum's not there, all the places where kids could play are closing down. Nine times out of ten they leave school without qualifications. So if you're broke, if you can't get a job, you're going to take the opportunity. My parents had no clue what I was up to – I didn't come back with any marks on my face... It's not a black thing, it's not a white thing, everyone's doing it. There's no "I'm black, he's white, we can't get along" anymore. The Albanians, the eastern Europeans, they're different, they're on their own.'

The commercial, rather than the territorial or 'respect' side of life, had become increasingly important, said BX. 'The Albanians have taken over the weed, they've taken over the coke, they've taken over the heroin – they must be doing something right.' But there were still ample opportunities for smaller-time dealers: 'You can make a grand a week. It could be weed, it could be skunk, it could be cocaine, it could be heroin, it could be spice. Some people might sell cocaine and heroin for a while but they can't handle it because they don't like the customers because they're all junkies, so they switch to something else. There is so much skunk around that we're now exporting it! "Blue cheese" is the new one. It was actually created in Birmingham and now it's being taken to Holland and sold there.'

Quite often what was sold as crack or heroin was cut heavily with paracetamol or even chalk or any other substance that looked realistic, he said. To demonstrate, he scratched at the café wall and a tiny piece of dusty white paint came off, which could, to the untrained eye, just have been cocaine: 'I've done this and sold it. I know people who go to the West End and they do that if they're selling to people they'll never see again.'

Territory was important commercially. 'If you're doing five keys (kilos) a week and then suddenly you're only doing three a week, it doesn't take long to realise that someone's out there taking your customers. So you have to eliminate the opposition. How do you do that? By either taking them out, or tipping off the police. You are never supposed to snitch but I know one guy, from Southall, who's a millionaire now; he was in competition with a guy from the same area so he informed the police. All the old-school rules – they're gone. I know people who work with the police to get immunity for themselves. I know one who everyone knows works with the police, he's even been shooting people but you type his name in Google you won't find anything about him and believe me, his record is way longer than my arm.'

The risks are high. 'Of the people I grew up with only three of us haven't been to gaol although I've been arrested many times. My older brother has been in and out of gaol – nine months here, six weeks there. But there are less police than ever so that gives you the incentive and even if you get arrested, you're not going to do that long.' He talked of a friend who was shot dead and whose killer was acquitted because he just denied that the hooded figure on the CCTV was him and the jury accepted his story. 'People just say "It's not me". And they reckon they're OK when they're in big man's gaol – young offenders (institutions) is totally different because everyone's crazy there.'

Of the reasons why so many were dying in knife attacks, he said: 'The people with knives are people who can't fight so they carry a knife. But if you're a drug dealer you have to find people who will do your dirty work for you. The way it works is the elders, who are, say, twenty-four or twenty-five, they see you doing well so they might take you under their wing. The young kids acting as look-outs, they're thinking – "I'm part of that guy's enterprise. That could be me in however many years, I could get promotion." As they say, "Loyalty brings forth royalty".'

Girls were also part of the picture, he said, drawn in because they 'love a bad boy', and because of the lifestyle they can enjoy the spoils – 'They get to go to Ibiza, to Miami… They hold things for you – guns, for instance, nearly everyone has access to a gun – because girls don't get stopped and searched.'

One of the major issues in the gangland trials is that of 'joint enterprise', whereby half a dozen people may be charged with a murder even if only one of them applied the fatal blow. This has led to many cases where hangers-on and little brothers have found themselves gaoled for life when they may have been unaware of how the violence was going to escalate, or were not even at the scene of the killing. A study by the Bureau of Investigative Journalism (TBIJ) found that between 2005 and 2013, 1,853 people were prosecuted for homicides involving four or more defendants, accounting for around a fifth of all homicide prosecutions each year.

'Joint enterprise is a problem,' said BX. 'One of my cousins is in gaol for murder right now doing twenty-two years. If something happens and you're there, you can't turn around and run. You kind of have to get involved. It's like a mandatory thing, not even something you have to think about.'

As for whether there were identifiable gangs or how much of that was a creation of the media or the police, 'There are recognised gangs or groups like Tottenham Mandem, the Peckham Boys, the Kensal Rise Boys, the Mozart Boys (from the Mozart estate in Kilburn). There's lots of hate between the crews, but sometimes they meet up to squash a beef.'

Gang names, both inventive and banal, geographical and personal, came and went much in the same ephemeral way as pop groups, creating a sort of demi-underworld. From the Mountain View Posse, the Back to Back Gang and The Gucci in Bristol to the Holy Smokes, Sin Squad and Moscow 17 in London, there was never a shortage of evocative titles to what were sometimes well-organised and violent teams and sometimes a few bored and truculent teenagers reinventing themselves as a posse. In 2012, the BBC's Andrew Hosken noted that three members of a south London gang called GAS had been gaoled for attempted murder for an attack which left a five-year-old paralysed. What did GAS stand for? 'The two most repeated are Guns and Shanks (gang jargon for knives) and Grip And Shoot. But then again some would tell you it means Grind And Stack.' In 2018, the Met Police Commissioner, Cressida Dick, suggested that there were 190 gangs in London.

But what exactly was that word so casually and frequently employed – a 'gang?' In the twentieth century it seemed simple to identify gangs by the name of the family or the leader (the Sabinis, the Whites, the Krays, the Richardsons, the Arifs); or by area (the Brummagem Boys, the Gorbals Cumbies). But in the new millennium, the term became problematical. One definition came from the Centre for Social Justice's 2009 report, *Dying to Belong*, and sought five key features: a relatively durable, predominantly street-based group of young people, who engage in criminal activity and violence, identify with or lay claim to territory, have some form of identifying feature and are in conflict with other, similar, gangs.

In Waltham Forest in east London, a study called *From Post-codes to Profits*, published in 2017, found that the biggest change since an earlier investigation in 2007 was 'a more organised and ruthless operating model focused on the drugs market and driven by a desire for profits.' This new operating model reckoned that obvious signs of gang membership was 'bad for business' as it attracted the attention of the police. It noted the rise of one gang, the Mali Boys, but added that in the ten years since their previous study, a number of the named gangs had disappeared from view and others not on the radar then had since emerged.

'As gangs develop,' the research concluded, 'they move from a "recreation" stage where crime is rarely acquisitive to a "crime" stage, where criminal activities are a means to support the gang... In the next stage, successful gangs move into an "enterprise" stage where criminal activities become an end in itself... Instead of an emotional sense of belonging to a postcode that needs to be defended, territory is valued as a marketplace to be protected.'

As the London drugs markets became saturated, gangs began to move outside to the provinces and small towns, where there was little competition and where they were, at least initially, not on the local police's radar. This became the so-called 'County Lines' business model. 'Cuckooing', whereby vulnerable people, perhaps junkies, had their flats used as a safe place for dealers to store drugs, became common.

The study, which suggested that in the London area there were in 2017 around 250 recognised gangs made up of around 4,500 people, noted two other developments as the third decade of the new millennium approached. There was the increasing involvement of women and girls who could be used, as BX suggested, for transporting drugs and guns, and the role of social media and technology, which some gangs used to promote their 'brand' or intimidate the opposition. In some music videos, gang members would boast about their activities and antagonise other gangs, a phenomenon known as 'net banging'.

'We did an awful lot of work in London around gangs,' said Steve Rodhouse, the lead officer in the Met for gangs and organised crime before he became Director General of Operations at the National Crime Agency. 'Some were street gangs, a lot of them organised around the postcode they worked in or by ethnicity and they were responsible for a significant amount of violence. They weren't commonly family-based gangs... We had a strategy that we wouldn't give airtime to the "brand" and encourage competition and a sort of league table because we felt people would be competing to be "Number 1 most horrible gang". But you only need to go onto YouTube or social media sites and you see that building a brand, taunting other gangs, demonstrations of wealth, success and violence are really very common... They change, they split, they splinter, they form coalitions.'

While most of their violence was gang-on-gang, on some occasions they embarked on attacks outside their world. Such a crime occurred in 2006 when a lawyer, Tom ap Rhys Pryce, was stabbed to death in Kensal Green, north London, by two young men, Delano Brown, seventeen, and Donnel Carty, eighteen, so they could steal his mobile phone, Oyster card and £20 in cash. The pair were members of a gang called the KG Tribe and Carty called himself 'Armani' while Brown was 'Shy'. In the wake of the murder, the Reverend Les Isaac, who ran an initiative called Street Pastors, noted: 'The street culture has a pull and even some of the children we know who come from relatively stable backgrounds are being sucked into this lifestyle.'

Few people were better placed to assess the changes that had taken place in this world than Trevor Hercules, the former armed robber who turned his life around after more than a decade in prison and who, since 2000, had been working with young people at risk to try to persuade them that prison was a waste of their time and by challenging what he calls their 'social deprivation mindset' before it becomes ingrained. Having been arrested as a teenager in the 1970s and racially abused by the police, he knew where some of the young men were coming from.

'The biggest change since those days is the age of the people involved,' he said. 'It's youth on youth violence. You have to make a distinction between those who choose to join a gang and those who are driven into it just because they live on a certain estate. Before you had a choice, now you are forced to join a gang, although it's more of a cultural group than a gang. They have nowhere else to go. They come from estates and live on the bread-line. They have to make their own way in life and they think that the only way is through villainy, and crack pays the most money. They understand "respect" and they need respect and they get it serving up (dealing drugs). They don't call the police in the black community so they have immunity. In the old days in London there were certain places like All Saints Road (in Notting Hill) and Sandringham Road (in Stoke Newington) but now drugs are everywhere.' There were other changes in gang structures: 'Now you have black and white teaming up. And you see Somalians and Ethiopians who have come from war-torn places where guns and violence were very commonplace.

'You can see people in court now crying because they don't realise what they've done, what murder is,' said Hercules. 'They don't even know who the guy is they've killed.' He visited young offenders serving life for killings: 'Not one of them understood the concept of murder. They are doing a minimum of eleven years and I had to spell out to them what that means. Most of them would say "Sir, can you talk to my brother" to try and persuade them not to make the same mistakes.'

In the previous century, some prisoners found God, which cynics sometimes suggested was their way of obtaining parole more swiftly, and others became Buddhists. Hercules said he became a Muslim in prison for dietary reasons but he added that the appeal of Islam to young men who were in gangs and who felt lost was that 'Being a Muslim in prison is like being in a club and they give you good reasons for joining – "everyone from the West made you slaves" and so on.'

It was the theme that Ebony Reid, a sociologist at London Metropolitan University, encountered in her extensive published research on the subject of gangs, entitled '*On road*' *culture in context*, based on the north London estate on which she herself grew up.

'I ain't a bad man, I'm no longer that man,' the nineteen-year-old TJ told her. 'I ain't robbing innocent people, selling my soul. My heart is clean. Islam helped me start again, cleanse my sins... I've done my dirt, done some real terrible shit, I was reckless, robbing people, man, sticking man up, I didn't give a shit who I hurt. That's not how I wanna live. Some days I couldn't even sleep, because my soul couldn't rest, I didn't feel at peace with myself. I kinda feel OK now, I pray to Allah and ask his forgiveness, hoping he will forgive my demons.'

For others, a gang life remained a life worth living regardless of the risks and they justified their career choice. 'I weren't put here to be no waste man. I am making my own money and feel good that I can look bout myself,' Bradley, aged twenty-five, told Ebony Reid. 'I don't think our drive is that much different from that geezer in the pinstripe suit. We want money, and we'll do what it takes to get it.' And however grim the stabbing statistics, the fact remained, as journalist and author Gary Younge pointed out in his exploration of knife crime for the *Guardian*, a teenager was sixteen times more likely to be shot dead in America than they were to be stabbed to death in Britain.

The culture of the gang within the underworld had clearly changed with the times. Even more dramatic was what had happened to organised crime in Britain in an increasingly globalised world.

16

THE UNDERWORLD BECOMES THE OVERWORLD

LAST ORDERS AND CROOKS ANONYMOUS

The titles of the memoirs were like an epitaph: *The Last Real Gangster* by Freddie Foreman came out in 2015; *The Last Gangster: My Final Confession* by Charlie Richardson arrived just after his death in 2012; *The Last Godfather, the Life and Crimes of Arthur Thompson,* was published in Glasgow in 2007. The days of the high-profile criminal had come to an end. We had entered what Sir Rob Wainwright, Europe's most senior police officer, would describe as a world of 'anonymised' crime.

By the twenty-first century, members of the underworld were deciding that discretion was the better part of villainy. While the Sabinis and Billy Hill, the Krays and Richardsons, the Great Train Robbers, Howard Marks, 'Mad' Frank Fraser and Curtis 'Cocky' Warren had embraced their notoriety, there was now a reluctance amongst most of the criminal fraternity to court publicity. As photographer David Bailey said of the Kray twins, whose portrait he so famously took: 'Their big mistake was posing for me. If you're a real gangster, nobody knows who you are.'

Legislation played its part in this newly discreet world. In 2003, a change in the law of double jeopardy meant that, if there was significant new evidence, someone could now stand trial for a second time on a charge on which they had already been acquitted. This meant that confessions of having got away with a murder or a spectacular robbery had to be airbrushed from memoirs. The derring-do became the derring-didn't. Mindful of the longer and longer sentences meted out to 'send a message', there was a newly bashful approach to confessing to old crimes. The 2009 Coroners and Justice Act prohibited villains from profiting from accounts of their crimes, erecting another hurdle in the path of the memoirising gangster. (The bill was attacked by Baroness (Ruth) Rendell as it made its way through the Lords; she cited Jean Genet as just one writer who would have been affected by it.)

'There was a definite element in the sixties and seventies of the Robin Hood figure when being "notorious" was part of the culture,' said Tony Saggers, the former drugs chief at the National Crime Agency. 'People are more businesslike now... But perhaps the equivalent to those memoirs is Drill music on YouTube. They think "I'm going to sing about drug dealing and stabbing people" and put it on YouTube.' And, as the sociologist Dick Hobbs noted in his book, *Doing the Business*, the only Robin Hoods in the East End were pubs.

Fred Foreman, one of the very last surviving figures from the era, reflected on these changes over veal, spaghetti and red wine in a restaurant overlooking the canal in Little Venice, west London. Far from the Battersea of his wartime boyhood but close to the sheltered accommodation which had become his new home, he no longer wanted to recall the murders of which he had been acquitted as he had done in his first memoir, *Respect*, published in 1997.

The man who had collected more nicknames than anyone else – the Undertaker, the High Executioner, Brown Bread Fred, the Guv'nor, the Mean Machine and the tortuous 'Managing Director of British Crime', which was forced on him by his publisher – was not only reluctant to talk about old crimes but also decried the new methods of underworld retribution: 'I have no respect for anyone just stabbing someone with a 12-inch blade – a child can stab another person. Years ago, when you had an argument, it was a matter of a straightener – a street fight, bare-knuckle.' He did not believe that the young postcode gang members, who also sought that loaded word 'respect', would ever write their memoirs. 'I don't think anyone who has turned to crime these days is going to live long enough to build up a reputation, are they?'

An example of the low-profile approach was the Adams family – the 'A-team' as they were known – from the Angel, Islington, who were often accused – without any evidence actually offered – of having been responsible for as many as twenty-five unsolved murders. They made no attempt to have the sort of public profile that the Krays and Richardsons attracted and consciously eschewed publicity. Although three Adams brothers ended up serving hefty prison sentences for a variety of offences – none of them murder – they never had the public presence of their predecessors. They diversified through clubs, mini-cab firms and property and had a reputation amongst other criminals of looking after their own if they ended up behind bars. It was not until the new millennium that the brothers ended up serving significant sentences as law enforcement became subtler in pursuing them.

They attracted the greatest attention when Terry Adams was jailed for seven years in 2007 for money-laundering. 'It is suggested that Terry Adams was one of the country's most feared and revered organised criminals,' said Andrew Mitchell, QC, outlining the prosecution case at the Old Bailey. 'He comes with a pedigree, as one of a family whose name had a currency all of its own in the underworld. A hallmark of his career was the ability to keep his evidential distance from any of the violence and other crime from which he undoubtedly profited.' He was ordered to pay £4.8 million in legal fees to the law firms that had represented him initially under legal aid plus a further £800,000 in prosecution costs. Ten years later, in 2017, he lost his appeal against the order to pay £700,000 under the Proceeds of Crime Act and handed over the money.

In 1985, his younger brother, Tommy, had been cleared of involvement in the handling of the Brink's-Mat gold bullion in the trial that saw the jailing of Kenneth Noye and Brian Reader. Tommy later made a home for himself in Spain, but was convicted in 1998 of being part of a £2-million cannabis-smuggling operation for which he was jailed for seven years. Like his brother, he was also ordered to pay back over £6 million 'criminal assets', later reduced to £1 million. In 2017, he was jailed again for another seven years for money-laundering.

A third of the brothers, Patsy, found himself in Woolwich Crown Court in 2016 when he was charged with an attempted murder in Clerkenwell three years earlier, for which he was arrested in Amsterdam and brought back to Britain. The victim, Paul Tiernan, who had been shot and wounded while sitting at the wheel of his BMW, refused to co-operate with the police and Adams duly agreed that he would plead to a lesser charge of grievous bodily harm and was jailed for nine years. He said he had fled to Holland because the family name meant he would 'not get a fair trial'.

Two Adams family associates met untimely and unsolved ends: Solly Nahome, an accountant and diamond dealer, said to have had a major money-laundering role, was shot dead outside his house in Finchley, north London, in 1998. Eight months earlier, Gilbert Wynter, generally described as an 'enforcer', disappeared, his body supposedly buried in building works – the Millennium

Dome became the most fanciful rumoured location. Wynter had been acquitted at the Old Bailey four years earlier of killing a former athlete, Claude Moseley, with a samurai sword and was a supposed link between drug dealers and organised crime in north London. He was said to provide hitmen from Jamaica, who would fly into London, be pointed at their target and speedily fly out again, having done the business. In 2011, the Met linked the two murders and reopened the investigation into both but without success. Steve Rodhouse, who took over as the head of operations at the National Crime Agency in 2018, noted that 'Groups like the Adams still have a notorious name and a brand that is used to good effect.'

Also still active, despite long prison sentences, were the Arifs, who had surfaced most prominently in the 1970s and were periodically described as 'Britain's Number One Crime Family'. A quarter of a century after his brothers, Dennis and Mehmet, had been jailed, Bekir 'Dukie' Arif was sent down in 2016 for eleven and a half years for conspiring to supply amphetamines after 48 kilos of the drug were found in a caravan in Somerset. Bekir had been already jailed in 1999 for twenty-three years for heroin trafficking and, while in Whitemoor Prison, had contributed to a *Guardian* article, 'A Day Inside', which described the tedium of life behind bars: 'another interrupted night's sleep; the night screw, who must wear size-eighteen boots, given the noise he makes, shone his torch in my face every hour. Unlocked at five to eight and I made an application for money to go on my PIN numbers, so I can make phone calls. Called to labour at 8.55, checked off the wing with a rubdown and metal detector. The work – breaking up used CDs – is about as mind-numbing as it gets.'

The title of 'Britain's Number One Crime Family' was awarded to many, from the Adams to the Arifs, the Thompsons to the Noonans. More controversially, in 2007, many newspapers attached the label to the 'Johnsons', a group of fifteen Travellers from Cheltenham, who were alleged to have been involved in two decades of thieving, with stately homes being a favourite target, netting themselves supposedly some £80 million, although those financial claims, like those in drugs seizures throughout the years, should have an asterisk attached to them to denote 'wild guess'.

'You are,' said Judge Christopher Critchlow as he sentenced them at Reading Crown Court, 'a lawless group with no respect for people or the law.' Five police forces – Gloucestershire, Wiltshire, Thames Valley, Warwickshire and West Mercia – took part in what was known as 'Operation Haul' in pursuit of the gang, whose most lucrative haul came from Ramsbury Manor, home of the property tycoon, Harry Hyams. As a result of the theft, Hyams, the man who built London's controversial Centre Point and who died in 2015, slid forty-nine places down the annual *Sunday Times* Rich List.

Three years earlier, the BBC broadcast a documentary called *Summer with the Johnsons,* which chronicled the family's everyday life and in which Ricky Johnson cheerfully defended robbing the rich: 'I feel I've got the right to rob the sirs, the lords and ladies,' he said, on the grounds that their wealth had come from 'pillaging' others. Gypsies and Travellers in Britain have long complained about being casually labelled as criminals, and for a while 'Travellers' was included on the police list of organised crime groups, thus casting a whole group of people into the underworld in a way that no official body would dare to treat any other single community. It took the formation of the Gypsy Roma Traveller Police Association in 2014, with a membership of over a hundred, for those assumptions to be challenged internally.

It has been rare for anyone accused of running a criminal network to sue for libel. But in 2013, David Hunt, who described himself as an East End businessman and was nicknamed 'the Long Fella' because of his height, sued the *Sunday Times*, whose reporter, Michael Gillard, had suggested in an article in 2010 that he ran a major criminal network and was regarded as 'untouchable' by the Metropolitan Police. The article, published under the headline, 'Underworld Kings Cash in on Taxpayer Land Fund', was in part based on leaked Serious and Organised Crime Agency (SOCA) and other police documents. A spectacular five-week trial ended in victory for the paper in July 2013. The trial judge, Mr Justice Simon, said that he accepted that Hunt was the head of 'an organised crime network implicated in extreme violence and fraud' and Gillard duly won a Journalist of the Year award for his story.

The old underworld was changing in other ways. In 2018, the National Crime Agency – which had taken on the previous roles of the National Criminal Intelligence Service and SOCA – was estimating that £90 billion of criminal money was being laundered through the UK every year, 4 per cent of the country's GDP. The country was awash with dirty dosh and London had become the global capital of money laundering and the beating heart of European organised crime. The underworld had been embraced by the overworld and was attracting criminals from everywhere. It seemed that Britain, just as it had needed to recruit doctors, plumbers, fruit pickers and footballers from abroad, was also having to import its criminals. So how big was this new underworld becoming? The NCA estimated in 2018 that there were around 4,629 gangs and organised crime groups, comprising about 33,598 'organised criminals', most of whom were UK nationals.

'The international nature of crime and technology are probably the two biggest changes,' said Steve Rodhouse of the way the underworld had shifted. 'Pretty much all of the NCA's most significant "high-harm" operations now involve people, commodities or money transferring across international borders. The days of having a drugs gang, a firearms gang, a people-trafficking gang have changed because of the concept of polycriminality – groups satisfying criminal markets, whatever they may be, is now much more common. These are businesses and people are looking to exploit markets so why confine yourself to one market?'

The search for new criminal markets and its causes had already become apparent. 'One group of people saw real opportunity in this dazzling mixture of upheaval, hope and uncertainty,' noted Misha Glenny in his book, *McMafia*, on the effect of the collapse of the Soviet Union and the Balkan Wars and the newly opened borders. 'They were criminals, organized and disorganized, but they were also good capitalists and entrepreneurs, intent on obeying the laws of supply and demand, so they sought out overseas partners and markets to develop industries that were every bit as cosmopolitan as Shell, Nike or McDonald's.' There was no shortage of British criminals willing to become those partners, full of respect for the new foreign arrivals and ready to take part in the trafficking of drugs, guns, women for prostitution, migrant workers, high-end cars and even cigarettes.

As the stakes grew higher in the underworld, so did the desire to acquire weapons. 'There has been an influx from eastern Europe and particularly from Poland, and there are also a lot coming in from people who have served in Afghanistan and Iraq,' said 'Mick', a south London gun-dealer. 'In Liverpool docks, you can put in an order for ten guns and some grenades and they'll say OK and two weeks later, they will be there... Someone will have a tool and there is always one guy in a posse willing to use it. They will have one guy who doesn't give a fuck... They want handguns – shotguns are too big and bulky. The sawn-off doesn't look so good but use a machine-gun and you get known as a heavy guy. They have them just to be a chap on the street, to pose.'

The penalties for supplying weapons to the underworld duly increased massively. In 2017, Paul Edmunds, a sixty-six-year-old antique firearms dealer from Gloucestershire, was jailed for thirty years for supplying weapons and ammunition which had been found at more than 100 crime scenes, including gangland murders.

Edmunds crafted bespoke bullets for use in vintage weapons such as Smith & Wesson pistols from the US and nineteenth-century French and Russian guns that he brought into the UK supposedly as collectors' curiosities. He supplied the guns and ammunition to an apparently respectable Birmingham physiotherapist called Mohinder Surdhar after the pair met at a legitimate gun fair in 2008. Surdhar passed them on to Birmingham's Burger Bar gang, who kept some and sold others to underworld contacts. West Midlands Police likened the pair to the characters Walter White and Jesse Pinkman, from the US television show *Breaking Bad*, as people who appeared to be respectable but were making fortunes through crime.

The previous year, in June 2016, Harry Shilling, aged only twenty-six, the ring-leader of what was then the biggest of the gun-smuggling operations, was jailed for thirty years for shipping £100,000 worth of weapons from the same source used in the attack by Islamic extremists on the French satirical magazine, *Charlie Hebdo*, in Paris in 2015, in which twelve people died. Shilling had bragged 'we [are] now officially gangsters' after twenty-two assault rifles and nine Škorpion sub-machine guns from eastern Europe sailed up the River Medway from Boulogne.

There were other, darker forms of trafficking afoot. One of the grimmest examples came to light in 2003 when an 'immigration expert' was jailed for ten years for smuggling and exploiting more than thirty Eastern European women. The twenty-six-year-old Albanian, Luan Plakici, was said to have made more than £1 million from importing 'poor, naive and gullible' young women who thought they were on their way to jobs as waitresses or barmaids. Some had to service up to twenty men a day to pay for the £8,000 'travel bill' from Romania and Moldova. One witness told Wood Green Crown Court that she would be given condoms and lubricating cream each morning and in the evening, Plakici would count the condoms to ensure she had 'worked hard enough' and made the £500 a day he required. With brothels in London, Bedford, Luton and Reading, Plakici had made enough money to build fancy homes for himself, including a palatial one in his home country. He had acquired a British passport in 1999 after arriving in the UK as an asylum seeker, had been used as an interpreter in court and even took part in a BBC documentary about his field of work. Such a successful prosecution was rare as it was dependent on the bravery of two young Romanian women and many other victims were too fearful of revenge attacks on their families to go to the police.

By the turn of the millennium it was already clear that thousands of Eastern European women were being sold over the internet into the sex industry in Britain and put to work in massage parlours and brothels. The international nature of the trade was exposed fully in 2014 by a trial which ended with the leader of a gang that imported more than 100 women into Britain being jailed for twelve years. Vishal Chaudhary, who lived the high life in London's Canary Wharf, contacted young women through social networking sites in Hungary, the Czech Republic and Poland, offering work as receptionists, nannies or cleaners in England. Instead, the women were forced to work in brothels. Chaudhary's team, all of whom were jailed, consisted of his brother, Kunal, who worked for Deloittes in Manchester, a Hungarian heavy called Krisztian Abel and the latter's sister, Szilvia, who helped recruit the women. Their passports would be kept by the gang and the women would be made to have sex with up to twenty men – paying up to £100 an hour – every day. 'Many of the victims have been deeply traumatised by what this gang did to them,' said Detective Sergeant Alan Clark of the Met's trafficking unit after the trial. 'One victim's graphic account actually brought the interpreter to tears.'

The following year, another gang behind the sexual exploitation of at least 250 women, servicing around fifty brothels, was jailed. This was a Hungarian outfit which was exposed when one of the women escaped from a brothel in Newham, east London, by climbing over the back-garden fence and going to the police. She had had a relationship with one of the traffickers, Jenö Burai, who sold her to Zsolt 'the Snake' Blaga, in Peterborough, to settle a debt. The Met's trafficking unit worked with the Hungarian police and eleven members of the gang, four of them women, were arrested and convicted. Blaga was sentenced to fourteen years and Burai six.

'Pop-up brothels' – that rather breezy title disguising the baleful reality of soulless premises rented for brief periods to avoid detection – became a feature of the underworld's expansion into the twenty-first century sex trade. By 2017, the Home Office estimated there were up to 13,000 victims of slavery in Britain in 2017, most of them from Eastern Europe, Nigeria and Vietnam; police raiding brothels in Leicestershire and Northumbria found that more than three-quarters of the women working there were Romanian but it was the Albanians who attracted the greatest attention as the new gangsters on the block.

There had been earlier hints of Albanian criminal activity. Around midnight on the morning of 14 October 2006, shots were fired in an Albanian/Kosovan club in Park Royal, north-west London, and one man, Prel Marku, was killed. The shooting was the result of a feud between two gangs over who had the right to rob the parking meters of the West End, a scam that netted the thieves more than £1 million a year from Westminster alone and had the advantage that the stolen money – all coins – was untraceable.

It was a significant murder for a number of reasons: an indication that there were now organised foreign criminals ready to kill for a slice of what the British underworld might regard as small beer.

The man who fired the fatal shots was Herland Bilali, a disco doorman with a reputation for violence. Accompanying him into the club was a young man, 'Timi' Spahiu, who had arrived as an asylum-seeker a few years earlier and would claim that he thought the visit was to be an attempt to sort out the dispute peacefully with a discussion between the two rival gangs. According to witnesses, Bilali came in, shouted an obscenity in Albanian, pulled out a gun and started firing. Marku, the man shot dead, was an innocent bystander. Spahiu was another victim of the 'joint enterprise' law that pulled in so many on the periphery of gangland murders. Both men fled but both were tracked down and jailed for a minimum of thirty-three years. For some in the British underworld the message was: the Albanians are here.

While the Krays and Billy Hill were more than happy for everyone to be aware of their reputation, even they might have baulked at the way that the most high-profile of these new millennial arrivals soon presented themselves. The Hellbanianz gang, based in Barking, in east London, and consisting of cocky young Albanians, went online in 2017 via Instagram and YouTube rap videos to flaunt their ill-gotten gains and fire power in spectacular fashion.

The flashy cars and bundles of banknotes on display in their videos were the result of the importation of cocaine and cannabis but the gang was also involved in the weapons trade. The pictures showed £50 notes wrapped round a cake and their 'HB' logo written in cannabis. Even after they were arrested and jailed, they would post pictures of themselves, taken with smuggled mobile phones, from inside prison, where they would inscribe their gang name on the walls.

The most prominent member, Tristen Asllani, who lived in Hampstead, was jailed for twenty-five years in 2016 for drug dealing and firearms offences – possessing a Škorpion machine-gun. He was caught after a police chase in north London, which ended when he crashed his car into a computer repair shop in Crouch End. His photo, showing him stripped to the waist after he had apparently spent long hours in the prison gym, appeared on a site called 'My Albanian in Jail' and under the heading of 'Even inside the prison we have all conditions, what's missing are only whores'.

Another major player, who operated under a bewildering number of aliases, was Klodjan Copja, who was jailed for seventeen years in 2017 for importing drugs, after he had been extradited from Greece. Many of the Albanian mob operated with bogus Greek passports and were well-connected: Ermal Hoxha, grandson of Albania's late communist dictator, Enver Hoxha, was jailed in Tirana for cocaine trafficking. Muhamed Veliu, an Albanian investigative journalist, who knew London well, said that Hellbanianz had been on the crime scene in east London for many years. 'They are sending a bad message to young Albanians in Albania. By seeing such photos, they think the streets of UK are paved with gold but that's not the case. Bizarrely, despite the fact they are in the prison, they show the outside world photos of their life behind the bars.' He said that there was a concern that the British media stereotyped all Albanians as criminals but, he added, the 2005 Securitas robbery, in which two Albanians played key roles, was regarded with some national pride back home. 'It was "the crime of the century", it was seen as very different from making money from prostitution, which is the lowest form of crime. It is wrong, of course, but they did need bravery to get involved and at least they went for a bank, that was the feeling in the Albanian community.'

'Albania is Europe's largest producer of cannabis,' said Tony Saggers. 'It is important not to stereotype but the Kosovo War led to Albanians pretending to be Kosovan in order to get asylum in the UK. Many of the people who came weren't criminals but just wanted a better life, but there were criminals amongst them who were able to set up illicit networks.' He said that after the civil war, when smuggling had become an essential part of life, the trafficking routes were established. 'The Albanians learned that if you are efficient, you reinvest. The UK criminal has a get-rich-quick mentality while the Albanians' strategy was get-rich-slow so they have driven down the price of cocaine in the UK. They knew that if they expanded, they could undercut the market.'

It helped that their reputation preceded them. 'The Albanian criminals may be ruthless and potentially murderous when controlling their organized crime, but when they come to the UK they try to be more charismatic and they use fear – "we're here, we need to get on", that sort of approach – so there is little violence from the older Albanian criminals in the UK because they know that violence attracts more attention.'

There were other types of people trafficking and modern slavery in this new underworld. The lawyer, Philippa Southwell, specialised in cases of 'forced criminality', which applied in particular to young Vietnamese people brought illegally into the UK by traffickers and forced to work in cannabis farms to pay back debts of up to £30,000 that their parents have undertaken in order for them to have a new life in Europe.

'The modus operandi of criminal organisations is to target children or young adults, trafficking them across the world in a journey that can take months,' she said. 'Those being trafficked from Vietnam, often transit via Russia, Germany and France, by boat, lorry and even by foot. Once at their destination they will be locked in a premises and made to tend the cannabis plants, by watering them and ensuring the lighting is on. These cannabis grows are sophisticated multi-million-pound drug operations, with the electricity often being extracted illegally and high-value equipment used. The windows of the buildings may be nailed shut. The farms normally operate in rural areas, where the chance of detection is reduced.'

The boys and young men were in a form of debt bondage and had to work to pay off their debt, a debt that was almost never paid off. 'There is a misconception within the criminal justice system that they are free to leave because the doors may not always be locked,' said Southwell, 'but the reality is that they have nowhere to go, they are controlled through threats of violence, debt bondage, isolation, fear and other complex control methods that are regularly used by traffickers.'

The police tended to arrest whoever was on the premises and often the victims would be advised to plead guilty by their lawyers while the large profits from the cannabis farms would be laundered through nail bars or restaurants. Estimates of the numbers of such farms vary but they clearly ran into the thousands.

Sir Rob Wainwright, who served as Europol chief for nine years, also noted this internationalisation of crime. Speaking at a Police Foundation gathering just after his retirement in 2018, he said that Europol, the European equivalent of Interpol, dealt with 65,000 cases a year, having expanded since its foundation in 1998 when 'it consisted literally, of two men and a dog – admittedly, a sniffer dog – in Luxembourg.' By 2018, he reckoned that 5,000 organised crime groups were operating across Europe and the Mafia model had been replaced by a 'more nimble' model, with 180 different nationalities operating, mixing legal with illegal business and working with between 400 and 500 major money launderers. This was multinational business with specialists in recruitment, movement, money laundering and the forging of documents.

The internet, of course, was a major factor. Wainwright likened its effect on crime to that of the motorcar in the 1920s and 1930s, when suddenly criminals could escape at speed and take advantage of new markets. He cited the Dark Net, which he said was selling 350,000 different illegal items – 60 per cent of which were drugs – but including everything from guns to pornography and even operating a ratings system for speed of dispatch and quality. This is 'anonymised crime,' he said.

The combination of new faces of whom the British police – and often Interpol and Europol – were unaware, along with an increasingly tech-savvy pool of criminals made for a toxic cocktail. It was not just a criminal fraternity from Eastern Europe or Latin-American drug dealers that were attracted to the United Kingdom. Nigerian criminals, mostly involved in fraud, could take a reasonably-priced course in Lagos which would instruct them on how to go about applying for asylum, what stories to tell, whether to take children with them and what boroughs in London to aim for. But the underworld remained, as it had through the previous century, firmly in the hands of the natives, some of whom had by now taken their own criminal ways to Spain and the Netherlands, Thailand and South Africa.

And just as the old Borstal, which was abolished in 1982, had been seen in the twentieth century as a place where criminals could gain an apprenticeship – Billy Hill described it as 'the finest finishing school for adults any underworld could hope for' – so did the vast increase in the UK prison population lead to an ever-expanding masterclass in the 'university of crime'. In 2018, it emerged that more than 6,000 prisoners out of the 86,000 jail population were believed to have links to organised gangs. Beleaguered prison governors claimed that the gangs now had a substantial foothold behind bars. Members of the underworld were also much more likely to go to jail than their predecessors. While in 1901 the rate of imprisonment was 86 per 100,000 of the population, by 2016 that had more than doubled to 182 per 100,000 as Britain established itself as the most punitive country in western Europe.

Mitch Albutt, of the Prison Governors Association, suggested that organised crime gangs had even built a lucrative trade in psychoactive drugs inside the jails based on coercion, beatings and violence that could turn substances worth £200 on the street into £2,000 profits inside. It emerged that they not only used drones to fly illicit drugs to specific cell windows but had even resorted to coating children's paintings in psychoactive substances, rather than relying on long-suffering wives and girlfriends to smuggle the drugs in on visits, hidden in their mouths or underwear. In 2009, a report by Dame Anne Owers, the Chief Inspector of Prisons, on Long Lartin, one of the five high-security establishments in England, found that inmates felt that it was becoming an 'American-style jail' in that prisoners had to attach themselves to a gang for their own protection.

What effect did the long sentences have on discouraging the underworld? 'The British criminal carries on despite the risks through a mixture of complacency, relying on the law of averages that he won't get caught – and greed,' was Tony Saggers's conclusion. More than a century earlier, another senior police officer, Sir Robert Anderson, who had been an assistant commissioner in the Met, questioned the methods of tackling crime in those days and whether they were counter-productive. 'Crime there will ever be,' said Sir Robert presciently. 'Organised, systematic crime is the creature of our present methods.'

The underworld has always been adaptable, happy to combine old tactics with new targets. In January 2018, Britain experienced what appeared to be the first robbery of the controversial digital currency, Bitcoin. Four balaclava-clad armed men broke into the family home of a young Bitcoin trader in the village of Moulsford, in Oxfordshire, and forced him at gunpoint to transfer the currency. At the time, the value of a single Bitcoin was around £8,000 and Bitcoin transactions were anonymous, meaning that users could stay hidden, making it very attractive for criminals.

And as the old forms of robbery declined, they were replaced with moped theft: violent, modern highwaymen, stealing jewellery in smash-and-grabs and mobile phones from passers-by or stores. In December 2017, ten members of a gang, from mixed ethnic backgrounds and none older than twenty-four, were jailed for up to eighteen years each for smash-and-grab raids mainly aimed at high-end mobile phone stores, using stolen mopeds for a speedy getaway. They were eventually caught by tracking devices that had been attached to some of the stolen phones – the biters bitten in a way that old Ruby Sparks never had to worry about. Sentencing them, Judge Michael Simon described them as 'young in chronological age, but old in criminality.'

'What are new are some of the kinds of crime and tactics,' said John Grieve, the former Director of Intelligence at the Met, who became a professor at London Metropolitan University. 'Some are carefully anonymised, others are blatantly open in their "defence" of their local post-coded drugs trade. The moped highwaymen, for example, are a disorganised throwback to Victorian times, stealing watches, jewellery and other high-value goods on the street as well as their more organised vicious gang raids on malls and top-of-the-range shops. It is a patchwork of hatreds and alliances as it ever was. So it has changed, yes, but it also stays the same.'

One of the new tools at the disposal of law enforcement was the 2002 Proceeds of Crime Act (POCA), which allowed the police to pursue and confiscate the ill-gotten gains of professional criminals and allowed the courts to add up to fourteen years in jail for those who did not comply with orders to pay. It was used most notably against the Hatton Garden burglars and drugs dealer Curtis Warren.

'POCA came in in 2002 and is extensively used,' said James Saunders, a lawyer who has as much experience as anyone in handling underworld cases and whose offices are just a half-brick's throw from the Royal Courts of Justice. 'The police now have all the means to follow the money. A holdall full of cash is no use to you now, unlike in the days of the Great Train Robbery. If they find £200,000 under your bed which can't be explained, they confiscate the money.'

The NCA's Steve Rodhouse saw the tracking down of criminally acquired money as vital: 'It's the whole sweep of tactics to take the funding away from criminality. It's around unexplained wealth orders, it's using civil powers to take funds, account freezing and forfeiture orders. This reverses the burden of proof on to them (the organised criminal). We are very much making the pursuit of criminals' assets and illicit finance a key strand in our strategy, which means making more of our people financially literate.'

A typical example of POCA's use came in 2018, when a mid-level drug dealer called Paula White from Greater Manchester was ordered by a judge to pay back £1.7 million of her supposed criminal profits or face another eight years behind bars. White had already been jailed for nine years in 2015 for selling Class B drugs over the internet and the order targeted her 'realisable assets', which included her home, with its swimming pool and orangery, a villa in Marbella and an Aston Martin Virage sold at auction for £58,000. This was a highly-publicised warning to criminals that, if they hoped to emerge from prison after a few years and find their loot awaiting them, the rules had changed.

Another new law that also changed the game was the 2015 Modern Slavery Act, which targeted criminals exploiting vulnerable people, such as those Vietnamese children or illegal immigrants, to assist them in their businesses. Within a couple of years there were successful prosecutions under the Act, although very much at the lower end of organised crime: in 2018, Zakaria Mohammed, a twenty-one-year-old drugs dealer who trafficked teenagers from Birmingham to a grim little 'crack den' in rural Lincolnshire was jailed for fourteen years. In the same year, a London-based nurse called Josephine Iyamu was convicted of being part of a network that trafficked Nigerian women to Europe and turned them into sex-workers. Hers was the first conviction of a British national for offences committed overseas under the Act. The young women had been trafficked overland across Africa, by boat to Italy, and then to Britain.

What had also changed dramatically was the array of methods of detection, that incriminating alphabet soup of DNA, CCTV and ANPR, not to mention the cell-siting of mobile phones – whereby a suspect's location at a certain time could be traced through the use of their phone – of bugs hidden in cars and homes, and the eternal trail of internet searches. While the Hatton Garden burglary was 'old school' – a project crime, no grasses, old English criminals – they were caught via 'new school' methods – their cars traced by ANPR, their incriminating conversations recorded by hidden bugs, their computers as silent witnesses.

Of the other ways the underworld had changed over the years, James Saunders concluded: 'It's got younger. Old-timers would say they "don't show respect like what we used to" and it is mind-numbingly violent. There is a generation of no-hopers and these guys stab each other for incredibly small amounts of money. Fraud is alive and well, particularly internet fraud and scamming – the youngsters who don't want to go around stabbing each other are digital and if they get a hit from one in 10,000 that works for them.' But what about the motivation for wanting to be part of an underworld in the first place?

'It's a good question as to why people want to be criminals,' said Saunders. 'Typically, they've not had a good education. I think at least half wanted to be "somebody" rather than just commercially successful. The way you were somebody in the past was getting up early on Thursday and going and robbing the cash-in-transit van and you then went down to the Usual Suspects Arms and be seen spending money that you couldn't possibly have unless you were involved in crime so that you were a "face", you got respect.' Whatever punishments may follow, the recruiting sergeants of the underworld – poverty, greed, boredom, envy, peer pressure, glamour, prejudice – will never be short of volunteers. Crime – and an underworld – there will ever be.

Two postscripts from those 'last real gangsters', men who had served at both His and Her Majesties' pleasure. Fred Foreman: 'I don't want to glamorise what I did because it's not fucking glamorous, is it? I've done sixteen years inside, so when you weigh up the pros and cons of it, I don't see it balancing out in my favour. All the money I got out of crime, it doesn't pay off in the long term. The lessons speak for themselves: missing all your birthdays and Christmases and New Years, missing out on your children growing up.'

And, from beyond the grave, 'Mad' Frankie Fraser, who shared his thoughts with the congregation of Wesley's Chapel in east London in 1995. He was asked by one of the worshippers if he would have lived his life differently. 'Yes,' he replied. 'I wouldn't have got caught.'

BIBLIOGRAPHY

Anon., *Lives of Robbers and Murderers*, Milner & Co., undated

Ball, John, Chester, Lewis, and Perrott, Roy, *Cops and Robbers*, André Deutsch, 1978

Bartlett, Jamie, *The Dark Net*, Windmill Books, 2015

Barnes, Tony, Elias, Richard and Walsh, Peter, *Cocky*, Milos Books, 2000

Bassey, Amardeep, *HomeBoys*, Milo Books, 2005

Bean, J. P., *The Sheffield Gang Wars*, D & D Publications, 1981

Beltrami, Joseph, *The Defender*, M. & A. Thomson, 1988

Biggs, Ronnie, *Odd Man Out*, Bloomsbury, 1994

Biggs, Ronnie, *Odd Man Out: The Last Straw*, Mpress, 2011

Booth, Martin, *The Triads*, Grafton Books, 1990

Boyle, Jimmy, *A Sense of Freedom*, Pan, 1977

Breslin, Jimmy, *Damon Runyon: A Life*, Hodder & Stoughton, 1992

Burt, Leonard, *Commander Burt of Scotland Yard*, Heinemann, 1959

Byrne, Richard, *Safecracking*, Grafton, 1991

Campbell, Duncan, *That Was Business, This Is Personal*, Secker & Warburg, 1990

Campbell, Duncan, *We'll All Be Murdered in Our Beds!*, Elliott & Thompson, 2016

Cannon, Joe, *Tough Guys Don't Cry*, Magnus, 1983

Cater, Frank, and Tullett, Tom, *The Sharp End*, Grafton, 1990

Challenor, Harold, with Alfred Draper, *Tanky Challenor*, Leo Cooper, 1990

Chapman, Eddie, *The Real Eddie Chapman Story*, Tandem, 1966

Chinn, Carl, *The Real Peaky Blinders*, Brewin Books, 2014

Cox, Barry, Shirley, John, and Short, Martin, *The Fall of Scotland Yard*, Penguin, 1977

Daly, Max and Sampson, Steve, *Narcomania*, Windmill Books, 2013

Darbyshire, Neil, and Hilliard, Brian, *The Flying Squad*, Headline, 1993

Davies, Andrew, *City of Gangs*, Hodder & Stoughton, 2015

Dickson, John, *Murder Without Conviction*, Sphere, 1988

Donnelly, Jimmy, *Jimmy the Weed*, Milo Books, 2011

Donoghue, Albert, and Short, Martin, *The Krays' Lieutenant*, Smith Gryphon, 1995

Du Rose, John, *Murder Was My Business*, Mayflower, 1973

Eddy, Paul, Walden, Sarah, and Sabogal, Hugo, *The Cocaine Wars*, Arrow, 1989

Fabian, Robert, *London After Dark*, Naldrett Press, 1954

Fabian, Robert, *Fabian of the Yard*, Cedar Books, 1956

Ferris, Paul, with Reg McKay, *The Ferris Conspiracy*, Mainstream, 2000

Fielding, Leaf, *To Live Outside the Law*, Serpent's Tail, 2011

Findlay, Russell, *Acid Attack*, Birlinn, 2018

Findlay, Russell, *Caught in the Crossfire*, Birlinn, 2012

Finmore, Rhoda Lee, *Immoral Earnings*, MH Publications, 1951

Firmin, Stanley, *Scotland Yard*, Hutchinson, 1948

Firmin, Stanley, *Crime Man*, Hutchinson, 1950

Flanagan, Maureen, *One of the Family*, Century, 2015

Forbes, George, and Mehan, Paddy, *Such Bad Company*, Paul Harris Publishing, 1982

Fordham, John, *Let's Join Hands and Contact the Living*, Elm Tree, 1986

Fordham, Peta, *The Robbers' Tale*, Hodder & Stoughton, 1965

Fordham, Peta, *Inside the Underworld*, Allen & Unwin, 1972

Foreman, Freddie, *The Last Real Gangster*, John Blake, 2015

Foreman, Freddie, *Respect*, Century, 1996

Fowler, Michael and Brearley, Giles, *Safecracker*, Milo Books, 2012

Fraser, 'Mad' Frank, with James Morton, *Memoirs of a Life of Crime*, Little Brown Books, 1994

Fry, Colin, with Charlie Kray, *Doing the Business*, Smith Gryphon, 1993

Gamman, Lorraine, *Gone Shopping*, Bloomsbury Reader, 2013

Glenny, Misha, *McMafia*, Vintage, 2008

Gooderson, Philip, *The Gangs of Birmingham*, Milo Books, 2010

Goodman, Jonathan, and Will, Ian, *Underworld*, Harrap, 1985

Gordon, Charles G., *Crooks of the Underworld*, Geoffrey Bles, 1929

Gosling, John, *The Ghost Squad*, W. H. Allen, 1959

Grant, Douglas, *The Thin Blue Line*, John Long, 1973

Greeno, Edward, *War on the Underworld*, John Long, 1960

Greenwood, James, *The Seven Curses of London*, Fields, Osgood & Co, 1869

Guerin, Eddie, *Crime: The Autobiography of a Crook*, John Murray, 1928

Hercules, Trevor, *Labelled a Black Villain*, Fourth Estate, 1989

Higgins, Robert, *In the Name of the Law*, John Long, 1958

Hill, Billy, *Boss of Britain's Underworld*, Naldrett Press, 1955

Hill, Justin, with John Hunt, *Billy Hill, Gyp & Me*, Billy Hill Family Ltd., 2012

Hobbs, Dick, *Doing the Business*, Oxford University Press, 1988

Hobsbawm, E. J., *Bandits*, Pelican, 1969

Howe, Sir Ronald, *The Pursuit of Crime*, Arthur Barker, 1961

Hutchinson, Roger, *High Sixties*, Mainstream Publishing, 1992

Johnson, Graham, *Powder Wars*, Mainstream Publishing, 2005

Johnson, Graham, *The Devil*, Mainstream Publishing, 2009

Johnson, Graham, *Young Blood*, Mainstream Publishing, 2014

Kelland, Gilbert, *Crime in London*, Grafton, 1987

Kirby, Dick, *Operation Countryman*, Pen & Sword, 2018

Knight, Gavin, *Hood Rat*, Picador, 2012

Knight, Ronnie, with Barrie Tracey, *Black Knight*, Century, 1990

Knight, Ronnie, with Knight, John and Wilton, Peter, *Gotcha!*, Pan, 2003

Knight, Ronnie, with Peter Gerrard, *Blood and Revenge*, Gardners Books, 2004

Kohn, Marek, *Narcomania*, Faber & Faber, 1987

Kohn, Marek, *Dope Girls*, Lawrence & Wishart, 1992

Kray, Charlie, with Robin McGibbon, *Me and My Brothers*, Grafton, 1988

Kray, Kate, *Married to the Krays*, Atlantic Publishing, 1988

Kray, Reg, *Born Fighter*, Arrow, 1991

Kray, Reg, *Thoughts*, River First, 1991

Kray, Reg, and Kray, Ron, with Fred Dineage, *Our Story*, Sidgwick & Jackson, 1988

Krishnamma, S. R., *The Ballad of the Lazy L*, Rani Press, 1994

Lambrianou, Chris, *Escape from the Kray Madness*, Sidgwick & Jackson, 1995

Lambrianou, Tony, *Inside the Firm*, Smith Gryphon, 1991

Lee, Dick, and Pratt, Colin, *Operation Julie*, W. H. Allen, 1978

Leach, Charles E., *On Top of the Underworld*, Sampson Low, Marston & Co., 1933

Leigh, David, *High Times*, Heinemann, 1984

Lock, Joan, *Scotland Yard Casebook*, Robert Hale, 1983

Lucas, Norman, *Britain's Gangland*, W. H. Allen, 1969

Macintyre, Ben, *Agent Zigzag*, Bloomsbury, 2007

McArthur, A., and Long, H. Kingsley, *No Mean City*, Neville Spearman, 1956

McDonald, Brian, *Alice Diamond and the Forty Elephants*, Milo Books, 2015

McKay, Reg, *The Last Godfather*, Black & White Publishing, 2004

McNee, Sir David, *McNee's Law*, Collins, 1983

McVicar, John, *McVicar By Himself*, Arrow, 1979

Mark, Sir Robert, *In the Office of Constable*, Collins, 1978

Marks, Howard, *Mr Nice*, Vintage 1998

Martienssen, Anthony, *Crime and the Police*, Penguin, 1953

Meier, William M., *Property Crime in London, 1850–Present*, Palgrave Macmillan, 2011

Morton, James, *Bert 'Battles' Rossi*, National Crime Syndicate, 2017

Morton, James, *Gangland*, Little Brown, 1992

Morton, James, *Bent Coppers*, Little Brown, 1993

Morton, James, *Supergrasses and Informers*, Little Brown, 1995

Murphy, Robert, *Smash and Grab*, Faber & Faber, 1993

O'Mahoney, Maurice, *King Squealer*, W. H. Allen, 1978

Palmer, Marnie with Tom Morgan, *Goldfinger and Me*, The History Press, 2018

Parker, Robert, *Rough Justice*, Fontana, 1981

Patrick, James, *A Glasgow Gang Observed*, Eyre Methuen, 1973

Payne, Leslie, *The Brotherhood*, Michael Joseph, 1973

Pearson, John, *The Profession of Violence*, HarperCollins, 1972

Progl, Zoe, *Woman of the Underworld*, Arthur Barker, 1964

Qasim, Mohammed, *Young, Muslim and Criminal*, Policy Press, 2018

Radcliffe, Charles, *Don't Start Me Talking*, Bread and Circuses Publishing, 2018

Read, Leonard with James Morton, *Nipper*, Warner Books, 1991

Read, Piers Paul, *The Train Robbers*, Coronet, 1986

Reid, Ebony, *'On Road' Culture in Context*, Brunel University, 2017

Reynolds, Bruce, *The Autobiography of a Thief*, Bantam Press, 1995

Richardson, Charlie, *My Manor*, Sidgwick & Jackson, 1991

Richardson, Charlie, *The Last Gangster*, Century, 2013

Richardson, Eddie, *The Last Word*, Headline, 2005

Samuel, Raphael, *East End Underworld*, Routledge & Kegan Paul, 1981

Scott, Sir Harold, *Scotland Yard*, Penguin, 1954

Scott, Peter, *Gentleman Thief*, HarperCollins, 1996

Sharpe, F. D., *Sharpe of the Flying Squad*, John Long, 1938

Short, Martin, *Crime Inc.*, Thames Methuen, 1984

Short, Martin, *Lundy*, Grafton Books, 1991

Sillitoe, Percy, *Cloak Without Dagger*, Cassell & Co., 1955

Skelton, Douglas and Brownlie, Lisa, *Frightener*, Mainstream, 1992

Slipper, Jack, *Slipper of the Yard*, Sidgwick & Jackson, 1981

Smith, Noel 'Razor', *A Few Kind Words and a Loaded Gun*, Penguin, 2005

Smith, Terry, *Blaggers Inc*, Pennant Books, 2009

Sounes, Howard, *Heist*, Simon & Schuster, 2009

Sparks, Ruby, with Norman Price, *Burglar to the Nobility*, Arthur Barker, 1961

Stafford, Dennis, *Fun Loving Criminal*, John Blake, 2007

Stedman Jones, Gareth, *Outcast London*, Oxford University Press, 1971

Taylor, Laurie, *In the Underworld*, Basil Blackwell, 1984

Thompson, Tony, *Gangland Britain*, Hodder & Stoughton, 1995

Thompson, Tony, *Gangland*, Hodder, 2010

Tullett, Tom, *Murder Squad*, Triad Grafton, 1981

Van Den Berg, Tony, *Who Killed Freddie Mills?*, Penguin, 1993

Viccei, Valerio, *Knightsbridge, Robbery of the Century*, Blake Publishing, 1993

Viccei, Valerio, *Too Fast To Live*, Blake Publishing, 2000

Watts, Marthe, *The Men in My Life*, Christopher Johnson, 1960

Webb, Duncan, *Dead Line for Crime*, Frederick Muller, 1955

Wheen, Francis, *Tom Driberg*, Chatto & Windus, 1990

Whittaker, A. J., Cheston, L., Tyrell, T., Higgins, M. M., Felix-Baptiste, C. and Harvard, T. *From Postcodes to Profits: How gangs have changed in Waltham Forest*, London South Bank University, 2018

Wickstead, Bert, *Gangbuster*, Futura, 1985

Woodhall, Edwin T., *Secrets of Scotland Yard*, Bodley Head, 1936

Wright, Alan, *Organised Crime*, Willan Publishing, 2006

INDEX

Humphreys, Jimmy xii, xv, 226–7, 237, 238–40, 241–2
Hunt, David 'the Long Fella' 343–4
Hunt, Jimmy 20, 21
Huntman, Benny 82
Huntman, Roger 82
Hussey, Jimmy xiv, 143, 147, 152, 280
Hutchinson, Leslie 'Hutch' 107
Hyams, Harry 343
Hysenaj, Emir 307

Ilford Barclays Bank robbery (1970) xi, 158
Illustrated Police News 4
Ince, George 166
internet crime xviii, xix, 285, 287, 326, 347, 352, 356, 357
IRA 21, 103, 223, 267, 268, 318
Isaac, Reverend Les 334
Isaacs, Johnny 194
Iyamu, Josephine 356

Jack the Liar 231
Jackpot, Operation 249
Jackson, Sir Richard 32, 35
Jacobites 124
Jacobs, Philip 'Little Caesar' 112, 113
JaCogLaw 201
Jagger, Mick 260
James, 'Blonde Vicky' 58
James, Roy 143, 144–5, 147, 172, 189
Jeffery, Henry 161
Jeffrey, Jimmy 197
Jeffrey, Ronnie 102, 103
Jenkins, Harry 'King of Borstal' 55
Jenkins, Roy 71, 157
Jocelyn, Ralph 5
Johnny 'No Legs' 31
Johnny the Boche 159
Johnson Crew 138
Johnson family 342–3
Johnson, Ricky 343
Johnson, Willy 251
Johnson, James 279
joint enterprise 331–2, 349
Jones, Danny 308–10
Jones, Rhys xv, 140–1
Jones, Russell 328
Joynson-Hicks, Sir William 10
Julie, Operation xiii, 275–7
jump-ups 56–7

Kasule, Moses 328
Kate Hodders 112

Keen, Boyd 279–80
Kelaher, Detective Chief Inspector Vic xii, 234–5
Kelland, Commissioner Gilbert 240–1
Kelley Boys 118
Kemp, Dick 275, 276, 277
Kempton, Freda 206, 253
Kentucky Club, Stepney 66, 70
Kerley, Lynne 247
Kersey, Diane 114
Kersey, Leonard 113–14
Ketley, Christina 314
Kimber, Billy 10, 11
King, Bobby 158–9, 167, 174–5, 305
King, David 319
King, George 3, 4
Kinsella, John 'Scouse John' xvi, 140
Kirby, Dick 248
KLM bullion raid, Holborn (1954) x, 53
Klondyke, Operation 279
Knight, David xii, 194
Knight, Jimmy 196, 292
Knight, Johnny xiv, 194, 196, 292
Knight, Ronnie xiii, xv, 102, 193–8, 292
Knightsbridge Safe Deposit Centre robbery (July 1987) xiv, 298–303
Kostanda, Alec 'The Count' 226
Kray, Charlie 62, 71, 72, 75, 85, 86, 88, 89, 90–1, 113, 166, 193
Kray, Reggie xi, 61–91, 113, 190, 282
Kray, Ronnie xi, xv, 61–91, 105, 112, 113, 190
Kray, Violet 70, 105
Krays, the ix, xi, xv, xx, 61–91, 92, 93, 94, 95, 100, 101, 105, 108, 110, 111, 112, 113, 127, 128, 130, 139, 153, 165, 171, 174, 190, 282, 329, 338, 339, 340, 349
Krays, The (film) 86
Krishnarma, Surya 'Chris' xii, 264–6

Lady Bucks 124
La Grange, Jean 100
Lambrianou, Chris 79, 80, 86, 88
Lambrianou, Tony 78–80, 81, 86, 87–8
Lambton, Lord 238
Lamont, Andrew 305
Landa, Vince 136, 137
Lane, Judy 271
Lane, Kevin 318–19, 320
Latif, Parvez 300–1, 303
Latin Quarter Club, Soho 194
La Torre, Antonio 135
Lau Ping, Ada 252

Richardson, Alan 95
Richardson, Charlie ix, xiii, 74, 93–101,
    106–10, 156, 231, 282, 338
Richardson, Eddie 94, 95, 96, 99–100,
    102, 103, 104, 108, 109, 110, 136,
    281–2
Richardson family ix, xi, xiii, xx, 72–3,
    74, 75, 92–110, 111, 136, 156, 231,
    234, 281, 282, 318, 329, 332, 338,
    340
Ridgewell, Detective Sergeant Derek
    236
Robb, Gary 202
Robbery Squad 161
Roberts, Harry xi, xv, 157, 163
Robinson, Billy 314
Robinson, Brian 'The Colonel' xiii,
    293–4, 295
Robinson, Detective Superintendent
    Bob 161
Robinson, Flo 314
Robson, Detective Inspector Bernard
    232, 234
Rodhouse, Steve 334, 342, 344–5,
    355–6
Rolfe, Craig xv, 321
Rolling Stones 194, 260
Rolt, Terence 55
Rooney, 'Babs' 127
Rooum, Donald x, 229
Rose of Denmark pub 113
Rose, Denis 44
Rose, James 190
Rossi, Antonio or Tony Ross 211
Rossi, Umberto 'Battles' 13–14, 48–9
Rothermere, Lady 24–5
Rowlands, Robert 290–1
Rubin, Eric 303
run-out 41
Russian gangs xix, 4, 5–6
Russo, Victor 'Scarface' 49

Sabini, Darby (Charles) xix, 10–11, 12,
    13, 15
Sabini, Fred 10
Sabini, George 10
Sabini, Harry Boy 10, 12, 14
Sabini, Joe 10
Sabinis ix, xix, xx, 10–11, 12–13, 14–15,
    39, 116, 332, 338
Sadler, Fay 58, 218
Saggers, Tony 284–5, 286, 339, 350,
    354
Saliba, Romeo 223

Sampson, Freddy 165
Samuel, Raphael 3
San Toy 118
Sands, Basil 235
Saunders, James 176, 355, 357
Savage, Jean 298
Saxe, Clifford 197
Scadlynn Ltd 295
Schach, Bernard 'The Yank' 47
Scheherazade Club 222
Schnurmann's rubber factory, Totten-
    ham 5
Scotland Yard xii, 2, 8, 15, 22, 31, 32,
    54, 59, 83, 84, 115, 173, 177, 180,
    181, 182, 185, 212, 220, 231–2,
    233, 234–5, 246, 247, 258
Scott, Peter x, 72
Scott, Ronnie 44
Scott, Sir Harold 38, 208
scuttlers 115
Sebire, DCI Jackie 322
Second World War xx, 7, 8, 15, 18, 23,
    24, 31, 33, 34, 37, 38–9, 42, 44–5,
    122, 173, 204, 205, 208, 228, 249,
    262
Securitas depot robbery (2006) xv,
    305–7, 350
Security Express depot robbery, east
    London (1983) xv, xvii, xviii, 196–7,
    198, 291–3, 308
Seed, Michael xvi, 308, 310–11
Serious and Organised Crime Agency
    (SOCA) xx, 145, 344
Serious Crime Act (2007) 287
Sewell, Freddie xii, 240
Sewell, Georgie 11
Shakespeare, Letitia xv, 138
Shanghai Restaurant, Limehouse 253
Sharpe, Fred 'Nutty' 4, 6, 17, 206,
    207–8, 254
Shatford, Detective Superintendent Jon
    305
Shay, Danny 67
Shea, Frances xi, 72
Sheffield 115, 116, 117, 118
Sheppard, Alf 245–6
Sheppards 303
Sheridan, Walter 8
Sherwood, Fred 315, 316
Shilling, Harry 346
Shinwell, 'Manny' 69
Shinwell, Ernest 69
Shirley Ann club 94
Shonck, Philip 3